Grounded

A SENATOR'S LESSONS ON
WINNING BACK RURAL AMERICA

JON TESTER

WITH AARON MURPHY

ecco
An Imprint of HarperCollins*Publishers*

GROUNDED. Copyright © 2020 by Jon Tester. All rights reserved. Printed in the United States of America. No part of this book may be used or reproduced in any manner whatsoever without written permission except in the case of brief quotations embodied in critical articles and reviews. For information, address HarperCollins Publishers, 195 Broadway, New York, NY 10007.

HarperCollins books may be purchased for educational, business, or sales promotional use. For information, please email the Special Markets Department at SPsales@harpercollins.com.

Ecco® and HarperCollins® are trademarks of HarperCollins Publishers.

FIRST EDITION

Designed by Paula Russell Szafranski

Frontispiece and all insert images are courtesy of the author unless otherwise noted.

Library of Congress Cataloging-in-Publication Data has been applied for.

ISBN 978-0-06-297748-9

20 21 22 23 24   LSC   10 9 8 7 6 5 4 3 2 1

To Kilikina,

Brayden,

Tucker,

Dallin,

and Abbey.

Remember you're renting

this planet from

your grandchildren.

Contents

Grounded

Introduction

On the evening of April 25, 2018, I made one of the biggest decisions of my life—one that changed the future of millions of American veterans. For days, that decision dominated national news headlines and hurled my political career into uncertainty, prompting pundits to change their ratings for my upcoming election from "likely Democrat" to "tossup," or worse, and puzzling even some of my closest campaign advisers. For me, the decision was easy. I was simply doing my job holding the Trump administration accountable according to the responsibilities expected of me in the US Constitution.

A week earlier, I received a concerning phone call from someone whose identity I confirmed, though the caller asked to keep the name confidential. I told the caller I would. The person was a high-level White House insider who warned me about President Trump's latest cabinet nominee: Rear Admiral Ronny Jackson, MD, the president's personal physician, who had also attended to President Obama and President George W. Bush. A few months earlier, Dr. Jackson took the podium in a bizarre news conference to tell America that President Trump "might live to be two hundred years old" if only he ate healthier food.

As ranking member of the Senate Veterans' Affairs Committee, I was one of the first senators to meet in person with Dr. Jackson after the president nominated him to be secretary of veterans affairs, a job with oversight of the federal government's second-largest department, with more than 375,000 employees. I found Dr. Jackson to be affable and confident, and he seemed to be on a glide path to Senate confirmation.

"You cannot confirm this guy," the insider told me. "Ronny Jackson would be a disaster. His nickname is 'Candyman' because of how loose he is with prescription drugs. And I'm certainly not the only one who knows it."

I asked my contact to meet with my trusted team on the Veterans' Affairs Committee, some of the sharpest minds in the country, who were tasked with vetting Jackson prior to his confirmation hearing. Over the next few days we received more than two dozen similar calls from current and former White House medical unit employees, many still in uniform, telling us about Jackson's behavior and questionable medical practices. If any of the allegations were true, Dr. Jackson was most certainly not fit for the job. To make matters worse, we weren't getting answers to our growing list of questions about him and his qualifications from the White House, even after a tough phone call I had with Chief of Staff John Kelly. And someone was starting to leak accusations to the media, which endangered our control of the important responsibility of vetting Dr. Jackson internally.

"If in fact this turns out to be real, the hearing is going to be really ugly," I told General Kelly. "If it doesn't turn out to be real, then it won't be."

But the reports about Jackson kept coming to my committee. So on April 25, 2018, I consulted with my staff and decided to send to the press a summary of the various allegations—all of which had been corroborated independently by at least two of our sources. Minutes later, our phones started beeping with *New York Times* and Associated Press news alerts telling the entire world what we had been hearing for days.

That evening was a little more than six months away from Election Day. And until that night, the pollsters projected me comfortably ahead of a relatively unknown challenger in Montana. Until that night, the president of the United States really had no idea who I was, and he hadn't spent much time concerned with my second campaign to be reelected as a US senator. Then, the next morning, with a Senate confirmation hearing still on the horizon, Dr. Jackson removed himself from consideration, sparing himself from having to answer tough questions under oath. Minutes later, the president phoned in to *Fox & Friends* and started attacking me.

"I watched what Jon Tester of Montana, a state that I won by like over twenty points," Trump said. "You know, really, they love me and I love them. And I want to tell you that Jon Tester—I think this is going to cause him a lot of problems in his state."

The next day, during an appearance with Chancellor Angela Merkel, the president railed on me again, suggesting my constituents in Montana weren't "going to put up with it."

And early Saturday morning, as I was planting wheat on my farm outside Big Sandy, Montana, my chief of staff called to tell me that the president had taken his beef with me to Twitter. Now the president of the United States, humiliated by his own poor vetting, was after me—a Democrat in a bright red state, up for reelection. He made it personal. He was calling on me to *resign*.

So why did I make the accusations public? Why did I risk my entire political career on a move that resulted in the full wrath of a president who made history in our sparsely populated state by barnstorming there four times before Election Day? I did it because it was my duty. Everything I'd learned about public service, from my earliest days as student body president of Big Sandy High School to the president of the Montana Senate, taught me that if I ignored serious and unanswered allegations, I wouldn't be doing my job. I would do it all over again, even if it cost me my political career.

But it didn't. And today I am one of the few citizens of this nation who has successfully held Donald Trump accountable without suffering politically for it. In fact, on November 6, 2018, a majority of Montana voters (including 7 percent of self-identified Republicans) sent me back to the Senate for six more years, despite the president's full-throated attempt to exact political revenge. He was right; Montanans do love President Trump. They'd supported him over Hillary Clinton overwhelmingly two years earlier.

Trump, to many Montanans, was exactly what Washington needed: a straight-talking antithesis of an establishment politician who seemed to resonate with rural America. He was seemingly eager to fix everything broken with our political system with simple common sense. They saw Trump's willingness to say whatever was on his mind as authentic. To many of his supporters, Trump's ethical and moral foibles, his inflammatory rhetoric and the bombastic handling of our economic and national security, are either excusable or overblown, or both. But I see right through it. The president isn't authentic, but he's good at playing the part. He takes rural America for granted.

How I got into the "world's most exclusive club" is not an ordinary story. Many politicians are quick to distance themselves from the distinction of *being a politician*. I never feel compelled to do that, because I am and *always will be* a farmer, like my folks and like my grandparents. In fact, I'm the only US Senator who manages a full-time job outside the Senate—as a farmer. Every spring, I spend at least two weeks planting, and every August I spend at least three weeks harvesting. I maintain my own heavy equipment and deliver my wheat in an eighteen-wheeler. I buy grease by the case and seeds by the ton. I slaughter and butcher my own beef and pork. And other than my wife, Sharla, I have no help. The task of scheduling my "senatoring" work around the inflexible timing of farm responsibilities drives my staff crazy, but they know my farm work is nonnegotiable. It keeps me, quite literally, *grounded*.

I still work the same land homesteaded more than a century ago by my grandparents, Arnfred and Christine Pearson. At the turn of the twentieth century, the Pearsons were sold a bill of goods by another wealthy businessman with a penchant for lying: James J. Hill, a railroad tycoon nicknamed "the Empire Builder." Hill lured hopeful farmers, including Fred and Christine, to the wild grassland of north-central Montana via his railroad. On their homestead outside Big Sandy, the young Pearsons survived a devastating tornado, bitter cold, a young son who got crushed under a windmill and spent weeks in a coma, a rattlesnake bite, drought, and a forty-foot column of flames that roared from a natural gas seam in what was supposed to be their water well.

I grew up in a twenty-four-by-thirty-six-foot house next to my dad's butcher shop, where, in 1966, I lost three of my left fingers in a gruesome meat grinder accident (yes, nine-year-old farm kids use meat grinders). But my childhood on our farm, twelve miles west of Big Sandy, was otherwise a stable one. Dad wasn't afraid of a fight, and he taught me how to pick the right fights, but mostly he knew how to bring out the best in people. My mother, Helen, understood politics as both an art and a science—an appreciation she cultivated from *her* mother. She knew how to keep people together and to ultimately *win* the fights she picked, and she was a staunch fiscal conservative.

Water was so scarce Mother grew up knowing how to wash a sinkful of dishes with a single cup of it. Both Mother and my grandmother would have made fine politicians had they been afforded the opportunity. Instead, they put their focus on public education and family agriculture. After losing my fingers, I had to give up my plans to play the saxophone and I took up the trumpet. And my folks convinced me to go to college to earn a degree in music; I had wanted to become a diesel mechanic. But I listened to them.

As a young father, I taught elementary school music in Big Sandy before running for a seat on the local school board. I served on the local soil conservation board. I converted my farm to organic in the mid-eighties because Sharla got sick for an entire week after breathing in the dust from spraying treatment on our wheat seed, and I would get sick every time we sprayed pesticides on the crops. An early adopter of organic agriculture, I joined the board of the international Organic Crop Improvement Association. I eventually ran for the Montana Senate as a Democrat, where I represented a district the size of Connecticut and Rhode Island combined. In my second term in the Montana Senate, my colleagues elected me president. And while holding all these jobs, I kept on farming.

I was never supposed to win my US Senate seat—the same seat once held by Majority Leader Mike Mansfield. In 2006, the political powers that be predicted a landslide primary election victory by Montana's state auditor, a well-groomed man with a well-groomed political pedigree named John Morrison. Morrison ran into scandal late in his campaign, and with help from the emerging "netroots" movement, I won that primary by a whopping 25 percent of the vote. A few months later, with a mere 3,562 votes, I unseated Senator Conrad Burns—may God rest his soul—as Burns fought his own ethical problems and a questionable relationship with the disgraced lobbyist Jack Abramoff. On November 8, 2006, the day after Election Day, I declared victory at the very moment Donald Rumsfeld resigned as secretary of defense, sending a signal that even a bright red state like mine was weary of the status quo.

My political career has been shaped by many influences. I learned patience and humility and persistence by "pickin' rock," a dreaded childhood chore for which there was no automated machine. Pickin' rock means tossing large rock after rock into the bed of a truck. There's an endless supply of rocks on every farm; no matter how many of them you dig up and haul away, you'll find countless more each time you work the dirt. If you don't lug the rocks away, they'll get caught up in the farm machinery during planting or harvest and cause all sorts of problems. They're always there and they're always a pain in the ass. Pickin' rock is simple work, but only someone with patience and resolve can survive it with sanity intact.

From Montana's veterans I first learned respect and the value of sacrifice, and the pain of government injustice. Growing up I played "Taps" on my trumpet at the funerals of hundreds of veterans. It wasn't a paying job, but I did it because it was important to their families and it was important to me, even as a kid. It wasn't until I became a US Senator that I learned just how unfair our nation has been to its veterans, turning its back on them after they've returned home with wounds seen and unseen. That's why I've directed most of my staff in Montana to spend most of their time helping our state's veterans navigate the mess of the VA in order to get them the benefits they've earned. And it's why I make damn sure the Department of Veterans Affairs has good leadership at the top.

From my time on the Big Sandy school board, I've learned the importance of bringing all perspectives together to find the truth. That experience also taught me the consequences of stubbornness. As a young trustee in 1986, I made a decision to expel a teenage boy for wearing an earring to school and violating our conservative dress code. The ordeal ultimately resulted in a lawsuit by the American Civil Liberties Union. The flap made headlines across Montana, and it divided our little community much the way partisan politics divides our nation today. A judge ultimately relaxed the antiquated dress code of the Big Sandy School District (which even prohibited "weird haircuts"), but that's how I learned to navigate tough situations with my mother's political fortitude. Suspending that boy for wearing an earring is a decision I regret.

Speaking of haircuts, I got my first flattop from Big Sandy's barber, George Ament, whose son Jeff became Big Sandy's celebrity when he formed a grunge band called Pearl Jam. In August 2005, Jeff and his band held a benefit concert for me, which put my name on the map. Pearl Jam returned to Montana for their only North American concert during my second reelection in 2012, and again in 2018.

From my farm I've learned, firsthand, the dire warnings of our rapidly changing climate. In 2018, Sharla and I had to manage record snowfall in March, and as the snow rapidly melted, a raging river flowed right through our land, just feet from our home. We can no longer predict the weather patterns, and we face strange climate-related changes every year, like the rise of sawflies. Sawflies are little critters that bury themselves in staffs of wheat before crawling out and sawing the stem in half, destroying entire crops at a time. We didn't have sawflies on the farm when I was a kid. From my farm I've also learned the importance of family agriculture; the critical right for farmers to control the seeds they put into the ground without worrying about patents or lawsuits or the strict codes of big agribusiness. Don't get me started on the dangers of genetically modified organisms.

In 2010 I offered an amendment to the Food Safety Bill that drew the ire of major food manufacturing companies, and they pulled out all the stops to try and defeat it by unleashing scores of forceful lobbyists on Capitol Hill. My amendment simply exempted local farmers and food producers (the folks who push their produce to a farmers' market in a wheelbarrow) from the same expensive standards that apply to companies that manufacture, say, peanut butter and ship it all over the country in short order in eighteen-wheelers. Those corporations saw my amendment as a threat to their profit margins. But I faced them down, and with the help of well-known supporters of my amendment like Michael Pollan and Eric Schlosser, I won.

From my political campaigns, I've learned that the biggest threat to our democracy isn't a petulant president who has no moral compass, or members of Congress who turn a blind eye to him. The biggest threat is runaway, unaccountable campaign spending that gets worse every even-numbered year. Montana has a front-row seat to this debate over "dark money." The US Supreme Court's 2010 decision *Citizens United v. Federal Election Commission* nullified our state's century-old Corrupt Practices Act of 1912, which banned corporate influence over our own elections. Montana's media markets were flooded with unaccountable dark money TV ads during my first reelection campaign in 2012, a feat only to be outdone six years later, in 2018. The first step to fixing our broken democracy is to fix the influence of secret campaign spending and to shine sunlight into the corners of dark money.

And from the rural community I still call home, I learned that the worst thing a politician can do is to abandon authenticity and hard work, and to take anything or anyone for granted. In Montana, character and authenticity matter. Leaders who lack good character are usually shown the door by the voters who expect it. In Montana, these aren't the traits of successful politicians; they're the deeply held values of a state whose ancestors survived by them. It's how I won a third term in a red state after voting against Neil Gorsuch and Brett Kavanaugh, and after the president, and his kid, and the vice president, tried their damnedest to beat me.

And if America is to survive today's current test of our fragile experiment in democracy, we must put our trust in these values. I believe they will show this nation a new path. It will take courage. It will take political risk. It will take personal sacrifice, and fighting and winning the right fights. It will test us as a nation as I was tested and tempered by pickin' rock, with my sanity intact.

CHAPTER 1

Grit, Glue, and a Meat Grinder

I can only imagine how my folks spent the evening of June 16, 1966, in the waiting room of the hospital in Havre, Montana. I've often wondered. I picture my mother, Helen, wringing her large hands in her lap and quietly staring straight ahead, stoically facing down the emotions that could have gotten the best of her. My dad, Dave, is pacing back and forth under the buzzing neon lights, cursing as anxious farmers do. I was a couple of months away from turning ten and starting the fifth grade. Like all summer days for a Montana farm kid, it began as just another workday.

That afternoon Dad had driven from the farm into Big Sandy to pick up some feed, leaving Mother and me in the butcher shop to finish cutting, grinding, and wrapping a cow he had slaughtered, skinned, and broken down into large but liftable hunks of dark red beef marbled with fat. Mother never liked the idea of me using our shiny new electric meat grinder. But even as a nine-year-old, like most farm kids back then, I knew how to operate trucks, tractors, and power tools. And as so many parents do when confident children insist, Mother reluctantly allowed me to grind chunks of beef shoulder as she wrapped and labeled steaks a few feet away. I probably told myself that if I plowed through the butchering chores as quickly as I could, I'd have more time to horse around in the evening with Bob, my sixteen-year-old brother, whose idea of fun was to try to smother the life out of me whenever he could.

Dad had built the butcher shop the year before, between our red hip-roof barn and the little yellow house I grew up in. The shop was a twelve-by-eighteen wood-sided building with a twelve-foot ceiling and a sturdy wooden frame strong enough to support the weight of hanging beef. It was supposed to be small because of all the weight one needed to throw around; moving from station to station was efficiently designed to take only a few steps. The large walk-in cooler took up a corner, there were a couple of freezers, a scraping table, a saw, a scale, and the grinder. The shop, lit with three lightbulbs that hung from the ceiling, kept the warm air out in the summer and the cold air in during the winter. We covered the concrete floor with sawdust to make cleanup a little easier.

That afternoon in June I remember switching on the electric meat grinder. Something about the whirring of that machine put me into a kind of trance—maybe it was the power of the four whistling steel blades spinning inside. It's funny how memory works, because mine did me a favor and blotted out much of what happened next. Today it's only a blurry sequence of images and sounds. For a reason I'll never be able to explain, I simply put my left hand into the maw of the meat grinder, and when I pulled it out a half second later, my middle three fingers were gone. There was no pain. I do remember blood splattering everywhere—on the walls, *off* the walls, onto the ceiling, all over me. The splattering didn't stop as the grinder kept whirring, indifferent to my shock and Mother's screaming.

Mother told me to hold my left hand with my right hand as tight as I could. I grabbed my left hand so tightly I could feel my own exposed bones pressing sharply into the flesh of my palm. We ran into the house to get the keys to the car, but Mother grabbed the wrong set and once we were in our '65 Pontiac Bonneville, she had to run back into the house again. Before we left for the hospital, I asked if she had shut the grinder off. She had not, so in what must have been a fog of horror, she ran back into the butcher shop, trying her best to keep panic out of the equation. Bob was way out in the field driving a tractor, oblivious to the commotion, or so I thought.

I rode shotgun as Mother booked it to town, exactly twelve miles straight east down Kenilworth Road, most of which wasn't paved back then. I braced both hands between my knees as blood dripped all over the floorboard of our new car. Mother saw Dad driving up Kenilworth toward us, returning with the feed and unaware of the whole situation. She flagged him down. Dad left his grain truck on the side of the road and jumped in the Pontiac and we sped to the newly built Big Sandy Medical Center. The bleeding had slowed a bit by the time I arrived, and the nurses put my whole left hand in a big pan of Betadine. Then they wrapped me up and we raced another thirty-five miles north to the bigger hospital in Havre for surgery. In Havre, the staff remained calm as Dr. Jim Elliott prepared for the emergency operation. He warned me I was about to "smell something like cat pee." Right before the ether took me under, I thought, *I wonder what cat pee smells like?* And that's the last thing I remember.

I'll never know the words my folks might have exchanged with each other that Thursday evening in the hospital. I know there wasn't any anger or blame, at least not in the waiting room.

I came to in a small hospital room, confused and unable to move. Mother and Dad were there, and they told me to stay put until I was ready to sit up. I couldn't see my fingerless left hand at first, because it was wrapped in thick bandages. My hand was sore and warm and it throbbed intensely as if I were holding my heart between my two remaining fingers. But the worst part came a couple of weeks later when it was time to pull out the stitches. That's when I discovered how tender the scar between my thumb and my pinky really was. When Dr. Elliott pulled those stitches out, even after he applied some local anesthetic, it felt like the flesh and bones of my left hand were being stabbed, crushed, burned, and pulled apart all at once. I howled as both Dad and Mother pinned me to the table and tried to keep me still. To this day, I can honestly say that the removal of those stitches was, by far, the worst physical pain of my entire life.

I wrapped my hand with gauze and bandages for the rest of the summer and into the first few weeks of fifth grade as I healed up. The scar hurt for months and remained tender to the touch well into my twenties. For more than a decade, every time I bumped my left hand against something hard, like a desk or the handle of a pitchfork, searing, aching pain would buckle me over.

All things considered, Dr. Elliott sewed me up nicely and he later told me that the wound was actually a fortunate one. He was a general practitioner, but his skillful surgery preserved full dexterity in my thumb and my pinky, which the blades didn't touch. The fact that I still had full use of both of those fingers meant I would still have a powerful *grip*. Being able to lift, haul, drive, push, and twist things with both my hands after the accident probably saved my career as a farmer. But it forever changed my hopes of playing the saxophone. I had to switch to playing the trumpet and quickly convinced myself that playing the horn is easier without all those left-hand fingers getting in the way. I can play the piano too, so long as my left hand is limited to playing simple octaves.

My parents, wisely, never allowed me to feel sorry for myself. They certainly didn't consider my missing fingers a disability. Other than playing the saxophone, I could do almost anything else. I take exception when news reporters write with fascination about my "mangled hand," because I've never really seen it as a liability. Now there's no pain whatsoever. The scar is calloused and leathery just like the skin on my right hand.

Nonetheless, my digitally challenged left hand has become an unexpected focal point in my political career. During rallies on the campaign trail, I wave at folks with my left hand and they often wave back with three fingers on the left hand tucked down, hang loose—style, in what feels like a gesture of solidarity.

During my first reelection campaign in the fall of 2011, the National Republican Senatorial Committee (NRSC) ran an attack ad on TV that featured a doctored photo of me shaking hands with President Obama (apparently meant to highlight my affection for a president who never enjoyed much popularity in Montana). The image showed me grinning and grasping the president's right hand with mine, and my five-fingered left hand reaching for an embrace. It didn't take long for us to notice the GOP had cropped the picture with someone else's left hand. Whatever message they were trying to convey in their ad got lost in the fact they had used a fake image—and it effectively reminded Montanans that we shouldn't always believe what we see in TV attack ads.

Early in 2018 as I campaigned for a third term in the US Senate, I shot a TV ad in which I counted on my fingers the various bills I introduced that President Trump had signed into law. When we aired that ad in March, the president had signed thirteen of my bills. So I looked into the camera and started counting them. When I got to number eight, a bipartisan law increasing veterans' disability and survivor benefits to keep up with rising costs, I held up my hands and said, "I'm out of fingers!"[1] The ad was memorable because it was cute, but it was effective because it conveyed how important it is for me to actually get things done in the US Senate regardless of the political noise that consumes the news. The ad also summarized my work on behalf of America's veterans—something I valued long before I got involved in politics.

Most of my bills President Trump signed into law dealt with veterans. In 2017, I became the ranking member of the Senate Veterans' Affairs Committee and made an earnest decision to quietly get as much done as possible with Chairman Johnny Isakson of Georgia, whom I considered a true friend in the Senate. Immediately after President Trump took office, Johnny and I got to work and hammered out numerous bills at the request of veterans and the service organizations that represent them. In our first year leading the committee, in addition to increasing disability benefits, we also passed legislation improving the VA's Choice Program, giving the VA more authority to fire poor-performing employees and streamlining the hiring process for difficult-to-fill VA positions. We also removed the expiration time of GI Bill benefits, improved the process for appealing VA disability benefits, funded better care for rural and homeless veterans, and provided VA benefits to veterans who were exposed to toxic chemicals during classified missions. Yep, more than I can count on my fingers, but it really doesn't matter, because there's so much more work to be done.

I wasn't the only kid who suffered a traumatic accident on our farm. My uncle Lloyd spent a month in a coma when he was about the age I was when I lost my fingers. In 1914, a tornado swept across the farmland west of Big Sandy and completely destroyed my granddad's first barn. The cyclone also toppled the farm's fifty-foot iron-frame windmill. That windmill fell right on top of Lloyd, pinning him to the ground and knocking him out cold.

All the old-timers told me that my granddad, Arnfred, was by far the strongest man they knew. He hoisted the whole windmill up and pulled poor Lloyd out from under it. Lloyd didn't wake up for weeks, but he miraculously survived despite having no access to modern medicine or professional health care. Back then, getting to Big Sandy took the better part of a day if you were lucky enough to have horses, and Granddad had traded his team of horses for his brother Henry's 160-acre homestead next door.

By the way, Uncle Lloyd lived another seven decades (he died in 1983 at the age of seventy-seven), and he farmed the family land for most of his years. Granddad put that old iron windmill back up when he rebuilt the barn in 1916. Both are still standing today, not far from the butcher shop where I still use the same meat grinder that took my fingers. There's nothing wrong with the grinder. I have too much skin in the game to throw it out.

A creative reporter once asked if I had the hypothetical opportunity to have a conversation with a long-lost relative, who it would be and what we would talk about. I told her I would ask Arnfred and Christine Pearson, my mother's parents, why they chose this particular piece of flat grassland twelve miles west of Big Sandy. Out of all the acres of land available across the West, why did they homestead here? It was Fred who picked out the place in 1912, apparently drawn to the lure of north-central Montana by the "Empire Builder" himself, James Jerome Hill.

James Hill, a Gilded Age railroad tycoon, saw a golden opportunity for himself following Congress's passage of the Enlarged Homestead Act of 1909, which doubled some homesteads to 320 acres, and the Homestead Act of 1912, which reduced the amount of time required to live on a homestead from five years to three. A shorter commitment to working the land meant that more homesteaders were willing to try their luck out West. Hill also built the Great Northern Railway, a privately funded railroad that sliced across the plains of northern Montana through the city of Havre (we pronounce it HA-vur), in what is now Hill County. Hoping to make a few extra bucks, though he already had millions, Hill turned to poor farm families across the upper Midwest and talked up the fertile soil, the wide-open lands, and the milder winters of north-central Montana. Of course, those hopeful families could reach this promised land only by taking Hill's railroad.[2]

James Hill's successful greener-grass campaign sounded pretty darn good to those farmers, many of whom were first-generation Americans born to Scandinavian and eastern European immigrants who'd settled across Wisconsin, Minnesota, and North Dakota. The families lured to Montana by Hill's convincing advertising campaign were called, derisively, "honyockers."[3] The word comes from another politically incorrect term, "hunyak," possibly a combination of "Hun" and "Polack," used generally to describe poor immigrants from Europe. Fred, the son of Swedish immigrants, and his wife, Christine, who'd come to America from Sweden at the age of sixteen, were among them. And they, like so many of their neighbors, were hungry for new opportunity and tired of the long winters of the Red River valley between North Dakota and Minnesota.

After Fred's first visit to Big Sandy, he went back to eastern North Dakota, got Christine and his brother Henry and a few cousins, and to Montana they all came for a piece of the Empire Builder's golden promise. As it turns out, James Hill sold most of his desperate honyockers a bill of goods. Granddad said when he first came to

Montana, the native grass was so tall it would brush the underbelly of a horse. The loamy, alkaline clay soil of north-central Montana is particularly suited for growing grains, pulses, and alfalfa hay. But to cultivate the soil for dryland farming (farming with no artificial irrigation), you have to know exactly what you're doing for a successful yield. Many honyockers had no clue. And so much for mild winters. They were often worse in Montana.

My grandparents and the other folks who homesteaded this part of Montana scraped out tough lives on their new land. Many of them lived in one-room shacks. In those days Fred and Christine slept in a rickety little home whose curtains flapped inside when the wind blew outside. They shared a single horsehair blanket and kept warm with a little stove. You can see why so many of the honyockers didn't make it in Montana. Henry and the cousins eventually gave up and returned to North Dakota.

Fred and Christine stayed put. They rebuilt the barn after the tornado blew it down. They nurtured their boy back to health after he woke up. They figured out how to cultivate the finicky soil. When Granddad punched his first well into the ground, he didn't realize he had hit a deposit of natural gas until he lit a cigarette and dropped a match, sending a column of flames forty feet into the air (he dumped a wagonload of gravel into that well to snuff out the flames before digging another one).

One afternoon while working under a wheat thresher, Fred rolled over onto a rattlesnake, which bit him in the back of his shoulder. *Well*, he thought, *this is the end*. But he knew that if he got up and ran for help, his heart would pump faster and circulate the venom throughout his entire body, increasing the chances of a painful death. So he stayed right where he was, alone under the thresher, motionless. He waited out the snakebite as the flesh on his shoulder snowballed and turned red, then black and blue. Eventually he pulled himself out from under the thresher with one hell of an ugly wound, but he survived.

The Pearsons had suffered devastating windstorms, bitter cold, shooting fire, poisonous snakes, a coma—everything but locusts at this point. And then in the late teens drought hit, and it hit hard, wiping out the farm entirely. The wild Montana frontier finally forced them back to North Dakota. But it was only a temporary absence. In the spring of 1920 they had saved up enough to return to their homestead, and they started all over again on the same little piece of land. They had a couple hundred acres to their name, a newly built barn, a slightly banged-up windmill, their healthy son, Lloyd, their daughters, Geneva, Virginia, and newborn baby Helen, strong muscles, and a powerful work ethic that built rural America.

Several hundred miles to the southwest, a Mormon couple named Vernon Raymond and Caroline Worthington Tester carved out their own living in Salt Lake City. Vernon, a miner by trade, described himself as a "coal driver and laborer" on his World War I draft card. Dad remembered his mother more fondly. The Utah Testers had eight children: Vera, Edna, Mary, Vernon Jr., Becky, Johnny, my father, David Orson, and little Caroline, who went by "Liney." Dad was born in May 1916, less than a year before the United States entered the Great War. My father's folks were long gone by the time I was born. But I inherited something from Grandpa Vernon: his middle name. *Raymond Jon* is what my folks put on my birth certificate. Only Jon stuck.

How Helen Pearson met Dave Tester is not as intriguing a story as why Dave Tester ended up moving to the Pearson family homestead in Montana. In a word: duty. He had never planned on farming, and he certainly didn't aspire to spend most of his life on the flatland raising crops, but he turned out to be pretty damn good at it.

Dad grew up exploring the Wasatch Mountains east of Salt Lake. He was always at home on the back of a horse, deep in the woods or pulling fish out of mountain streams. He joined the Civilian Conservation Corps (CCC) in 1933, the same year his father died, and he traveled the country for honest work to help support his mother and little Liney during the Great Depression. In the CCC Dad learned how to properly butcher beef and pork. His older sister Becky married a man from Butte, Montana, and there Becky befriended Geneva Pearson. One day, Geneva introduced her little sister Helen to Dave

Tester. In what I'm sure is a long story short, they got married in 1943, the same year Dad's mother passed away.

Dad always seemed like an unsettled soul on Mother's family farm, yet he knew he had a responsibility to work and protect our land as its temporary steward. Our place is flat for almost as far as you can see, but blue silhouettes of mountains burst out of the horizon in every direction. The Sweet Grass Hills are visible some fifty miles to the northwest. The Bear Paw Mountains are the closest, about thirty miles directly east. Flat-topped Square Butte almost looks like a giant sci-fi building on the southern horizon, and the wild blue Highwoods are just beyond. And about forty miles to the west, there's a knobby assortment of bluffs we call "the Knees." All of these mountains surrounded Dad, teasing him from a distance, for most of his working life. He never got to live in them until he and Mother retired from the farm in 1978 and moved to northern Idaho.

For all those years in between, Dave Tester dutifully worked the land his wife's parents homesteaded. He ran his custom butcher shop, cutting meat for extra income (he considered closing the shop after my accident, but he couldn't afford to). He taught his three sons everything he knew about planting and carpentry and butchery and tractors and equipment maintenance. But he disappeared into the mountains as often as he could, usually with his horses. He always kept at least three horses on the farm: one for him to ride, one for us kids to ride, and one that wasn't quite ready to ride yet. I think Dad needed the comforting wildness of an unbroken horse on the tamed flatland he reluctantly called home.

Though Dad was raised a Mormon, and insisted that his sons were all baptized in the Church of Jesus Christ of Latter-Day Saints (I was, though I've never considered myself a member), he rarely went to church. He quietly preferred weekends in the woods whenever he could get them. He called the rugged mountains of what is now the Bob Marshall Wilderness, 175 miles west of Big Sandy, "God's cathedral," and it was there you would find Dave Tester truly at home, alone with his horses.

The late Robert C. Byrd, the stalwart senator from the "Mountain

State" of West Virginia, affectionately called me "Mountain Man" during the three and a half years we served together in the Senate. I suppose it had more to do with my physical stature than my home state. But Mountain Man is a better nickname for Dad. I never had the gumption to correct Senator Byrd, but I am a farmer.

I came into the world on August 21, 1956, which is a good day for a farmer to have a birthday because it usually falls smack dab at the end of harvest. On the day I was born, there was still a day's worth of wheat to cut (sixty acres back then) when Dad announced, "Well, it looks like the baby's coming."

That was a reasonable enough excuse to skip harvesting for the day. So Dad left his tough-as-nails father-in-law, Fred, his two older sons, and a generous neighbor named Willard Ostrom to finish the work. Harvesting wheat isn't a task that can wait another day, by the way; when it's ready to cut, you've got to cut it, or you could lose the protein content in the germ that gives wheat its value.

Dad rushed Mother to the Havre hospital (the very place where, precisely 352 days earlier, Montana's future governor Brian Schweitzer had been born). A few hours after my arrival in the world, Dad drove back down to Big Sandy, where he met Fred for a celebratory beer or two. But it wasn't the birth of a new grandson Fred Pearson was ready to celebrate.

"It's a boy!" Dad told him, the buttons of his shirt ready to pop off.

"So?" replied the salty old honyocker. "We got the harvest done."

Dad was the grit of our family. And while he preferred the solitude of the mountains, he had a big, outgoing personality. He believed in showing respect and following the rules. Once, after I sassed my mother, he told me to meet him in the barn. I said, "Yes sir," knowing full well what I was in for. Dad literally kicked my ass with a cowboy boot still on his foot. It was the last time I ever talked back to my parents.

But about a year after losing my fingers, I heard a muffled argument downstairs I wasn't supposed to hear. Dad told Mother that if she "had been on the ball, Jon would still have all of them . . ." That's when I did something I'd never done before or since. I'm not sure what compelled me, but I stormed downstairs to the kitchen, where my folks were arguing.

"You can fight about whatever else you want!" I yelled, shaking my left hand at them. "But don't you *ever* fight about this! *It's off limits.*"

Dad and Mother said nothing. They just stood there, quietly. I remember that moment feeling older than them, as a furious ten-year-old boy standing in their kitchen. They stopped arguing and I went back upstairs. Our little yellow house remained quiet for the rest of the night, and to my knowledge they never talked about the accident again.

Mother was the glue that kept us all together. Aside from a stint teaching high school English in the central Montana town of Denton and earning her college degree from the University of Montana in 1942, Helen Pearson Tester spent her entire life on the farm until her move to Idaho. All three of the Pearson women earned college degrees in the thirties and forties, another of the many remarkable successes of their parents. Fred and Christine Pearson not only turned their precarious homestead into a successful farm, they sent all their girls to college, they set up a neighboring farm for Lloyd, and they eventually built and rented houses: two in Big Sandy, two more in Havre, and two homes in Billings. They were successful at business because they knew how to work hard, and they knew how to manage money. That's a simple combo, and it's all it took for them to not only survive but to prosper in frontier America.

While Fred was a farmer's farmer, Christine, like my mother, was the political heart of her family. She kept current copies of *The Progressive* and *The Nation* on the table next to her reading chair, and she always knew which politicians in Washington were pushing which bills, and what those bills would do if they became law. Christine preached that public education and family agriculture are the two cornerstones of American democracy. Her Swedish upbringing reinforced her conviction that government should exist to *serve only the people*, not corporations or the wealthy; it should not interfere with the lives of its citizens, but it should make all lives easier, more efficient, more equitable and safer. Christine was so insistent on quality education that she convinced Fred to move into Big Sandy so their four kids could attend better schools in town, and not the one-room farm schoolhouses that dotted the prairie.

The Pearson farmstead had no electricity when my mother, Helen, grew up there. The only water available came from Granddad's second well, whose water the windmill slowly pumped four hundred feet up to the surface. It wasn't much. Water was so scarce the Pearsons would share bathwater, then scoop it out and reuse it again to flush their toilet. A lot of folks in this country take for granted the modern infrastructure that delivers just the right amount of water when we need it. Farmers usually curse having too little water; sometimes we curse having too much of it. In Mother's days it was often the former, and cursing was frowned upon.

Mother read whatever she could, and she vigilantly stayed on top of the news as best she could, following politics particularly closely. She got involved with the Chouteau County Democratic Central Committee and volunteered for candidates she believed in, like Majority Leader Mike Mansfield, Senator Lee Metcalf, and Senator John "Doc" Melcher. Mother, like her folks, was a proud "FDR Democrat," and she always brought common sense and smart coolheadedness to every conversation; it's also how she solved problems or defused arguments or taught her boys the lessons of life. She would have made a powerful elected leader had she been afforded the opportunity in her day.

I wish she would have had that opportunity. She never believed she could, nor did she think she could leave the farm and its responsibilities for politics. Though Montana was the first state to elect a woman to the US House of Representatives, in 1916, our state has not been represented in Congress by a woman since Jeannette Pickering Rankin. Congress could learn a lot from strong pioneers like Christine Pearson and Helen Tester. If history remembers kindly my service in the US Senate, I hope it notes that whatever political instinct I may have, I inherited from both women.

Mother passed away on June 27, 2009, about a half year before the Senate approved the Patient Protection and Affordable Care Act with sixty votes. Before her death, I had a long conversation with her about my political future. I told her I was having second thoughts about running for a second term in the US Senate. My schedule was brutal, and every minute of every week was consumed by the Senate or the farm, or traveling between the two.

"You know, you can do a lot of good if you stay in the Senate," she told me.

Mother never gave up her love of following politics. She reminded me that we still had a health care law to pass, and conservation policies to address, and campaign financing practices to reform, and communities across rural America to keep strong through family agriculture and public education.

Of course, she left the decision about whether to run again to me and my wife, Sharla. I thought about what Mother said for a long time. And once again, I'm glad I listened.

I didn't realize until my midfifties, not long after Mother died, the pain and guilt she must have lived with her whole life following the accident that took my fingers. She rarely spoke of it, and I never asked her about it. My folks weren't the type to talk with therapists, or even to talk through emotions with friends. It took me becoming a father to understand how difficult it must have been for her to see her physically perfect child lose three perfectly good fingers in a bloody fraction of a second, knowing it would alter his life forever.

If a creative reporter asks me again about a chance to have a conversation with a relative, I would have a different answer. I would choose to simply tell my mother: "It's okay, Mom. I did fine. It really is no big deal." I would thank her for raising me with the values that sustained our farm for more than a century, for teaching me the value of a dollar, and for not allowing me to think I was different from anyone else just because I can't play the saxophone. Whenever I smell the soil after a rain—Mother's favorite smell—I allow myself to say: *She knows.*

Perspective helps too. Years later, Dad told me about his encounter with another father in the waiting room of the Havre hospital as I underwent surgery.

"What's wrong?" the man asked, seeing how shattered Dad was as he paced back and forth.

"Our boy just lost three fingers in a meat grinder," Dad replied.

"Gosh, I'm sorry to hear that."

"What brings you here?"

"My son has leukemia," the man told him.

I wasn't even in the room and those words haunt me.

In the mid-sixties, a leukemia diagnosis was essentially a death sentence for a child (a cousin my age died of leukemia at the age of two). That man in Havre wasn't mourning the loss of limbs; he had already prepared for the death of his young son. All I had was a glorified impediment to my band career, and it put everything in perspective for Dad.

"Whenever you think you got it bad," he liked to say, "someone else has got it worse."

But today I look at that waiting room conversation with a different perspective. Today, children rarely die from leukemia. In fact, according to one study published in the *Journal of the American Medical Association*, the mortality rate for childhood leukemia fell by *50 percent* between just 1965 and 1979.[4] Why? Because this nation had the *right priorities*. Our government invested heavily in the human infrastructure—the research and development—needed to get the upper hand on leukemia treatment. Our communities, even the small ones, built hospitals that save the lives of kids who lose fingers in farm accidents. We put our tax dollars to work building, educating, and making scientific discoveries.

Our nation in my parents' time, under the leadership of visionaries like Franklin D. Roosevelt, ensured that people like my father, whose back was stronger than his classical education, could enjoy a lifetime of meaningful work. Our nation then ensured that Thomas Jefferson's "cultivators of the earth" and the hardscrabble communities they called home could survive natural disasters and unnatural economic cycles. And our nation richly gave back to the people who built it. Good leaders like FDR can look into the future, and they can anticipate what lies around the corners. Thanks to his New Deal, even remote, rural farms like ours finally got electricity in 1947. Running water soon followed. And so did prosperity.

Those smart investments were the priorities of resilient people like the poor honyockers, who learned how to survive harsh winters with only a little stove and a single horsehair blanket. They were the priorities of families who knew how to wash a sinkful of dishes with a single cup of water and who reused their bathwater to flush the toilet. They were the priorities of a nation that eventually allowed a seven-fingered farmer from Big Sandy to open the doors of what should always be the greatest deliberative body in the world.

In 1965 the community of Big Sandy replaced its little clinic on the second floor of what we called the "Big Store" with a nine-bed hospital down the street. Today the Big Sandy Medical Center is a designated Critical Access Hospital whose future is uncertain in our consistently shrinking community (the "city limits" population of our town today is about 600; down from about 1,000 in 1960).[5] The hospital can no longer count on a reliable funding stream from the federal government to keep its doors open. But the hospital is no less critical today than it always has been. And if a town like Big Sandy loses its hospital, or its bank, or its public school, the entire community will likely bust.

Today rural America is in desperate need of visionaries who can see—and who are willing to look—around the corners for our kids and grandkids. President Donald J. Trump certainly doesn't have that vision; he's just another James J. Hill trying to get away with using the most powerful office in the world to hawk false promises to the honest people of America.

On July 5, 2018, Donald Trump visited Montana for the first time as president of the United States. He didn't come to Big Sky Country to learn anything new about rural America, or to see for himself the communities and livelihoods affected by his trade war with China, or to listen to the concerns of any of the more than 100,000 veterans who call Montana home. No, President Trump flew Air Force One into Great Falls to settle a score with *me*. A few months earlier, I had raised some important questions after the president hastily nominated his personal White House physician, Rear Admiral Ronny Jackson, to oversee the more than 375,000 employees of the Department of Veterans Affairs as secretary. Dr. Jackson quickly withdrew his nomination amid the sudden scrutiny, which embarrassed the president. And because President Trump thinks of himself as a hard-nosed fighter who has to throw the last punch even when he's on his back, he came all the way to Montana with his fists clenched.

President Trump's visit to Great Falls that day was the first of four unprecedented campaign visits to Montana in 2018 designed to exact political vengeance on me and to bolster my relatively unknown Republican challenger, Matt Rosendale. By July 5, the president had signed sixteen of my bills into law. So I directed my campaign to take out full-page newspaper ads in the *Great Falls Tribune* and thirteen other local newspapers across the state *thanking* the president for doing right by Montanans and veterans by signing these bills.

"Welcome to Montana, and thank you President Trump for supporting Jon's legislation to help veterans and first responders, hold the VA accountable, and get rid of waste, fraud and abuse in the federal government," the ads read. "Washington's a mess—but that's not stopping Jon from getting things done for Montana."[6]

"I'll continue to work with anyone from any party to get things done for Montana," I added in an accompanying press release. "President Trump, I'll clear my schedule for whenever you are ready to sit down and talk about how we can get to work for Big Sky Country."

This, of course, didn't sit well with the president or his greasy-haired kid.

"When I look at Jon Tester in this race, he says all the things he voted for Trump on," Don Junior angrily yelled while introducing his old man in Great Falls. "Where was he on tax reform?"

"I see Jon Tester saying such nice things about me," the president said moments later in his long, meandering attack on me. "I say, yes, but he never votes for me."

Of course, I didn't vote "for Trump" on any of my bills. By then I simply got sixteen good bills passed, and the president signed them because it's his job. My gratitude was sincere. As for legislation considered supportive of the president, I'll support it if it's smart. I actually voted to confirm most of his early cabinet nominees. But if he expects me to support his priorities and policies blindly, as far too many lawmakers do, that's wishful thinking.

I can certainly handle the president's and Junior's attacks on me; I'll never believe much of what they say, anyway. What upset me about that afternoon were the inaccuracies that the president fed with a straight face to the people I represent. And in Great Falls, Montana, home of the Little Shell Band of Chippewas and a short drive from the Rocky Boy's Indian Reservation, President Trump glibly refused to apologize for using the slur "Pocahontas" to describe Senator Elizabeth Warren. Trump's use of the word to attack Senator Warren was nothing new; but it was startling and saddening to hear from the president of the United States in a state where nearly 7 percent of the population is Native American.

In the Four Seasons Arena in Great Falls, Donald Trump also told Montanans that North Korea is "going to denuclearize," that he lost the 2016 popular vote because some Americans voted "four times," and that $5 trillion would somehow pour into the US economy because of the GOP's controversial tax law of 2017, which is what Junior called "tax reform."[7]

Where was I on the so-called Tax Cuts and Jobs Act? I very proudly voted against it. I had my staff print out the entire 479-page bill as soon as we got the text (just a few hours before we voted on it), complete with illegible edits in the margins scribbled by the GOP staffers who wrote the bill. Minutes later I posted a video on Twitter bemoaning the impossible-to-read, handwritten words and the insufficient time we had to absorb the bill's tremendous cost and consequences.

"Look at this, folks—this is your government at work," I said into a video camera, slamming the thick stack of paper on a desk.

"This is unbelievable. We're doing massive tax reform on an absolute, incredible time line. This is going to affect everybody in this country. It's going to shift money from middle-class families to the rich. It's amazing."

Minutes after we posted the video, Jimmy Kimmel retweeted it, adding that the bill was like "the end of a movie and they have to wrap the plot up QUICK."[8] And with Kimmel's help my video went viral, garnering more than eleven million views on Twitter and Facebook.

A couple of weeks later, frustrated by the Senate's narrow, overnight passage of one of the most expensive spending measures in our nation's history, I told a *Washington Post* reporter the Tax Cuts and Jobs Act was "one of the shittiest bills ever to come before the Senate."[9] I meant it.

That law put another $2 trillion of debt on our kids with a single signature from President Trump.[10] It benefits the James Hills of America far more than it does the hardworking honyockers who will have to pay for it. And the Republicans muscled that law through despite America's rip-roaring economy in 2017. My folks and grandparents always paid off any debt in good times. They certainly didn't add to it. Of course Democrats aren't blameless either; most are far too quick to solve problems by throwing more money at them. Not a single member of Congress today could wash a sinkful of dishes with a single cup of water.

My pal Heidi Heitkamp, a great senator for the people of North Dakota, told me once that "our generation has inherited from our parents and is borrowing from our children." That is tough to admit to my own kids and grandkids, and the million other Montanans I represent, but it is the truth, and it is not sustainable.

But I believe in the people of this nation, especially those who've built the middle of it: the family farmers and ranchers, the educators and innovators, the union workers, our service workers and public servants, our warriors, our health care providers. As these working folks have done throughout Montana's and America's history, they learned how to survive because they had no other choice. And they never turned their backs on future generations as they did it. We can do that again with visionary leadership. In fact, we have no other choice in order to survive the mess of the status quo.

We can do it by better understanding the important lessons hard learned by rural America, by investing in the right priorities, by picking and winning the right fights. We must do it while allowing our nation's sacred experiment in democracy to exercise its checks and balances as intended. And we must always keep some skin in the game.

CHAPTER 2

Pickin' Rock

In my youth I spent many difficult days with my ass higher than my head, soaked with muddy sweat, hands buried in the dirt, picking rocks larger than my fists and tossing them into the back of a pickup. The loathed chore of "pickin' rock" is familiar to most farm kids—at least across north-central Montana. It's backbreaking, boring, dirty, and completely unsatisfying work. Yet removing problematic stones from the soil is an essential task for a farm. Those rocks will damage or downright disable equipment and make planting and harvesting much more difficult. Today, automated machinery can churn through the soil to sift out larger stones. We had no such machinery on our farm when I was a kid. Pickin' rock was as much a part of the workday as driving a tractor or changing a tire or feeding the cows.

Pickin' rock may be physically challenging, but it isn't complicated work. Any dolt can go out and dig up rocks and chuck them into the back of a truck for a while. But only people with strong backs and stronger minds can do it for hours and days on end without losing their sanity. The work does require focus, but not the kind of focus that keeps your brain fired up; it demands a high pain threshold and mental fortitude.

As with Sisyphus eternally pushing his boulder uphill, pickin' rock is also an endless chore. No matter how many rocks you pluck out of the dirt and haul away, you'll turn up more goddamn rocks every time you work the soil. I long ago gave up on the hope that someday I might finally pick all the rocks buried in our farm. So when my folks sent me out to pick rock, my goal was never to finish the job; my goal was to survive the job without losing my mind. I'd gather my wits and hold them tight as I stooped low to the ground, pulled rock after rock from the dirt, and tossed them into the pickup with a clank. Over and over and over again. *Clank. Clunk. Clank.* After a few minutes, I'd get bored, only to realize I had many more hours and many more truckloads to fill.

As I got older and stronger, my folks added another chore: lifting seventy-pound hay bales at least three feet off the ground and onto a flatbed hay wagon. When I was in the eighth grade, Dad bought a used swather and a new hay baler, which meant we baled hay for our neighbors. And that meant I lifted hay—between 800 and 1,200 bales per day—all summer long, or so it seemed. My brother and I stacked the bales on top of one another, five high, onto the wagon. After delivering the bales to a barn, I unloaded them and stacked them up all over again. I went to bed every night with my arms numb and throbbing, knowing I would have to do it all over again in a matter of hours. Of course, machines do this chore now too.

Having kept my sanity through all these years, I now know the valuable lessons pickin' rock and lifting hay bales taught me: patience, pride in work, humility, and persistence despite physical discomfort and mental atrophy. Maybe that's why so many farmers are so good at putting up with the things out of their control. My older brothers, Bob and Dave, picked their share of rock too. It gave all of us a strong work ethic, and it helped us approach difficulties in our lives without complaint. I like to think a childhood of pickin' rock prepared Bob to take on one of the toughest tasks of his life, only hours after I lost my fingers.

That afternoon Bob, who was sixteen that summer, was driving the tractor way out in the fields, within distant view of our flatland homestead. Of course, neither Mother nor I thought of Bob when we left in a panic for the hospital. Later I learned that Bob actually watched from afar as we tore out of the yard in a cloud of dust. Moments later he saw our Pontiac meet Dad's GMC feed truck on the horizon. He knew something was wrong when he saw Dad park his truck on the side of Kenilworth Road and jump into the car to speed toward town.

So Bob made his way back to the yard. He saw blood splattered all over the outside of the house. The blood was his only sign that something terrible had happened to someone—he didn't even know whose blood it was. To this day I have no idea how blood from my hand ended up on the side of our house, but it's one of the clues I have as to how gory my accident really was. Bob waited alone for hours, wondering what had happened, until Mother and Dad finally had a chance to call him from Havre. Bob drove up to Havre while I was in surgery, then drove back to the farm. Then late that night, without anyone asking, he cleaned up the mess in the meat grinder. He scooped whatever was left of my fingers and buried them in the yard. He didn't want Mother to have to deal with any of it.

I once wrote a high school essay about my five closest experiences with death. Bob, who's seven years older than me, played a starring role in most of them. Like Dad, Bob was more of a horseman than a farmer, and he spent every spare minute he could riding his mare, Minnie Pearl. Bob loved to play tag, with a catch. He chased me while I was on foot and he was atop Minnie Pearl, and he laughed at the funny sounds I made while trying to run and scream at the same time. Once while swimming in our coulee, Bob playfully pushed me underwater and held me down near the muddy bottom. What he didn't know was that the powerful suction of the sticky mud trapped my whole head, forcing me to hold my breath until he mercifully yanked me out. I gasped for air, terrified and covered in mud.

But Bob also gave me important advice that comes best from a big brother. And I've always looked up to him. For a while in grade school a few of the bigger kids entertained themselves by throwing me and several classmates into the monkey bars and trapping us there over our lunch recess. The same bullies also found fun in identifying and then hunting down one smaller kid to beat up each recess, which terrorized the entire school. I asked Bob what I should do about it. I don't know why I felt I had a responsibility to end it; maybe it was because I was bigger than most of the kids in my grade. And in my grade school mind-set I certainly wasn't going to seek advice from an adult.

"Here's what you do," Bob said confidently. "You find the biggest, meanest SOB you can find, and you beat the hell out of that guy. The big guys aren't used to getting a fist in the face, and it'll show the rest of 'em what you're made of."

So I walked up to the biggest, meanest bully I could find. I wound up a haymaker that started at my waist and concentrated all the strength I had into my tightly closed fist, and I clocked that kid right in the chin. He staggered back with stars in his eyes and the bullying ended that moment. That turned out to be the first political problem I solved effectively, though artlessly, but it worked.

Years later, my highly organized campaign manager Christie Roberts hung a Mike Tyson quote in her office as a cheeky reminder to her staff:

"Everyone has a plan until they get punched in the mouth."

When it comes to punch throwing, only Bob Tester had wiser words.

Bob left home not long after I lost my fingers. My oldest brother, Dave Jr., is twelve years my senior (he was born before our farm got electricity and running water), and he left home the same year I started school. One of my earliest memories is when Mother and Dad brought me along to the bus station to say goodbye to Dave as he headed off to Montana State University. After a couple false starts in college, Dave eventually went to veterinary school and enjoyed a long and successful career as a large-animal vet. Dave's son, DJ, was born when I was eight, and DJ often spent summers with us on the farm.

We all lived in the cozy yellow twenty-four-by-thirty-six house my parents had built near the barn the year they got married. When my brothers lived at home they had rooms on the second floor. I slept downstairs until it got too hot in the summer months, then I would sleep upstairs in a room whose window overlooked the flatland to the east. On those air-conditionless, alfalfa-scented nights, I hoped for an eastern breeze to blow into my window and cool things down, but it rarely did. In the mornings all of us gathered downstairs at the kitchen table, where we would plot out our work for the day over a hearty breakfast and whatever political opinions were on Mother's mind.

After Bob left and before DJ spent his summers with us, I felt like I was raised as an only child. Both of my brothers returned often to help with seasonal work, but neither of them was interested in taking over the farm from our folks. I knew at the age of eight I would stay put on our farm. Some kids dream of being astronauts or inventors or nurses or actors; I wanted only to be a farmer. So from as early as I can remember, I took farming responsibilities seriously—probably too seriously for a young boy. I knew the chores that needed to be done and I did them without being told. Before I was ten years old I put myself to bed early every night because I knew I had to wake up early to get a start on the next day. I was an average student at school, but at home on the farm I soaked up everything I could about maintaining vehicles and farm equipment, about soil science and weather patterns, and about how to cultivate our loamy, rock-filled piece of land into some of the most productive wheat fields in the country.

Bob reminds me that I once set him straight when he visited the farm for a weekend. I was sixteen, and Bob had assumed the big-brother role of temporary straw boss, and he started telling me what work I needed to do.

"I live here and you do not," I told Bob. "I know what work needs to be done. And Bob?"

"Yeah?"

"I'm in charge."

Bob tells me he never felt disrespected by that exchange. I certainly didn't mean any. He simply realized that I was only stating the facts, and from then on we both understood exactly what our roles were. The simple rules of our household were: respect each other, do your work and do it well, spend only as much money as you absolutely must, make time to enjoy the simple pleasures of life, and take care of the animals first. Dad and Mother kept a milk cow and some chickens in the yard. Dad always said the best thing about having a cow is that it forced him to come home every night to milk her, keeping him away from whatever vices or indulgences might cost money.

Good horses and nice cars were among Dad's rare indulgences, and he had always wanted a Cadillac. When I was twelve, he set his sights on a lightly used 1968 Cadillac DeVille for sale in the mining city of Butte. Knowing Dad, he found himself a screaming deal, saved up his money, and made an offer. Mother hated the idea of buying a Cadillac—even a used one; she saw luxury cars as wastes of money, but she went along. My folks took me with them on the four-hour journey to Butte in our 1965 Pontiac station wagon, which Dad wanted to trade for the dark blue DeVille. I remember the Cadillac had retractable footrests that came down from the backs of the front seats, so passengers could rest their feet on them instead of on the floor of the car. That's the sort of thing Mother hated.

I had never been to Butte before, and even then it seemed like a sprawling city. Dad bought the Cadillac from a man who owned an auto dealership, and who lived in a penthouse apartment on the top floor of the grand Hotel Finlen. For decades the Finlen stood as Montana's tallest building, towering over uptown Butte at an impressive ten stories. We got to stay that Saturday night in the man's penthouse apartment, and I remember vividly the sweeping view of the city lights below. Mother, a lifelong flatlander, worried aloud that I might sleepwalk myself out the window.

Our road trip to Butte, on November 2, 1968, coincided with the Democratic Party's "Victory Banquet" in the grand ballroom of the Hotel Finlen. They weren't celebrating a victory quite yet; some four hundred people gathered that Saturday evening to hear from party leaders prior to the upcoming general election the following Tuesday.

Though Helen and Dave Tester were Democrats, they didn't know the political banquet was taking place in Butte. They were excited by the hubbub and allowed me to poke my head into the ballroom to see what it was all about. I saw a long table of food. At one side stood Senate Majority Leader Mike Mansfield, elegantly dressed in a dark suit. Senator Lee Metcalf stood on the other side, peering through thick-rimmed glasses. Both men seemed huge to me. Of course they didn't notice me peeking into the ballroom—probably with more interest in the smorgasbord of food than the fiery political discussion. But I regret not telling Mother I wanted to meet both men. Had I done so, she would have made sure of it.

That evening in Butte, Senator Mansfield told those Democrats he believed America would soon elect Vice President Hubert Humphrey and Senator Edmund Muskie as president and vice president of the United States. Mansfield rarely missed the mark, but his prediction that night did. Then Mansfield criticized, as he often did, America's increasingly questionable involvement in Vietnam.

"We have too many commitments overseas," Mansfield told the hometown crowd, no doubt in his famously deliberate way of speaking. "We have mutual agreements with forty-two countries and we have neither the manpower nor the resources to continue a burden and responsibility of this sort . . . we must recognize the fact that we are not—and cannot be—the world's policeman."[1]

A couple of days earlier, on October 31, President Johnson had temporarily stopped American bombing in North Vietnam in what seemed like a hopeful detente leading up to planned peace talks in Paris. But then South Vietnam's president, Nguyen Van Thieu, suddenly announced that his country would not participate in the Paris talks. This development upset Mansfield, who said in Butte that Democrats and Republicans would work together to push for talks with or without the South. Mansfield believed the possibility of peace transcended the differences between the two parties, saying "there is no room for politics on the war in Vietnam."[2]

History didn't agree with Senator Mansfield's assessment. In late 2016, Nixon's biographer John A. Farrell unveiled notes he discovered from a Nixon aide indicating that as a presidential candidate in October 1968, Nixon pulled strings behind the scenes. Nixon, Farrell wrote in a *New York Times* column, feared Johnson's peace talks could give Humphrey "an edge" in the November 5 election. So Nixon told his confidants, including Anna Chennault, to quietly message Thieu and promise him a better deal once Nixon was elected president. This prompted a receptive Thieu to withdraw from the peace talks, prolonging the bloody conflict. Nixon denied any involvement in the matter.[3]

Prior to his long political career, Mike Mansfield worked in Butte as a hardrock miner. Before that, he served in the military. Mansfield joined the US Navy at the age of fourteen to serve in World War I as a young seaman. A few years later he joined the US Army as a private, then the US Marine Corps as a private first class.[4] America will always celebrate Mansfield for his storied tenure as Senate majority leader during some of our nation's most trying times. He successfully oversaw the passage of the Civil Rights Act in 1964. He served as a delegate to the United Nations. After his Senate service, he redefined diplomacy as ambassador to Japan from 1977 through 1988. President Reagan honored Mansfield with the Presidential Medal of Freedom in 1989. Yet despite all these accomplishments, he asked to be buried in Arlington National Cemetery beneath a plain headstone that identifies him simply as[5]

MICHAEL

JOSEPH

MANSFIELD

PVT

US MARINE CORPS

MAR 16 1903

OCT 5 2001

It was his military service he wanted our nation to remember. Born in New York City, Mike Mansfield grew up a Montana miner, not a farmer. Yet he too knew the value of pickin' rock.

I never did get to meet Senator Mansfield, whose Senate seat I now hold. I always hoped to have the opportunity when I was a state lawmaker. He passed away at the age of ninety-eight in 2001, less than a month after the terrorist attacks on the World Trade Center and the Pentagon, and less than a year after his beloved wife, Maureen, passed away at the age of ninety-five. Mike Mansfield always credited Maureen with his political success; she was a teacher in Butte who encouraged him to go back to school, and she even funded his college education by cashing in her own life insurance policy.[6]

In the spring of 2018, I invited Vice President Joe Biden to Helena to headline the Montana Democratic Party's annual fundraising banquet, affectionately called the Mansfield-Metcalf Dinner. The political event, held every spring, energizes the party faithful with a well-known speaker or two, just as that Butte victory banquet did in 1968. Biden's keynote address in 2018 sold out the Mansfield-Metcalf Dinner within minutes, drawing a crowd of more than 1,100 Democrats from across Montana.

Biden reminded them of his own bond to Senator Mansfield: In 1972 it was Majority Leader Mansfield who refused to let young senator-elect Biden resign from office following the tragic deaths of Biden's wife, Neilia, and baby daughter, Naomi. Both were killed when a tractor-trailer broadsided their car while they were out Christmas shopping. Mansfield stepped in as Biden's mentor, encouraging the new senator from Delaware to continue serving and allowing him ample time and space to grieve with his two young sons.

In Montana, Biden credited Mansfield for saving his sanity and for giving him "something to look forward to." Biden also shared a story he has often told: Soon after he took office in 1973 he watched Senator Jesse Helms, the newly elected conservative firebrand from North Carolina, castigate Bob Dole and Ted Kennedy on the Senate floor for their bipartisan work on what became the landmark Americans with Disabilities Act. Senator Helms, Biden said, didn't think taxpayers had an obligation to fund improvements like wheelchair access to businesses. Moments later Biden fumed in Mansfield's office.

"This man has no social redeeming value!" he complained of Helms to the majority leader. Mansfield quietly listened while chewing on his corncob pipe.[7] Biden never forgot what Mansfield said next, which he detailed in his memoir *Promises to Keep*:

Your job here is to find the good things in your colleagues—
the things their state saw [when they elected them]—and not
focus on the bad. . . . And, Joe, never attack another man's
motive, because you don't know his motive.[8]

He went on to tell Biden that in 1963 Jesse and Dot Helms adopted a boy with cerebral palsy after reading the boy's plea for parents
in a newspaper.[9]

I wish I could say I never question the motives of some of my colleagues. The difference now is that some of their motives are perfectly
clear—motives like protecting a disastrous presidency at all costs and
despite the good of the nation. On January 10, 2019, smack in the
middle of the longest government shutdown in US history, I went
to the Senate floor to implore my colleagues to simply hold a vote to
reopen the government. I knew enough Republicans would cross over
if they had the chance. I didn't expect to lose my cool, but I did.

A month earlier, the US Senate unanimously agreed to the
House's legislation to keep the government open by level-funding it.
As ranking member of the Appropriations Subcommittee that funds
border security, I worked with Republicans to agree on $21 billion
for border security, including $1.6 billion for a physical structure on
the southern border—money the Trump administration wanted but
didn't even know how to spend (we asked and they couldn't answer).
But in December nobody in Congress insisted on the whopping
$5.7 billion President Trump wanted for his wall, even though candi-
date Trump repeatedly told voters that Mexico would somehow pay
for it. After the Senate unanimously approved the House's funding
bill in December, conservative pundits ripped into the president for
failing to deliver on his campaign promise. So the president changed
his mind and demanded the $5.7 billion after all. All Republican
senators changed their minds too and rushed to his defense, even as
he rationalized the shutdown.

Senator John Thune spoke on the floor just before I did on January 10.

"When did securing our borders become immoral? It used to be that members of both parties recognized that border security was a basic obligation of our government," the South Dakota Republican said, "and that we had a duty to ensure that our borders were protected and that dangerous individuals or goods were not entering our country, but apparently—apparently—Democrats don't agree with that anymore."[10]

What? Talk about questioning motives. Nothing could be further from the truth, I responded. I reminded the senator from South Dakota of the facts and events he'd apparently forgotten over the holiday recess. In fact, in 2018, I earned an endorsement from the National Border Patrol Council, a nonpartisan organization of border patrol agents, for my bipartisan commitment to funding strong border security.[11] The GOP playbook, however, must have instructed its members to obfuscate funding a border wall (which polls poorly) with funding border security (which polls well), and then hope no one really noticed. I had none of it.

"Is this how you make America great again?" I shot back in a speech that quickly got several million views on social media. It was the Senate version of finding the biggest bully I could find and punching him in the mouth. "Is this how it's done? It is not working."[12]

I also pointed out that Majority Leader Mitch McConnell refused to even hold a vote on reopening the government. Instead McConnell held a vote on a bill authorizing US assistance to Israel.

"I am a big supporter of Israel, but I take an oath of office to protect *this country first*!" Spit flew. "And we are turning our back on this country.

"I wonder what the forefathers would think today if they saw this body—a shell of its former self," I went on. "And it is not due to the rules; it is due to the fact that we have leadership that will not live up to the obligation of this body as set up to begin with."

I was simply calling out dishonest judgments and questioning why so many senators refused to swallow their pride. They were putting the president's broken promises and his disastrous, impulsive, expensive, and politically motivated policies ahead of the good of America. I lost my cool because the people I represented were hurting. Nobody was winning. Eventually the president saw how much he was losing and he finally relented, ending his shutdown on January 25.

A couple of months earlier, Donald Trump Junior had called me a "piece of garbage" during a pre–Election Day political rally in Montana. Someone asked me if I had a response. I mostly shrugged it off, but I did challenge Junior to spend a day with me, pickin' rock on my farm in north-central Montana, the old-fashioned way. Let's put our asses higher than our heads and see who lasts the longest, I said. Though my challenge didn't get much traction in the media, it still stands.

During his speech in Montana, Vice President Biden also joked that I look "like a guy who can lift an ox out of a ditch."[13] Thanks to years of pickin' rock, I know a thing or two about heavy lifting, and I suppose I look the part. But I also know a thing or two about the patience and resilience of strong leaders like Mike Mansfield. I know a thing or two about persistence thanks to my unlikely rise in politics. I know a thing or two about pride in work thanks to my family.

A few days after Dad drove his new, dark blue Cadillac DeVille home from Butte in 1968, one of the neighbors saw it parked in our garage. Mr. and Mrs. Chandler were picking up packages of beef from our butcher shop. Mrs. Chandler was so frugal that she saved the plastic wrap we used to package her beef, washed it, and brought it back to us so we could reuse it.

"Wow," Mr. Chandler said. "She's a beaut." He and his wife, like Mother, were the children of homesteaders.

"Thank you." Dad beamed. Then Mr. Chandler's face got serious.

"If you can afford a car like that, Dave, you don't need my business."

So much for Dad's Cadillac DeVille. He was proud of that car, but in Big Sandy, it was simply too much of a status symbol among folks who work the dirt. Dad returned the car a few days later and got his money back. Where we're from, it's okay to swallow a little pride when it matters most.

CHAPTER 3

_____

24 Notes

In early February 2017 the White House sent a message to my office inviting me to have lunch with the new president of the United States. It didn't take us long to figure out that several other senators, four Republicans and six Democrats, had gotten the same invitation. That February 9 was the first time I met Donald Trump. He had been president for less than three weeks, and he had no real agenda for us; in fact, it seemed as though everyone at the White House was still trying to figure out where the exits were.

White House staffers nervously stood against the walls as we all sat with the president around a cramped table. The president spent the first half of our meeting making a pitch about immigration. Then he went through his familiar campaign talking points, a habit most of us assumed he would kick after his honeymoon period. The biggest news from that meeting was the president's use of the slur "Pocahontas," again, to describe Senator Warren (who wasn't there) to ten of her colleagues.[1]

Then we each got several minutes to update the president on whatever issues were important to us. I shared with him several concerns, including the need for campaign finance reform. But I spent the bulk of my limited time telling the president how the federal government's current hiring freeze was hurting America's veterans, and I asked him to exempt the Department of Veterans Affairs. As the new ranking member of the Senate Veterans' Affairs Committee, I told the president it was critical for the VA to be able to recruit qualified health care providers in order to be competitive with the private sector. The president didn't push back at all. Instead he turned to Reince Priebus, at that time his chief of staff, and said something along the lines of, "Well, Priebus, who did this?"

I couldn't believe it. Seventeen days earlier, with the stroke of a pen, the president himself had halted all new hires within the federal government—including the VA—for ninety days. Either he'd completely forgotten, or he wasn't aware that his own hiring freeze applied to the government's second-largest department. The VA was already understaffed and frantically looking for employees to serve the more than nine million American veterans who rely on it every year.[2] Trump's controversial hiring freeze, apparently meant to symbolize a commitment to smaller government, only compounded the VA's problem. And it meant many veterans across the country weren't receiving their benefits or health care.

Priebus simply nodded and scribbled his cell phone number on a little piece of paper, apparently trying to protect his boss from embarrassment, then he said he would get back to me. At first, Priebus impressed me, because he seemed to be somewhat in control of a wildly out-of-control, *uncontrollable* office. I even told a reporter I thought Priebus was a "very capable man."[3] That first impression didn't last long, though. Even after we left a message at the number he provided, Priebus never got back to me.

I wished I'd had a whole day to share with the new president my concerns about the state of the VA. I wanted to tell him, directly, about the importance of reforming and extending funding for the Veterans Choice Program, and how we have to do more to break down the stigma of treating mental health challenges. I wanted to tell him about the scourge of military sexual trauma, and I wanted to remind him that an average of twenty veterans take their own lives every day in this country.[4] I wanted to tell him about one of the most profound moments of my time as a US senator, when a Vietnam veteran at my very first town hall meeting told me something I'll never forget.

I held that meeting on January 27, 2007, in Hamilton, Montana, as a newly minted member of the Senate Veterans' Affairs Committee. All three of us Tester boys had grown up hearing Mother tell us: "You have two ears and one mouth, so use them accordingly," which, little did I know then, turned out to be the best political advice I have ever received. Alan K. Simpson, the retired senator from Wyoming and former chairman of the Veterans' Affairs Committee, put his own colorful spin on the same advice.

"Throughout my political life, I have held town hall meetings so people could raise hell with me—or cheer me," Senator Simpson wrote in *Right in the Old Gazoo*, his book about "scrapping" with the press. "The point was, I listened. If your jaws are always swinging, you can't possibly be listening."[5]

When I arrived at Valley Veterans Service Center in Hamilton in 2007, dozens of veterans greeted me and told me they had been waiting for decades for an elected leader to actually make time to listen to them. One of the older Vietnam veterans stood up, gestured to some of the younger folks in the room, then pointed his finger right at me and said, "You're not going to treat this group of veterans the way we got treated." He was justifiably pissed off.

That moment will always stick with me. I didn't get to tell President Trump about that veteran, but I brought it up shortly after the Associated Press declared my victory the day after Election Day in 2018—the moment I knew Montanans had sent me to the Senate for six more years.

"Every day for the past twelve years, I've thought of that man," I said during my news conference. I didn't expect to get a lump in my throat, and for the first time ever I had to hold back tears on live TV. "We've done everything we can do and we've got a lot more to do to live up to the promises we've made our veterans of this country. The fight is not over yet."[6]

Montana is home to about 100,000 veterans.[7] With a population of just over a million, that means we consistently have one of the highest percentages of veterans per capita in the nation.[8] My grade school bus driver was a World War II veteran named Lindy Ray, a devoted member of the Big Sandy VFW who regularly served in the honor guard of funerals for fellow veterans. For years Mr. Ray watched me carry my trumpet back and forth to school every day. I had to store it at the front of the bus for the ride into town and back.

"You must be getting pretty good at playing that horn, Jon," Mr. Ray said in the spring of 1969. "Any interest in playing 'Taps' as we lay to rest some of our heroes?"

"Sure," I said, surprised and honored to have been asked out of the blue.

"Taps" is only a twenty-four-note tune, but it is the one song you must never, ever mess up when playing it for real. One missed note can alter the tone of a funeral for a grieving family. One missed note will instantly turn somberness into collective embarrassment. For the performer, one missed note will likely result in more missed notes.

I inherited the job of playing "Taps" from a "first chair all-northwest" trumpet whiz named Ralph Schwarz, one of Big Sandy's best musicians. Ralph was five years older than me. Mr. Ray wanted me to study a bit under Ralph before Ralph left Big Sandy for college, and I eagerly accepted the opportunity to learn from one of the best. Neither Ralph nor I got paid for playing "Taps" at local funerals and memorial events. It was just something we did.

"Nobody's gonna give you feedback when you play 'Taps' because it's never that kind of song," Ralph told me. "You'll know you did a good job if you look up and the old ladies are crying. That will be your only sign you did good."

My first "Taps" performance came a few weeks later, during a Memorial Day ceremony. It was a disaster. Ralph played "Taps"; my job was to echo him in the same key. That May I was wrapping up seventh grade and Ralph was wrapping up his senior year in high school. For some reason, when the time came Ralph played in a lower key instead of the normal key of C like we had practiced. He didn't think I could play in the higher key. I knew my twenty-four notes inside and out, but I was too nervous to think about shifting keys, so I played my echo in C as Ralph stayed in D. I didn't miss a note, per se, but the performance was a total wreck on my part. Nobody said anything because they were polite and it was "Taps," but I could almost feel them shifting uncomfortably in their seats.

Most of the funerals I played for were for World War II veterans who lived in and around Big Sandy. Some of them had served in Korea. One was a World War I veteran. For each funeral I wore a coat and tie and quietly sat with the color guard through the church service. I joined the color guard as they led the pallbearers to the hearse outside, then we all rode together to the cemetery. At the gravesite, the final part of the ceremony was a twenty-one-gun salute, fired three times by local members of the VFW like Lindy Ray. After the crack of the third volley the commander shouted, "*Pre*-sent arms!" And that was my cue to start playing "Taps."

I got to know the older veterans who helped plan those funerals pretty well over the years. They called me whenever they needed a bugler, and I always said yes—especially when I learned that the only other option was to play a recording of "Taps" instead. I've always thought recordings are tacky and veterans deserve better, so I made myself available whenever I could, for countless funerals all the way through high school and even into college. Playing "Taps" was my first call to public service; a small part I could play in a much bigger story.

The year 1969 was also the year Bob enlisted in the Montana Air National Guard. He had been going to school at the College of Great Falls (CGF) in hopes of becoming a veterinarian like our older brother, Dave, when his draft number came up. Bob knew he'd be drafted as soon as he finished college, so he chose instead to enlist full-time in the air guard, based in Great Falls. That enlistment turned into a long and fulfilling career that took Bob all over the world. He became a medic and later a flight medic before operating the Montana Air National Guard clinic. He then oversaw the environmental division of the guard, which meant he was responsible for the safety and cleanup of hazardous materials. Bob retired in 2006 as a chief master sergeant in the US Air Force after putting in just shy of thirty-six years of honorable service. Bob took pride in his work, and it hit me hard when strangers sometimes heckled him for wearing his uniform in public during the Vietnam War.

That antiveteran sentiment is what fueled the frustration among some of the folks who attended my first town hall meeting in Hamilton in 2007. They gave me an earful that every elected officeholder should hear. They told me about their troubles navigating the VA, and the VA's less-than-ideal handling of post-traumatic stress disorder, and the bureaucratic red tape that drives away too many veterans in need. They also brought up the scarcity of veterans' cemeteries across Montana.[9]

After that meeting I held similar listening sessions all across the state. Each meeting drew more veterans as word spread. They told me about the lack of qualified health care providers in rural and frontier communities, long wait times and backlogs, the need for better care for women veterans, and the growing epidemic of PTSD and traumatic brain injury, especially among those returning from the wars in Iraq and Afghanistan.

One of the most consistent problems they told me about was the fact that the VA reimbursed disabled veterans only 11 cents per mile driven to a VA facility for a health care appointment. A veteran in the town of Plentywood, in far northeastern Montana, has to drive five hundred miles to get to Montana's VA hospital in Fort Harrison, which is in the middle of our enormous state. At 11 cents per mile, that veteran would receive only $55 to pay for fuel and wear and tear. That mileage reimbursement rate had not increased since 1977, when a gallon of gas cost 62 cents.[10]

So I introduced legislation to crank up that mileage reimbursement rate. At first we passed a law increasing it to 28.5 cents per mile, which went into effect in February 2008. And two years of wrangling and finagling later, I added a provision to the Caregivers and Veterans Omnibus Health Services Act to bump up the rate to 41.5 cents per mile.[11] That still doesn't quite pay for the cost of travel, but it helps.

(We tried for a higher rate, but Republicans on the Veterans' Affairs Committee wouldn't go higher.)

Another consistent concern I heard from countless veterans was the lack of good health care facilities across Montana, and the inexcusable state of some of the existing ones. In early 2008, President Bush's VA secretary, Lieutenant General James Peake, accepted my invitation to visit Montana for a veterans' town hall meeting and to tour Billings' subpar VA clinic.[12]

If that old clinic was a joke (it was), then Secretary Peake's tour of it was the punch line. The clinic was supposed to serve Montana's largest city, but it was located in a hard-to-access strip mall with limited parking. The VA clinic took up several cramped suites that didn't even connect to one another.[13] When Secretary Peake arrived, he and his sizable entourage couldn't even fit inside. So I led them through the front door of one suite, then out the back door, then into the back entrance of the suite next door—snaking in and out, conga line–style, so Secretary Peake and his people could see. Peake agreed with what veterans had told us: Billings and Yellowstone County, home to 20 percent of Montana's veterans, were long overdue for a whole new VA clinic. That odd tour prompted Peake to give "priority attention" to the project.[14]

Several months later, in mid-November, we broke ground on the site of the new, 25,000–square foot VA clinic on its own campus in West Billings, and a few years after that we expanded the building to 70,000 square feet.[15] Today the VA's community-based outpatient clinic in Billings is the department's largest health care facility in the region, saving thousands of veterans from having to drive the 245 miles to Fort Harrison—thanks to the vets who spoke up after too many years of being ignored.

Those early town hall meetings turned out to be fruitful. Thanks to the feedback from veterans, we built four more VA clinics around the state, two telehealth clinics, a new mental health care facility at Fort Harrison, and three new vet centers that specialize in mental health care. I backed legislation improving health care for veterans across rural America and implemented additional mental health screening for National Guard members returning from combat. And we were just getting started.

I heard horrific stories about the struggles of women veterans, especially survivors of sexual assault. After a Marine Corps veteran in Montana told me about her assault while in service to our nation, I teamed up with Congresswoman Chellie Pingree of Maine to introduce the Senate version of the Ruth Moore Act. Our bipartisan bill lessened the burden of proof for survivors of military sexual trauma in order to qualify for VA disability benefits.[16]

I also realized how many veterans weren't getting any help at all. Early on I hired a specialized liaison to work full time on behalf of veterans in Montana, and I directed almost all the folks who worked for me in Montana to spend significant time on casework for veterans. We helped with missing files, improper disability ratings, scheduling health care appointments, and turning up the heat on the VA to provide better service. We even helped track down medals veterans had earned but had never received for one reason or another.

In 2008 I got to meet one of Montana's more colorful veterans. Dr. Joseph Medicine Crow was ninety-four that year, and still telling me his famous World War II stories through a broad, toothless smile. Medicine Crow is familiar to many World War II history buffs. He played a prominent part in Ken Burns's documentary series *The War*. Medicine Crow was the last living war chief of the Crow tribe, which meant he'd completed four wartime deeds as a young soldier in the European theater: touching a living enemy, taking an enemy's weapon, leading a successful mission inside the enemy's territory, and stealing an enemy's horse. Medicine Crow actually stole dozens of horses from Nazis who were resting at a farmhouse, and he'd led a team of American soldiers carrying explosives into German territory to weaken the Siegfried Line. He also surprised a German soldier in an alley and knocked the man's rifle out of his hands. Instead of shooting the German on the spot, Medicine Crow wrestled him to the ground.

"He had me down, but I turned him over and grabbed him by the throat," Medicine Crow recalled in an interview for *The War*. "I was ready to kill him."[17]

But Medicine Crow loosened his grip after the man gasped a word that transcends language barriers: "Mama!" Medicine Crow said that word opened his ears, and he let go of his terrified enemy—no doubt a young man in his early twenties or even teens, as so many millions who fought in World War II were.

Joe Medicine Crow lived near Lodge Grass, Montana, not far from the Wyoming border. He was the first member of the Crow tribe to earn a master's degree, and he wrote several books on the history and culture of the Crow people. He was also instrumental in developing the renowned Plains Indian Museum at the Buffalo Bill Center of the West in Cody, Wyoming, and that's how he knew Senator Alan K. Simpson. In March 2008 I invited Senator Simpson up to Billings to join me for a news conference where we announced we were formally asking President Bush to award Medicine Crow the Presidential Medal of Freedom, the nation's highest civilian honor. When Medicine Crow spoke in Billings that day, he donned his war chief's headdress and sang an honor song in the Crow language, thumping his hand on the podium for a drumbeat.[18]

President Bush didn't get around to acknowledging our bipartisan nomination, but his successor did. A little over a year later, on August 12, 2009, President Obama gave Medals of Freedom to—among others—Justice Sandra Day O'Connor, the physicist Stephen Hawking, Senator Ted Kennedy, Bishop Desmond Tutu, and Dr. Joseph Medicine Crow, who wore his war chief's headdress during the ceremony at the White House.[19] There's a great photo that makes me smile every time I see it. In it, President Obama is trying to avoid getting tickled on the cheek by eagle feathers as he fastens the medal around Medicine Crow's neck.

I said long ago that Montanans will remember Joe Medicine Crow and the stories of his pioneering heroism for generations. In March 2015, at the age of 101, he took part in a ground-breaking ceremony for a new middle school in Billings named in his honor.

That's another picture I'll never forget: A frail war hero wrapped in an honorary wool blanket, wearing sunglasses and his eagle feather headdress, speaking about children at the future site of Joe Medicine Crow Middle School. Around his neck: his Medal of Freedom.[20] Joe Medicine Crow passed away the following year.

Another senator who wrote a letter in support of Joe Medicine Crow's nomination was one of my heroes and closest friends in the US Senate. I usually sat with Senator Daniel Inouye of Hawaii during our weekly lunches with the Senate Democrats, trying to glean whatever advice and scoop he was willing to share.

"Big One!" he'd say with a vigorous grin. That was his nickname for me.

"Senator," I'd reply with reverence.

For a few years Senator Inouye's office was directly across from mine on the seventh floor of the Hart Building, and it was easy to see him coming or going because he had a conspicuous security detail (as president pro tempore of the Senate, Inouye was third in line to the presidency, behind the vice president and the Speaker of the House). He often joked about our missing limbs. The loss of his right arm, of course, was a much more heroic tale than that of the loss of my fingers.

In April 1945, Second Lieutenant Inouye's platoon came under heavy machine gun fire near San Terenzo, Italy. Inouye was part of the US Army's *Nisei* 442nd Regimental Combat Team, which was composed mostly of second-generation Japanese Americans. The twenty-year-old Inouye led his men crawling on their bellies toward a German fortification high on a ridge when bullets started raining down on them. Inouye tossed a grenade into the German bunker, then began shooting at it, unaware of a bullet hole in his own bleeding gut. As Inouye threw a second grenade at the bunker, a German soldier shot Inouye with an explosive round that shattered his right forearm. The late historian Norman K. Risjord wrote about the firefight in his book *Giants in Their Time*:

> Inouye's grenade destroyed the bunker, but one dying German squeezed off a final round from his machine gun,

hitting Inouye in the leg. Inouye rolled several yards down the hill, passed out, and woke up to see blood spurting from the severed artery of his arm. He tried to put a tourniquet on, but there wasn't enough left of the arm to work with. So he grabbed the artery with his fingers and pinched it closed. His men crowded around and prepared to carry him back to the rear. "Get back up that hill!" Inouye screamed through his envelope of pain. "Nobody called off the war!"[21]

In 2000, President Clinton honored Inouye with the Medal of Honor, citing "extraordinary heroism and devotion to duty.

"By his gallant, aggressive tactics and by his indomitable leadership, Second Lieutenant Inouye enabled his platoon to advance through formidable resistance, and was instrumental in the capture of the ridge," the Medal of Honor citation reads.[22]

"When someone told me that I did and said those things, I didn't believe it was me," Senator Inouye told me once. "You'd have to be crazy to do that!"

Adrenaline does strange things to people in trauma.

When I returned to the Senate in November 2012 following my first reelection victory, Senator Inouye had lost his vigor. He was eighty-eight years old, and his health had taken a turn for the worse in the weeks we'd been away from Washington. Senator Inouye relied on a wheelchair, and he had just started using an oxygen tank. But soon after I returned he sent me a handwritten note:

> *Congratulations, Jon.*
> *I can rest now.*
> *—Dan*

A few weeks later, the senator passed away. He was the thirty-second American to lie in repose in the rotunda of the US Capitol. And on Sunday, December 23, I brought a borrowed trumpet with me to Honolulu. I had offered to play "Taps" for my friend and mentor, and Senator Inouye's family graciously accepted. The military organizers tasked with planning the senator's funeral weren't so sure.

"Senator, exactly how many seconds will your performance be?" asked a young man in a crisp uniform as we rode in a government van to the service at the National Memorial Cemetery of the Pacific, commonly called "the Punchbowl."

"Thirty-six? Thirty-seven?" I replied. "Maybe thirty-eight?"

"Exactly, sir?"

"I can make it exactly thirty-seven seconds. Why do you ask?"

"We have four F-22s flying over, and we need them to be directly overhead as you sound your final note. So we'll need that exact time."

It was the young man's polite way of telling me to keep my performance of "Taps" to *exactly* thirty-seven seconds, because he was about to formalize it, with military precision, with the flight commander. Another uniformed honor guardsman with a bugle joined me as I made my way up to the stage with my trumpet.

"I'll be standing next to you just in case you need any assistance," he whispered. "If you need me to come in, I'll pick it up right where you leave off."

"Got it, thanks," I told him, feeling a little bad for taking the bugler's job. "But you don't need to worry about this." Apparently the military was just as concerned about a single missed note as I was. My first, off-key performance of "Taps" on Memorial Day 1969 was also the last time I messed it up.

After the twenty-one-rifle salute, and overlooking thousands of mourners under shade tents in the Punchbowl, including Mrs. Irene Inouye, most of my Senate colleagues, and the president of the United States, I played "Taps" for my friend, trying my best to keep my own emotions in check. I kept my eyes closed until the end. As I sounded the twenty-fourth note, four F-22 Raptors from the Hawaii National Guard's 199th Fighter Squadron screamed over us in tribute, flying in the asymmetrical "missing man" formation.[23]

In late July 2014, the US Senate was on the verge of finalizing the Veterans Access, Choice and Accountability Act, a bipartisan bill aimed at improving health care for veterans across the country. That legislation created the VA's Choice Program, allowing rural veterans to receive "community care" closer to home through qualified non-VA health providers. The bill also improved the VA's ability to recruit qualified employees and addressed mental health care workforce shortages. The Democratic-controlled Senate passed the legislation with a vote of 93–3 in June. The Republican-controlled House passed its version a week later, meaning the two bills went to a smaller group of lawmakers (called a conference committee, on which I served) to work out the differences and settle on a final version. But after six weeks of negotiations, House Republicans ultimately didn't want to pay the full cost of improving health care for veterans. And instead of negotiating a final bill, they held a side meeting on July 24 and threatened to propose a whole new bill, a process which would have set us back months, if not years.

So I lit them up on the floor of the Senate. The hypocrisy and screwy priorities had boiled over and burned veterans across the country. Shenanigans like this, I said, were "a prime reason Congress's approval rating is in the single digits.

"Today some lawmakers decided to forgo the hard work of compromise. Instead of putting veterans first, they have made improving veterans' care political," I said, trying to keep my voice at a respectable level in the Senate chamber. "For six weeks, members on the other side of the aisle in both the House and the Senate have balked at the cost of taking care of our veterans. Many of these lawmakers are the same ones—*the same ones*—who put our wars in Iraq and Afghanistan on a credit card. Many of them didn't blink twice when we sent hundreds of troops into Iraq earlier this month. Way back when, when the Iraq War was authorized, Congress spent less than three weeks debating Iraq. But now when it comes to taking care of our men and women who served—many in the same wars they put on the credit card—they worry about the cost. Well, I got news for them: Taking care of our veterans is a cost of war. You do not send young Americans to war and then not take care of them. And it should not be the case that we rush to war but drag our feet when it comes to our vets."[24]

I was on a tear. That summer I held more town hall meetings

with veterans across Montana, and this time they told me they had lost faith in Washington's ability to get anything done. Many of them had shrugged off their hopes of seeing improvements in VA health care. Blame fell on both parties.

"But I told them it could be done," I said. "If we don't change course—if we don't leave politics at the door as we promised—then it's going to be hard for me to go back to Montana and look those veterans in the eye. We can do better, and we must do better."

Negotiations ultimately got back on track, and both the House and the Senate overwhelmingly approved the final bill in late July. President Obama signed it into law a week later.[25] But the stain of partisan politics kept creeping back into policy making for veterans.

When Senator Johnny Isakson became chairman and I became the top Democrat on the Senate Veterans' Affairs Committee in 2017, we had one of those well-intentioned conversations about checking politics at the door. Often when that happens in Washington, it lasts only until the first disagreement. But there's something about Johnny Isakson's steady leadership and southern authenticity; together, we agreed to keep partisan politics out of the art of policy making. There's plenty we disagree on, but when it came to veterans we both honored our commitment.

The Trump administration, however, had a different approach. With support from Trump-allied organizations like the Concerned Veterans for America, funded by Charles and David Koch, high-level insiders close to the president furtively pushed the administration to make overtures that would either privatize the VA or eventually force the privatization of the VA. Both Senator Isakson and I strongly opposed privatization of the VA, as did VA secretary David Shulkin and all of the mainstream veterans' service organizations. The VA certainly has its share of problems, but privatizing the department would only spell disaster for millions of veterans. Privatization means paying gobs of money to third-party administrators with little accountability; it would mean millions of veterans—especially those scattered across rural America—getting stuck without access to quality, affordable health care. With a privatized VA, the need to turn a profit would supersede the responsibility to provide service, which would mean the VA would place less of a priority on veterans who live in rural parts of the country, resulting in fewer health care providers, fewer facilities, and substandard care.

"The private sector, already struggling to provide adequate access to care in many communities, is ill-prepared to handle the number and complexity of patients that would come from closing or downsizing VA hospitals and clinics, particularly when it involves the mental health needs of people scarred by the horrors of war," Shulkin wrote in the *New York Times*. "Working with community providers to adequately ensure that veterans' needs are met is a good practice. But privatization leading to the dismantling of the department's extensive health care system is a terrible idea."[26]

Yet we kept getting word that privatization was the direction the administration—or at least a powerful cabal of White House insiders—ultimately wanted to go. So in March 2018, during a hearing with veterans' service organizations and amid reports of merciless infighting inside the VA, I opened the meeting by putting it all on the table.

"The dysfunction of this administration has now bled over to the VA," I said to the leaders of the organizations in a tone meant to sound like a warning, because it was. "And I'm very, very, very concerned. I can tell you that Johnny Isakson and I have worked hard together. And we worked for you; we've taken our direction from you every step of the way. And there's not been any Democrats or Republicans; it's been about veterans, a hundred percent of the time. Unfortunately the dysfunction is hindering our ability to do our job."[27]

I reminded the veterans' service organizations that Senator Isakson and I had been working with them on another major piece of legislation designed to improve the VA and the new Veterans Choice Program. But the Trump administration kept pushing back, even after Secretary Shulkin assured us he opposed privatizing the VA. Dr. Shulkin was the only secretary in President Trump's cabinet who received a unanimous confirmation vote from the Senate, and it was clear that some of the president's closest advisers and loyalists were knifing the secretary in the back.[28]

"The president really needs to decide if he's going to empower Secretary Shulkin to actually do his job, or whether he's going to side with political interests—something these committees have never done," I said sternly. "Political interests like the Koch brothers, who, by the way, I do not believe understand what our nation's veterans are going through. We need to know who's calling the shots. I'm going to tell you what, the stakes are high. They've never been higher."

And I remembered, as I often do, the Vietnam veteran who stood up and pointed his finger at me in Hamilton in early 2007.

"This is very disturbing to me because we send young men and women off to war and they come back changed," I said. "Some of those changes you can see; some of them you can't. But we have an obligation as the people of this country, and we have an obligation to the next generation of fighting men and women to take care of you if we have changed you."

Exactly two weeks after that hearing, on the afternoon of March 28, President Trump suddenly tweeted an enormous shakeup in his own cabinet:

> I am pleased to announce that I intend to nominate highly respected Admiral Ronny L. Jackson, MD, as the new Secretary of Veterans Affairs . . . I am thankful for Dr. David Shulkin's service to our country and to our GREAT VETERANS![29]

Yep, President Trump dismissed Shulkin by announcing his would-be successor on Twitter. In another asinine attempt to tell America the earth is flat, the White House somehow insisted Shulkin "resigned from his position," though Shulkin said he would not resign because he was "committed to making sure this job was seen through to the very end."[30]

David Shulkin had been embroiled in his own scandal. Earlier in the year the VA's inspector general found that Shulkin had taken a trip that "resulted in a misuse of VA resources." Shulkin and his wife, along with senior VA leaders and a six-member security detail, spent eleven days in Europe, which an anonymous whistleblower said was "for more personal than official activities" (including accepting free tickets to Wimbledon). The trip cost the VA "at least $122,334."[31] Though I will never defend any misuse of government resources, Shulkin claimed the report was exaggerated, and he openly said the impetus of the inspector general's investigation was political retribution. We never had a chance to verify the facts, because the president replaced him. (Shulkin later said he reimbursed the government $4,312 for his wife's airfare.)[32]

"There are people within my organization who are not happy with the progress we're making and the direction of the organization, who are deliberately undermining me," he told reporters. "They're killing me."[33]

Hours after the president's tweet, Shulkin sent a column to the *New York Times* saying his firing boiled down to the simple fact that he opposed privatizing the VA:

> It seems that these successes within the department have intensified the ambitions of people who want to put VA health care in the hands of the private sector. I believe differences in philosophy deserve robust debate, and solutions should be determined based on the merits of the arguments. The advocates within the administration for privatizing VA health services, however, reject this approach. They saw me as an obstacle to privatization who had to be removed. That is because I am convinced that privatization is a political issue aimed at rewarding select people and companies with profits, even if it undermines care for veterans.[34]

Shulkin's last line, though, stood out most: "As I prepare to leave government, I am struck by a recurring thought: It should not be this hard to serve your country."

Of course, as it often does in the "chaos presidency" of the Trump administration, focus immediately shifted from Dr. David Shulkin to Dr. Ronny Jackson.

"Who the hell is this guy?" I asked my team on the Veterans' Affairs Committee. Nobody in the wide world of veterans' affairs had really heard of Dr. Jackson, and his nomination was a complete surprise.

They shrugged and said they'd dive into Jackson's record and give me a report.

I went back to my office, shut the door, and sat down. I looked at the two framed pictures on my desk, both of my tractors on the farm—my thinking pictures.

This is madness, I thought. *Our "great veterans" deserve so much better than a president who has no clue what he's doing.*

It should not be this hard to serve your country.

The fight is not over yet.

CHAPTER 4

Falling Down, Marrying Up, Taking Over

Had I been able to open my eyes, I probably would have seen blurry clouds rolling across the sky through my face mask. I'm sure a whistle blew and the play ended with the clattering of plastic shoulder pads in the distance, but I didn't hear it. Nobody came over to check on me as I lay on my back in the grass, unable to move. For several long minutes I winced in pain with words from my parents bouncing around in my head. I may be built like a linebacker, but that late September afternoon in Big Sandy was the beginning and the end of my football career.

Shit, I thought as I eventually wiggled all seven fingers. They still worked, thank God. *My folks were right.*

A few days earlier I had begged Mother and Dad to let me play football. At the kitchen table both of them grumbled at the prospect, but they reluctantly agreed that I could join the team as soon as we got the winter wheat planted. That meant I joined the Big Sandy

Pioneers six weeks later than everyone else. But my parents' permission to play football came with a warning.

"There's a very good chance you will get hurt if you do this," Mother said with that disapproving tone most kids hear and ignore. "And you may not walk again."

I shrugged off the advice. I also didn't concern myself with the fact that high school athletics left both of my older brothers with injuries. I just wanted to suit up and play ball. That afternoon our football coach had us run plays. I watched from the sideline as a defensive tackle went down.

"Tester!" he called. "Get in!"

As a 140-pound freshman with more weight in my shoulders than my belly, I thought the stars had aligned for a promising career in football, though I didn't even watch much on TV back then. And I really had no idea what I was supposed to do other than to try and intercept the ball if I could and tackle the quarterback whenever I could. The coach gave me no instruction. I assume he sized me up and figured I was well versed in the rules and strategies of the game. When he blew his whistle, I jumped over the guard and took down the quarterback. I felt pretty good about the success of my first play. The coach said nothing and we lined up for another one. When the whistle blew, I did the exact same thing. I expected the coach to tell me to stop tackling our own quarterback in practice, but again, he said nothing. *Two for two*, I thought. *I guess I'm pretty good at football!*

On the third play, the guard disappeared and a hole opened up right through the middle. I looked up and saw a straight path to the quarterback, so I took off for him. Little did I know that the coach's trap play involved a massive running back—a senior twice my size named Rocky Zaparynuk. Rocky was a good guy, but man, even his name sounds like it could hurt you. Out of the blue Rocky slammed into me head-on with full force. Every bone in my body cracked as the world faded to starry black and I hit the ground with a thud. Rocky then put one foot on my crotch and the other on my forehead and ran over the top of me, ending my role in that play with a painful exclamation point. My parents, yet again, were right. After the world came back into focus, I limped off the field and took a shower. If the football coach wanted to teach me a lesson, it worked. I never came back.

Well, there's always track and field, I thought. After all those years pickin' rock, I certainly had the heft needed to throw a decent shot put. But for some reason our coach thought even us field types should get a good feel for running long distance. I could run up to 440 yards at a reasonable dash before petering out, but I've never, ever considered myself a runner, much less a distance runner.

Big Sandy's varsity basketball coach was a formative figure in my life. He taught social studies at Big Sandy High and coached on the side. Because his influence on me wasn't necessarily a positive one, and because he never signed up for the public scrutiny that so many of us in politics are accustomed to, I'll call him simply "Coach." Coach was fresh out of college and spent a lot of time throwing weights around. He had bulging muscles and enormous muttonchop sideburns that seemed out of style even in the seventies.

In his social studies classroom, Coach had a severe style of teaching. His method inspired his athletes, whom he seemed to favor, but it certainly didn't bring out the best in me. He didn't motivate me whatsoever. And for some reason he seemed to save most of his ire for me. I wonder if his disdain was fueled by a deep-seated resentment that, though I looked the part, I didn't apply myself in sports. Coach would hurl pop quiz questions at me that sounded like military orders.

"Tester! Thomas Jefferson's second vice president."

"I dunno, Coach."

"Tester! Year of the Louisiana Purchase."

"Sorry, Coach."

"Tester! Author of the Bill of Rights."

I should have known the answers, but I didn't. And I hated being embarrassed in front of the class over and over again, so I mentally checked out and I stopped putting any effort into his class.

"Sheep," he would say to us. "You're all sheep."

That really drove me crazy, because I never thought of myself as a follower.

Coach made it clear by his attitude that he thought I would never amount to anything. He never said those words to my face, but I believed deep down that Coach didn't expect me to succeed. He saw me, I thought, as a waste of his time and energy.

In full disclosure, I wasn't inspired to really apply myself in high school. I saved all my mental energy for the things I felt were more important, and back then most of those things were related to the farm. After I became a teacher, I realized most of my teachers probably saw me as an average student, and when average teachers believe students are only average, those students stay average. If I had a good teacher, it made a world of difference. I cared. I excelled. If I got an average teacher, I put in average effort. Coach, of course, was less than average in my opinion, and that meant I didn't give a damn about applying myself for him, or for civics in general, for that matter.

Coach was also in charge of the track team. My first day on the team, he piled us into the back of his pickup and drove us way out to Hurd's Barn, six miles up Kenilworth Road. Then he told us to run back to the high school. I tried jogging for a few good minutes and soon the rest of the team disappeared ahead of me. I was far at the back of the pack when my elderly neighbor Archie Archibald came tootling by in his '58 Chevy and rolled down the window.

"Whaddya doin' walking way out here, Jon?" he asked, unaware that I was *supposed* to be running. "Need a ride?"

"Hell yes, I need a ride."

I climbed into Archie's pickup and he drove me back to Big Sandy High. I waved at my teammates as I passed them en route. When I got back to the locker room I took a hot shower, got dressed, and left just as the fastest runners—the poor suckers who actually *wanted* to run long distances—arrived, sweaty and exhausted.

"You're in deep trouble," my athletic buddy Curt Reichelt told me, panting. "Coach is gonna run your ass off now."

"Nah, he won't," I assured Curt, "cuz I'm done with track and field, and I ain't coming back."

Well, there's always basketball, I thought. I've always loved playing basketball. Still do, in fact. I often played pickup games whenever I

could with whoever happened to be hanging around the school parking lot, including Jeff Ament, who had more of a knack for playing
a bass guitar. Jeff later went off to Seattle and formed Pearl Jam with
Stone Gossard.

After I tried out for the high school basketball team my sophomore year, I just never got into it. Maybe it had something to do with
having to spend more time with Coach. I knew I was better than
some of the other kids, but I didn't get to play very often. I wondered
if it was because of my missing fingers.

Early in the season during a game in Chinook, I got bored sitting in the bleachers and, as bored kids do, decided to make my own
trouble. In what wasn't the smartest decision of my life, I thought it
would be fun to antagonize the strongest guy in our class, who played
on the varsity team. He did not (and still does not) have an ounce of
fat on his body, and I don't think he even felt pain.

"You smell awful," I joshed. "You could knock a fly off a shit-
wagon."

He lunged toward me and I took off running. But while chasing
me the poor guy jammed his thumb in the railing of the bleachers,
and his injury was so bad he couldn't play in the varsity game. This
also meant Coach was, appropriately, furious with me. Later that evening, another smaller teammate started trash-talking me in the locker
room about something I don't even remember. So I picked him up,
lifted him above my shoulders, and helicoptered him around my
head. That's when Coach walked in on the shenanigans and unloaded
on me.

"Tester!" he screamed. I dropped the poor kid. Coach narrowed
his eyes and pointed a thick finger at me. "You've done enough jack-
assin' around today."

Coach sat me out; I didn't step foot on the hardwood once that
night. I deserved the punishment. Chinook slaughtered Big Sandy,
and I realized I might not be cut out for high school basketball. Between my junior and senior years, Coach left Big Sandy for a new
job several hours away and we got a new coach, Luke Gerber. I got
along swimmingly with Mr. Gerber. I didn't try out for the team, but

he invited me to practice with them, and I did. At Thanksgiving, I walked up to him and asked if I could join the team, and he said no. That decision devastated me.

"There's an important lesson to be learned here," Mr. Gerber said the next morning when he saw how dejected I was. "I love ya, Jon, but you didn't sign up when we started. If you're going to do something, *do it*. Don't screw around." I nodded. The important lesson Mr. Gerber taught me that day has applied to just about everything I have done since. That was, however, the end of my basketball career. And I decided instead to go out for the speech and debate club.

A fellow trumpet player named Johannes Grosen and I both joined that debate club our junior year. The first time I watched a debate, I got so confused I thought maybe it wasn't for me. But Grosen and I stuck through it, and as debate partners we learned the finer points of building arguments and rebuttals, and the art of sparring with words and simple psychology. I probably wasn't worth a damn in debate, but by the end of the season I got the hang of it. In our district competition, Grosen and I put in what we thought was a hell of an effort, and we were 100 percent certain we had won, but the judges thought differently and declared us the losers. That's where I learned to never take a victory for granted.

It was my speech coach, though, who taught me how to articulate political arguments. Jim Barsotti, or "Mr. B" as I called him, was at the other end of the spectrum from Coach. Mr. B was one of Big Sandy's beloved English teachers who later became the high school principal. He founded the speech and debate team, and when he got excited about something, which was often, he would yell "Balla balla!"[1] Mr. B taught us how to structure speeches to build an arc of suspense. He taught us the importance of clarity and simple language. Big Sandy High School had a hell of a little speech and debate team in the seventies, and we held our own when competing against much larger schools all over the state. I studied Mr. B's advice carefully, and I turned out to be better than average, because Jim Barsotti was far better than average. He was a big man with a big personality—the definition of a master teacher. Mr. B was, no doubt, one of the most influential people on my political career. Studying both sides of an issue and changing minds with facts and words sparked in me a flame of politics.

So at the end of my junior year, I ran for student body president on a ticket with my next-door neighbor, Mark Ostrom, as vice president. Our other neighbor Curt Larson ran with us as secretary-treasurer. Curt was the only one among us who actually understood electoral politics. We met one afternoon to talk about how to beat the jocks, who were also running for the student offices. Curt suggested we court the support of all the girls, and the seventh and eighth graders, who also got to vote in the school we shared with them.

The plan worked. Our ticket won a majority of votes that spring. My first order of business as president was to hold a schoolwide ice cream social at the end of the year. During that party, a bunch of younger kids came up to us to say thank you for reaching out to them. Even seventh graders understand when elected officeholders care about their opinions. It was the first time I got positive feedback from my constituents, and that will motivate any elected leader—it certainly motivates me today. Working in the US Senate can be overwhelmingly frustrating, slow-moving, politics-strained work. All of that is overshadowed when Montanans come up and say thank you for a tough vote, or for helping to secure veterans' benefits.

Big Sandy's movie theater had burned to the ground years earlier, and as the new leaders of Big Sandy High's student body, Mark, Curt, and I salvaged the big letters once used for the theater's marquee. We repainted them and fashioned a large sign out of wire to hang from the roof of the high school. Every week we climbed up to the roof and painstakingly strung our letters into messages announcing dances or sporting events or bake sales, which we hung over the side of the building to update our fellow students. We also finally completed the task of helping raise enough money to recarpet the school library, which had been an ongoing project for previous student councils for years.

For Government Day, on behalf of Big Sandy's students, I invited one of our area's most familiar elected leaders to visit with us about his long career in public service. State senator David James, a wheat farmer from the nearby town of Joplin, had served as a Democrat in the legislature since 1939—a stint that included two terms as House minority leader, two terms as Senate majority leader, and three terms as Senate president pro tempore.[2] Senator James was a tall, soft-spoken old farmer who accepted my invitation graciously and visited with us Big Sandy students for the better part of a day. He made the art and war of state politics sound *fun*.

But it was during a field trip to Helena to see the Montana State Capitol when I decided I wanted to run for a seat in the legislature some day, or at least maybe a seat on the Chouteau County Commission. At that point in my life, the Capitol was the most impressive building I had ever stepped foot in. There I stood—a big high school junior with hair a lot longer than it is today, a budding knack for speech and music, and a growing appreciation of politics—beneath the gilded rotunda of the Capitol. I remember seeing for the first time the chamber of the Montana House of Representatives, adorned by the largest of Charles M. Russell's paintings: a twenty-five-by-twelve-foot depiction of Salish people meeting on horseback with Meriwether Lewis and William Clark in southwestern Montana in 1805. The massive mural is notable because it's actually hard to spot Lewis and Clark; Russell carefully subdued their presence in the background and shifted the focus of his painting on the people who called Montana home tens of thousands of years before white explorers ever arrived.[3]

I didn't pay much attention to which party controlled the Montana Senate or the House at the time (Democrats controlled both chambers through the mid-seventies).[4] In fact, back then, I didn't even think about which party suited me best. But I clearly remember seeing busy legislators buzzing through the wide hallways and all sorts of folks bustling in and out of Governor Tom Judge's office on the second floor. I remember hearing the clacking of cowboy boots and dress shoes on the marble floors, and seeing the sunlight pouring in through the windows. There was something about that day in Helena. I felt small but proud of the fact that I was part of something big. Montanans had built this building, created their own government inside it, and carefully deliberated the direction of the entire state. I knew then that I wanted to be part of it.

I started paying a bit more attention to what was happening in Helena after that field trip. And like Mother, I started paying more attention to what was happening in Washington, DC, too. The languishing war in Vietnam and Nixon's Watergate scandal consumed the news. Back at home, I spent much of my senior year in high school upping my game on my trumpet. We had a new music teacher that year, an Australian named Graham Nicholson, and he too knew how to turn the screws to get better-than-average out of me. As the VFW bugler, I still regularly played "Taps" at local funerals, and I could hold my own in performing all kinds of music. Mr. Nicholson first suggested that I at least think about becoming a music teacher someday.

I had planned to attend the Helena Vocational-Technical Center to become a diesel mechanic after I graduated from high school. After all, diesel technology is a pretty good skill to know for a farmer. Maybe I could scrape out a few extra bucks fixing various engines for my neighbors in addition to running the farm. Still, the nagging feeling that Coach believed I would never amount to anything bothered the hell out of me. I was going to prove him wrong, somehow.

"Think about getting a degree in music, Jon," Mother suggested, after she sat me down with Dad at the kitchen table.

"Anyone can learn how to fix an engine," Dad added. "A music degree could give you something to fall back on, because you won't always know if the farm's gonna be here."

They were right again, but pride ultimately tipped the scale; I simply didn't want Coach to be right, and a four-year college degree would show him. So I drove down to Great Falls with my trumpet, auditioned for and got a performance scholarship—$600 per year for four years—from the College of Great Falls, which had one of the best music programs in the state.[5] That $2,400 made all the difference; it was enough to make college affordable, as long as I lived off campus with Bob. Bob had already settled into his career as an air guard medic. He let me stay in a spare room in his little house in Great Falls, and he offered fresh advice when I told him I was going to put my name in the hat for a seat on the student senate.

"Hardly anyone knows who I am," I complained. The College of Great Falls, now called the University of Providence, was a small Roman Catholic college in Great Falls. Back then about a thousand students attended CGF, and many of them lived together in dormitories on campus; I was an outsider. "Nobody even knows my name."

"Here's what you do," Bob said with a cigarette between his lips. "Buy a couple cartons of these, go to the dorms, door-to-door, and hand 'em out to everyone you see. 'I'm Jon Tester, I'm running for the student senate, here's your free cigarette.'"

"Really?"

"Oldest trick in the book."

Health concerns aside, a simple strategy like handing out free cigarettes to young adults to build name recognition and ultimately to earn votes is a textbook example of retail politics. I didn't take Bob up on his advice, but it probably would have worked. I lost miserably in my one and only attempt to be part of the student government at CGF. But it was probably for the best. For those four years I immersed myself in music. I studied theory and history and ear training. I realized it helped to have a better-than-average understanding of math, because it translated straight to music. I performed in ensembles and with quartets and in concert, in music halls and churches. For years I had played the trumpet, but college was where I became a musician. I earned a teaching certificate, and I graduated from college with honors. That's when I realized, as my older brothers had before me, that even though I was an average student at Big Sandy High School, I could open new doors if I applied myself in college. I proved Coach wrong. I *succeeded*.

In the fall of 1975, while home in Big Sandy one weekend, I went to a Pioneers football game and saw a stunning woman cheering with her girlfriends. She had no idea who I was, nor did she notice me sneaking glances at her.

"Who is that?" I finally whispered to a buddy.

"Sharla Bitz."

"I'll be damned."

Bitz was a familiar name across north-central Montana—there were lots of them, all descended from German homesteaders who'd made their way west during James Hill's railroad boom. I had never met Sharla, who was two years younger than me and who had, until recently, lived in the little town of Chinook. I couldn't take my eyes off her; she was slender, with long, golden brown hair and bright blue eyes. I didn't see her again until the following spring, when I joined my folks for a Sunday service at the First Church of God in Big Sandy. There she was, sitting in a pew in front of me, just as beautiful as the first time I saw her. *I'll be damned again*, I thought, forgetting I was in church. I still didn't have the intestinal fortitude to strike up a conversation.

That summer, some folks from church organized a youth barbecue at Archie Archibald's farm, halfway between our place and the Bitz farm, as the magpie flies. I decided to go just in case Sharla showed up. *Maybe this time*, I thought, *I'll muster up the guts to introduce myself*. Quite a few young parishioners, all about my age, were there, and we eventually staked out a diamond in Archie's pasture for a softball game. Softball, like basketball, is a favorite pastime in north-central Montana and another game I'll never grow tired of. Sharla and I ended up on opposite teams that afternoon; she had a hell of an arm and pitched for her team. At bat, of course, I tried to impress her with what I planned to be a line drive to the third baseman.

"Jon Tester?" Sharla shouted from the mound. "I'm gonna save ya the trouble of running!"

I didn't know how to respond, so I didn't. If I wasn't already sweating, you might have noticed that I blushed. She hurled the ball toward me and it whizzed through the strike zone, smacking the catcher's mitt. My powerful swing missed it completely. It was a damn good pitch. Sharla signaled strike one by putting her finger in the air, then she smirked.

"We'll see," I muttered.

Her second pitch was just as good as the first. And so was the third. Sharla Bitz, whom I'd been thinking about for the better part

of a year, and whom I was trying to get the courage to formally introduce myself to, never got to see me hit the softball. She struck me out,
just as she predicted. I bit my tongue because I was surrounded by a
bunch of nice churchgoers, but I silently cursed up a storm. Then I
looked back to the mound and Sharla gave me one of her smiles that
made it all worthwhile.

A few months later Steve Sibra and Rick Chauvet and I drove down
to the autumn dance at Kenilworth Hall, a multipurpose community
center that served as a dance pavilion, a local meeting space, and a
polling location. The autumn dance was something of a postharvest
tradition in Big Sandy, full of food and live music. And that's where I
saw Sharla Bitz again. As I often do when paper plates and messy food
are involved, I managed to dribble pork and beans down the front of
my shirt, resulting in a long red stain down to my belly. But I'd already
been embarrassed in front of Sharla, so I asked her to dance with me
anyway. She took my left hand in her right and, without saying a word,
noticed I was short a few digits. She simply clasped her long fingers
over my scar, looked at me and smiled again.

We all left Kenilworth Hall at about the same time that night.
Steve and Rick hopped into my Chevy Vega and we headed toward
town. Sharla also drove a Vega, and she left a few minutes before us
with her girlfriend Karolee Ophus.

"Woooo, that Sharla Bitz," Rick said from the back seat. "She's a
good-lookin' gal!"

"Yes she is," I agreed. Steve, one of my best friends to this day,
nodded in the passenger seat.

"I'm goin' out with her this weekend," said Rick.

"Oh?"

"Yep. Going down to Belgrade for the game."

I floored my Vega, figuring we could catch up to Sharla and
Karolee in a matter of minutes. Sharla's little brother Larry played
quarterback for the Big Sandy Pioneers, who were up against the Belgrade Panthers in a class B playoff game that Saturday. Then as they
are now, class B playoff games were worth traveling long Montana

distances for. Belgrade was a four-and-a-half-hour drive away. That was a lot of time to get to spend in a car with Sharla.

Soon I saw the red taillights of Sharla's Vega, and I flashed my headlights to get her to pull over. She did. I pulled up next to them on Kenilworth Road and rolled down the window.

"Hey Sharla!" I shouted across Steve's lap. Rick nervously fidgeted in the back seat and Karolee giggled. "Wanna go to Belgrade with me this weekend?"

"I'd love to, Jon!" She smiled.

And that was that.

"You asshole, Tester," Rick seethed.

The Pioneers lost by three points that weekend, ending their season in disappointment. But I didn't pay much attention to the game. Sharla and I started dating seriously after that weekend. From the minute she struck me out in softball to this day, her kindness has touched me. She's made me laugh. She shoots me straight when I need it most. She's been with me during the best times and the toughest. And since the day she stepped foot on the old Pearson homestead outside Big Sandy, she has been at home there.

Just a few months after we started going steady, I proposed to Sharla, and she said yes. On Saturday, September 3, 1977, less than a year after our first dance in Kenilworth Hall, we got hitched in Big Sandy. Our wedding took place in the Masonic temple (the church was undergoing renovation). My friend Mark Ostrom stood behind me as best man along with my brothers, Bob and Dave.

For the first few months of our marriage, Sharla and I rented Bob's little house on Sixteenth Avenue South in Great Falls. Then in early 1978, Mother and Dad sat us down for a life-changing announcement. After thirty-five years running the farm outside Big Sandy, they were coming in from the fields for good. Dad had faithfully remained on our flatland farm for decades, but the mountains called. Mother and Dad decided to uproot and move to northern Idaho, where Dave Junior ran his veterinary practice. Of course it was no secret that I was set to take over the homestead; I had expected and prepared for this transition for most of my life. But I was surprised that my folks had planned to move to an entirely different state. It wasn't difficult to picture Dad making himself at home in Idaho. Mother had never really wanted to leave the land where she'd grown up and raised her family; she was as much a part of our land as the good soil itself. But she'd agreed to go.

That spring, after Dad and Mother got the spring seeds planted and after our neighbors held a huge going-away potluck in their honor at Kenilworth Hall, Sharla and I helped pack their belongings into our grain truck, a horse trailer, and a couple of pickups, then we caravanned to Rathdrum, Idaho, just north of Coeur d'Alene. As my folks moved out, Sharla and I hauled our belongings into the familiar little yellow house. I was only twenty-one and Sharla was nineteen when we began our new life as farmers in our own right. We were keenly aware that our first order of business was to find extra income; we had only $600 in our checking account that spring. The farm itself was in great shape, but our little yellow house had started to show its age. The alkaline soil had slowly eaten away its concrete foundation, which meant the basement walls had started to crumble. That's why Sharla and I decided early on to keep operating the butcher shop.

"I'm looking at a chunk of beef I've never seen before," I told Dad halfway through cutting up the first steer I had to butcher on my own. I had to call Dad often for basic farm advice that first year alone on the farm.

As I have done countless times since, I gave the steer an instant death, shooting it carefully above and between the eyes with a .218 Bee—a powerful Winchester cartridge with a hollow-point bullet. I hung its carcass by its hind quarters from my front loader to let it bleed out, pulled off the hide with the help of a wickedly sharp knife, then let the beef dry-age in the cooler. But after trimming the steaks I made a wrong cut somewhere along the line, which resulted in a mysterious piece of meat I couldn't identify. After explaining every step of that solo butchering project over the phone, Dad told me I had cut the front quarter too far.

Soon after that, the electric pump for our gasoline tank quit working, so I called him again for guidance.

"Well, is it an electrical problem?" he asked patiently. "If you still have power, then your pump is burnt out and you have to take it apart to see where you went wrong. If you don't have power, you need to go down the line and see where the juice stops, then restore power to the pump."

Ultimately, Dad made me troubleshoot all the little challenges of farm life on my own; he let me make mistakes so I could learn from them. He and Mother pointed me in the right direction, but I didn't get to learn anything the easy way, thank God. But Dad's patience for the farm and its concerns wore thin during those first few years in Idaho. For a couple of seasons, they both came back to Big Sandy to help with the harvest—after all, it was Mother's favorite time of the year. But one year Dad was so cranky and quick-tempered during harvest we drove him to Great Falls and sent him on a plane back to Idaho, alone. That's when we truly understood what we saw coming for years: Dave Tester's *duty* to the farm had finally surpassed its shelf life. After that, Dad and Mother came back at harvest, but only for a few days each August before going back home to Idaho.

Mother also understood how difficult it can be for children when parents live too close. When she and Dad took over the farm in 1943, her folks lived only twelve miles east in Big Sandy, and they kept close tabs on the homestead. Mother knew she'd never be able to live up to their expectations for the piece of land they'd tamed. She could have insisted on living with us on the farm until her final days, but she knew better. She understood the importance of giving space to Sharla and me, and to the new family we hoped to start. Though they had retired from farm work, Mother and Dad weren't done contributing to their community. For several years in Idaho they managed the Kootenai County Fairgrounds, and they quickly made new friends.

It took me years to realize the trust and the guts involved with handing over a family farm to a twenty-one-year-old and a nineteen-year-old. I later learned that neighbors had warned my folks against their decision, but my parents insisted they knew what they were doing. I like to think they were right. Ever since we took over, Sharla and I have operated our farm as equals. We don't hire out any help; the two of us do all the work unless our kids or my brothers pitch in, which doesn't happen often. Sharla knows how to operate all the equipment. She knows how to use a grease gun and how to change the shovels on a duckfoot (a huge piece of machinery, pulled by a tractor, that tills the soil), and she can operate an auger and a meat grinder. Sharla, you might say, is one badass farmer. And I certainly wouldn't be a farmer without her.

In late 2006, not long before I took office in the Senate, Majority Leader Harry Reid assigned me to serve on six committees. Senator Reid did not assign me to the Agriculture Committee—the one committee where I already considered myself an expert. But I like to think the majority leader did the same thing my father had done to me twenty-eight years earlier: he forced me to figure out how to fix the fuel pump on my own.

In a funny way, all those decades of figuring out how to troubleshoot our own problems on the farm made it easier to figure out how to troubleshoot some of the gnarliest and most complicated issues affecting the United States. Sometimes in butchering, even when you know what you're doing, you end up with a chunk of meat you've never seen before.

"Just remember," Dad replied patiently, when I first called him in Idaho for advice about that piece of beef, "everything can be made into hamburger."

That may be true. But I prefer a good cut of steak.

CHAPTER 5

A Slow-Burning Fuse

Rear Admiral Michael Weahkee didn't expect to become part of a viral moment the morning of July 12, 2017, just three weeks after he took over as acting director of the struggling Indian Health Service (IHS). And he most certainly didn't expect me to call bullshit when he refused to answer my simple questions. In Montana, we have a long and proud tradition of calling a timeout when something doesn't make sense or someone isn't ringing true. That morning, the Senate Interior Appropriations Subcommittee, which funds much of the Indian Health Service, had asked Weahkee to come to Capitol Hill to discuss President Trump's controversial budget request. A few weeks earlier, the president had proposed cutting more than $300 million from IHS and the 2.2 million Americans it serves. And to make things worse, Senate Republicans were on the verge of holding a vote to repeal Obamacare.

I had been familiar with the problems plaguing the IHS long before I became a US senator. The agency persistently struggles with chronic workforce shortages, crumbling buildings, substandard training, and insufficient federal funding. The previous year, we'd increased IHS funding by 5 percent, and then President Trump proposed cutting it by 6 percent his first year in office.

Chairwoman Lisa Murkowski, the Republican from Alaska, opened our hearing by saying she was "very concerned that [President Trump's] budget request does not adequately meet the needs for health care in Indian Country." She noted Native Americans and Alaska Natives had seen drug-related deaths increase by a staggering 454 percent since 1979. They are three times more likely to die from diabetes than the rest of the population, and they suffer a suicide rate twice as high as the national rate.[1] Senator Tom Udall of New Mexico added that the president's proposal would mean "less money for inpatient services, preventive health care programs, drug addiction treatment, mental health programs, and specialty care."[2]

Then Senator Udall asked for an estimate of the "total amount of reimbursement" IHS facilities have received due to the Obamacare expansion of Medicaid. Weahkee didn't know the answer. It didn't take long for all of us to realize that the rear admiral wasn't comfortable answering any specific questions. Instead he gave flowery nonanswers that sounded like someone at the White House had ordered him to avoid admitting, under any circumstance, that the president's proposed budget would *hurt* the IHS.[3]

"Were you told not to answer any questions here, by the way?" I finally asked.

"No, no," Weahkee murmured. I didn't believe that for a second.

"Okay," I replied, "because I think it's absolutely unbelievable that you can't separate how much money that Medicaid has helped you with third-party billing. I mean, to the point where I think we should almost demand an audit, because that's not how things work. And you should have those numbers at the tip of your tongue, to be honest with you. If we're going to make policy here, we've got to figure out what the impacts of that policy is going to be. And by the way, it's your agency that deals with Indian Health. *Indian Health.* Nothing else." I felt my collar get hot. I simply wanted to cut to the chase and the top brass at IHS was sitting right there, with an obligation to answer questions. "What would you say the number one need is at IHS right now?"

"Absolutely it's shoring up our long-standing vacancies in some key leadership positions," he answered.

"So it's people?"

"People, yes sir."

"What does this budget do to your ability to hire staff?"

"Um, we have a lot of efforts underway—"

"Is there an increase in dollars for hiring staff, or a decrease?" I figured Rear Admiral Weahkee might take the opportunity to talk about how the hell you hire more staff with less money, with actual lives at stake. But instead he gave me more government mumbo jumbo.

"Um, we prioritized maintaining direct care services—"

"Okay, as far as total dollars go, is there an increase in dollars for hiring staff or a decrease?"

"Our priority has been on ensuring that we can continue to—"

"That's not my question," I snapped. "Does the budget—Does it increase the number of dollars for hiring people, or is it a decrease? I would assume you would know that."

"Well, sir, we had to make a lot of tough—"

"Okay, so is it a decrease? Is that what you're saying?"

"No, sir, I didn't say that."

"Look, come on, man," I pleaded. "I mean, just answer the question. I'll back you until your guts cave if the administration comes after you. But is it an increase or a decrease?"

"Um, it's, uh," Weahkee stammered, now visibly agitated. "You know, we've really prioritized our direct services to—"

"Really? I mean, I'm on your side, okay? I'm a former chairman of the Indian Affairs Committee. Former ranking member. I've been on this committee now for eight years. Just tell me if it's an increase or a decrease. It's that simple."

"Well, sir, looking at our line items, our priority has been to ensure that we can continue to provide direct health care services. And those funds have been prioritized and maintained at the levels that we can ensure that we don't have to decrease the level of service."

If you have a hard time understanding government-speak like I do, here's a translation: "We're obligated to say we want to provide health care to more people in need, but I'm certainly not going to complain about getting significantly less money, and I'd rather gaslight you than piss off the White House."

"And that's your answer?" I asked, giving the rear admiral one more chance.

"That's my answer, yes sir."

"Wow." I don't lose my temper very often. Mother gave me a slow-burning fuse, but at the end of that fuse is a powerful firecracker—I inherited that from Dad. "If you guys don't advocate for a budget, how the hell are we supposed to fix it?"

As Weahkee smugly sat there, I thought about the Native Americans in Montana, many of whom told me tearful stories about the insufficient service of the IHS. My fuse finally reached its firecracker. I realized Rear Admiral Weahkee, clearly unprepared and unwilling to even play ball, symbolized the entire problem with the IHS. That dysfunction was made worse by the Trump administration's weird and dangerous strategy of insisting that lies are facts and, under no circumstances ever admitting any wrong. The president and his people figured that a painfully awkward exchange during a sleepy congressional hearing was a small price to pay in order to get what they wanted, and they wanted to muscle through a proposal to hurt 2.2 million people without any tough questions asked, or answered. So I raised my voice.

"In ten years on this committee, I have never had somebody come up here and when I asked them a direct question, they don't answer it," I said. "I asked you a *direct question* on whether this budget was up or down and you would not answer it. You refused to answer it. That is totally unacceptable. I did not come in here with my hair on fire, but I'm leaving here with it. And I'm going to tell you something: Indian Health Service is in a *crisis*! And if you have served in Indian Health Service for ten years and you have answered the questions in Indian Health Service like you have here today, it's no wonder that it's in crisis. I cannot believe what has transpired in this hearing today."

Then I completely lost it.

"All I want is some damn answers!" I yelled. "That's it! And if we can't get answers from Indian Health, where do we go to get those answers? I don't expect you to answer that either. This is an unbelievable hearing, I just gotta tell you. I've not had one like this in my tenure in here. When I ask a question, I want an answer. It's unbelievable."

"Thank you, Senator," Chairwoman Murkowski said. "I think all of us share your frustration."

I was too riled up to think about it in real time, but losing my cool during a Senate hearing became a thing for the media. News outlets around the country picked up the exchange, with particular attention to the "all I want are some damn answers!" line, shining light on the Trump administration's unpopular budget proposal.

"This isn't the only time it's happened with this administration," I told NPR's Scott Simon a few days later. Back then, many Americans were still shocked by Sean Spicer's lie that President Trump's Inauguration Day crowd was "the largest audience to witness an inauguration, period" despite unquestionable photographic evidence to the contrary.[4] Our nation doesn't—and should never—tolerate obfuscation and lies from anyone in government.

"I think and I hope folks on both sides of the aisle in Congress will not tolerate this anymore," I continued to tell NPR. "And this budget that was put out by the Trump administration is a train wreck, for rural America in particular. And I will tell you that we need to make sure that the people who are in the leadership positions in these different agencies know exactly what's in this budget so we can hold them accountable as it unfolds."[5]

After the fiery hearing with Rear Admiral Weahkee, I got calls of support from tribal governments across the country thanking me for sticking to my guns as the Trump administration quietly tried to undermine them. To me, I was simply calling bullshit as both of my parents would have done.

The first time I called bullshit in my professional career was after a couple of years teaching music at F. E. Miley Elementary School in Big Sandy. After taking over the farm in the spring of 1978, Sharla and I needed the extra income, and I was eager to put my new music degree to work. My teaching gig was only half-time, but the school district agreed to fully contribute to health insurance for both Sharla and me. That coverage came as a relief, because even though we were pretty darn healthy, we both knew how easy it was to get sick or hurt.

My job as a music teacher didn't pay much, but I loved every minute of it. Almost. I had virtually no budget to work with, and I certainly didn't have my own classroom. I pushed a spinet piano on wheels from room to room to teach my music classes. I also taught a remedial math class. Because Miley Elementary didn't have much space, I taught that class in the gym's shower room, which was convenient because after the kids left I could use the john without even having to go to the teachers' lounge. I eventually got a half set of music books to work with, which I thought was pretty good considering I'd started out with nothing.

Early in my first year I drew musical symbols and staves on big pieces of construction paper and hung them around the classrooms as visual aids for the kids. I figured I'd brush up on drawing treble clefs by drawing one on the tile floor with a fat, washable marker. As I tried wiping up the ink after class, I realized I had used a permanent marker, and my awful practice treble clef stayed on the floor all year, which the first graders found at least memorable. They were my favorite kids to teach; first graders are young enough to enjoy the enchantment of music without any of the self-consciousness. They would surround me at the piano with excitement and soak up every lesson and eagerly sing every song I taught. I had a whole lesson involving a bunch of flimsy kazoos. Let me tell you: if you want to hook a kid on a lifetime of music appreciation, give her a kazoo when she's a first grader and tell her there's no wrong way to play it.

One day I had the first graders march around the classroom to the beat of a tune I played on the piano. I wanted them to get a feel for rhythm and tempo. Almost all the kids were having a great time marching to the beat, hooting and hollering. But when I looked up I saw one of them sitting on the heat register with his arms crossed.

"Sean, what are you doing up there?"

"This," the unimpressed little first grader told me, "is stupid."

More than forty years later I still give Sean crap about that when

I see him around town. But back then it concerned me enough to ask his teacher about the behavior.

"Sean's either really smart, or he's really a problem," I said.

"It depends on the day." She sighed. "He thinks he's too smart to pay attention when it matters most." I remembered Sean as I watched Senator Josh Hawley of Missouri during President Trump's impeachment trial in early 2020. The trial clearly bored Hawley, the Senate's youngest member, who had just turned forty. His unfortunate body language was clear: *This . . . is stupid.*

It was also during those early teaching years that I got my first look at how resilient some kids are, despite awful situations at home. One boy, Clyde, walked to school by himself on his very first day of first grade—a day most parents happily accompany their kids and kiss them goodbye. Clyde's mother had an alcohol problem, but he did his best to get himself to school every day anyway. Clyde even got himself to our Christmas concert, alone, dressed to the nines, as a first grader. Years later he became a self-motivated, standout drama student in Big Sandy.

"Kids like Clyde are exactly why we need the arts in schools," my old debate coach Jim Barsotti said after he became principal of Big Sandy High. "Clyde is one of the brightest kids in this town and a star in drama, and without drama in school, he'd have no place to go. He'd be lost in the wilderness without the *purpose* that this place provides."

On March 28, 1980, Dr. Jim Elliott, the same physician who'd stitched up my left hand fourteen years earlier, delivered our first child at the hospital in Havre.

"Well, she *can't* be Jon's kid," Dr. Elliott joked after the delivery. "She's got all ten fingers!"

Sharla and I named our daughter Christine after her great-grandmother. She didn't get to come home right away, though. Not long after she was born the nurses had to place her under bright blue lights because her bilirubin count shot through the roof. The jaundice got worse from there. Poor Christine needed three blood transfusions during the first week of her life. Sharla and I stayed by her side until she turned the corner, and soon her health returned to normal. Thank God we had health insurance to help pay for it.

That spring was my last as an elementary music teacher. Though I was a new dad, the pay was so low I literally could no longer even afford the gas needed for my commute into Big Sandy. I could make more money cutting meat on a Saturday than I could make in a whole week of teaching, so I politely told the superintendent that I had no choice but to step down from the elementary school job, and that I would happily apply for the full-time high school music teaching job if it ever opened up.

The following week, I saw an ad for the job I had just quit in the *Big Sandy Mountaineer*:

WANTED:

MUSIC TEACHER—PART-TIME

F. E. MILEY ELEMENTARY SCHOOL

(NO MUSIC DEGREE NECESSARY)

I've seen a lot of offensive stuff printed in newspapers over the years, but that one still gets the scratch-'n'-sniff sticker. When I took the half-time job, the school district required a degree in music—a degree I spent four years earning. Now anyone could apparently do it, which was insulting to me and a disservice to the kids who deserved better. That ad lit my fuse.

"*What the hell is this?*" I said, furiously smacking the newspaper in the superintendent's office. "No music degree necessary?"

The superintendent didn't say a word. He simply turned around with his back to me, apparently waiting for me to leave. And that was the end of my fuse.

"*I wouldn't take your high school job even if you wanted to give it to me!*" I roared. I slammed the newspaper on his desk with a few F-bombs and stormed out of his office.

When I was a teenager Dad had come with me as I tried to trade in my '67 VW Karmann Ghia at a dealership in Great Falls. The dealer took my car out for a test drive and returned a few minutes later to announce, more or less, that my car was a piece of junk with terrible steering. There was nothing wrong with the steering, and that exploded Dad's firecracker right then and there, on the showroom floor. He dressed the dealer upside down and yelled till he was blue. When Dad finally stopped shouting, no one was left in the showroom. Dad never stepped foot in that dealership again.

Of course, my outburst in the superintendent's office didn't make a lick of difference. But it made me realize that yelling rarely does any good. If I really wanted to lead the horse instead of chase after it, I should run for the school board, I thought. At about that same time, someone called me up and asked me to consider serving on the board of the Big Sandy Conservation District. Why not? After all, I had closely followed news about John Greytak and his controversial First Continental Corporation, which was in the lucrative but irresponsible business of flipping grassland ranches into cropland farms by plowing out the native grass—a practice better known as "sodbusting." After Greytak purchased 66,000 acres of rangeland in Petroleum County in early 1983, he hired crews to work round-the-clock to bust up the grass. Many Montanans saw the business model as a scheme to make it easier to bilk federal government farm subsidies. Many of us in agriculture saw it as a dangerous threat to the future of land management.

"In many people's eyes, that makes Greytak a speculator, a plunger, an investor, an opportunist—and only by coincidence a farmer," the *Great Falls Tribune* wrote that year.[6]

Look no further than the Dust Bowl to see the devastating consequences of unchecked, large-scale sodbusting. Without careful planning, erosion management, and regulations governing tillage, irrigation, and topsoil quality, agricultural land will literally dry up and blow away like it did in the thirties. As part of his response to the Dust Bowl, President Roosevelt in 1937 encouraged Montana to adopt legislation that eventually created fifty-eight soil conservation districts across our state, organized under the US Department of Agriculture's Natural Resource Conservation Service and overseen by the Montana Department of Natural Resources and Conservation. Chouteau County is so big it has two districts, each governed by five elected supervisors. Without much of a challenge, I was elected as a supervisor of the Big Sandy Conservation District in 1980—my first real foray into elected public service.[7]

The conservation board met only twice a month, but we were efficient. All of us were farmers or ranchers, or both. We weren't interested in partisan politics; we simply advocated for responsible land management that improved the chances of being able to keep our farms and ranches in our families. We formally condemned the sod-busting efforts of the First Continental Corporation and we promoted conservation practices that improved the health of soil and grass, and strengthened our "grass-based economy."

During my time on the conservation board, I got to go down to Helena to meet with Governor Ted Schwinden, a Democrat, and his agriculture director, Gordon McOmber. Schwinden was the first governor I'd ever met, and I was impressed by how open and willing he and McOmber were to listen about our work in our district. Governor Schwinden didn't want to preach to us; he just wanted to hear our perspective as actual ag producers in north-central Montana—and there were fifty-seven other districts he was listening to! That meeting was such a simple and effective use of time, and it taught me how easy it is for someone with political clout to actually take time and hear from people who still have dirt under their fingernails. Schwinden then held a reception for us in the newly built governor's mansion, but all I remember about that place was how ugly the giant black and white floor tiles were.

My term on the Big Sandy Conservation Board expired in 1983, and with a new taste for public service and experience under my belt as a teacher, I finally decided to run for a seat on the Big Sandy board of school trustees. I easily won that election too, and within a few years, I became vice chairman, then chairman. To this day, I'm asked about my most difficult job in politics. Without a doubt, my answer is the nine years I spent on the Big Sandy school board; it seemed everyone had strong opinions about public school policies, disciplinary actions,

Arnfred and Christine Pearson (née Anderson), Tester's maternal grandparents, on their wedding day, December 14, 1905, seven years before they moved from North Dakota to their homestead near Big Sandy, Montana.

Christine and Arnfred Pearson, seated, pose for their fiftieth wedding anniversary, in December 1955, with their children. (LEFT TO RIGHT) Lloyd, Virginia, Helen (Tester's mother), and Geneva. "All three of the Pearson women earned college degrees in the thirties and forties, another of the many remarkable successes of their parents," Tester writes.

All photos are courtesy of the author unless otherwise noted.

Helen Pearson, Tester's mother, poses with her shotgun in her early twenties (circa 1942). She spent most of her life on her family homestead outside Big Sandy, Montana, until moving to Idaho in 1978.

Helen Tester with her sons, Dave Junior (LEFT), Bob (MIDDLE), and Jon, on Christmas Day 1962. This is the only known photo of Jon Tester with all five fingers on his left hand.

Tester's father, David Orson Tester, with his horses Cheyenne and Carmen in 1970. David Tester was a lifelong horseman who spent his free time exploring nearby mountains.

Tester, seven years old, as a second-grader in 1963.

Tester with his father, David Orson Tester, in 1968.

Tester, seventeen years old, as an incoming senior at Big Sandy High School in 1973. Boys often got around the school district's "no weird haircuts" rule by having their senior pictures taken for the yearbook in the late summer, when they were allowed to have fashionably shaggy hair.

Tester, sixteen years old, performs "Bugler's Holiday" at a district music competition in Big Sandy in 1973. He received a superior rating.

Jon and Sharla (née Bitz) Tester on their wedding day, September 3, 1977. Sharla, who met Jon while striking him out at a church softball game, "is one badass farmer," Tester writes. "And I certainly wouldn't be a farmer without her."

(ABOVE) Tester, twenty-two years old, prepares for a day of teaching elementary school music in the fall of 1978. Tester loved the work, which relied on his new college degree in music, but left because he "could no longer even afford the gas needed for my commute into Big Sandy."

(RIGHT) Tester, in work boots "so comfortable I call them my dance shoes," dunks a basketball (with the help of an out-of-frame fifty-five-gallon barrel) in 1979. Always an energetic presence on the court, Tester still plays basketball with his US Senate colleagues.

Roger Clawson's March 16, 1986, At Large column in the *Billings Gazette* criticizing the Big Sandy board of school trustees, including a misspelled "John Tester," for expelling students who violated the school's dress code.

Reprinted with permission from the Billings Gazette

Tester referees a junior high school basketball game in Big Sandy, Montana, around 1990. "I often saw the best in young kids and sometimes the worst in adults," Tester writes of refereeing, a job that paid between ten and fifteen dollars per game.

Tester goofs around with his son, Shon, and daughter, Christine, on Christmas Day 1990.

Tester enjoys a card game with his grandchildren in 2017. (LEFT TO RIGHT) Brayden, Tucker, and Kilikina Schultz.

money, pay, taxes, ethics, graduations, grades, teacher performance, coaches, bullies, scholarships—it was a nine-year roller-coaster ride, and I loved every twist and turn.

When we had public meetings, lots of folks from the community would show up and make sure they were heard. If there was controversy, we'd prepare for days if not weeks or months of fireworks. When we had disagreements, which was often, I would hear about it at home and out in the town. If the US Senate is "the upper house" of American government, known for polite decorum and a tradition of civility and slow, deep debate, then the Big Sandy school board was a boiler room where things got done in a sweaty, fast-paced crucible of heat, noise, and full transparency and accountability. It was an exhilarating, raw experience in true democracy without all the garbage that comes with partisanship.

My role on the school board started with a political failure, though. One of my first controversies as a young trustee involved the superintendent's house in Big Sandy. The school district owned the building and agreed to sell it to the superintendent, who had lived there for many years.

"Aren't we going to get it appraised first?" I asked. The rest of the board looked at me as if I had spoken out of turn.

"No, Jon," one of them said. "He's got sweat equity in that house. We're just gonna get it done and move on."

"You can't do this," I told my colleagues, "without at least knowing how much the house is *worth*. We've got to get an independent appraisal or it'll look like a favor. It *is* a favor. We need to retract the sale, get an appraisal, then we can sell it."

They didn't listen. It felt like I was standing in the superintendent's office all over again, with his back turned to me. The other members of the board ignored my concern, outvoted me, and sold the house to the superintendent for what I'm sure was a hell of a good "sweat equity" deal, shortchanging local taxpayers in the process.

"Why can't I get through to them?" I asked Mr. Barsotti a few days later. I'd walked over to his house because I needed to blow off steam and he graciously heard me out. As a twenty-seven-year-old trustee, I felt like the rest of the board didn't take me seriously, even though I knew they'd screwed up.

"Because you caught them doing something they knew was wrong," Mr. B told me, "and they're denying you because you have no seniority yet."

That was true. I was recently elected to public office with no seniority under my belt, even though I owned a couple of small businesses. That meant times were tough for Sharla and me in the early eighties. We were forced to give up our health insurance, even with a toddler in our home. We simply could not afford it.

In 2009, as Congress debated the Affordable Care Act, I spoke often about what it feels like to be a young parent in a relatively dangerous line of work without health insurance. I told my colleagues in the Senate that Sharla and I "had no other choice but to hope and pray for health and safety" during those years.

"Thank God our prayers were answered," I said in the Senate chamber on December 21, a few days before we finally passed the bill. "Mine is one of the thousands of real Montana families that were forced to wing it rather than depend on a health care system that works."[8]

By 1985 Sharla and I had enough income to afford insurance again, and along came our second kid—a boy we named Shon (a combination of Sharla's name and mine). Christine was already five when Shon was born and, even then, she was old enough to keep tabs on her wily kid brother; she was and still is thoughtful and caring like the other strong women in our family. It didn't surprise Sharla or me when Christine told us she wanted to become a psychiatric nurse, a professional career in which she excelled.

Shon quickly took after his uncle Bob; he was always on the hunt for fun. But Shon never took much of an interest in sports.

"Look, buddy," I told him once, when he was about twelve. "You gotta do something to keep you busy."

"I want to fix up old cars," he said.

"Old cars? Tell you what. You teach yourself how to do all the work, I'll pay for the parts and the equipment you need."

And that's how Shon began a hobby he quickly mastered—one he still enjoys today; one that resulted in many happy father-son moments hunkered over parts and tools and sanders and paints in our shop, learning the ropes of classic car restoration. It was a good match for both of us. I have a weakness for anything made out of metal. Shon has patience and an eye for precision. I told him to figure it out, and he did, just like I had to figure out how to butcher my own beef after Dad left the farm. First Shon and I restored a Ford Model T, then a Model A, then a Willys CJ-2A Jeep. All of them were mint after Shon spent hours fixing them up. He even won awards for his work.

My focus in those days stayed on the farm and in the butcher shop. One morning in the spring of 1990 a friend of ours named Charlie Danreuther called me up and told me he had been diagnosed with cancer. Charlie was a longtime Chouteau County commissioner who also farmed south of us, in Loma.

"I'm gonna bow out," Charlie said. "And I was wondering, Jon, if you might be interested in running for my seat on the commission this year. You'd make a good commissioner."

"Of course I'd be interested in running, Charlie," I replied, pleased by the blessing of a well-known political figure in our area. I was always intrigued by the possibility of serving on the county commission. All of Montana's fifty-six counties are governed by three elected commissioners. That year Charlie was poised to face a challenger named Alfred Rice in the Republican primary.

"And I know you can beat Al."

"Charlie, if I run, I think I'll run as a Democrat."

Charlie said nothing for a few long seconds before saying, "Now why would you do that, Jon?"

In those days I didn't really consider myself a Democrat or a Republican. I had inherited my parents' fiscal conservatism, I was pro-gun, and I even considered myself anti-choice. But I also knew damn well how the policies of the Democratic Party had kept our little corner of agricultural America from disappearing altogether. And I had followed the news enough to know that I wasn't impressed by Montana's Republican governor, Stan Stephens, even though he was from nearby Havre. I also didn't really think much of our junior US senator, Conrad Burns, a Missouri transplant who'd made a name for himself as an auctioneer and farm broadcaster down in Billings. Both men had been elected two years earlier, and neither of them really understood agricultural policy, though they acted the part. I saw right through it.

"I just don't really like the leaders of the Republican Party, Charlie. They're embarrassing."

Had Charlie put a little more effort into what he did next, he very well may have convinced me to run as a Republican. Had he said, *I'll endorse you and campaign for you if you run as a Republican*, or, *Yes, we can do better than Governor Stephens and Senator Burns, which is why we need you to run as a Republican*, I might have made a decision that very moment to invite myself into the tent of the Grand Old Party. But instead, Charlie simply said: "Well, Jon, you can only win as a Republican in Chouteau County." The tone of his voice changed from polite to disappointed.

Chouteau County had indeed shifted red in recent years, but for most of the twentieth century it was bright blue. My folks certainly weren't the only people whose farm had been saved by the policies and vision of Franklin D. Roosevelt. I leaned Democrat because it was FDR's policies that had ultimately allowed me to be a farmer. And those policies had been enacted two generations before I even took over the farm.

"You running as a Democrat will make a big difference, Jon," Charlie warned.

"Why? I'm the same Jon Tester you called up five minutes ago. And you just said I would make a good commissioner." Again, Charlie paused.

"You just don't understand, Jon. It makes a difference. And Gar Wood is running as a Democrat."

I did understand. And I knew I could beat both Alfred Rice and Garvey Wood if I had tried. I wished Charlie well in his recovery, then drove down to the courthouse in Fort Benton and filed as a Democratic candidate. On the day of the candidate filing deadline that March, Charlie drove his pickup into my yard to pay me a courtesy visit.

"Jon, I decided to run for reelection after all," he told me, sheepishly. "I thought about it long and hard, and I just don't think you can beat Gar Wood. Anyway, I just wanted you to know."

Charlie's change of heart hit me hard. I knew it had nothing to do with Gar Wood and everything to do with the fact that he wasn't about to let a Democrat take his seat. I was so pissed off I announced in the *Big Sandy Mountaineer* that I was no longer running for a seat on the Chouteau County Commission, though my name would still appear on the Democratic primary ballot. I didn't campaign and I didn't raise any money that year, because I knew Charlie Danreuther, our popular incumbent, would easily coast to victory on November 6—Election Day. And he did. Charlie also triumphed over his battle with cancer and ended up serving a dozen years as Chouteau County commissioner. He passed away in 2012 at the age of eighty-two.[9]

But overall, that Election Day in 1990 was much better for Montana Democrats. They regained solid majorities and control of both the Montana House and the Senate.

"If 1988 was a high-water mark for the GOP, Tuesday's election was nearly a Pearl Harbor," the *Great Falls Tribune* editorialized a couple of days later. "The 1991 Legislature will resemble the lawmaking body of nearly two decades earlier—younger, more liberal, more urban-oriented, less male-dominated, concerned about social and resource issues. In other words, political history is repeating itself in Montana."[10]

Gar Wood, as expected, beat me in the primary election before losing miserably to Charlie.[11] That year gave me my first bitter taste of dirty politics, and it tasted awful. But it lit another slow-burning fuse; it strengthened my determination to run for public office again some day, and to do it *for real*.

CHAPTER 6

Preservers of the Past

In the late winter of 1986, scandal rocked Big Sandy and split apart our community—and it all began with an ice cube, a safety pin, and a twenty-dollar bet among teenagers at a 4-H meeting.

"We got a problem," Principal Barsotti anxiously told us the next day, after he stopped a fellow trustee named Arland "Arne" Gasvoda and me in the school hallway. "*A big one.*"

"What's the matter?" we asked. Mr. B told us that during the 4-H meeting a fifteen-year-old boy, a sophomore at Big Sandy High, accepted a dare from his buddies to pierce his left ear and wear an earring to school for at least one week. If he succeeded, he'd get the twenty bucks and all the glory that came with the challenge. The Big Sandy School District, however, had different plans. In Big Sandy, Montana, boys simply weren't allowed to wear earrings to school in 1986.

That year I was twenty-nine and the vice chairman of the Big Sandy school board. Though it had been last updated in the fifties, our school district's dress code wasn't much of a problem in our quiet community—or so I thought. Boys were required to wear "nice dress pants" to school on Tuesdays and Thursdays. Girls were never allowed to wear jeans, and they had to wear dresses on Tuesdays and Thursdays (unless it was ten degrees or colder). The code prohibited "T-shirts or similar attire with slogans or signs that could in any way be construed as socially unacceptable in our school." It also instructed all students to avoid "weird" haircuts.[1]

"It is desirable that students attending Big Sandy High School dress appropriately at all times and present a favorable appearance and impression to all," our dress code stated.[2] "Extremes in student dress and general appearance cannot be tolerated, since they distract other people and generally interfere with order and instruction. . . . Students tend to act the way they dress; fad uniforms seem to license antisocial behavior, and the nonconformist minority becomes an 'out' group because the other students tend to shun them."[3]

"I think you have only one option," I told Mr. B. After all, we had a dress code for a reason. A young man had violated it, and that violation had caused a major distraction in our little school. Our job was to enforce the rules. "If he's not going to pull it out, we have no choice but to suspend him."

A decade earlier as a student I'd *hated* our damn dress code. The boys got around the "no weird haircuts" rule by having their senior pictures taken for the yearbook in the late summer, when we were allowed to have fashionably shaggy hair, before tidying up for the school year. As student body president I'd even attended a Montana Association of Student Councils seminar in Great Falls about how to challenge our schools' dress codes. I knew what it would take. And I knew the consequences. As a young adult, though, I thought the dress code seemed to make sense. After all, it was about eliminating distractions.

So the Big Sandy school board voted unanimously to give the superintendent and Principal Barsotti the authority to suspend the boy for violating the dress code, indefinitely, until he took his earring out, acknowledging the inevitable grumbling that would come with our swift decision.

"Students grumble about the dress code like they grumble about everything else," the superintendent grumbled when he agreed with our decision to suspend the poor kid. "They grumble about homework too."

Then we moved on with our other business of the evening. Word of our swift discipline, however, traveled very quickly throughout Big Sandy—long before the convenience of social media—and the high school student body quickly organized.

The following Tuesday, March 4, dozens of students, about sixty-five of them, protested our antiquated dress code by wearing blue jeans to school instead of slacks and dresses as required.[4] Mr. B threatened to suspend *all* of them, then ordered them to go home and change into dresses and "nice dress pants." All but a dozen students complied, and we suspended those twelve rebellious teens too, for a single day. *That'll teach these kids a lesson*, we on the school board thought. Part of public service, I reminded myself, is sometimes making unpopular decisions.

Well, the American Civil Liberties Union took notice of our unpopular decision and immediately engaged a public defender in Havre named Mark Suagee, who filed a lawsuit on behalf of four of those students. Our dress code, Suagee argued, violated First Amendment rights. All of a sudden the Big Sandy school district made headlines across the state. Rumors started swirling about exorbitant financial settlements and the cost of attorneys' fees bankrupting our high school sports programs, none of which were true. Suagee actually took on the case pro bono and filed a request for a restraining order with District Judge Chan Ettien of Havre. On March 14, Judge Ettien agreed and told us we were not allowed to enforce our own dress code until the case was formally resolved.[5]

In an effort to tamp down community anger and to resolve the dispute out of court, we invited the public to our next school board meeting on March 19, which we held in the school auditorium in anticipation of a huge crowd. More than three hundred people showed up, spilling into the aisles and the lobby. Nearly sixty of them spoke, making it abundantly clear that the issue drew a bright red line down the middle of Big Sandy.[6] On one side: supporters of the old dress code (including yours truly); on the other: rabblers rousing for progress, led by Suagee, who made a point of wearing his Levis to the meeting.[7]

The auditorium booed Suagee off the stage after he introduced himself. But the tensest moment that night came after the stepfather of one of the plaintiffs got up and took the mic. I don't even remember what he said, but it was something old-fashioned if not derogatory about boys who wore earrings. His stepson stood up and yelled across the auditorium, "Sit down and shut up!"—which prompted a collective gasp from the entire room.

But we did make some progress that evening. The board dropped the Tuesday and Thursday nice-clothes requirement, meaning everyone could wear jeans and young women no longer had to wear dresses twice a week. We also created a ten-member committee made up of two trustees, a teacher, Principal Barsotti, and the presidents of each class from grades seven through twelve, to figure out a fairer, longer-term solution.[8]

The sharpest criticism, however, didn't come from any student or parent or administrator or old codger in Big Sandy; it came from a newspaper columnist down in Billings named Roger Clawson. Clawson was an unapologetic agitator, a sharp observer, and a master of wit; he effectively slayed public officials with ink and laugh-out-loud humor. His column, Clawson at Large, appeared three times a week in Montana's largest newspaper, the *Billings Gazette*, which meant I was keenly aware when Roger Clawson began dedicating lots of newsprint real estate to his satirical rebuke of the entire Big Sandy school board.

"It's my hope that the trustees will grab a root and growl," Clawson wrote on March 9, catapulting our local flap into the realm of statewide watercooler chitchat. "Their dress code is a relic deserving of their most ardent defense." Clawson then referred to our dress code as the "B.S. Code," which I'm sure stood for Big Sandy.[9]

"B.S.'s code is a masterpiece of 1950s fascism that was as much a part of my teen years as Buddy Holly, Little Richard, girls in short-shorts and baby moon hubcaps," he continued. "Codes of that golden age were usually produced by the school's resident Nazi." Then, a few days later, Roger Clawson used his column to turn up his heat to power boil.

"I suggested that Big Sandy's trustees should have this relic stuffed and mounted," he wrote in a column with the headline "Preservers of the Past Receive Up-to-Date Advice." "But it now appears that the B.S. code's preservation will demand more than taxidermy. . . . The American Civil Liberties Union has declared war on the code's keepers: Arland Gasvoda, John Tester, Robert Quinn, Glen Ophus, Ron Person and Stan Weaver."[10]

Even spelled incorrectly, there it was: my name in black and white, framed as a villain. (Clawson also misspelled the name of my cousin and fellow trustee Ron Pearson, Uncle Lloyd's grandson.) It was *accountability.* It was the first time I had ever been named in a statewide news article, and it was one that got lots of statewide attention. It stung.

I met Roger Clawson only once. At some point after that column was published, I passed through Billings with the other Big Sandy school board trustees on our way to a meeting in southeastern Montana. We decided to pop into the *Billings Gazette*'s office unannounced, and we asked to meet with him.

"We're the 'preservers of the past,'" we said when Clawson appeared from the newsroom. "And we just wanted you to know who we were."

Clawson smiled and greeted us with firm handshakes and lukewarm appreciation for the fact that we'd showed up in his newsroom in person, but the salty old journalist stood by his columns. He wasn't about to be intimidated, so he wished us well and went back to work. Roger Clawson passed away in 2015. He wasn't afraid of accountability, and he exacted it with courageous words, even when it prompted menacing responses from people who didn't like to be held accountable.[11] During this ongoing stress test of our very democracy and all the rights we take for granted, we need more Roger Clawsons.

Back in Big Sandy, things went from ugly to worse. Though Judge Ettien had pushed pause on the whole ordeal, it continued to sharply divide our community. Over the next few months, two students removed themselves from the lawsuit because of "pressure on their families and on the businesses of their parents."[12] The ACLU also said a third student moved away "partly because of hostile reaction to the lawsuit."[13] Finally, in mid-November, with input from our ten-person committee, we reached an agreement with Mark Suagee and the ACLU, and we overhauled the B.S. Code. The new dress code, which Judge Ettien formally approved, simply stated that students should exercise "good taste and discretion of the individual and his or her parents."[14]

"I question this part of the judge's ruling," Clawson wrote of our revised code on November 18. "Anyone with a deep savvy of the growing-up process knows that children must rebel against their parents before they can become adults and be parents to their children." Then he offered this advice:

> So here's what you revolting guys and gals of Big Sandy can do:
>
> Cut your hair weird, guys. Have a barber chop it off evenly about a half-inch long. Far out!
>
> Then buy a pair of brushed cotton slacks and a freaky narrow belt. Wear these with a Ban-Lon sweater over a white shirt.
>
> Girls can blow their parents' minds with brown-and-white shoes, bobby socks and full skirts with poodles on them. Tuck your hair into a weird hank hanging down your back like a horse's tail.
>
> That ought to make the old folks choke.[15]

Big Sandy, of course, survived the whole ordeal. Thanks to public accountability and an independent judiciary, the "preservers of the past" lost and the rebels won, and I learned a whole lot about politics over the course of that year. It was my first glimpse at how a single issue can rip holes in a community, and how a community can sew itself back together again, maybe even stronger. I got a firsthand lesson in PR management and the judicial system and the wrath of strangers who lived far from Chouteau County.

With the benefit of decades of hindsight, I regret suspending the poor young man who wore the earring to school. The young man called me and the other members of the board during the ordeal, and I gave him the courtesy of at least listening to his perspective. To this day, he says the whole controversy was never really about the damn earring, but rather about a community that judges too quickly and still struggles to accept change. He wore his earring, by the way, all the way through high school—just to punctuate his point. He says he learned more *outside* school than in school that year. And yes, he got his twenty bucks.

I also regret suspending the boy's classmates who believed in his right to be part of the "out group." My colleagues and I thought we were doing the right thing. After all, we'd survived the dress code when we were in school. And our community trusted us to make decisions based on the rules we had in place and the information we received. From the experience, I learned to bring in as many viewpoints as possible, and that it's okay to rocket out of the orbit of comfort zones, especially when something as basic as First Amendment rights are involved.

A couple of weeks after Montanans elected me to the US Senate in 2006, before I was even sworn in, I met in Great Falls with a group of unlikely bedfellows who wanted to share a proposal with me. They were owners of Montana timber mills, conservation leaders, and recreation enthusiasts who, after years of fighting one another over controversial wilderness proposals in the eighties, realized that nobody was getting what they wanted. The conservationists weren't getting more designated wilderness, because of the formidable opposition once led by the timber industry. And the loggers and mills weren't harvesting a fair supply of timber from the forests—to the point it was threatening the viability of their industry—because of the formidable legal opposition of the conservation movement. Armed with rolled-up maps and documents and handwritten notes from years of respectful and productive meetings with each other, they showed me a simple, grand compromise that they all agreed to: more permanent wilderness designation in exchange for a guaranteed supply of timber, especially in overgrown forests that needed to be better managed anyway.

Federal land in the United States designated as "wilderness" is some of the most protected land in the world. According to the landmark Wilderness Act of 1964, wilderness is "where man himself is a visitor who does not remain." And that means wilderness is controversial, because it is preserved forever, protected from development, roads, or even the intrusion of any form of "mechanical transport."

"Yeah, our plan is a little outside the box, but everyone gives a little and everyone gets a lot," one of the negotiators told me. "Nobody is winning, and we're sick and damn tired of losing. Now we just need someone to carry it for us in Washington."

"I'll take a look," I assured them.

After all, I was raised in a community built, for the most part, by compromise and cooperation. The honyockers of north-central Montana had no other choice in order to survive when they left Hill's railroad and staked their claims. When a family needed a new barn, all the neighbors would give up precious time to pitch in and help build it under the direction of a Scandinavian master carpenter named Ole Haakenson, who built hip-roof barns all across Chouteau County. The same thing happened when Dad poured the concrete for his butcher shop; several other farmers came by to help because Dad needed strong backs and extra hands. Families across the county pitched in to build Kenilworth Hall, where I dribbled pork and beans down my shirt before dancing with Sharla. When it came time to measure the steps up to the doorway of Kenilworth Hall, they borrowed boots from Wayne Dixon, the tallest person they knew, to ensure the steps would fit even his enormous feet.

If someone in the community got seriously sick or hurt, the community held (and often still does) a fundraiser to help pay the bills. Each year the Big Sandy Medical Center holds a popular community-wide pie-and-coffee sale, which brings in thousands of dollars to help purchase everything from new medical equipment to cleaning supplies. Sharla, who for years served on the clinic's guild before I was elected to the Senate, still makes sugar-free sour cream raisin pies for the cause.

Both Uncle Lloyd and my father-in-law, Ron Bitz, belonged to Treasure Lodge 95 in Big Sandy, which was chartered during the homestead heyday of Chouteau County in 1914.[16] I became a Freemason not long after Christine was born. I worked my way through the ranks and became Master of Treasure Lodge 95. The traditions and rituals of the Freemasons have always fascinated me, but I joined because I truly enjoyed the fraternity of sitting in the lodge basement once a month, playing cards, slurping down weak coffee and chewing the fat with other Masons from across the county, most of whom were in their midsixties. Other than the acknowledgment of God with a capital "G," religion largely stayed out of our conversations. And aside from the occasional candidate who joined us to talk about "Americanism," so did politics.

Over the past few years partisan politics has seeped into many nonpartisan traditions across this country. Not long after my first US Senate reelection in 2012, I received a blistering letter from a fellow Mason warning me to stay away from Treasure Lodge 95, apparently because he disagreed with my politics—a clear and offensive violation of the code of conduct. I had just won a long, bitter campaign against Montana's sole member of the US House of Representatives, Dennis Rehberg. Rehberg was also a Freemason—one of the few things we shared in common. Though the Freemasons were formative to me as a young adult, and though I have great respect for their worldwide charitable work, my excitement for being a Freemason has waned over the past few years. What was once a cherished time for undistracted fellowship among men who look like me, talk like me, live in rural America like me, and did much of the same work I do now seems oddly outdated now that I'm a senator. This role in public service demands a broader perspective that opens doors to all Americans regardless of what they look like, what they believe, where they live, or what they do.

Those young adult years of my life also led me to a new pastime that kept me fully engaged in our little community. Though I didn't have much of a basketball career in high school, I played pickup games through college, and when I returned to Big Sandy, the district asked me to become a junior high school referee. I loved every minute of the work, and it put some jingle in my jeans—between ten and fifteen dollars per game. Eventually the school district asked me to ref junior varsity games too, and that meant I earned anywhere from ten to forty-five dollars in extra income for every night I reffed, minus a bottle of beer I bought at the local bar before heading home.

Big Sandy used to be a class B school, meaning it was medium-size. Now it's a class C school, which means it's among the smallest. Basketball, especially across the class B and class C schools in Montana, was and still is a sacred tradition that connects rural communities with one another. Though many of these places shrink by the year, their school gymnasiums still fill up to the fire code limit on game nights. Local fans crowd inside to watch their kids—girls and boys—pour everything they have onto the court. Certain friendly rivalries among neighboring towns have lasted generations. Some of the rivalries haven't been as healthy, testing Montana with racial tension between white communities and Native American ones, where school basketball is just as popular.

The great NBA star and coach Phil Jackson, born in Deer Lodge, Montana, and whose mother was captain of the girls' basketball team in Wolf Point in 1927, counts playing basketball in Montana among his earliest memories because the joy of the game "can spiral out and reach out into other places in a person's life.

"Some people say basketball's a metaphor for life, but it's more important than that," Jackson said in a 2008 Montana PBS documentary about rural basketball called *Class C: The Only Game in Town*. "It's a sport that you see a person without very much protection. They're out there in their shorts and T-shirt, basically exposed, and playing a game in which their emotions are revealed—their character, how they carry themselves, how they work through disappointments. You can watch a basketball game or two and pretty much get a determination on the character of an individual."[17]

This was certainly true from the perspective of a referee, where I often saw the best in young kids and sometimes the worst in adults. Coaches and parents verbally took out their own frustrations on me and at me, which taught me a thing or two about the importance of thick skin in the public arena. And sometimes those frustrations were justified. While reffing a game in Big Sandy one night, I fouled out a young man from the visiting team—by far one of the best in the state—only to realize a couple of minutes later that I'd made the wrong call. His coach went berserk and shouted at me with his hands in the air, with just enough restraint to avoid being ejected.

"You made a mistake, ref!" the coach yelled, so pissed off that spit flew out of his red face. I shrugged it off but as the game went on, I felt worse about my call. The coach was right, dammit, and my reputation was at stake. So when the game was over, I went up to him.

"I screwed it up," I admitted to the coach, who was appropriately proud of and passionate about his team. "I thought I made the right call, but it wasn't. I'm sorry." I assumed he would accept my sincere apology and brush it off as part of the game, but he had none of it.

"What the hell do you think you're doing?" he screamed, red in the face all over again. "You know, these kids work their tails off every day, every weekend. We do our best. We come down here and you unravel all our hard work with your stupid call. *You're not even an MOA!*"

Being "an MOA" means you have a refereeing certificate from the Montana Officials Association, which allows those who are especially familiar with the rules to referee high school varsity games. Earning the certificate involves a major test requiring a broad knowledge of how to respond to lots of hypothetical scenarios during a game. I simply reffed for the junior high because the Big Sandy School District needed a warm-bodied adult on the court. The dressing-down I got after that wrong call prompted me to get formally certified by the MOA because I refused to be humiliated like that again. I also learned a valuable lesson: never, ever admit an honest mistake as a referee.

Another lesson from basketball came after Roy Lackner, one of

Big Sandy's best coaches, discovered I was interested in earning my MOA certificate.

"Look, I'll show you every situation you will ever see during this season," Lackner told me. "By the end you'll know exactly what to do. You'll be the best ref in the state, Jon. But in order for me to help you, I'll need flexibility. If you see me push you, it's because I'm testing you. Don't throw me out of the game."

Lackner first tested me by pointing out what he said was a recent change in the rules that governed all school-sanctioned games in Montana. Each team, he reminded me, was allowed five timeouts instead of four. Lackner apparently knew his rules, after all, and giving all teams a fifth timeout wasn't an unreasonable change. So near the end of the next game he asked for his fifth timeout and I granted it.

The crowd erupted with disapproval. I looked at Lackner and he looked at me back, and he shrugged. So I went over to the timekeeper's table to verify the rules. The timekeeper also shrugged, so I ran up to an off-duty MOA official I spotted in the bleachers as the crowd booed.

"Four timeouts or five?" I asked him. "The rules changed, right?"

The off-duty MOA official had a long-running feud with my nephew DJ, who announced basketball games on the radio and who had earned the ire of the MOA because he wasn't afraid of castigating referees over the air when they made bad calls. He also thought DJ was my brother.

"Go ask your brother," the MOA guy growled with his arms crossed, relishing the sound of boos directed at me.

To hell with it, I decided. *Five it is.* And I stuck with my own ruling. Turns out, the official rules never changed to allow five timeouts. Coach Roy Lackner taught me that when you're in charge of the rules, *you're in charge of the rules*. And you can't depend on someone else for the rules when it's your job to know them.

Communities come in all sizes. In the late nineties, our own family became a community to a young woman who did not have a home.

Melody Fell moved to Big Sandy her freshman year of high school and became fast friends with Christine. Mel spent almost every weekend at our house twelve miles west of town. She did her laundry there. She ate meals with us. Sharla and I, of course, were happy to have her. She was utterly polite and mature well beyond her years. It didn't take long for us to realize Melody's home life was 180 degrees different than ours.

"After a challenging childhood that involved a lot of moving around the country, I ended up in Big Sandy as a young teenager," Melody wrote in a *Great Falls Tribune* column in October 2012.

> Lost and lonely, my life started unraveling. My relationship with my real mother was suffering. Although she tried her best as a single mom, I spent most of my childhood acting like the grown up. I cared for my younger sister and baby brother, worked my own job, and paid rent to sleep on the floor of our living room. . . .
>
> I spent a lot of time at the Tester farm, where Jon and Sharla made me feel welcome. They saw right away that I was alone and empty. . . .
>
> Then I made the most difficult decision of my life. I left the pain of my home. The minute I walked away from my family, Jon and Sharla welcomed me into theirs. They've called me their daughter ever since.[18]

Melody, like Christine and Shon, now calls Sharla and me Mom and Dad.

Most people remember the exact dates that scarred their lives with tragedy. I, fortunately, don't have many of those days. There's June 16, 1966—the day I lost my three fingers. April 12, 2004, was the day Dad died. Mother passed away on June 27, 2009. But April 19, 2000, brought a different kind of tragedy to Big Sandy. Sharla, Shon, and I had spent that day pickin' rock; the three of us were way out in the fields and away from our landline (none of us had cell phones then). When we got into the house late that evening, we saw that the tape in our blinking answering machine was full. Sharla pushed the play button and we sat down as the news unfolded in a series of awful messages:

> Jon, Sharla: Call us right away, would ya? . . . Not sure if you heard but you need to know. . . . It's Michelle—God, I'm sorry. . . . Pick up if you're there, guys. . . . Michelle and Kyle were in that rollover . . . it was instant. . . . We need to get word to Melody. . . . Not looking good. . . . I'm praying for you guys.

Sharla and I sat silently in our kitchen as the answering machine reached the end.

Several hours earlier, at seven thirty that evening, Melody's sixteen-year-old sister, Michelle, lost control of her little 1999 Pontiac on a stretch of empty highway southeast of town. The Montana Highway Patrol later described the accident as a "series of overcorrections" that ended when Michelle's car skidded off Judith Landing Road, hit the barrow ditch, and rolled, landing on its roof.[19] Michelle was driving. Her friend Candi O'Neal, also sixteen, sat shotgun. A third friend, a fifteen-year-old named Kyle Boschee of Havre, rode in the back seat. They weren't drinking. They weren't doing drugs. They were just kids being kids. But none of them wore a seat belt.

The crash ejected Michelle, who died at the scene. Kyle died a short time later at the Big Sandy Medical Center. Candi was still in the upside-down wreckage of the car when help came, and she walked away with only minor injuries.[20] My faith has endured its share of stress tests in recent years—mostly in the form of strange twists of fate. The warm relief of Candi's survival is tempered with strange questions of *how* and *why*.

It was Sharla who finally said, "We've got to call Mel." Mel was away at college in Billings, four hours to the south. Both of us were stunned with sadness, struggling with the reality that was about to hit us again. We figured Mel was desperate to talk with us—to be with us—as the people she trusted in her life, so she could grieve. Maybe she was already on her way up to Big Sandy. Maybe she needed us to come get her.

"Yeah," I agreed with a painful sigh. Sharla and I knew it would be the most difficult call we would ever have to make. Then Mel answered her phone.

"Hi!"

She sounded surprised by the late call, but the cheer in her voice hit us in the gut like a hot iron. *Melody doesn't know.* In another strange twist of fate, I realized that moment that we were the first to tell Mel that her sister was dead. I looked at Sharla. Sharla looked at me and nodded, giving me the strength I needed. Mel hung up on us at first, angered by what she first thought was a sick joke. So I called her back and broke the news again.

If you're a person of faith, you might believe that what happened next was the work of angels. I do. At the exact moment I made that awful phone call to Mel, two of her friends from Big Sandy came into her dorm room in Billings. They already knew about Michelle's death and they had come, presumably, to comfort Mel. After I broke the news, she screamed, dropped the phone, and collapsed into the arms of those two friends, who were there to catch her. And within the hour they were driving her back to Big Sandy. I met her at three o'clock in the morning at the restaurant on the south end of town and gave her a big hug as she sobbed.

When we got home, Mel curled up on our living room floor in the fetal position and fell asleep; she didn't even have it in her to go downstairs to her room. During Michelle's funeral, most of which Mel planned, Sharla and I sat directly behind Mel and cried with her.

For as long as I've known Melody, I've watched her navigate the hurdles and bumps in life. I've helped her celebrate the joys too. In 2004 she married her longtime boyfriend, Glen Wall, a man we consider our son-in-law, and they had two children of their own—kids we consider our own grandchildren. After college Melody became a kindergarten teacher. Good role models, she reminds Sharla and me, make all the difference in the lives of young people, and she dedicated her career to being one. Melody is one of those people who were dealt all sorts of difficult hands in their life, and she played hers the best she could. Then she made it her job to see that everyone she touches has at least an ace to play.

Our daughters, Christine and Mel, both raise families while also managing demanding full-time jobs. I know they both play on an uneven field, splitting time between work and raising their families, struggling to find time even for themselves. I don't know how so many single moms across Montana and across our country manage the same thing—raising children and paying bills while figuring out how to feed mouths, fill a tank of gas, and find adequate health care. Winning bread for the whole family is a burden that quietly falls onto the shoulders of many single women across rural America. And in Montana, according to a 2018 report by the American Association of University Women, women on average still make only 79 cents for every dollar a man makes.[21] Nationwide, a Native American woman makes only 57 cents for every dollar earned by a man; Hispanic women make only 54 cents.[22]

In addition to the pay disparity, the women across rural America who support their families face even more hurdles: lack of access to quality health care, lack of access to nutritious food, lack of affordable childcare—if any at all. Simple but critical policies like the sadly perennial Paycheck Fairness Act, and legislation to prevent employers from discriminating against pregnant employees or expanding family medical leave, are an easy start. So is investing in lifesaving initiatives like the earned income tax credit and the Supplemental Nutrition Assistance Program (SNAP). In a nation of abundance like ours, the fact that *fifteen million* households don't get enough food is staggering and shameful.[23] It is unacceptable.

But there's hope to be found in the communities of rural America, where families with plenty look after families with little; where women and men often put their own politics aside to lend a hand—or an enormous foot—when their neighbors need help. And when there's injustice in rural America, don't underestimate the "out groups" that still have the power to challenge the status quo. There's hope in Native America, where entire communities in poverty find strength in culture and tradition. There's hope in crowded gymnasiums on Friday nights, where boys and girls in little communities celebrate competition and work through disappointments, then shake hands with the strangers who beat them.

One of the most valuable lessons I've learned in public service began in my little community, with a boy who wore an earring to school for twenty dollars: Effective leadership requires being open to everything. It requires examination, and a willingness to give up something, even if it means a little discomfort. Maybe that means revisiting an old dress code that should no longer apply. Maybe that means rewriting policies in Congress that support women who win the bread for their families. It means making room for the voices that haven't been heard enough across our nation and in our rural communities.

In my community in 1986, those voices belonged to kids who defied the Big Sandy dress code. But as a nation, those voices belong to the people—especially to women and people of color—who have long fought for equality and justice. Pioneers like Lilly Ledbetter, whose namesake Fair Pay Act of 2009 jump-started Congress's work in the unfinished business of mandating pay equity and eliminating discrimination from the workplace.

Those pioneers include the late Elouise Cobell, a Montana activist and member of the Blackfeet Nation who challenged the federal government's decades-long mismanagement of Indian trust assets. Cobell's landmark lawsuit resulted in a $3.4 billion settlement for hundreds of thousands of Native American people. Elouise Cobell passed away in 2011. I asked President Obama to consider her for a Presidential Medal of Freedom in the spring of 2016 because "she reminds us that anybody can rise up and make their voices heard."[24] And on November 22, the president awarded that medal to her posthumously.[25]

"Elouise Cobell spent her life defying the odds and working on behalf of her people," Cobell's Medal of Freedom citation states. "As a young woman, she was told that she wasn't capable of understanding accounting. So she mastered the field and used her expertise to champion a lawsuit whose historic settlement has helped restore tribal homelands to her beloved Blackfeet Nation and many other tribes. Today, her tenacious and unwavering spirit lives on in the thousands of people and hundreds of tribes for whom she fought, and in all those she taught to believe that it is never too late to help right the wrongs of the past and to help shape a better future."[26]

That lesson was clear among the coalition of conservationists and loggers who sat down with me in 2006 to ask that I turn their grand compromise into federal legislation. After numerous meetings with them, I introduced my Forest Jobs and Recreation Act on July 17, 2009. The eighty-page bill represented groundbreaking legislation based on years of input and collaboration from what had been, for decades, strange bedfellows. The Forest Jobs and Recreation Act would have designated nearly 700,000 acres of federal land as protected wilderness, which was welcome progress for the conservation community. It also required the US Forest Service to open up two national forests to an average of 10,000 acres per year for logging, providing timber and jobs to Montana's struggling mills and loggers. The bill prioritized logging and restoration work near roads and wildfire-endangered communities, created new recreation areas, and released protections for some Bureau of Land Management Wilderness Study Areas—lands that are highly protected as wilderness without formal, permanent wilderness designation.[27]

"Nobody gets everything they want in this business," I reminded reporters while introducing the Forest Jobs and Recreation Act at the RY Timber mill in Townsend, Montana. "Everybody gives a little and everybody gets a lot."[28]

I knew we were doing something right when hardcore conservatives flipped out over the creation of new wilderness, and the extreme left-wingers flipped out over mandated logging. Most of us in the middle understood the importance of compromise, and we made the legislation work. Unfortunately, the Forest Jobs and Recreation Act ran into the gauntlet of partisan politics and never became law despite numerous hearings and introductions in Congress. The fact that the Forest Jobs and Recreation Act never even got a vote in the full Senate is one of the biggest disappointments of my time in the US Senate. I have spent much of my time since then reminding the Montanans who wrote this bill that collaboration can and will still win, even if we're long overdue for a victory.

The bill itself was a lesson in listening and compromising when communities are in need. It was a lesson I first learned in 1986 when a sixteen-year-old boy wore an earring to high school in violation of our dress code. It was a lesson I learned time and time again when refereeing basketball, and watching women like Elouise Cobell and Melody Fell pave their own roads when the potholes of life got in their way. A community, no matter how small and no matter who's a part of it, can gain a lot by giving a little.

CHAPTER 7

A Peterbilt and a Prius

If you draw a line on a map of Montana from Great Falls northeast to Havre, then west over Cut Bank, then southeast back to Great Falls, you'll draw a rough perimeter around one of the world's most suitable regions for growing high-quality, high-protein wheat. In Montana we call it the Golden Triangle, and our 1,800-acre farm is right inside it.

It's safe to assume that the "Empire Builder," James J. Hill, wasn't aware of how fruitful the region would be as he sliced his railroad across it more than a century ago. It took generations of farmers and their hard-learned failures to figure out how to work the finicky soil and to make it productive. Many of the farms in the Golden Triangle, like mine, don't rely on artificial irrigation. On our place, artificial irrigation would make the soil too wet, drawing salty alkali out of it and making it impossible to grow anything. All the moisture we get for our farm comes from snow and rain.

I study the markets, the moisture, the soil health, and where the weeds are coming up to determine which crops to plant every year. Sharla and I grow several varieties of wheat along with barley, safflower, buckwheat, alfalfa hay, lentils, millet, and peas. The peas suck nitrogen out of the air and store it, so I don't harvest them. I plow them back into the dirt, where they release their nitrogen and replenish the soil as green manure. We don't use any chemical fertilizers.

If I see too much weed pressure in a field, I won't plant a pulse crop like lentils, because the weeds will take over. Weeds get smart like everything else. If you plant a crop in the same place at the same time of year twice in a row, the weeds will start coming up at the same time. If you stagger the planting time, or plant late-seed crops like millet or buckwheat, you can stay a step ahead of the weeds. You can manage weeds pretty well with smart planning, good timing, tillage, and proper crop rotation, which I carefully track with pencil-drawn maps tacked to the walls of my home office. We don't use any chemical herbicides either.

Sharla and I made the switch to organic farming in 1986 for two reasons. First, Sharla would stay sick in bed for a week after breathing in dust from the chemical treatment we applied to our seeds, and I got sick with flu-like symptoms after spraying pesticides on the crops. As soon as we made the switch to organic farming, our illnesses went away. The second reason was simple economics: we wanted to make more money. Growing organic crops opened our business to a whole new market of buyers willing to pay more for our higher quality, harder-to-grow grains and lentils. When I sold my first truckload of organic durum to Eden Foods, the contractor, Ann Sinclair, told me it was the best wheat her company had ever purchased. That's when we knew we had made the right choice.

As I wrapped up my time on the Big Sandy school board, I overlapped it with a couple of years of work on my local Agricultural Stabilization and Conservation Service committee (ASCS; now called the Farm Service Agency). The ASCS provided the US Department of Agriculture local input on decisions affecting farmland and federal farm programs. I spent five rewarding years on the Big Sandy ASCS committee before being elected to the Organic Crop Improvement Association (OCIA)—then the largest organic farming organization in the world. In the dizzying two years of 1996 and 1997, I served on OCIA's executive committee while also serving on its international board of directors—which included members from the United States, Canada, the Philippines, and Ecuador. We met four times a year. And that's where I learned more about the art of compromise, because we had to negotiate organic standards to apply to all thirty-seven member-countries of the OCIA, including Communist and third-world nations. The experience opened my eyes to the struggles of many other less fortunate farm families and their unsupportive governments across the world.

"It was the first time I had to deal with people who saw things from a totally different standpoint," I admitted to the Associated Press as a newly elected state senator in 1999. "A lot of the things we take for granted—like eating, safety . . . and privilege to speak our mind."[1]

When Fred and Christine Pearson homesteaded our farm in the early years of the twentieth century, organic farming was all they knew. Mother, like her parents, knew the soil was good because she scooped it up in her hands, held it to her lips, breathed it in, and tasted it. If it tasted sweet—earthy, funky, and mysterious—she would say it was healthy enough to grow food.

"Yeah," she would say, "this is *good stuff.*"

An afternoon rain shower releases the soil's sweetness of decay and growth into the air. I've never quite smelled anything like it anywhere else but our farm. It was Mother's favorite smell. Conventional farms, as ours was for several decades before our conversion back to organics, don't have that sweetness. That's one of the many problems with conventional farm chemicals like anhydrous ammonia. When you dump a bunch of that shit on the ground, the soil loses its smell—like streetlights lose the stars.

To get to our farm from Kenilworth Road, you have to twist and turn up a few dirt roads until you see some gnarly caragana trees doing their best to keep the wind away from our century-old red hip-roof barn and our little collection of storage sheds and grain bins. You'll see the old iron windmill that crashed down on Uncle Lloyd, a corrugated steel Quonset hut, the butcher shop Dad built, and a plain white house Sharla and I built ourselves in 1993. That was when the salty alkali in the soil ate away enough of the concrete foundation of the little yellow house I grew up in, and we could no longer live in it. We bulldozed the little yellow house in 2015.

A typical farm day requires an early start. If I spend the day on a tractor or a combine, I'm in the cab for most of it. I don't even stop for lunch; I eat my sack lunch on the go. On those days I slowly drive up and down the fields, planting, tilling, or harvesting them acre by acre. I know exactly which corners of my farm get cell service and for exactly how long. If it's not too windy I get a couple of bars while driving south; north, not so much. So I often make phone calls during my southbound stretches, and that means I've got to keep my calls brief.

"Turnin' around!" I often warn a caller as I crank the wheel. "Gonna lose you—" If the call is important, I'll call back a few minutes later when I head south again.

For many years before I got involved in politics, I used to solve math problems in my head during the long days of driving back and forth on farm equipment. As the powerful combine engine rumbled under me, I'd give myself long multiplication and division problems to figure out without paper or a calculator. How many square feet in a square mile? (27,878,400.) How many square feet in an acre? (43,560.) How many acres in a football field? (1.32.) So how many square feet are in a football field? (57,600.) I solved problems just to see if I could, and I did because I had the time and mental capacity to do it. And then I moved on to more practical problems.

When a wooden stringer above my butcher shop started to sag, I had to figure out how to replace it. For years that stringer, a sixteen-foot piece of thick wood in the attic, held up the weight of hanging sides of beef, and it finally started to show its age. But the only way to get a new piece of wood into the attic was through a small vent in the side of the shop. If I slid a new sixteen-foot stringer into the vent, I wouldn't be able to swing it into place in the attic, because there were too many trusses in the way. I finally figured out that the only way to replace the stringer required pushing two twelve-foot boards through the vent and using wood glue and bolts to groove them together inside the attic. It's not like putting a man on the moon, but I finally solved the problem while operating a combine. Thirty years later, that stringer is still holding strong.

Since 2007, I spend all my tractor time thinking about work. That's where I come up with questions for upcoming committee hearings and questions I need my staff to answer. I read memos with one hand on the wheel, I listen to the news on the radio, I practice upcoming speeches, and I catch up on phone calls—when I'm headed south.

During planting and harvest seasons, I'm usually in the fields well into the night. On certain days, depending on the price of grain, I'll hook up my forty-two-foot trailer to my 2004 Peterbilt 379 to make several hauls thirty miles down to Fort Benton to unload the wheat and barley. When I'm working the farm, I usually don't eat dinner until ten or eleven o'clock, then I take a hot shower and hit the hay. This schedule is typical for countless American farmers. Washington, a wise friend of mine once pointed out, needs to do a better job of speaking to the working people of America who take showers at the *end* of the day, not just the people who shower in the morning.

The shower-at-night life isn't for everyone. Dad, the mountain man, learned how to farm the flatland as an adult. Farming never coursed through his blood as it coursed through Mother's. But he made a promise to my granddad Fred, as Fred lay dying of cancer in 1963.

"Never sell the farm," Granddad pleaded to his son-in-law. "Will you promise me that?"

Because of Dad's duty to the land, he assured the old honyocker he never would. And if the thought ever crossed Dad's mind, he quickly put it out. Because I knew I wanted to be a farmer since I was eight, selling the farm has never been a question for three generations in a row. None of my children, however, have shown much interest in taking over the land. Shon suffers from severe allergies and Christine loves nursing, which means I'll be at it for as long as the good Lord allows. I, like so many other aging farmers, can't even bear to think about what will happen if nobody takes over.

Of course, not every day on the farm is peachy. When I come in from the fields for good, I won't miss waking up before dawn with our entire house creaking in the wind. I won't miss putting on a dozen layers of clothes because it's minus 30 degrees outside. When it's 30 below zero and snowing sideways, you find out everything wrong with your equipment. I had to butcher a beef cow on one of those awful mornings. My client dropped off the animal the night before, and within hours a wicked cold front blew in, slowing down the entire bloody chore. Dropping that beef in the incessant, subzero wind felt more like a mercy kill than a slaughter. I fired up my Massey Ferguson 35 loader, but I didn't realize how thick the hydraulic fluid had become in the cold, so it took forever for the tractor to lift up the carcass high enough so I could skin it, gut it, and split it in half. Yet I still had to race the clock to cut the massive carcass with my butchering knife before its meat froze solid. I accidentally banged my sharpening steel against the side of my loader, and it shattered into pieces like glass. I won't miss mornings like that.

Icy days have their benefits, though. Enough of them will kill off the tiny sawfly eggs that lay dormant in the stubble. Female wheat stem sawflies have tiny, serrated knifelike appendages on their heads. They hatch after the wheat grows, then they saw the wheat stems right in half with their little bug-head saws to lay more eggs inside, leveling entire crops at a time. You'll rarely hear organic farmers complain about critters like aphids and ladybugs. But why the good Lord sent us sawflies beats the hell out of me. We didn't have wheat stem sawflies on the farm when I was a kid.

Sharla and I have seen a lot of weird changes since taking over the farm. Those of us who work the land know when the weather is screwy. We can feel the climate changing under our hands and in our bones. The plants are telling us. The bugs are showing us. Something is terribly wrong with the earth, and the earth is warning us. Climate change is banging at the door, and we're foolish to ignore it as it quietly creeps under the floorboards.

When I was little we'd enjoy long, snowy winters in the warmth of our home. The snow would pile up in the mountains and gradually melt well into the summer, feeding the rivers and reservoirs that irrigators need to survive. In my youth, we started planting in late April or early May, and we usually harvested during the first three weeks of August—right up to my birthday on August 21. Today, climate change has gunked up all that dependable clockwork. Farmers across the country are now working around unreliable weather patterns and strange storms that don't comply with any season. We've become used to unusually devastating hailstorms in the summer and warm, 60-degree days around Christmas.

In the winter of 2018 and 2019 we saw record snow dump across north-central Montana. Sharla and I hadn't seen that much of it on the farm since 1978—the year we took it over. Normally we welcome any extra moisture; for farmers, deep snow is money in the bank. But in 2018 something happened that we hadn't experienced in forty years: We had an incredibly long, unseasonably cold winter that kept the snow deep through March. Then we got hit with several days of unseasonably warm—almost hot—weather, which melted all the snow across the prairie at once. Hundreds of thousands of acre-feet of water converged into coulees, creating rivers that raged across the farmland. All winter long, I carefully carved channels into the snow behind our farmstead to keep any running water away from our buildings. In March, the raging coulee water missed our barn by only feet. The looming threat to our fragile land forced me to cancel multiple work trips around the state so I could keep my eyes on it. The chore got me thinking about whether the Trump administration ever thought about the untamable power of water flowing across flatland as they conceived their border wall. Where, exactly, would the water flow in a record rainy season along our southern border if a physical wall is in the way?

In the early fifties Dad dug a reservoir just west of our barn that remained full of water for my entire life. Fifty years later, for the first time ever, that reservoir went dry for several consecutive years. That's also when we noticed an ominous change during the harvest season. August used to be the driest month on the farm; in recent years it has been one of the wettest.

Climate change isn't just inconvenient weather, or too little or too much water, or more bugs; it also affects the bottom line for those of us in agriculture. It creates unpredictability and wild swings in the market. It drives up the cost of crop insurance. It threatens our very food security. And of course, climate change is disastrous for other industries across Montana too. In the summer of 2016, Governor Steve Bullock closed a 183-mile stretch of the Yellowstone River to fishing and floating for several weeks after thousands of fish went belly up due to a microscopic warm-water parasite that caused a god-awful-sounding affliction called proliferative kidney disease.[2]

The following summer's wildfire season smoked records in Montana, burning 1.4 million acres of wildland.[3] To put that into perspective, that's more than *seven times* the area of all five boroughs of New York City put together. Fire watchers that summer used a term I'd never heard before: "flash droughts"—freakish periods of intense, dangerous, and dry heat—which made conditions and wildfire danger even worse.[4] Thick smoke hung over Montana for weeks, smothering our multibillion-dollar tourism industry and forcing kids indoors for much of the summer. I saw a biker riding down the street that August wearing a flimsy paper face mask in what seemed like a futile effort to protect his lungs from the smoke. A smudge of black soot covered the spot in front of his mouth—the buildup of all the smoke the poor guy had sucked in. Worse, the 2017 wildfire season claimed the lives of two firefighters.

For most farmers, the threat of climate change looms over the horizon like a dark storm. We know it's coming. We can see it inching toward us. But as long as we're not getting too wet or too dry, and as long as we're still able to raise crops and as long we still have a safety net most of us take for granted, we're still out working in the fields, unworried by the black clouds beyond. But unlike any other weather event in the history of humankind, we have the power to stop this storm from barreling toward us, if we have the courage to confront it now. For the sake of our kids, I hope to hell we do.

When I was a kid, I often heard an unsettling warning about family farm agriculture: "bigger is better." Perhaps this maxim began with President Eisenhower's ag secretary, Ezra Taft Benson, who famously told farmers in the fifties to "get big or get out," contradicting the sound principles of family agriculture that my family believed so strongly in. Today my farm is more than ten times bigger than my grandparents' original 160-acre homestead. It's about four times bigger than the average farm in America.[5] But at 1,800 acres, it's actually *small* for north-central Montana standards. "Bigger is better" is bullshit. It's dangerous advice, if we care about preserving the viability of rural America. Small-scale farms keep our entire food system in check. Without them, your next meal is beholden to a giant, maybe foreign-owned corporation that sets the prices, drives markets, and controls every aspect of your bite of food, from seed to swallow.

My support for small-scale farms and food-processing businesses played a role in the debate over the FDA Food Safety Modernization Act, a 2010 law overhauling our nation's food safety standards. Senator Dick Durbin of Illinois led the effort in response to several national outbreaks of foodborne illnesses. But after combing through his first version of the proposal, I found that it didn't sit well with me. As written, the strict federal regulations that would apply to major industrial food corporations would also apply to small, family-owned produce farms and processors, which state and local governments already regulated. It was a perfect example of how expensive, one-size-fits-all regulations mandated by the federal government could devastate small farms and businesses—especially in rural America.

"When you buy some vegetables or a jar of jam from your local farmers' market, you're buying the cleanest, freshest, healthiest food available, directly from the producer," I said while introducing a couple of amendments to Senator Durbin's bill. "Family farms and ranches have enough hurdles to jump over just trying to make a living. They don't need expensive, redundant regulation that could put them out of business."[6]

My proposed changes were pretty simple: Small farms and food processors who sell their food directly to consumers, grocery stores, or restaurants would be exempt from the onerous new federal regulations, as long as they grossed less than a half-million bucks per year, and as long as they sold their products within their own state boundaries, or within a 275-mile radius.[7]

"Family growers have more eyeballs to the acre," I told *Food Safety*

News. "They have more control over the food they produce. And if there is a problem, it's not like some food factory that can send bags of lettuce to 40 different states in a matter of hours. The real problem was never with the folks who take their goods to the farmers' market in a wheelbarrow. The real problem was with our centralized food system—the factories that churn out hundreds of jars of peanut butter every day and ship them to every corner of the country."[8]

Of course, the big industrial food corporations wanted small farms and businesses to comply with the same standards they were required to meet. They saw the food safety bill as both a threat and as an opportunity to crush small competitors by keeping their fat thumbs on the scales, forcing the little guys out of business by essentially weaponizing federal regulations. So as soon as my amendments started getting traction, the giant food corporations and their slick advocacy organizations dispatched lobbyists to Capitol Hill to gin up opposition. All of a sudden, I had to tamp down false rumors and wild disinformation campaigns, including claims that my amendments would exempt my own farm (they didn't; I don't sell my grain directly to the marketplace). Then I said something that really pissed off the corporate food businesses.

I told the *Washington Post* that small producers "have the ability to meet their consumers eyeball to eyeball. They're not raising a commodity; they're raising food."[9] And then I told the agricultural newspaper *Capital Press* that "industrial agriculture takes the people out of the equation."[10]

I stand by every one of those words. Large-scale, industrial agriculture couldn't care less about the people who actually grow the food; the priority for big agribusinesses is the bottom line, and that bottom line gets bigger whenever a family-owned farm goes bust or gets gobbled up by a corporate syndicate. In November 2010, as we debated the food safety bill, twenty industrial-scale ag organizations, led by the powerful United Fresh Produce Association (known simply as United Fresh) sent a letter to Senate leaders saying they were appalled by my outspoken opinions about industrial agriculture.

"Comments from Senator Tester and supporters are now making

it abundantly clear that their cause is not to argue that small farms pose less risk, but to wage an ideological war against the vast majority of American farmers that seeks to feed 300 million Americans," they wrote on November 18. They added that if the Food Safety Modernization Act included my amendments, they would "be forced to oppose final passage."[11]

United Fresh went even further, calling my quote "hogwash," and adding it "should not only insult the farmers of America, but the intelligence of members of Congress," which, with all due respect, can be a pretty low bar.[12] "The Tester amendment utterly fails to protect consumers by including blanket exemptions from the rest of the bill's strong safety net, without regard to risk," United Fresh claimed. Bullshit. Size, I insisted then as I insist now, correlates directly with risk.

"When we have the kind of *e. coli* outbreaks we've got where it impacts many, many, many states and thousands of families, that's *risk*," I told the *San Francisco Chronicle*. "When we've got a producer that's raising lettuce that's looking at the guy who's going to eat it right square in the eye, that's a different level of risk entirely."[13]

Did I wage an ideological war? If waging war is siding with small farms and businesses that are inherently better than industrial growers at keeping food good and clean, and protecting those small farms and businesses from redundant regulations that would blow them out of business, then that's a war I'll fight any day. Plus I had common sense on my side. The food policy gurus Michael Pollan, the author of *The Omnivore's Dilemma*, and Eric Schlosser, the author of *Fast Food Nation*, both called the bill "the most important food safety legislation in a generation," adding that my amendment "will make it even more effective."[14] Then they came to my defense in a joint column published by the *New York Times*:

> In the last week, agricultural trade groups, from the Produce Marketing Association to the United Egg Producers, have come out against the bill, ostensibly on the grounds that the small farms now partially exempted would pose a food

safety threat. (Note that these small farms will continue to be regulated under state and local laws.) It is hard to escape the conclusion that these industry groups never much liked the new rules in the first place. They just didn't dare come out against them publicly, not when 80 percent of Americans support strengthening the FDA's authority to regulate food.

By one estimate, the kinds of farms that the bill would exempt represent less than 1 percent of the food market-place. Does the food industry really want to sabotage an effort to ensure the safety of 99 percent of that marketplace because it is so deeply concerned about under-regulation of 1 percent? The largest outbreaks are routinely caused by the largest processors, not by small producers selling their goods at farmers' markets.[15]

At the end of the day, I won the fight for safer food from indus-trial farms without unnecessary new regulations for family farms. The Senate passed the measure, as amended, on November 30, with 73 aye votes, including 15 Republicans.[16] The House followed suit three weeks later, passing the Food Safety Modernization Act with 205 votes.[17] Montana's sole Congressman, Dennis Rehberg, voted against it. From my perspective, it was a small victory for family farms fight-ing the tightening grip of corporate consolidation.

The consolidation of family farms at the hands of multinational food giants threaten the very existence of family farms. Their "bigger is better" philosophy of farming is wiping out rural communities like mine and making it an impossible industry to sustain. In 2017 the average age of a farmer in Montana was 59.4 years—slightly older than the national average of 57.5 years.[18] We are not doing nearly enough in this country to bring up a new crop of producers who are eager to inherit their family farms or ranches. Congress has imple-mented some policies to incentivize careers in agricultural produc-tion, but with the average age of an American farmer now nearing 60, we've got a lot more work to do.

We ought to start by rejiggering how we invest in America's

land-grant and agricultural research universities. My grandparents' generation relied on research from these institutions to improve crop yields, efficiencies, and farming practices. Publicly funded research helped crack the codes so farmers could survive natural disasters and tackle new problems, like the rise of wheat stem sawflies and fungi that wipe out entire crops. Today we ought to be studying the effects of changing food production on the health of consumers; for example, why so many people are developing allergies to foods humans have been eating for thousands of years. We ought to be looking at how to introduce *more* small producers into the market as the world's climate changes, and as we count the number of mouths to feed by the rising billions.

Many land-grant universities are now conducting agricultural research with private funding, not public funding—because the public funding has dried up. That steers their research to benefit big agribusiness—to make farms bigger and, for those businesses, better. Too many of America's land-grant and agricultural and research universities are figuring out how to put more profit into the equation by taking *people* out of it. And there go the folks who can produce a safer, more nutritious food supply while keeping their rural communities strong.

This results in a food system that efficiently grows calories with chemical inputs in frankensoil that has no smell. But the scary part is that the food system we are creating and dumping money into is a vertically integrated system. One or two companies own and control every part of the process: the genetically modified seed, the herbicide that works only for the modified genes in that seed, the grain, the shipping method to get that grain to a factory, the factory, and the food product that comes out the other side of it. A small-farm producer like me wants nothing to do with that kind of system. Our little farms are part of a horizontally integrated system—the last holdouts that still produce actual food in this country.

In May 2011 the *Washington Post* hosted the Future of Food Conference at Georgetown University. Prince Charles headlined the daylong event, which featured all sorts of speakers with various opinions about agriculture, food security, hunger, and sustainability. I'm sure the Prince of Wales is a decent dude, but I have little in common with him other than our shared appreciation of organic agriculture. But he made a very important point about the significance of small farms and food security that struck me:

"Imagine if there was a global food shortage," Prince Charles said. "If it became much harder to import food in today's quantities— where do countries turn to for their staple foods? Is there not more resilience in a system where the necessary staple foods are produced locally, so that if there are shocks to the system, there won't be panic? . . . Strengthening small farm production could be a major force in preserving the traditional knowledge and biodiversity that we lose at our peril."[19]

That is a hell of an important point. *Vertically integrated food systems have a single point of failure.*

I had the honor of giving the closing remarks at the Future of Food Conference, as the US Senate's only farmer. I acknowledged how remarkably the United States has increased its food production capabilities over the past century using better farming techniques, chemicals, and fertilizers. I spoke about how a hundred years ago, my grandfolks raised flax, hay wheat, and barley because they knew that diverse rotation is good for insect and pest control and healthier soil.

"Generations ago, a healthy crop rotation was critical if you wanted to make a profit," I pointed out. "Over the past one hundred years, we have seen far less diversity as far as crop rotations go, and far less diversity in competition when it comes to marketing our crops. Monoculture agriculture is a phenomenon that accelerated after World War II with the advent of farm chemicals and water-soluble fertilizers."

But what really disturbed me, I told the seven hundred folks who attended the conference, was the rise of genetically modified organisms:

> With GMOs, farmers don't control the seed; multinational agribusiness does. You've probably heard about these

transgenic plants. A gene is taken from a microorganism—a plant or even an animal—and inserted into another plant. You and I have heard over and over that our only hope to feed the planet as our population grows is GMOs. Well, I'm here to tell you that I don't buy it—

The hundreds of people in the auditorium interrupted with applause.

What it has done—and what it continues to do—is take away options for family farmers. And it takes away options for consumers. If we keep moving down this path, farmers won't be able to control their seeds, something they've done since the beginning of time. And no longer will you truly know what you're eating.[20]

The real reason the United States has kept pace with the world's growing demand for food is because generations ago, our government knew it had a responsibility to guarantee the food security of our nation. Our government did it with farm programs that provide safety nets to small family farms—to ensure that no matter what kind of natural disaster or war or economic uncertainty might affect agriculture, our nation will still have access to food. That is a vision worth fighting for, and it strengthened the middle class by harnessing the power of those of us in rural America and feeding the world with it. Growing up, my parents believed that participating in the farm program was a patriotic duty. They worked hard, they paid their taxes, and they made an honest living. If times turned, the US government would be there to make sure they'd at least survive till next year.

With President Trump and his allies in Congress, I'm not so sure farmers are looking forward to "next year." The president's self-imposed trade war, with no plan for relief in sight, is inflicting tremendous hurt on small farms across the nation. In May 2019, I appeared on CBS's *Face the Nation* to speak on behalf of millions of other farmers about the impact of President Trump's disastrous trade war.

"The reason we have bad commodity prices right now at the farm gate is because we've got a president who went into a trade war without a plan—without our allies," I told the host, Margaret Brennan. "And it ends up where family farm agriculture ends up paying the price. And that doesn't help with food security, and it certainly doesn't help with our economy."

"How long can farmers go before you see the bankruptcies that you have been predicting?" she asked.

"I think we're already starting to see it," I pointed out. "And the sad part about this is it wasn't caused by weather events. It wasn't caused because of consolidation in the marketplace, [or because] prices were too low and inputs were too high. What we've seen is a president who's acted irresponsibly in the trade. He had a plan to hold China accountable but yet didn't know how to implement the plan to hold China accountable. And in the end we don't have an endgame. And farmers have been paying the price."[21]

The $16 billion farm bailout Trump single-handedly delivered to farmers in 2019, by the way, was hardly a safety net. It was a short-term sugar high designed to temporarily placate the millions of grumbling American farmers who had voted for the man with the expectation that he would be in their corner. Instead, he used them as pawns—as collateral damage—in his trade war. And he tried to buy us off by putting our kids further into debt—all without a peep from the lawmakers who normally complain about deficit spending.

"People talk about socialism and who is advocating for socialism around here, but the fact is that this is pretty much socialistic," I said in a speech to the Senate in September 2019, not long after returning to work in Washington following the harvest.

> The sad part is that the amount farmers are getting [from Trump's $16 billion bailout] is probably about a tenth of what they are losing in the marketplace. In fact, when I was

determining what we were going to plant this spring, I was trying to find what we could make money off of. And quite frankly, commodity prices are down across the board, and there wasn't anything that you could turn a profit on. I don't say that being a farmer who wants to complain about prices, because we do that occasionally. I say that because the price of hard red ordinary winter wheat, which probably doesn't mean much to anybody unless you are in agriculture, is about the same price it was in about May of 1978, when I took the farm over. That is not an inflation-adjusted price. That is what it is selling for—a little over $3.50 a bushel. If you take a look back at 1978, it doesn't take a nuclear physicist to figure out that things cost a little less back then. You could buy a car for probably about 15 percent of what you are paying for one now, and farm equipment was the same way.[22]

I ended my remarks by inviting President Trump to Montana, once again, to see for himself how the hard truths of his trade war are hurting rural America and its agriculture. I invited him because I have *hope* for the future of our family farms and ranches. Despite the setbacks of crappy ag policies, unnecessary trade wars, and uncertain commodity prices, I also see more farmers and ranchers willing to stick out their elbows for their noble line of work. I see consumers willing to do their part by supporting and appreciating local food and the families that grow it. Every day I see common sense prevail when enough people are paying attention.

With the exception of many of America's political leaders, I also see a world responding to our changing climate. To those who make a living with their hands in the dirt, I ask you to pay a bit more attention to what younger folks all across our world are already doing. Millions of them are sticking up for the very world they will inherit. They have numbers. They have noise. I can't wait for the day they vote, because that will be the day the rest of us wake up in a world that will start coming back to us.

Several years ago I broke down and bought a used Toyota Prius to haul myself around Washington, DC. I'm pretty sure I'm the only member of Congress who drives both a Peterbilt and a Prius. Will my little Prius fix the problem? Of course not. But if an oversize farmer can pitch in a little by putting up with an undersize car, so can millions of other Americans. If that farmer can pick a fight with powerful, multinational food companies and win, so can the rest of the world.

So can you.

CHAPTER 8

My One-Eared Dog

I'm not much of a pet person. All animals on our farm serve a purpose. Chickens, when we had them, provided eggs and chicken dinners. A couple of nameless cats, when they show up, keep the mice down. Dogs keep other dogs and the damn foxes away, so they shouldn't ever be inside—and God forbid I'd ever pay money for one. Nor would you ever see me walking a dog around holding a leash in one hand and a plastic baggie full of dogshit in the other. That's just not how we do it twelve miles west of Big Sandy.

As a young kid I had a horse named Beauty for a few years. I was about six when Beauty knocked the cover off a fifty-gallon barrel of wheat and helped herself to the feast. After we found out, Dad told me to ride her for the day and to make sure she avoided water along the way. Drinking water, he explained, would expand the wheat in her belly and cause problems. After a daylong ride, Beauty was thirsty, and I figured she'd had a chance to digest the wheat, so I let her drink deep. That night, Dad and brother Dave stayed up through the evening trying to save Beauty and her burst belly, but she was a goner before I woke up the next morning.

In the late nineties I did have a dog that sorta grew on me. Gus was a wily fox terrier who liked me even though I didn't pay much attention to him at first. Gus once got into a scrap with our other dog, a pit bull named Buster, a mean sonofabitch that had a talent for killing our cats. Buster whupped Gus pretty good, and Gus spent a week licking his wounds in the chicken coop. When Gus emerged, his once perky left ear had gotten so infected it had rotted. Then he scratched at his ear and it just fell off his head. Gus then looked down and ate the damn thing. Coincidentally, this happened at about the same time as the infamous "Bite Fight" on June 28, 1997, when Mike Tyson got DQed for nibbling off a chunk of Evander Holyfield's ear in the third round. Maybe it was Gus's traumatic loss of a body part that created an odd bond between us.

A couple weeks earlier, on May 2, 1997, Governor Marc Racicot signed into law a disastrous bill deregulating Montana's electric utility.[1] State government regulation had kept prices low for consumers because there was only one game in town: the Montana Power Company (MPC), which employed some three thousand people with good jobs and good pensions. Senate Bill 390, introduced by Republican state senator Fred Thomas and supported mostly by Republicans, allowed the Montana Power Company to sell off its assets and operate in what proponents said would be a competitive market and lower prices even further. But the whole plan backfired. Miserably.

My friend Ken Toole, a former state senator who later became a member of the Montana Public Service Commission, called the deregulation of the Montana Power Company "one of the greatest economic disasters in our state's history."

The deregulation resulted in hundreds of millions of dollars in losses statewide. Stockholders lost $2 billion. MPC sold off its power generation assets to Pennsylvania Power and Light, then used the money to invest in a new company called Touch America, which went bankrupt in a matter of months. South Dakota's NorthWestern Energy eventually bought the assets. More than 2,800 MPC employees lost their jobs and pensions by 2001, and Montanans paid the highest electricity prices in the region by 2006.[2]

"They promised us lower rates, they promised us better service and they promised us more stability," Toole said of the law's proponents when he announced his candidacy for the Public Service Commission, which oversees Montana's utilities. "Instead, they gave us the highest rates in the Northwest, plant closings and an economic disaster. . . . The deregulation steamroller crushed everything in its path, including senior citizens, low-income people, as well as conservation and consumer groups."[3]

Montanans, who had enjoyed some of the lowest power rates in the nation, were suddenly saddled with higher electrical bills. The whole mess was a case study in terrible public policy and smacked of undue lobbyist influence. The news upset me so much that I wanted to punch a hole through my newspaper; it was pure corporate greed wearing the cheap disguise of trickle-down promises in the free market. And it was the spark that set ablaze my decision to finally run for the state legislature, as a Democrat. I could no longer just sit there and read newspaper stories about this stuff; I wanted to stop things like this from happening. I had learned years earlier that you can make an impact only by either influencing your legislators or being the legislator, and I finally found an opening.

Our longtime Republican state senator and family friend, Loren Jenkins of Big Sandy, announced that fall he would not seek reelection. Jenkins represented Senate District 45, then a seven-thousand-square-mile chunk of Montana—larger than Connecticut and Rhode Island *combined*—which encompassed most of Chouteau County, all of Liberty County, and the western part of Hill County.[4] The district covered half the city of Havre and some of the Rocky Boy's Indian Reservation, thirty miles east of our farm.

The Montana Legislature is made up of fifty senators and one hundred state representatives, all of whom, for ninety days every other year, make laws inside the Capitol, then go home and try to make a living under the laws they create. For a farmer, especially an organic one, a ninety-day legislative session that begins in January times out just right. We usually start planting in late April. The legislature usually wraps up right before.

Montana's state lawmakers are as diverse as our enormous state, elected as citizen legislators whose only requirements are being US citizens, being Montana residents for at least a year, being residents of the counties they represent, and being at least eighteen years old. That means the legislature runs the gamut of experience—from brilliant policy wonks to young activists to weirdos to businesspeople to ideological zealots with nothing better to do. Montana voters in 1992 imposed term limits on legislators, limiting their service to no more than eight years in either chamber within a sixteen-year period.[5] That decision resulted in a dramatic loss of institutional knowledge among familiar—and familiarized—legislators, and a steep learning curve among freshmen lawmakers who replaced them.

I knew I wanted to serve in the legislature the minute I stepped foot in the rotunda of the Montana State Capitol as a junior at Big Sandy High School. But it was the catastrophic deregulation of the Montana Power Company, coupled with Senator Jenkins's retirement, that opened the door in late 1997. Our local state representative, a Republican farmer named Roger DeBruycker, announced in late December that he would vacate his House seat to run for the Senate District 45 seat.[6] That's when I called up some old friends in Havre named Ray and Betty Peck. The Pecks were both longtime activists for the Montana Democratic Party. Ray was also the House minority leader. He had represented Havre since 1982, and the new term limits would prevent him from serving again after the 1999 session.[7] (Ray Peck was also Big Sandy's school superintendent until I started the fifth grade with three missing fingers, and he rented a house in town from my grandmother.)

"You think I got a shot against DeBruycker?" I asked. Roger DeBruycker, after all, was an established politician with name recognition and a powerful "R" behind his name. Roger was also good friends with Chouteau County Commissioner Charlie Danreuther, who ran against me after asking me to replace him years earlier.

"Oh, you can beat Roger," Ray said. "You'll have to work your butt off, though. You willing to go out there and knock on every door?"

Every door? That meant driving thousands of miles and knocking on the doors of thousands of people—mostly strangers—across Senate District 45. I swallowed hard.

"That won't be a problem. How much money do you think I'll need to raise?"

"It'll run you five grand," Ray said. "But if you win, you'll learn more in one session of the legislature than you would during an entire year of college."

After a long talk with Sharla, Christine, and Shon, all of whom supported the idea, I announced my candidacy for the Montana Senate in February 1998. Sharla especially supported the decision, because if I won, the time commitment would force us to cut back on the amount of meat we would have to butcher, and the work was taking a toll on her physically. During my announcement to a crowd of local Democrats in Chester, I recalled my appreciation for the late Senator David James, whom I'd invited to speak to my high school on Government Day almost twenty-five years earlier. Senator James was the reason, I said, I became interested in politics. A woman in the crowd began dabbing her eyes. When I spoke with her later, she introduced herself to me as Senator James's daughter.[8]

The first order of business as a new candidate was to resign from my part-time work refereeing basketball. I realized that no matter what call I made on a court, it was sure to piss off half the gymnasium, and *all* of them were voters. The second order of business was to put together a list of all my butcher shop clients, present and past. I sent each of them a letter telling them I was running for the state senate. A few days later one of my clients sent me a check—my first ever campaign contribution. I couldn't believe it. It wasn't much, but it was *money I didn't even work for*; I simply announced that I wanted to be a public servant and a voter trusted me enough to send her hard-earned money because she believed in me.

Because I had the benefit of an uncontested primary election that year, the Montana Democratic Party offered the early help of a brilliant staffer named Jill Gerdrum, who gave my basement campaign some professional organization (I certainly couldn't afford to hire a full-time campaign manager). Jill and I pored over maps, and she helped me put together my campaign literature: a "door card" with all the relevant info and a picture of Sharla and me. Then she helped me simplify my pitch.

With a thermos full of coffee and a tank full of gas, I got busy knocking doors every spare evening and weekend I had starting in February 1998. Knocking doors is as simple as it sounds. My first campaign wasn't sophisticated enough to analyze voter data and patterns with reams of information about who lived behind each door. I simply walked up to every house, trailer home, apartment, and farmstead in the district I could find, avoided a growling dog or five, rang or knocked, and had a brief-as-possible conversation with any voter or potential voter who answered. Nine out of ten doors went unanswered, but I kept at it.

"I'm Jon Tester," I'd say when someone of voting age came to the door. "I'm running for Senate District Forty-Five, and I'm going to make sure the state pays its fair share in education funding. I want to keep your property taxes low and I want to make sure higher education is affordable."

That was about it—not a whole hell of a lot different from the messages that resonate with rural America today. I quickly learned that it was more important to introduce myself and to let them know I was willing to work hard. The simple courage of knocking on a stranger's door conveys all that without a single word. Remarkably, very few folks who answered their doors even asked which political party I belonged to. And in rural Montana, knocking rarely resulted in slammed doors in my face. Most of them were just pleased to see a neighbor, especially after they looked me in the eye and shook my hand.

The very first house I knocked was over by my in-laws' farm outside Box Elder. I had to drive about a quarter mile into the yard, and after the elderly lady answered the door, I got tongue-tied and stood on her porch, stammering.

"You're Jon Tester," she finally told me, which is not how campaigning is supposed to work. "I know who you are." But that first door was the worst of my experiences. I quickly got the hang of it and fell in love with campaigning. I would arrive in a small community like Gildford, Montana (population 180), and after sizing it up, I would challenge myself to knock every single door in town in an hour. That meant I would have to literally jog from door to door, knocking and cramming my cards into every doorjamb. Then I would drive my pickup six miles west to Hingham (population 120) and do the same thing. Every now and then I'd get into deep conversations with folks about things that were important to their communities, like state funding for watershed improvements. Every now and then I'd come across a voter whose mind I knew I could never change, and I cheerfully thanked him and moved on. But most of my contacts were simple, friendly greetings.

Sharla got in on the fun too. When we hit a town, she would take one side of a street and I'd take the other. If Sharla found someone who wanted to talk to me, she'd flag me down and I'd run across. Christine and Shon even got in on the action. The Model T I bought for Shon to fix up paid off, because as a family we participated in every community parade, driving our newly restored old car. I shook hands at every county fair and rodeo and powwow. And I made it a point to knock on most doors in the district five times each between February and Election Day, November 3, 1998.

I knew it was a success when someone asked me, "What are you doing here?" after I knocked on his door a fifth time. "You earned my vote the second time you showed up!"

For most of the year, Roger DeBruycker didn't seem to pay attention to what I was doing. Like many Republican candidates in Montana, I believe he assumed he would coast to victory on Election Night. But he must have realized in October that all my hustling was paying off across District 45. As a state representative, DeBruycker had earned the nickname "Red Light Roger" because his default position was to vote against damn near *everything* in the legislature.[9] That included a final vote against state funding for the popular Sage Creek Watershed Project. DeBruycker had technically voted for the bill in its earlier two forms, but his final and most important vote on the amended bill was nay. Nonetheless, he claimed in a late October campaign ad that he supported funding for the project, which caught

Jill's attention. After some thorough research, we decided to run ads in local newspapers noting that DeBruycker ultimately voted against the funding he had claimed credit for.

Red Light Roger doubled down with a series of obfuscating radio ads, accusing *me* of lying about *his* record. But we knew we had the facts on our side. I tried calling DeBruycker several times, but I couldn't get a hold of him. So I called up his campaign treasurer and warned her that the whole ordeal would make DeBruycker look foolish if he didn't pull the ads. Facts are facts, I said. But I didn't get their commitment to pull the ads.

So with my blessing the Montana Democratic Party filed a formal complaint with the state's independent Commissioner of Political Practices, taking issue with DeBruycker's misleading advertising. That complaint finally got DeBruycker to cancel his radio ads with the excuse: "I'm not going to get into a legal hassle over it. It isn't worth it."[10]

"You don't pull these kinds of ads unless you're caught lying," the Montana Democratic Party fired back.[11] I demanded an apology from DeBruycker for challenging "my integrity as a human being," but I didn't expect one and never got one.[12] Our damage had already been done, though, and our hard work had already paid off. A few days later on Election Night, I officially won our race at ten o'clock. I received 3,747 votes, or 55.8 percent of the share, stopping Roger DeBruycker at my own red light.[13] He received only 2,974 votes, even after spending $4,700 of his own money.[14] But despite my upset win in Chouteau County, the Republicans still controlled the state Senate.

"I think the main thing that beat me was Jon just had better organization," DeBruycker admitted to the *Great Falls Tribune* a couple of days later. "I was just outgunned."[15] That 1998 race turned into one of the most expensive in the state. I ended up raising and spending a lot more than $5,000. My campaign cost four times that, and I raised it all from good people who believed in me. I simply worked harder. I spoke to more voters. I spent more time campaigning. I wanted the job more. *I burned more shoe leather.*

In May 2019, I accepted an invitation to speak at the Center for

American Progress's Ideas Conference in Washington, where I made a case for winning back rural America. "If you don't show up, you don't get the vote," I told the room full of activists. "If you're running for the legislature, you knock on every door. If you're running statewide, you go to every town." I told them how concerning it is to me that smaller campaigns in rural communities often target only certain doors deemed persuadable, a strategy that flies in the face of introducing yourself to strangers and convincing them to support you the old-fashioned way. That strategy is why Democrats in rural places often lose, I said.

"You knock on every door if you're going to win," I added, over applause. "*You knock on every door.* And the folks out there that tell you you're wasting your time when you're knocking on that door? Well then, as [Senator] Max Baucus told me, go figure out where you can get some more time. Because the truth is those people are important and those people are the folks that—if you can get them to vote for you—you *win* that election."[16]

For years before my stint in the legislature, I played on a men's softball team called the Great Falls Sting with another state senator named Steve Doherty, who was elected Senate minority leader for the 1999 session. I asked Steve to put me on the Select Committee on Jobs and Income, which started meeting in late 1998, before the session even began in early January. Steve gave me the assignment, which meant I got a head start as a freshman lawmaker. And on December 23, Montana's Supreme Court made a decision that made national headlines. In a 4–3 ruling, the court overturned Montana's notorious, three-year-old "Reasonable and Prudent" daytime highway speed limit—which was essentially no speed limit at all—saying the law was "unconstitutionally vague." That decision meant my colleagues and I would have to find a solution in a matter of weeks.[17]

In that matter of weeks I discovered that Ray Peck was right: a single session in the Montana State Legislature was more educational than an entire year of college. I rented a house in Helena from a former Havre state legislator named Bob Bachini and his wife, Shirley, both of whom spent the winter in Arizona, and I drove home to my farm on Saturday afternoons in a gold VW Beetle. But I spent most of my time in Helena hard at work in the Capitol, and I got the hang of things pretty quickly. I learned how to build coalitions, and how to negotiate with Republicans to get most of what I wanted. I learned where the pressure points were, which lawmakers were worth my time, and which ones weren't. And I worked my ass off. Within days I introduced a bill to encourage the construction of low-income housing through tax incentives, and I pushed what I promised on the campaign trail: more state dollars for public education.[18]

I saw my share of controversy too. I joined another freshman senator, Democrat Glenn Roush of Cut Bank (a retired Montana Power Company employee), in supporting a Republican bill that raised eyebrows among other legislators in our party. That bill eventually did away with property taxes on business equipment and livestock. I didn't love the bill, but it benefitted family farmers and ranchers. I also supported an overwhelmingly bipartisan bill reestablishing a daytime speed limit of seventy-five miles per hour in Montana, which, as the *Great Falls Tribune* reported, "some constituents liken to fascism."[19] That included my own brother. I had recently helped Bob jerk the motor out of his Corvette, then we juiced it up to 400 horsepower and put it back in. It is fair to say that Bob and a lot of other libertarian-minded Montanans still miss that old "Reasonable and Prudent" speed limit.

That spring, another Montana farmer was storming across the political landscape. Brian Schweitzer, a political newcomer born in Havre several months before me, announced his candidacy for the US Senate on March 24. Schweitzer promised an "aggressive campaign to lead Montana into the new century" by challenging Senator Conrad Burns, who announced his reelection bid in February.[20] Schweitzer, a soil scientist by trade who spoke fluent Arabic from a stint in Saudi Arabia, never ran out of gas and immediately mastered the art of earning media attention with an energetic combination of policy ideas and schtick.

Two weeks after announcing his candidacy, Schweitzer organized a surreal news conference in the rotunda of the Montana State

Capitol. Standing at a podium surrounded by four security guards, he held up a signed pledge promising not to take campaign contributions from the tobacco industry. Then he scattered coins and bundles upon bundles of real paper money onto the floor—apparently $47,000 of it—to visually underscore the $47,000 in contributions Burns had accepted from tobacco companies.

"I challenge Conrad to give up the tobacco dollars to charity and sign an oath to defend Montana families against your big tobacco friends!" Schweitzer said from a podium surrounded by a sea of dead presidents staring up at him.

"This is not Missouri," he added. "We don't grow tobacco in Montana!"[21]

Of course, that line was Schweitzer's clincher. The whole stunt was really designed to emphasize the fact that Burns was not a Montana native. He'd moved to Montana from Missouri as an adult.[22] Schweitzer, a farmer-rancher who raised dill, peppermint, beets, barley, and cattle, quickly reminded everyone he was a third-generation Montanan. Like it or not, how many generations you are as a native Montanan matters in Montana politics. I am a third-generation Montanan. My 2012 challenger, Congressman Dennis Rehberg, was a fifth-generation Montanan, like my grandkids. The political scientist David C. W. Parker wrote about the odd custom of generation-claiming in his book about Montana's 2012 US Senate race, *Battle for the Big Sky*:

> Many who have lived here all their lives feel that, like tea, Montana values and connection to place must steep into a person's soul and bones. Until that process is completed over generations, it is impossible—and imprudent—to understand and speak for Montana.[23]

While I believe being a lifelong Montanan is an important indicator of how well a candidate understands our state and its people, it certainly isn't a prerequisite for public service—nor does whatever number of previous generations have anything to do with it. Senator

Mike Mansfield, after all, was born in New York City. Senator Steve Daines was born in Van Nuys, California,[24] (yet still touts his status as "a fifth-generation Montanan").[25] I never hear Native American leaders tout the *countless* generations they rightfully claim to what is now Montana.

Schweitzer lived up to his promise of running an aggressive campaign all the way through Election Day, November 7, 2000. In November 1999, Schweitzer organized a bus trip from Great Falls to Milk River, Alberta, so dozens of Montana seniors, including both of his elderly parents, could "stock up on cheap pharmaceuticals they need to battle arthritis, high blood pressure and other ills that come with getting older."[26] Each passenger paid $14 for the ride into Canada and another $15 to see a doctor there. Though the journey saved those forty seniors more than $3,500 in drug costs that day, for Schweitzer, the real endgame was to embarrass Congress generally and Conrad Burns specifically.[27] And of course, he organized more bus trips into Canada from other Montana cities.

Every chance Schweitzer could get, he attacked Burns for unpopular votes or for doing nothing at all. He blamed Burns specifically for a delay in long-awaited aid for the nation's farmers, forcing Burns to get into the weeds explaining the legislative process.[28] He highlighted Burns's unpopular openness to privatizing Social Security, and he relentlessly went after the senator for being ineffective after "12 long years of leadership that divides people."[29] And whenever Schweitzer made his way through a crowd—say, at a University of Montana Grizzlies tailgate—he tethered to himself a giant helium balloon in the shape of a lightbulb to symbolize his big ideas.

Back in Big Sandy, I had a little fun of my own. Now that the 1999 session was in the rearview mirror, I wanted to mail a survey to my constituents—to all those folks on whose doors I'd knocked—asking them about their priorities for the next legislative session in 2001. I looked at Gus, hoping for a spark of creativity, and he perked up his ear and wagged his whippy little tail at me. That was the inspiration I needed. I snapped a picture of him and printed the photo on the front of my survey with the words, "Politicians in Helena are like my one-eared dog: they only listen to half of what you say. I want to hear all of what you say." I'll be damned. The strategy worked; I got responses back from across all three counties.

That first term in the Montana Senate also took me on an agricultural trade mission to Asia, my first time ever across the ocean, where we visited several Taiwanese cities, including Taipei and T'ai-chung. It was also my first time immersed in cities so overpopulated and polluted they felt claustrophobic. Our job as Montana agricultural "trade specialists" was to strengthen Montana's trade ties and to promote our organic crops. But Mother Nature had other plans. A few days after we left, a massive, 7.6-magnitude quake struck Taiwan, killing thousands and putting the momentum of our entire trade mission on hold.[30]

Little did I know then that the news of Election Night of 2000 would change the course of my own political career. For the first time ever, Montanans elected a woman, the late Judy Martz, as their new Republican governor. Rehberg, Montana's former lieutenant governor who unsuccessfully challenged Max Baucus for his Senate seat in 1996, narrowly beat Nancy Keenan, the Montana superintendent of public instruction, in the US House race. And Conrad Burns edged out Schweitzer by just 13,652 votes for a third term in the Senate.[31] It was clear that two years of Schweitzer's persistent hooks and jabs had significantly weakened the junior senator's popularity in Montana. Brian Schweitzer certainly took a bite out of Conrad Burns.

In 2002 I won my first reelection in Senate District 45 with more than 71 percent of the vote, beating another farmer named Roy Hollandsworth.[32] By then, most of the voters in the district knew who I was, and, for the most part, they either appreciated my record or at least appreciated the fact that I shot straight about it. And in 2003 I was elected Senate minority leader. That year, our challenge was to balance the state budget despite a $300 million shortfall. And we did it, the same way my folks had on the farm for years: setting priorities, cutting the fat, and living within our means.

After my folks left for Idaho in 1978, I got in the habit of calling them every Sunday night. Before my tenure in the legislature, our conversations revolved entirely around the farm: the weather, the moisture, commodity prices, crop plans, equipment breakdowns, and the usual gossip about the neighbors. After my first election in 1998, our weekly conversations shifted entirely to politics and the work of the Montana State Legislature. Mother, of course, was keenly interested in my front-row perspective of politics, and she always wanted to know what I thought about news stories of the day, at all levels of government. Dad, however, became increasingly distant with every passing week. His health had finally started to catch up to his age.

In his younger years, going shopping in Great Falls was an all-day family event, because Dad would stop and chat with everyone he saw on the street, and he knew most of them. He loved to dance with Mother, and he always loved his horses. But in his eighties Dad lost that vigor. He quit both horses and dancing because he never trusted his heart after a surgery at the age of eighty-two. That was the beginning of the end for Dad. When I last saw him in the spring of 2004, he seemed to have already left. He recognized me, but the spark that made Dad Dad—the mountain man whose duty to his family redirected him to a quiet career on the flatland—had flickered out, and he looked at all of us with hollow eyes.

On April 12, suffering from congestive heart failure, Dad got a bloody nose that didn't seem to stop. It was so severe Mother called my brother Dave, who lived nearby. Both Dave and his wife, Becky, rushed to check on Dad, and soon called for an ambulance. In the middle of the commotion, Dad calmly looked up from his easy chair at Becky and said: "My goodness you're tall!" with one more wink in his eye, unclear if he even recognized her. Those were my father's final words.

Dad had requested a Do Not Resuscitate order, and he was gone by the time paramedics arrived. He would have turned eighty-eight in one more month. My older brother welled up in those strange few moments after Dad's death, before the ambulance showed up.

"Stop," Mother told him with her finger in the air, processing her own grief in the stoic way only Helen Tester could. "There's no sense crying. This is one of those things we will accept."

I had the job of writing Dad's obituary—something simple, as he would have wanted it. "Dave had a great respect for animals and a love for horses," I wrote at the end of the obituary. "In that vein he was involved in the Big Sandy Saddle Club and the Chouteau County Sheriff's Posse."[33]

Dad never got to see how dramatically Montana's political landscape changed again in late 2004. In the legislature we began the year by announcing the Democrats' new, proactive plan to "strengthen, stabilize, and diversify" Montana's economy; we then took the plan on the road to discuss it with communities across the state. Schweitzer, then a candidate for governor, joined the chorus. Our plan called for tax credits for new businesses, better business opportunities in Native American communities, improved workforce training, higher wages, and responsible natural resource development. It got us all talking to Montanans about jobs—*and only jobs*. Our message resonated.

"By investing in and adding value to our greatest natural resource—our human resources, our workers—we can create an economy to match our landscape," I said during one of our news conferences. "We want to help Montanans get a job, a career, whether they want to work with their heads or their hands."[34]

Our hustle and message discipline paid off again. Though Democrats lost nationally that Election Night, Montana Democrats won big. Brian Schweitzer (along with state senator John Bohlinger, his Republican running mate) beat Republican Bob Brown to become Montana's next governor. For the first time in a decade, Democrats won control of the Montana Senate.[35] In the state House, the Democrats held on to forty-nine seats as the Republicans captured fifty; one seat, House District 12 in Lake County, boiled down to a handful of disputed ballots. Eight weeks after Election Day, on December 28, the Montana Supreme Court finally declared Democrat Jeanne Windham the winner. That decision tied the number of seats in the House, which, thanks to Schweitzer's victory, meant Democrats were in charge for the first time in fourteen years.[36]

Also that year, by almost a two-to-one margin, Montanans became among the first in the nation to legalize the use of medical marijuana. And by almost the same margin, they amended the Montana Constitution to define civil marriage as "between one man and one woman."[37] When asked what I thought about the new ban on same-sex marriage, I regrettably deferred to the "will of the people of Montana," a majority of whom had made it pretty clear what they wanted their Constitution to say in 2004. Politically, it was the convenient answer.

Privately, I wrestled with that answer. Earlier that year, after Shon graduated from high school, we were driving home from Missoula, where Shon had just delivered a beautifully restored 1953 MG Roadster to a client. I could tell he was nervous for some reason. His face was white and he was shaking when he told me he was gay.

"I know," I told him.

"What?"

"I've known since you were in the sixth grade."

"Were you ever going to have a talk with me about it?" he stammered.

"That's not part of my journey," I said, for better or for worse. "But I'm happy we're talking about it now. When are you gonna tell your mother?"

"I already did," he said. "Eight months ago."

Sharla, it turns out, wanted Shon to come out to me on his own time line. Though Shon's sexuality surprised neither of us, it took several years for me to realize the psychological impact that Montana's new definition of marriage had on our son.

A few weeks after Shon came out to me, I had a much more difficult conversation with him. I told him I worried about him as he headed off to college in Missoula, and I said something stupid along the lines of, "This is going to be a difficult life you've chosen."

"When did you *choose* to be straight?" he fired back. I didn't have an answer. He made a good point that I'll never forget. Through Shon, my perspective on LGBTQ rights and acceptance has evolved significantly since that conversation. I am now proud to admit I'm the father of a man who happens to be gay. Shon told me later he may be the last person in our family who will have to struggle to come to terms with sexuality. For that, I'm grateful.

A few weeks after Election Day in 2004, my colleagues elected me president of the Montana Senate. The man I replaced in that role, Republican Bob Keenan of Bigfork, summed up the role of Senate President pretty well.

"In the president's seat, you're doing some refereeing," Keenan told Lee Newspapers as he passed the baton to me. "You're kind of a player-coach, as opposed to being the quarterback on the floor."[38] Given my short-lived history with football, I eagerly accepted the role of "player-coach." And with control of both chambers and the governor's office, the Democrats were on a roll.

The goodwill with Bob Keenan ended there. On November 9, 2004, the Montana Supreme Court ruled that state funding for public education in Montana was constitutionally inadequate and "evolved without the benefit of any determination of what constitutes 'quality.'" The court gave the Montana State Legislature just under a year to better fund public schools.[39] Senator Keenan's response? To hold a late-night gaslight debate on the "definition of quality education."

"Have at it," I answered. "We could use a good debate about the definition of quality education." And so the Montana Senate held one, beginning at two p.m. The problem was that Keenan was trying to showboat his way through the afternoon, then into the evening, then into the following morning. I'm not sure if he was trying to earn a headline, or bragging rights to his caucus that he put up a fight, or if he was simply trying to break us. But his strategy was an annoying one: to waste time by asking repetitive questions to the chair of the Education Committee, Senator Don Ryan of Great Falls. Senator Keenan kept us in session with his strategy until the early hours of the morning. And Senator Ryan respectfully and diligently went along, until at long last, Keenan wrapped up.

By then, it was three o'clock in the morning, and we had three or four more bills left on the board, so I kept the Senate in session and started debate on the next one. Senator Corey Stapleton, a Republican from Billings who later became Montana's secretary of state, asked if we could quit.

"No, Senator Keenan wanted a debate," I said. "So we are going to continue to debate." And to the annoyance of our Republican colleagues, I carried our session into dawn. The Democrats knew exactly what I was doing. So did the Republicans, but it was difficult for them to publicly grumble about it. Senator Keenan, their former leader, wanted to inflict pain on us through parliamentary procedure, and I wanted to remind them that both parties could play his game.

Years later in the US Senate, I suggested the same strategy to Majority Leader Reid when the Republicans threatened to keep the Senate in session through the early morning. "Call their bluff!" I implored. "We need more late nights and early mornings around here. Working through the night never hurt anyone."

As president, I also insisted on hiring Ray Peck to help in some capacity. At the age of seventy-eight, he was an experienced mentor who always had sage advice for everyone, and he still had a passion for legislative politics. First I asked Ray to run the Senate's computer to keep our schedules and votes on track. But he admitted he wasn't skilled in computers. So I told Ted Dick, the sergeant at arms, to hire Ray as one of the assistants who staffed the floor of the Senate. But Ray soon got stuck working the evening shifts because the younger assistants all wanted to leave early to enjoy their evenings on the town. About a week and a half later, Ted, who's about my girth, came up to me and put his arm around my shoulder.

"Um," Ted said quietly. "Ray quit."

"Ray quit? Why did Ray quit?"

"He didn't want to do the night shift anymore."

"Well, Ted," I said, "you gotta go *un-quit* him!"

"How?"

"Go to his house right now and tell him we'll give him whatever shift he wants, and from here on out, you give him whatever shift he wants." And that was all it took to un-quit Ray Peck.

I also had to step into schoolteacher mode when I got word that one of the Democratic senators, Carolyn Squires of Missoula, told a colleague to "fuck off" in a fiery exchange on the Senate floor—and loud enough that the entire chamber overheard it. That, of course, was a severe breach of decorum. So I called her into my office with House Majority Leader Jon Ellingson and the man Senator Squires had just cussed out, Senator Greg Lind, a Democrat also from Missoula.

"Yeah, what's this about?" Senator Squires asked with her arms crossed. She was a character who didn't take shit from anyone, and she was having none of our meeting in my office, with a bunch of men.

"You know what this is about." I sighed. "We can't have this kind of behavior on the Senate floor."

"It's okay," Lind said, embarrassed. "I'm over it." But I thought it was important to send a signal that Senate Democrats were above this sort of thing.

"Senator Squires, I have to ask you to apologize to Senator Lind."

Senator Squires looked over at Majority Leader Ellingson, slowly raised her hand, and pointed her finger at him.

"I've told *him* to fuck off." Then she moved her finger to point at Lind. "I've told *him* to fuck off." Then she pointed her finger at me. "And I've told *you* to fuck off. *I'm sorry.*" And with that, Senator Squires got up and walked out of my office. Carolyn Squires, who became a dear friend of mine, passed away in 2016. I have no doubt that she is still speaking the four-letter truth to power, somewhere out there.

Despite some bumps and salty language along the way, Montana Democrats made good progress during the long days and late nights of the 2005 Montana State Legislature. Unlike the slow and deliberate grind of the US Senate, the Montana Legislature was a hot, fast kitchen. We worked efficiently, transparently, and—more often than not—collaboratively (or at least respectfully) with the Republican caucus. The Democrats racked up more than our share of victories, and we made sure our constituents knew about all of them, major and minor. National Democrats can learn a lot from that strategy. Too often we don't take a win when we can get a win, because it's not a "big enough" win.

In early February, after close consultation with Schweitzer, I introduced Senate Bill 415, the Montana Renewable Power Production and Rural Economic Development Act. The legislation created a renewable portfolio standard in Montana by requiring NorthWestern Energy and other electricity providers to buy at least 15 percent of their power from renewable sources within the next decade.

"Some say that's unreasonable," I admitted a few weeks later to a reporter who asked about the grumbling energy companies warning of higher costs to consumers. "I would say 10 years from today, 15 percent would be looked on as a minimum."[40]

Both chambers passed Senate Bill 415, and Schweitzer signed it into law on April 28, 2005.[41] In September 2014, less than a decade later, the Montana Legislature officially reported that Montana's electrical utilities had met our reasonable goal, and that the renewable portfolio standard "has had a negligible impact on ratepayers in Montana." Their report added that though the standard did not replace existing power generation utilities, "most of them added wind generation to their portfolios."[42]

I also carried legislation that established a program called Big Sky Rx, to help seniors pay their Medicare Part D premiums. That helped approximately 188,000 Montanans at the easy expense of pissing off the pharmaceutical industry.[43] We passed Senate Majority Leader Ellingson's Senate Bill 302, which allowed for same-day voter registration in Montana beginning in 2006—a law that the Republicans have since tried their damnedest to dismantle even though it has afforded the right to vote to tens of thousands of Montanans. The fifty-ninth session of the Montana Legislature also passed a bill banning smoking in public places across the state. Pretty good progress, for a few weeks of work.

But when it came to adequate funding of public education, we had unfinished business. It was clear the legislature would need to convene a special session later in the year to address the State Supreme Court's mandate. And behind the steamroller of progress of that session of the legislature, news of brutal firefights in Afghanistan and President Bush's disastrous war in Iraq dominated national headlines.

By the end of 2005, ten Montana men had died in the line of fire in both countries, and neither conflict had an end in sight.[44]

And on March 1, 2005, the *Washington Post* published another national story that got immediate attention in Montana (the *Missoulian* newspaper reprinted the entire *Post* story, word for word). The story's reporter, Susan Schmidt, wrote that a "$3 million grant from a federal program intended for impoverished Indian tribal schools went to one of the richest tribes in the country under pressure from Sen. Conrad Burns (R-Mont.), who oversees the budget of the Bureau of Indian Affairs." Burns had pressured the bureau to send the grant to Michigan's Saginaw Chippewa tribe, a client of a lobbyist whose name was, until then, unfamiliar to Montanans: Jack Abramoff. Burns, then the chairman of the powerful Senate Interior Appropriations Subcommittee, shrugged off "objections of Interior officials" to steer millions of taxpayer dollars to the Saginaw Chippewas, whose members each received "$70,000 a year from gambling profits."

"Abramoff, his associates and his wealthy tribal clients have been an important source of Burns's campaign funds, providing 42 percent of the contributions to his 'soft-money' political action committee from 2000 to 2002, according to federal election records," the *Post* reported.[45] Burns and his staff immediately played defense, claiming the senator had met Abramoff "only once or twice." That claim smelled just as fishy, because the *Post* also reported that Burns's former chief of staff "traveled to the 2001 Super Bowl on the Abramoff corporate jet, along with several staffers from the office of House Majority Leader Tom DeLay (R-Tex.)."[46]

That story was just the beginning, and the first of many more stories in 2005 and 2006 about Conrad Burns and his ties to Jack Abramoff. Montanans read them with raised eyebrows. Senator Burns had already been weakened by Brian Schweitzer's bruising challenge in 2000. Then he blindly supported both the increasingly unpopular war in Iraq, and President Bush's unpopular efforts to privatize Social Security.

It seemed to many of us that Conrad Burns was only half-listening to Montana.

CHAPTER 9

More Zeroes

I had my disagreements with Conrad Burns, but we got along in the years after our bruising fight over his Senate seat in 2006. We'd bump into each other in the airport every now and then and swap stories. He was a character. And flaws and flubs aside, he cared deeply about Montana and his public service to it. In the days after I edged him out of the US Senate, I'm told Senator Burns personally directed his outgoing staff to work closely with my incoming staff, and they did, setting aside any bitterness to do best for their boss and our state. Senator Burns had set the standard for excellence in constituent service, and we still work every day to meet his high standard for responding quickly to emails and phone calls, answering Montanans' questions, and helping them poke through the red tape of the federal government.

Conrad Burns grew up on a farm he described as "two rocks and a dirt" outside Gallatin, Missouri. Though his family had very little money, he said he enjoyed a "very happy childhood." And after several years traveling the West as a salesman and writer for a cattle magazine, he moved to Billings in the late sixties to become an auctioneer.[1]

Burns made a name for himself in 1975, when he founded the North-ern Ag Network, a cluster of radio stations that broadcast farm and ranch news across Montana and Wyoming.[2] I remember listening to his distinctive voice on the radio while on my tractor; he had a Mis-souri twang and a colorful way with words. Burns sold his interest in the Northern Ag Network shortly before running for—and handily winning—a seat on the Yellowstone County Commission in 1986.[3] Burns served as a commissioner until 1988, when, with the support of the National Republican Senatorial Committee, he decided to chal-lenge the incumbent John Melcher for a seat in the US Senate. He announced his candidacy on February 25, 1988.[4]

Throughout that year, Burns simply outworked and outmaneu-vered Doc Melcher. He primarily focused on the red meat messages of lower taxes and less government. Then Melcher opened a wide flank for Burns late in the campaign. In August 1988, as wildfires rav-aged Yellowstone National Park and consumed the nation's attention, Melcher introduced controversial legislation designating 1.43 million acres of roadless national forestland as wilderness. Melcher stayed in Washington for most of the fall and managed to pass the bill through both chambers of Congress. In Montana, though, Melcher's bill was rocky from the get-go, drawing ire from Burns and the Right that the wilderness protections went too far, and frustration from the Left that it didn't go far enough to protect wildland.

Then, on November 2, 1988, less than a week before Election Day, President Reagan publicly refused to sign Melcher's bill, killing it with a pocket veto. Reagan claimed Melcher's legislation would "injure the economy of Montana."[5] The more obvious reason for the presi-dent's veto, of course, was to deliver a nicely timed political boost to the farm broadcaster from Billings. On November 8, Burns unseated Melcher in the US Senate race by 13,636 votes, winning with 52 per-cent.[6] And a few days later, the Helena *Independent Record* made an often-forgotten observation:

"State Rep. Dennis Rehberg, a Billings Republican who managed Burns' campaign, is a shrewd politician and tactician and deserves a lot of credit for the upset victory," the paper editorialized.[7]

For his part, Burns stuck to his memorable quotes as he antici-
pated his transition from Yellowstone County to Washington, DC.
When the Associated Press asked about the difference between being
a county commissioner with little political experience and being a US
senator, he replied, "There's no real difference. We're just dealing in
more zeroes. The responsibility's the same."[8]

But Burns's colorful quips had worn thin by the time I served as
president of the Montana Senate. He had earned numerous national
headlines by sticking his cowboy boots in his mouth. In fact, *Time*
eventually included Burns in its list of "worst senators," calling him
"serially offensive."

> In the last campaign, Burns called Arabs "ragheads" and
> had to apologize. In 1994 he played along when a rancher
> made a demeaning comment about African Americans. Last
> month he told a woman, within earshot of the media, that he
> was looking forward to getting "knee-walking drunk."[9]

But it was ultimately Conrad Burns's increasingly concerning relationship with "Casino Jack" Abramoff that earned him a spot on
the *Time* list. After Abramoff pleaded guilty in January 2006 to conspiracy, tax evasion, and fraud, Burns agreed to cooperate with federal
prosecutors. In Montana, voters had learned that Burns had accepted
more contributions from Abramoff and his clients than any other
member of Congress ($150,000, which Burns ultimately returned).
In 2001, Burns voted against a bill to improve labor and immigration
standards in the Northern Mariana Islands, where garment manufacturers got away with making clothes in poor working conditions with
MADE IN USA labels. But a year earlier Burns had *supported* identical
legislation; he switched his position after a $5,000 donation from an
Abramoff client who wanted to defeat the bill.[10] Burns's dented suit of
armor had started cracking. In fact, the Montana Democratic Party
began airing $230,000 worth of effective TV ads questioning Burns's
ethics long before our party knew who its Senate candidate was going
to be.[11]

In the spring of 2005, Sharla and I joined a handful of trusted friends at the Helena home of Jan and Bill Lombardi. Bill, the secretary of the Montana Senate, had previously handled communications for Senator Max Baucus. My old minority leader and softball teammate Steve Doherty was there. So were my buddies Tom Kimmell, Senate Majority Leader Jon Ellingson, Senator Dave Wanzenried of Missoula, and Senator Mike Wheat of Bozeman, the chairman of the Judiciary Committee.

"You're the guy to show old Conrad the door," Wheat told me, which was quite a statement because Mike Wheat was a prominent trial attorney, and the Montana Trial Lawyers Association had just announced its US Senate endorsement of Democrat John Morrison, Montana's state auditor.

"What about Morrison?" I asked.

Morrison, the son of a former gubernatorial candidate, Frank Morrison Jr., and the grandson of a three-term Nebraska governor, Frank Morrison Sr., announced on February 25 a challenge to Senator Burns.[12] Morrison certainly looked the part of a US senator, at least for Hollywood. He wore nice-fitting suits, had a photogenic haircut and straight white teeth, and it appeared that he had already scooped up the early support of prominent national Democrats, including Senator Baucus and the Democratic Senatorial Campaign Committee (DSCC)—the party's national Senate campaign organization. John Morrison had money, name recognition, good looks, and establishment support.

"But that support," someone noted, "is a mile wide and an inch deep."

"You can beat Morrison," Wheat added. "*You're the guy!*"

"But to be perfectly clear: you could get your ass kicked," Kimmell warned.

Then the conversation switched to Burns.

"Burns may be like the farmer, Jon. He may sound like the farmer. But you *are* the farmer."

"But the power players in DC will never support ya . . ."

"But this Abramoff thing is only gonna get worse for Conrad, and when Montanans go looking for another option they want to see *you*, not John Morrison."

"If you do this, do it now," Lombardi said. "My motto: *power and speed.*"

Of course, running for the US Senate was a whole different ball game compared with the state Senate races I had won. I knew a competitive US Senate race would require a whole lot more zeroes than I was used to, and a lot more ground to cover—147,000 square miles of it, to be exact. Sharla and I first had a long talk about whether to run for the US Senate at all. She worried about keeping the farm viable should my campaign ever get legs.

"We can't lose the farm over this," she warned. She brought over a hot pan of scrambled eggs and a bottle of ketchup from the kitchen to our living room table. I wrapped my hands around my mug of coffee.

"We won't," I assured her. "I'll make damn sure of it. But we can do both. It just requires a little extra work."

"How're you gonna raise the money?"

"I don't know," I said, staring at the steam from my cup. Then I chuckled. "They suggested we mortgage the farm." Sharla grimaced as I looked up. "But we sure as hell won't be doing that."

"Well," she said. "Give it a go. If we're not gonna lose the farm, we got nothing to lose."

Sharla and I also discussed how important a possible victory might be for our baby granddaughter, Kilikina Schultz, Christine's daughter. The war in Iraq and the ongoing war on terrorism had no end in sight. Kilikina, we realized, may never know a world without war and its consequences. She was going to inherit a government that had already spent uncountable gobs of money. Later, we looped in Christine and her husband, James; Shon; and Melody and her husband, Glen. Simply running for the Senate, I told them, much less *winning* the seat, would change our lives forever. It would change our definition of and expectation for privacy. It would mean round-the-clock scrutiny and plenty of ugly lies. But all of them said, *"Do it."* My brother Dave closed the deal when he told me: "If you don't try to win, you'll always wonder if you could've."

A few days later, I hired Bill Lombardi as my campaign manager. At the farm, Sharla, Shon, and I carefully affixed giant vinyl letters on the side of our forty-two-foot grain trailer:

JON TESTER

US SENATE

And on the back of the truck, in smaller letters, we wrote: YOU'RE BEHIND THE RIGHT GUY.

I figured with as much driving as I was about to do, hell, it was easy, free advertising. Then I called up a few friends, including my old Big Sandy basketball buddy Jeff Ament, and state senator Kim Hansen, who lived a couple hours north of me. I asked Kim if he'd help me drive the grain rig on a 950-mile press tour across Montana, in three days.

"Of course," Kim said. And beginning on May 24, Sharla, Shon, Kim, and I piled into the cab of our tractor trailer and drove up to Havre, then down to Billings, west to Bozeman, up to Butte and then Missoula, then over to Great Falls via Helena. Lombardi, a former newspaper reporter, called up local journalists, and I accommodated as many newspaper and TV interviews as I could land along the way. The theme for that first US Senate campaign road trip was and still is a familiar one to both Republicans and Democrats: Montana's and America's diminishing middle class.

"Small business, family farmers, agriculture, working people have been kind of under attack for the last 15–20 years," I told the veteran political reporter Chuck Johnson along the way. "The middle class has built this country and we need to make them whole."[13] I also noted that Senator Burns, plagued with ethical questions, held the Senate seat once held by Majority Leader Mike Mansfield. It was time to take back that seat. I did not tell Johnson that top Democrats in Washington had called me to urge me to get out of the race; to clear the field for Morrison. I was messing up their plans, they said. Their calls didn't concern me.

Jeff Ament joined me in Missoula. After graduating from high school, Jeff left Big Sandy and went to the University of Montana, then made a beeline for Seattle. He rode a mean skateboard, played a mean bass guitar, and joined a mean grunge band that made a name for itself in the late eighties. Pearl Jam hit it big, and suddenly Jeff Ament was a bona fide rock star who kept his roots deep in Montana. I first asked Jeff if he'd join me for my campaign stop in Missoula, where he owned a home, and he happily agreed. Jeff was one of the few people who saw early that I somehow struck a chord with younger voters across Montana. The leftwing political blogs (which we called the "netroots") were alive and well back then, and they had, for the most part, paid a lot of attention to me and my scrappy campaign.

On a river, anglers who wear polarized lenses can see right through the shimmery surface of the water to spot the trout darting underneath. Younger voters, I've always felt, have the same ability to see right through the artificial muck of politics when meeting a candidate. They know which candidates are genuine; who listens to them, who truly cares about them, and who wants to serve them. They also know which candidates are faking it. I suppose I was the catch younger voters were looking for, and John Morrison wasn't. I had no need to invent any part of my story; I didn't give a hoot that I didn't look the part, and I genuinely enjoyed talking to younger voters—especially in smaller, more rural communities across the state.

"Keeping rural Montana alive has so much to do with the youth of Montana," Ament said when he joined me for a news conference in front of my truck, wearing a white T-shirt with the words TESTER 2006 hand-drawn across the front in black marker. "You see these small, rural communities are dying and it's killing the hope for the youth. If he becomes part of the federal Senate, he could make a big difference."[14]

When I wasn't campaigning on the road, I spent long hours cold-calling Montanans and asking them for financial contributions. "Call time," as this process is known, is an essential and often dreaded chore for all serious candidates. Molly Harper managed my call time, which meant she supplied me with never-ending lists of people who, if they answered their phones, might listen to my campaign pitch, then send me a check—maybe. I spent countless hours making those calls in a hot, stuffy office in a building once frequented by Ted Kaczynski, the Unabomber. One day I spent ten hours on the phone unsuccessfully dialing for dollars before breaking the news to Molly that I had only raised fifty damn bucks.

"Good job!" she said.

"Bullshit. I could've made more money working at McDonald's today."

"Maybe, but more Montanans know who you are now than they did ten hours ago, right?"

Still, my lackluster call time was discouraging. Nobody I dialed up really knew who I was, and very few of them cared. By the early summer, I had raised $8,000, maybe $9,000, which was too much to give back and not even close to making a dent in the several hundred thousand I would need, at least, to win a contested primary, much less the millions I would need to unseat an incumbent three-term US senator. So I called up Jeff to ask for an even bigger favor: Would Pearl Jam host a benefit concert for my campaign in Montana? What I needed most, I told him candidly, was to simply get my name out there, and a rock concert would be tremendously helpful.

"Let me see what I can do," he replied. "We care about people like you, Jon."

I certainly didn't expect a yes, but to my surprise, and to Lombardi's great surprise, Jeff came back with a date for a Jon Tester Pearl Jam benefit concert in Missoula: August 29, 2005. That Monday night Pearl Jam brought down the house at the Adams Center on the University of Montana campus, drawing a crowd of more than 4,500 fans. Most of them had never heard of me, nor were they interested in politics. But Jeff and Eddie Vedder connected the dots during the show.

"This is what happens when a dirt farmer from Big Sandy runs for Senate, teamed up with a bass player from Montana who's a member of a world-famous band," I said while introducing Pearl Jam on stage. Jeff performed that night wearing a black T-shirt with two words which became my early campaign slogan: MONTANA FARMER.

"Whether we raise a nickel, if we can get the young people of Montana fired up about this campaign, we've succeeded," I told the

Missoulian newspaper before the show started. "We just want to raise awareness."[15]

At the end of the day, that's exactly what happened. From that point on, fundraising was less of a problem for me and my campaign. Behind the scenes, the Pearl Jam concert turned out to be a logistical nightmare. Though the band members graciously donated their time, my campaign had to comply with all sorts of federal laws to pull off the enormous fundraiser, and we paid all the associated costs to put on the show, including security, the road crew, and all the rental fees. But that night we pulled in an overall haul of $85,000.[16] More important, thousands of mostly younger people who had never heard my name now associated it with Big Sandy's better man, Jeff Ament.

The next surprise came when we publicly reported our third-quarter fundraising numbers. I had raised just over $324,000 between July 1 and September 30. John Morrison had raised just under $243,000.[17] Though the Pearl Jam concert was a major factor in my financial lead over Morrison that quarter, it felt like his momentum had already hit its stride, and maybe he was slowing down. The national pundits didn't agree. In October Chuck Todd, then a writer for *National Journal*, ranked the Montana Senate seat as the sixth most likely to flip from Republican to Democrat, behind Pennsylvania, Ohio, Rhode Island, Missouri, and Tennessee.

"At some point, we could envision moving this [race] up some but only if John Morrison and not Jon Tester gets out of the primary," Todd wrote. "As much as we know the liberal blogosphere loves Tester, the reality is that he'll get killed in the general by Burns and the NRSC, which will paint him as out of the mainstream." Todd went on to say that my Pearl Jam benefit concert, "while cute for a good press hit, will not excite the right-leaning Bush voters that any Democrat has to woo in order to win. . . . Morrison is the Democrats' best bet to keep this race competitive."[18]

Of course, I don't hold anything against Chuck Todd for the misfire back in 2005. What he may have missed was the fact that the voters of Montana—of rural America—wanted someone out of the mainstream. By and large, they were fed up with typical politicians and disenchanted with the status quo. The same resentment and cynicism that led to "Drain the Swamp" and "Feel the Bern" in 2016 fueled my own Senate campaign a decade earlier.

Todd certainly wasn't alone, and I suppose his analysis made sense from a Washington perspective back then. But I did take issue with the fact that Morrison sent that *National Journal* article far and wide to his supporters across Montana in an effort to paint me as vulnerable and somehow out of touch. Morrison also checked off his growing list of support from Washington politicians; I had none of them. But clearly, Morrison was worried—especially because the Democratic Senatorial Campaign Committee was paying more attention to Montana given the increasing vulnerability of Senator Burns and the mounting questions about Burns's relationship with Abramoff.

"Taking advice on winning elections from Washington, D.C., can be a bit like taking a business ethics class from Jack Abramoff, the Washington lobbyist tied to Conrad Burns and under indictment for wire fraud and conspiracy," I wrote to my supporters after Morrison amplified Chuck Todd's unflattering *National Journal* writeup. "I don't like Washington insiders telling me I can't be seen with my old friends from Big Sandy."[19]

In December 2005, Governor Schweitzer called for a special session of the Montana Legislature to address funding for public education and pensions for educators and other public employees. As Senate president, I responded by saying the governor's request was an "appropriate call."[20] Though we had already tackled school funding earlier in the year to satisfy the 2004 mandate from the Montana Supreme Court, the legislature still needed to pass a more permanent funding plan. And with power and speed, we did. In only two days, with a clear vision and a smart, organized plan, the Democratic-controlled Montana Legislature passed a much-needed 10.6 percent increase in public education funding, over the loud objections of the Republicans.[21] As a US Senate candidate, it was another important victory in making my case for leadership in Congress.

On the very day we adjourned that session, the *New York Times* broke a story that took my breath away. On the evening of

December 15, the *Times* reported—despite a request from the White House to refrain from publishing its story—that President Bush had signed a secret order in 2002 authorizing the National Security Agency (NSA) to "eavesdrop on Americans and others inside the United States to search for evidence of terrorist activity without the court-approved warrants ordinarily required for domestic spying." The powers that Bush gave to the NSA, the *Times* continued, "go far beyond the expanded counterterrorism powers granted by Congress under the USA Patriot Act."[22] The news only strengthened my resolve to run for federal office. A so-called free nation that allows warrantless, unchecked spying on its own citizens is a nation whose citizens are never free.

In March, I turned up the heat by calling on Burns to resign, saying his ties to Abramoff smelled "like a barnyard that needs a cleanup," and the *Cook Political Report* downgraded the race from "leans Republican" to "tossup."[23] Then my Montana Senate colleague Bob Keenan announced a challenge to Burns in the GOP primary, saying Montana Republicans needed a "viable option they can be proud of."[24] Though the Montana Republican Party quickly endorsed Burns in response, Keenan's announcement was a clear sign that the junior senator was in trouble. In early April, as Burns ran TV ads playing even more defense about Jack Abramoff, and as both Morrison and I went after Burns for his ethical lapses, Montana newspapers published a bombshell of a story that altered Morrison's political career, and mine.

Morrison admitted he'd had an extramarital affair with a woman in 1998. As auditor, Morrison's office later investigated the man his affair partner would eventually marry, a Montana businessman named David Tacke. Tacke sold investors on his idea of placing pairs of binoculars under stadium seats at sporting events, then renting the binoculars on a pay-per-use basis. The idea was a flop, but Tacke collected heavily from investors anyway, and those investors complained to Morrison. Morrison, investors said, was slow to respond to the accusation. He eventually disclosed his conflict of interest to his staff and handed the case to an outside attorney to negotiate the settlement agreement, which was widely criticized as ineffectual and poorly enforced. Federal prosecutors later pressed charges against Tacke, and he spent time in federal prison for money laundering, and mail and wire fraud. As one frustrated investor told the *Missoula Independent*: "David Tacke knew about the affair, and that gave him the upper hand in the settlement negotiations. . . . I think what happened is [Tacke and Morrison] created a settlement agreement and then went back and forth. Tacke didn't want to be found out as a fraud and Morrison didn't want to be found out as an adulterer."[25]

Though Morrison tried to downplay the story, its political consequences were swift and severe in a race whose singular focus was on an incumbent facing ethical questions. John Morrison simply lacked the credibility needed to go after Conrad Burns. As I pointed out during a debate in Helena with Morrison and a third candidate, Paul Richards, "I am the only person on this stage that can go belly-to-belly with Conrad Burns on the situation of ethics."[26] I looked at Morrison and added that I had no skeletons in my closet.

"I think Jon Tester can go belly-to-belly with anyone," Richards quipped, which cracked up everyone.[27]

Vanity Fair broke the other big story that April. In an article titled "Washington's Invisible Man," *Vanity Fair*'s David Margolick suggested that Abramoff was "the fellow responsible for what might be the biggest government scandal since Watergate." Margolick actually landed an interview with Abramoff, and Abramoff tied *himself* directly to Conrad Burns.

> Burns told a reporter he wishes Abramoff had never been born, and, more recently, has blanketed the airwaves in Montana with ads claiming that Abramoff "lied to anybody and everybody" and "ripped off his Indian clients," but that "he never influenced me." Abramoff won't comment specifically on the ads, clearly tempted as he is. "Every appropriation we wanted [from Burns's committee] we got," he says. "Our staffs were as close as they could be. They practically used Signatures [Abramoff's swanky DC restaurant]as their cafeteria. I mean, it's a little difficult for him to run from that record."[28]

In the spring of 2006 we produced my first campaign TV ad, and we had raised enough money to broadcast it across the state. We shot the thirty-second commercial around Great Falls and inside the Riverview Barber Shop, where every other week or so I paid my barber, Bill Graves, $6 (including tip) for a haircut. The ad, which we called "Creating a Buzz," features a man noticing that all of his neighbors are sporting new flattops, so he goes into the barbershop to get one for himself. The ad also showcases my farm, my tractor, my wife, and the red hip-roof barn Ole Haakenson had helped my grandfather build ninety years earlier.

"Look around Montana and you'll see Jon Tester is catching on," the folksy narrator says between shots of people admiring one another's high and tight haircuts (all the extras were early supporters and friends of mine, including one woman, who each volunteered to get an actual flattop for the ad). Bill Graves peers over his clippers as the narrator continues: "Maybe it's because Jon Tester is a third-generation farmer who worked with Brian Schweitzer for cheaper prescription drugs and better schools, or because of Tester's plan for affordable health care. Or because he'll put an end to Senator Burns's kind of corruption, and make the US Senate look a little more like Montana."[29] The ad wasn't much, but like the title, it generated its own buzz. And then our campaign contributions really started coming in.

Shortly before the primary election on Tuesday, June 6, a seasoned Democratic operative named Hal Harper, who worked for Schweitzer, pulled me aside with new polling data. "It'll be a close race and I wouldn't count on winning," Hal said. Then he paused. "But I wouldn't count on losing either."

At ten thirty that Tuesday night I got a call from John Morrison. I didn't even hear my phone ring, so he left a message. I was at a rambunctious watch party in Missoula with a bunch of supporters, including Jeff, and the returns were looking much better than any of us expected. Then I checked my voice mail. Morrison conceded his defeat, making it official: I had, as an underdog, won the Democratic nomination as a candidate for the US Senate by an overwhelming 61 percent, trouncing Morrison by more than 27,000 votes.[30]

To this day, that primary election was the most satisfying victory of my political career, because I began the race a year earlier with a fraction of the name recognition and a fraction of the money that Morrison had. And I won by sticking to the issues that resonated with *all* voters, not just Democrats: jobs, health care, fiscal responsibility, public education, energy and the environment, and public lands. Those issues, by the way, are the issues that *still* matter to most voters no matter where they live or which party they belong to. Our primary race got ugly early, and it got personal at times. And it showed me that younger voters had tuned in, then showed up to vote. I was so proud of that win, I kept Morrison's voice mail concession on my cell phone for three years.

But our focus immediately shifted away from Morrison and to Senator Burns. During an interview on live TV at our watch party, Jeff looked directly into the camera, pointed his finger at the lens, and said: "Conrad, we're coming after you!" (Burns, as expected, easily beat Bob Keenan.) And exactly seventeen minutes after the Associated Press declared me the winner, Burns sent a pointed statement to the media asking where I stood on the wedge issues of gay marriage, the burning of the American flag, and abolishing the estate tax, which, of course, he called the "death tax." He also floated an odd attack line that suggested I was more suited to being a senator from Massachusetts or New York.

"Massachusetts doesn't deserve a third senator," his campaign said, apparently in an attempt to frame me as a liberal.[31] To that end, Burns often compared me to Senator Edward Kennedy, whom I had never met. Funny, because of the two candidates for US Senate, I was the only one born in Montana, and I had never even been to Massachusetts.

The Democratic Senatorial Campaign Committee watched the race closely too, because Montana lit up on the map of its chairman, Senator Chuck Schumer. Suddenly, winning back the seat once held by Mike Mansfield was within reach, and it became a DSCC priority. That's when my campaign entered a second stage. With help from Senator Baucus and his chief of staff, Jim Messina (a University of

Montana alumnus who later managed President Obama's 2012 campaign), I cast a wide net for talent and built a forceful campaign team.

I hired Stephanie Schriock, a Butte native who'd served as the finance director on the presidential campaign of Vermont governor Howard Dean—which meant she was an early pioneer of online, "small-dollar" fundraising. I signed up Matt McKenna to run my communications team. Matt, a Bozeman native, was a longtime operative who'd earned his stripes on Brian Schweitzer's 2000 Senate campaign before working behind the scenes for Senators Tom Daschle and Max Cleland, and Alaska governor Tony Knowles. Bill Lombardi became my political director. Rob Hill and Preston Elliott ran my field campaign. Stephanie, who later became my chief of staff before running Al Franken's Senate campaign—then becoming the powerful president of EMILY's List—whipped my team into shape for a top-tier Senate race. Suddenly, that's exactly what we were.

"What'd I tell ya?" Sharla said after the primary election. She gave me the same smile she gave me before striking me out in our first softball game. "Just keep reminding them you don't have to use the old playbook."

"It's about to get a whole lot tougher," I reminded her.

"We can handle it," she said, smiling again. "Just keep your priorities straight and everything else will follow in a straight line. The farm and your family are priorities."

For all of Burns's tough talk, his first real headline following the primary election was about his decision to skip his first debate with me and the Libertarian US Senate candidate, Stan Jones. Jones first ran against Senator Max Baucus in 2002, when *The Daily Show with Jon Stewart* lampooned him for his striking bluish-gray skin—a bizarre and permanent side effect of "misusing" colloidal silver in 1999 to somehow protect himself from a Y2K apocalypse.[32] But on the debate stage, both Stan and I had fun poking at Burns's absence. The host of the debate, the Montana Newspaper Association (MNA), made it only easier for us by setting out an empty stool where Burns was supposed to sit. The senator, it turned out, dodged our debate to attend a golf fundraiser in Virginia instead. So, while glaring at his empty stool, I remarked, "It's unfortunate that Senator Burns feels it's more important to deal with the big-money lobbyists on the East Coast rather than stand here and deal with Montanans."[33]

Wildfires began ravaging our state a few weeks later that summer. Many of them tore across central and eastern Montana, destroying thousands of acres of rugged ranchland, frustrating some ranchers and farmers who thought the government's response was too slow and mired in too much bureaucratic red tape. The federal government coordinated its firefighting efforts out of the National Interagency Fire Center in Boise, Idaho, which dispatched numerous wildland firefighting crews from various agencies across the nation. One of those crews was an elite team of hotshot firefighters from Augusta, Virginia, who were among the 368 firefighters battling the 92,000-acre Bundy Railroad Fire in south-central Montana. On July 23, Burns approached three of those exhausted men as they waited for their delayed flight out of Montana at the Billings airport.

"Are you firefighters?" Burns asked. One of the hotshots replied yes.

"What a piss-poor job you're doing," Burns told them, beginning what was described as a verbal "altercation" by reports of the incident. "You're wasting a lot of money and creating a cottage industry. You need to listen more to the ranchers!"

"We're pretty low on the totem pole, sir," the firefighter replied. "Have a nice day."[34]

Burns's outburst prompted the Forest Service to immediately dispatch a public information officer to talk with the angry senator at the airport, presumably knowing full well that he served on the powerful Senate committees that authorize and appropriate funding for the federal government's firefighting efforts.

"See that guy over there? He hasn't done a goddamned thing," Burns complained to the public information officer, according to reports of the exchange. "It's wasteful. You probably paid that guy $10,000 to sit around. . . . Managing these fires from Boise doesn't work."[35]

The public information officer said Burns was particularly frustrated because he thought incident commanders prevented ranchers from fighting wildfires on their privately owned land. She respectfully corrected Burns, reminding him that private landowners are, in fact, "integral to our success," though fire bosses prefer to know exactly what's happening on a wildfire and may ask landowners to evacuate in the interest of safety. After Burns complained about how much federal wildland firefighters get paid, the officer said: "I offered to the senator that our firefighters make around $8 to $12 an hour and time-and-a-half for overtime. He seemed a bit surprised that it wasn't higher."[36]

When reports of Burns's airport meltdown became public, his staff issued a quick apology, explaining that the senator "freely admits he took out his frustration on the wrong people." The Forest Service, eager to put the issue to rest, noted Burns apologized and said, "as far as we're concerned, that's the end of the story."[37]

But politically for Conrad Burns, that was hardly the end of the story. In fact, as wildfires sometimes do, it blew up in his face. He immediately complained that the published reports made "political hay" of the incident. It was the job of my campaign, of course, to make sure as many Montanans as possible saw Conrad Burns as we did. But in this case, we didn't have to do much. Burns himself did that job for us.

"I'm the only guy in the world probably getting beat running unopposed," Burns admitted at a GOP picnic a couple weeks later, after doubling down on his defense of frustrated ranchers. "I can self-destruct in one sentence. Sometimes in one word."[38]

We know Burns said that because the Montana Democratic Party recorded him saying it. That year the party employed a young man named Kevin O'Brien, who followed Burns everywhere Kevin was allowed. Kevin put thirty-five thousand miles on his Nissan Sentra, showing up wherever Burns did in Montana to record every word with a camcorder. Sometimes he got more than comments; in August Kevin recorded Burns, then seventy-one, dozing off during a farm bill field hearing, then posted the video on YouTube to the music of "Happy Trails."[39] In June, Kevin recorded Burns as the senator spoke to a crowd of supporters about Hugo, a "little fella who does maintenance work" at Burns's home in Virginia. Hugo, Burns added, was from Guatemala. Burns then recounted his conversation with the handyman.

"I said, 'Can I see your green card?' And Hugo says, 'No!' I said, 'Oh gosh.'"[40]

That line suddenly raised important questions about Hugo's citizenship, and Burns's campaign declined to answer them. But Burns brought up Hugo several more times on the campaign trail—he even answered a phone call from Hugo in the middle of a stump speech—which showed us that Burns, an outspoken critic of illegal immigration, had let his guard down.[41] He also self-destructed by making sweeping generalizations rooted in fear, suggesting several times that the United States was fighting terrorists who "drive taxi cabs in the daytime and kill at night."[42]

But the defining issue of that campaign wasn't firefighters or taxi drivers or maintenance men; it was, ultimately, Montanans' growing dissatisfaction with the war in Iraq, the threat of diminished civil liberties in President Bush's administration, and overspending and corruption in Washington—which persistent news stories about Burns and many of his GOP colleagues exemplified on an almost daily basis. The issue of congressional earmarks became red hot that summer, thanks in part to Conrad Burns and Jack Abramoff.

I never had, and still do not have, any issue with congressionally directed earmarks, so long as they are transparent and publicly debated. I believe it's much more important for an elected lawmaker—someone like me, for example, who has driven every mile of every highway in my massive state—to help determine which highway projects are in most need of federal funding. Some bureaucrat holed up in a Washington cubicle has no clue. Without congressionally directed earmarks, that bureaucrat will end up slicing the federal pie and deciding where the money goes based on some government funding formula, not local input. And you can bet that government funding formula won't put a sparsely populated state like Montana at the top of the priority list.

Before 2007, however, earmarks were not transparent. Too often lawmakers or their staffers quietly tucked them into bills during last-minute negotiations with zero time for public scrutiny or debate. And earmarks were all too often ridiculous, and peppered into pieces of must-pass legislation as favors to lobbyists or donors. There's no argument that both Senators Burns and Baucus used their clout in the Senate to ensure Montana got what it needed in appropriate earmarks. As for transparency, both of them sent frequent press releases announcing the federal money they brought home, because it was important for them to get proper credit for securing it. In fact, Burns's campaign slogan in 2006 was two words: "Burns Delivers." The problem was, there were too many questions about who, exactly, Conrad Burns was delivering for.

The issue of transparency of earmarks came up during our debate in Bozeman on October 9. "The current process of earmarks in the middle of the night without the transparency of the people of this great country is the wrong way for a representative democracy to be working," I said.[43] During another debate in Butte, Burns and I got into a tussle over the Patriot Act. Burns, who voted for the disastrous law, vigorously defended it, then suggested I didn't understand the enemy.

"He wants to weaken the Patriot Act!" Burns said to a capacity crowd of more than 1,200 people. I wanted to remind him that the 2005 Montana Legislature overwhelmingly passed a resolution, with bipartisan support, saying the State of Montana will not comply with the Patriot Act. But instead I said something that got much more traction: "Let me be clear: I don't want to weaken the Patriot Act. *I want to repeal it.*" The crowd cheered.

"It takes away your freedoms," I continued. "This country was *based* on freedom. Hundreds of thousands of Americans have fought and died for our freedoms. Take away our freedoms and the terrorists will have won!"[44] Burns then tried to tie me to politicians who supported gun control, to which I replied: "With things like the Patriot Act, we damn well better keep our guns. That's all I've got to say."[45]

A pissed-off Senator Schumer called from Washington shortly after that debate, asking what the hell we were doing and why, goddammit, was I making hay out of the Patriot Act? After all, the law passed with bipartisan support. My message back to Senator Schumer:

Don't underestimate Montanans' libertarian appreciation of the American rights that the Patriot Act took away. I knew that about Montana more than anyone in Washington—including Conrad Burns.

A few days later, Burns and his team doubled down by organizing a conference call between Montana reporters and America's inaugural Homeland Security secretary, Tom Ridge, who called my desire to repeal the Patriot Act "ludicrous." Coming from someone I saw as a genuine threat to American freedom, I considered Tom Ridge's criticism a badge of honor. And his and Burns's messaging still wasn't convincing—even to many of those "right-leaning Bush voters" Chuck Todd had warned us about in 2005. When asked if the Patriot Act would have prevented the 9/11 attacks, especially considering that two of the hijackers were approved for student visas *after* the Patriot Act became law, Ridge answered, "the fact that it did not exist or may not have prevented them . . . is no reason to suggest we do not need it."[46]

When Burns and I debated in Billings on October 17, I pointed out that President Bush *still* had no plan for his disastrous war in Iraq. "We're in a quagmire over there," I said. "The fact is it's taken our focus off the war on terror. We haven't been diligent on that. It's costing us too much in blood. It's costing us too much in money."

"He wants everybody to know our plan," Burns responded. "That's not smart. . . . He says our president don't have a plan. I think he's got one, but he's not going to tell everybody in the whole world." Some in the auditorium snickered when Burns said this.

"The president's plan right now is to stay there—to keep doing the same thing," I responded, "and he's going to turn this war over to the next president, and I don't think that's a plan. . . . I'm not after telling our opponents what we're going to do. The fact is *we* don't know what we're going to do over there right now, and the military has done a great job. They've done a marvelous job. But our political leadership has not."

"There is a plan!" Burns insisted. "We're not going to tell you, Jon! We're not going to tell you what our plan is because you'll just go out there and blow it!"[47]

Here, it seemed as though the whole auditorium, many of whom wore bright yellow shirts that read FIRE BURNS, burst into laughter. McKenna immediately compared the line to stories from the seventies suggesting that Nixon had a "secret strategy" for ending the Vietnam War. After the debate a spokesman admitted Burns wasn't aware of any specifics about President Bush's plan for Iraq, but said that the senator "knows the general strategy."[48]

I thought Burns's debate performance in Billings was his most difficult. Both of us were tired, but Burns allowed his body language to show his frustration. He flailed his arms and raised his voice and rocked back and forth behind his podium. As my old debate coach, Jim Barsotti, would have pointed out, Burns's body language signaled to me that he knew he was losing. I kept my cool.

Burns landed his punches too. In late October, a political reporter called me up after hearing a tip that a former friend of mine had whispered to the Montana GOP. She wanted to know about the tense 1990 visit to my farm by the State of Montana meat inspector. Though I shut down the shop in 1998, the reporter wrote that I was required to have a license to custom-butcher meat for my neighbors. I never got one, because after thirty years of inspectors, inspections, threats, and even intervention from a member of Congress, we were specifically told we didn't need a license for the services we provided. We were never cited and never fined. That article bothered the hell out of me, because it was an example of government overreach that turned into a painfully timed political liability, and it should never have been an issue, much less a story.[49]

But soon the news was dominated by other stories about public polls suggesting I might just beat Burns. In the days leading up to Election Day, Governor Schweitzer and Senator Baucus joined me and other elected Democrats to crisscross the state and hold energetic get-out-the-vote rallies with huge crowds of excited supporters. Schweitzer, two years into his first term as governor, enjoyed tremendous popularity in Montana. He also had a vivid political memory, and he certainly wasn't over his stinging defeat by Burns six years earlier. Now that Abramoff was part of the equation, Schweitzer was a growling dog with a bone.

"This is a guy who specializes in making sure members of Congress don't have to take the top bunk!" Schweitzer stormed at a rally in Helena on November 3. "Take a good look at 'Casino Jack.' He's got the top bunk. Ol' Conrad Burns gets the bottom bunk!"[50] Schweitzer repeated the line up until Election Day.

On the eve of the election, Schweitzer and I addressed a massive rally in Billings before we headed up to Great Falls together for another boisterous rally. And on Tuesday, November 7, everything came together as it was supposed to. Under Stephanie's flawless direction and leadership, my campaign did all it could to ensure a massive turnout and fair voting at all polling places. We oversaw dozens of poll watchers and field organizers, who engaged hundreds of volunteers in every corner of the state. It was kind of like my strategy in 1998— going after as many voters as possible, this time with *more zeroes.*

Sharla and the kids and I camped out in our room at the Heritage Inn in Great Falls. Our room overlooked the sprawling lobby of the hotel, where that evening hundreds of supporters would gather for our Election Night party. Other than doing a few interviews with reporters that day, there was nothing left to do but wait for the polls to close at eight p.m. Sharla and I enjoyed the quiet downtime with our family. Mother, Dave and Bob, and their families came down from Idaho to watch the returns with us. Even Sharla's folks, lifelong Republicans, wished me well.

This is what I hoped for that evening, if all went according to plan: The Associated Press would declare my victory by about ten thirty. Hundreds of balloons stuffed into a net overhead would fall onto the celebrating partygoers below as the giant TV screens tuned to CNN announced our victory. Confetti cannons would burst. I would get a gracious concession call from Senator Burns. Then I would emerge from my room to speak to the crowd about the beginning of a new era in Montana politics, and the importance of restoring integrity to the Senate seat once held by Mike Mansfield. And then we would all celebrate well into the night before getting right to work the next morning.

That's not at all how it went. First of all, I forgot to bring a tie with me from the farm, and I had to borrow one from a friend for the numerous interview requests from TV reporters camped out below. Indeed, hundreds of supporters gathered in the lobby after the polls closed, and we heard them roar outside our room as word came in that the Democrats had won back control of the US House. Inside our room we watched as Bob Casey unseated Rick Santorum in Pennsylvania. Sherrod Brown beat Mike DeWine in Ohio. Jim Webb won Virginia, beating George Allen. Sheldon Whitehouse replaced Lincoln Chafee in Rhode Island. And Claire McCaskill whupped Jim Talent in Missouri. Now all eyes were on Montana. If I won, the Democrats would retake control of the US Senate.

Our race was still too close to call by ten thirty, and eleven thirty. Then Stephanie updated Sharla and me on the precincts that had yet to come in. Burns was ahead in Yellowstone County by 1,222 votes, but I was ahead overall by about 1,700 votes.[51] In an effort to protect my sanity, she did not tell me that she had learned that ballots from Butte were missing. So I emerged from my hotel room to speak to the folks who'd shown up to celebrate—speaking not as a senator-elect, but as a grateful, hopeful, exhausted candidate.

"We're feeling good!" I assured them. "But we're not there yet. And we probably won't know where this thing goes till morning." I thanked them for their hard work, I thanked them for coming, then I encouraged them to go home. By about twelve thirty Wednesday morning, they all did.

One of the many benefits of being a farmer is being able to sleep soundly at the end of a long day—even one as dramatic and uncertain as Election Day, and Sharla and I were exhausted. We knew we had done everything we could, and both of us had come to terms with the possibility that I might lose.

"We're gonna catch some Zs," I told my campaign team. "Wake me up when you figure out who won."

My campaign team worked through the night, ensuring accurate accounting for every single vote cast. Governor Schweitzer stayed up all night calling various elections offices for updates. Senator Baucus stayed up all night poring over numbers with his staffers. McKenna and his team stayed up all night accommodating interview requests from across the country. Then he woke me up with a loud knock, and I answered the door in my underwear.

"Who won?"

"We don't know yet," McKenna said.

"Then what the hell did you wake me up for?"

"Because we're doing a live interview on the *Today* show in a few minutes."

After throwing on a coat and my borrowed tie, I waited for my first TV interview in a stuffy hotel conference room my team had converted into a makeshift briefing room by stapling a bunch of campaign posters to the wall. Even at four thirty in the morning it was crammed with caffeinated reporters, network cameras, and cables running every which way. That little room was the only place available to us that morning. Hotel employees had spent the night breaking down what was left of our party in order to make room for a craft fair on Wednesday; after all, we had booked the space only for Tuesday. Our balloons still hung over the lobby in their net, and a hotel staffer got stuck with the weird job of pulling them out one by one, then popping them. As I slurped down a cup of awful coffee, a producer stuck a plastic gizmo in my ear and told me to wait until I heard from Matt Lauer and his producers. Over the past few hours, I had been up by several thousand votes, then a couple hundred votes, then 1,900 votes.

"With the new numbers, how many precincts are left, do you know?" I asked as I waited for the interview to start. My mic was hot, and the NBC camera was rolling.

Someone off camera told me all the precincts from Butte still had not been counted. As Terence Samuel summarized in his book about the 2006 elections, *The Upper House*, Butte's election administrator "figured that one stack [of ballots] from the staging table was accidentally stapled to another without being tabulated and had already been wrapped and sealed in a pouch to be sent to the secretary of state."[52] The administrator wasn't allowed to unseal the pouch in order to preserve the integrity of the ballots in case of a recount. And now we were waiting for a county judge to issue an order to unseal the pouch as soon as the sun came up.

"Butte's still out?" I looked up at McKenna, who nodded. Butte has always voted reliably bright blue, thanks to its rich history steeped in the birth and the rise of the American labor movement. There's no way Burns could catch up if Butte's precincts hadn't been counted. I closed my eyes, smiled, and said, "That's good."[53] That was the exact moment I knew I had won. That restrained little moment of relief, contained in one careful grin, somehow ended up on MSNBC's *Countdown with Keith Olbermann* that evening, as one of the "Hidden Moments" of Election Night.

At seven thirty that morning, the judge ordered the pouches unsealed and sure as shit, there were the ballots that hadn't been counted yet. I did interview after interview through Wednesday morning, telling media outlets that I felt good about the results and the prospect of shifting the balance of power in the Senate. I even went to the Riverview Barber Shop to get a much-needed haircut from Bill Graves with an entourage of reporters in tow. By the early afternoon, Stephanie and her team had crunched the numbers. They were confident that I had indeed earned enough votes to unseat Conrad Burns. Most counties across the state had reported their results, and though it was extremely close, we knew we had more votes—exactly 3,562 more. But the race was still too close for the Associated Press to determine a winner.

"Let's claim-jump this thing!" Governor Schweitzer finally said.

Minutes later, we told the AP that I would declare victory at a news conference in one hour, giving the news organization ample time to decide whether to be in front of or behind the story. Then we scrambled to set up a news conference in another hotel conference room a couple of miles away.

Knowing that I was about to declare victory was apparently enough for the Associated Press to be in front of the story, and moments before our news conference began, the wires lit up with news that I had won the US Senate seat. Senator Burns called me moments later.

"I don't know about you, but I slept like a baby, Jon," he wise-cracked. "I woke up every hour and cried." Leave it to Conrad Burns to find some levity even during one of the tougher moments of his career. Burns used that line publicly in the following days.[54] He graciously conceded the race, wished me congratulations, and offered to be as helpful as possible over the final two months of his tenure in the Senate.

At the very moment I addressed the excited crowd of supporters in Great Falls, Defense Secretary Donald Rumsfeld held a news conference announcing his resignation in response to a stinging defeat in the 2006 elections. By a margin of 3,562 votes, and with the help and hard work of countless Montanans eager to see a change in leadership in Washington, I won back the seat once held by Senators Mansfield and Melcher. I'd managed to surprise the pundits twice in five months, helping the Democrats win back control of the US Senate.

Conrad Burns suffered a stroke in 2009, and he enjoyed a quiet life in Billings following his retirement. He regularly held court from a wheelchair at the Rock Creek Coffee Shop in downtown Billings on Wednesday mornings, cracking jokes and offering his colorful commentary on politics with a group of friends who enjoyed his company—as most Montanans did. He passed away in his home in Billings on April 28, 2016, at the age of eighty-one.[55]

When I received word of Senator Burns's death, I told Sharla I wanted to pay my respects at his funeral. After all, Burns and I had developed a bond that exists only among people who are lucky enough to hold the awesome and strange work of the "world's most exclusive club." I thought my presence at his service might be awkward at best and seen as contemptuous at worst, so I planned to stay away. But then Senator Burns's wife, Phyllis, called my office. She personally invited me to the senator's memorial service, and I went to honor his life of public service. After all the Burns family had been through, they treated me like gold. Mrs. Burns's invitation was one of the warmest gestures I've ever experienced in politics.

CHAPTER 10

A Farmer's Guide to the US Senate

Sharla and I saw the inside of the US Capitol for our very first time when we zipped over to Washington for my orientation as a US senator-elect in November 2006. The Senate holds an intensive week-long orientation for all newly elected members and their spouses shortly after Election Day. It's when we all learn the ins and outs of how the guts of the place work, from parliamentary procedure to budgeting expectations to security protocols to how the hell to understand the strange clocks in our offices (a series of red lights on the clock face signal how much time we have left in a vote).

The orientation week is also an important time to connect with our new colleagues, some of whom, in 2006, had just gone through their own wild elections. That year, Tennessee's Bob Corker, the former mayor of Chattanooga, was the only Republican among us newly elected senators. Corker had just beat Harold Ford Jr., who happened to be the Democratic Senate candidate I'd gotten to know the best during the election. Ford was dynamic, smart, and one of the most amazing public speakers I had ever seen. We happened to attend an event out of state together and I had the misfortune of speaking after Harold.

Needless to say, I didn't think I would like Corker when I first met him. But he and I got along from the minute we shook hands at our orientation in Washington. The other new senators-elect were Sherrod Brown of Ohio, Ben Cardin of Maryland, Bob Casey of Pennsylvania, Amy Klobuchar of Minnesota, Claire McCaskill of Missouri, Bernie Sanders of Vermont, Jim Webb of Virginia, and Sheldon Whitehouse of Rhode Island.

Senator Burns used to joke that Washington is "a 13-square-mile area of logic-free environment."[1] His math was off—DC is 68 square miles—but the sentiment was memorable. The dysfunction of the federal government may be logic-free at times, but the city itself is a decent place to visit. Sharla still says we are "tourists" in Washington. I feel about it the same way Dad, the mountain man, felt about life and work on our flatland farm. It may be a nice place to work when it's not unbearably sweat-inducing, but it will never be *home*. Washington, DC, as Dad might say, is just not in my DNA.

So for both Sharla and me, orientation week was one of the strangest weeks of our lives. We were well out of our comfort zones, suddenly surrounded by busy, well-dressed people running on tight schedules moving quickly around a well-organized city. They treated Sharla and me in a way neither of us were used to—with obligatory reverence. US Capitol Police officers had already started learning to identify me and my new colleagues on sight, so they could allow us to bypass security lines throughout the Capitol complex. Both Sharla and I received ID cards identifying me as a member of Congress and Sharla as my spouse. And I quickly realized how out of place we really were, surrounded by a whole lot of self-important people with important-sounding titles. Many of them spoke to us about their power and wealth, the prestige of their educations, the people they knew and their career paths. It was difficult to relate to these people. In Montana, folks are never quick to openly discuss things like power and wealth. And both Sharla and I realized we would never be comfortable adapting to the culture of Washington, DC, politics.

Nonetheless, aides, officers, and handlers already referred to me as "Senator," and constantly assured me (and the other ninety-nine senators) that I *belonged* in this place, though it certainly didn't feel like it. They also made me realize that I had a lot to learn, from navigating the passageways throughout the Capitol complex to learning the old customs of the Senate to meeting all of my new colleagues. Intimidating? You bet your butt. But taking a page from my earlier days in public service, I jumped in with both feet and learned everything I could from the folks who were already there.

I'm certainly not the first farmer elected to serve in the US Senate, nor will I be the last. So here are some observations and advice from this farmer-senator from a rural state:

1. SENATORING AT HOME

I told Montanans in 2006 that I would come home every weekend.

"You'll never be able to fly home that often," Ray Peck warned. "That's gonna be impossible. It'll kill you."

But it was possible, with a lot of hard work. To this day, I still come home to Montana *damn near* every weekend. It works out well, because I believe Montana's citizen legislature is the strongest form of government. I believe the founders of this country meant the same thing for members of Congress. Coming home every weekend allows me to still be a farmer, and to lay claim to the title of a citizen-legislator.

A typical week for me begins Monday morning at two thirty. That's when I hop into the shower, slurp down a cup of coffee, then hit the road for a dark, ninety-minute drive to the Great Falls airport. From Great Falls I catch the early-morning flight to Minneapolis. I try to get some sleep on the first leg. In Minneapolis, I eat a breakfast of melon while catching up on my news, reading memos, and making calls to my chief of staff, my scheduler, and my legislative director. I take the early flight into Washington National Airport, and I'm in the office by two thirty p.m.

In Washington, my daily schedules are broken down into fifteen-minute increments in order to accommodate as many meetings as possible. I meet with my legislative team on Monday evenings, I prioritize all Montanans who are visiting Washington that week for work or play, and I attend as many hearings of my five committees whenever I can (sometimes committee hearings are held simultaneously). To keep us on our toes, votes are scheduled in the middle of all of this at the discretion of the majority leader, with very little notice. When that happens, we rearrange my schedule in real time, sometimes collapsing it, sometimes rejiggering it, and sometimes shitcanning it altogether. It helps to belong to the same party as the majority leader, because then you are privy to the vote schedule much earlier than members in the other party, and you can make a case for rescheduling certain votes if they're inconvenient. If the majority leader belongs to the other party, get used to uncertainty and short notice.

In DC I put in fourteen-to-sixteen-hour days through Thursday afternoon, when I fly back home to Montana—as long as there are no more votes, which is also up to the discretion of the majority party and its leader. This means I often operate with two working schedules: one in case I stay in DC and one if I get to fly back to Montana. I usually fly to wherever I plan on working on Friday. The "weekend" usually involves two full workdays—Friday and Saturday—covering as many places in Montana as possible. I usually begin Friday at five a.m. accommodating live interviews with local TV and radio stations. I put a few hundred miles on the road through Saturday, then I drive all the way home to Big Sandy by midnight. I'm used to lots of windshield time, and I often travel despite rain or snow or ice or darkness.

Sunday is my farm day, which means it's always a workday, but being home recharges my batteries, even if it means getting grease on my fingers and dirt under my nails. This is farming. The rest of the week is for "senatoring." Then my week starts all over again.

Senatoring is exhilarating, important work, and with the exception of moments when the majority leader sees it fit to waste everyone's time, I love every minute of it. I hardly ever miss votes. I am rarely late. And my two full-time schedulers (three, if I am running for reelection) know how much I expect an efficient, balanced, properly timed, and thoughtful schedule. A good scheduler knows how to perform miracles. At least mine do.

(LEFT) A view of the Tester farm near Big Sandy.

(RIGHT) An early photo of Tester's original family homestead, circa 1914. That year a tornado destroyed the barn and toppled the fifty-foot iron windmill, which fell on Lloyd Pearson. The windmill frame is visible in both photos.

Jon and Sharla Tester unload wheat into an auger in 1995. The Testers have always done their own farm work and do not rely on hired help.

Tester, in 2016, carves a side of beef in his butcher shop in Big Sandy—the same place where he lost his fingers as a child.

Tester, in 1998, loads a hay grinder as Gus, the Testers' one-eared fox terrier, and cattle look on.

(LEFT TO RIGHT) Christine Tester, Melody Fell, and Shon Tester prepare signs for a political event during Tester's first campaign for Montana Senate District 45 in 1998.

Thirteen-year-old Shon Tester campaigns for his father in a go-kart in 1998.

Gus, the one-eared dog, was the inspiration for the homemade flyer Tester produced and sent to his constituents that read, "Politicians in Helena are like my one-eared dog: they only listen to half of what you say. I want to hear all of what you say."

Jon and Shon Tester hold Gus for a photo in 1998.

Tester (BACK ROW, FIFTH FROM LEFT) takes his oath of office as a state senator in the Montana State Capitol on January 4, 1999.

(ABOVE) Shon Tester applies vinyl letters to his father's grain truck in the spring of 2005, at the beginning of Jon Tester's first US Senate campaign.

(BELOW) The Tester family poses in front of Jon's campaign-themed grain truck, featuring the slogan YOU'RE BEHIND THE RIGHT GUY! in the spring of 2005. (LEFT TO RIGHT) Jon, Sharla, and Shon Tester, and James and Christine Schultz with baby Kilikina.

US Senate candidate Jon Tester poses with Pearl Jam bassist Jeff Ament outside their hometown of Big Sandy, Montana, in the summer of 2005. Ament's father, George, a barber, gave Tester his first flattop haircut.

(LEFT) Pearl Jam's August 13, 2018, concert poster depicting Tester in a tractor flying over a burning White House. The poster was conceptualized by Jeff Ament and illustrated by artist Bobby Brown, known professionally as Bobby Draws Skullz. *Reprinted with permission of Bobby Brown and Jeff Ament*

(ABOVE RIGHT) Pearl Jam shows off T-shirts emblazoned with Tester's name during their August 13, 2018, concert in Missoula, Montana. The band held similar performances for Tester in Montana in 2005 and 2012. (LEFT TO RIGHT) Boom Gaspar, Matt Cameron, Eddie Vedder, Jeff Ament, Stone Gossard, and Mike McCready. *Photo by Rob Skinner, courtesy of Pearl Jam*

on and Shon Tester clear their heads by replacing the engine in a Chevy pickup on Election Day, November 6, 2018. Tester considered that morning "makeup for the time I didn't get to spend with Shon on Father's Day."

Tester meets in his Senate office with Rear Admiral Ronny Jackson, MD, on April 17, 2018. President Trump on March 28 nominated Jackson, then the president's personal physician, to serve as secretary of Veterans Affairs. Jackson withdrew his nomination on April 26 after Tester released White House whistleblower accounts questioning the admiral's qualifications.

US Senate photograph

The highway sign outside Big Sandy, Montana. Local supporters installed the sign in 2007, shortly after Tester took office.

2. THE SENATE WAS ORIGINALLY DESIGNED FOR FARMERS

Senate leaders announce the following year's schedule in November or December, and that schedule lets the rest of us know exactly which weeks we plan to be in session. This too, however, is ultimately up to the majority leader, who reserves the right to cancel these "state work period" days, which most people call "recesses." I never mind canceling a recess or working through a weekend, so long as the Senate stays in session to actually vote, which is too often not the case (see #8).

The Senate usually builds in two weeks of recess in the spring, which usually accommodates my spring planting—unless my soil is too wet to put seeds in, or unless it rains, in which case my schedulers build a pop-up schedule. Then there's the traditional August recess, which accommodates my harvest—unless harvest comes late or early, which is happening more and more these days. The Senate typically adjourns for August because in the days before air-conditioning, muggy Washington was an insufferable place to work. I like to think these recesses were really established to accommodate America's first senators and representatives, many of whom were farmers and needed the time for their own agrarian schedules. Today, I am the only senator who still does this kind of work.

My biggest test came in the spring of 2007, when, for the first time, I had to figure out how to jibe senatoring with spring planting, and I hadn't quite figured out how to balance the two responsibilities. Back then, my daughter, Christine, and her husband, James, were making plans to take over the farm, as Sharla and I had done in 1978 when my folks retired. I was looking forward to showing them the ropes. But that spring was a disaster.

Christine, James, and Bob came to the farm to help out with seeding. One Friday I left the farm to attend several meetings in Havre. When I came home, one tractor sat out in the field after running out of diesel fuel (which is a real pain in the ass to fix), and the other tractor's plow was buried to its frame in the field because a chain had broken. The plow was in so deep I couldn't even pull it out with my loader.

Later that year, James and Christine told me they weren't planning on moving back to the farm after all. James said his work as an electrician was picking up and Christine's career as a nurse at Shodair Children's Hospital was a good job that offered family health insurance. I don't blame them. That conversation is the same conversation countless farmers across this country are having with their own children. What this meant for Sharla and me was less sleep and more work.

My ability to farm *and* serve in the Senate is possible, of course, only because of Sharla. Often when I'm in Washington she stays in Big Sandy. Every morning she calls to report the weather, the soil moisture, where the weeds are, when the peas or alfalfa are blooming, and when the wheat starts to head out.

3. SENIORITY MATTERS, SORTA

Of the ten freshmen elected in 2006, I was ranked at the bottom of the barrel in terms of seniority. And that meant that out of all one hundred senators, I clocked in at dead last. For members elected on the same day, other factors determine their official seniority ranking, such as their history of elected office and the populations of their states. Vermont has a smaller population than Montana, but because Senator Sanders had served sixteen years in the US House of Representatives, he outranked me by eight seniority slots, coming in at ninety-two (Senator Cardin ranked highest among us, at ninety-one). Senator Whitehouse, Rhode Island's former attorney general, didn't hold an elected office when he was elected to the Senate. But Rhode Island's population in 2006 was slightly more than Montana's, so he ranked just above me, at ninety-nine.

Why does seniority matter? It really matters only in the US Senate. The leaders of each caucus determine who gets to sit on which committees based largely, but not exclusively, on seniority. More-senior members often have first right of refusal for various assignments or orders that their names appear on legislation, or in official records. Seniority often dictates things like speaking orders and how far back your desk is in the Senate chamber. Seniority also determines the crazy process by which senators get to select office suites (see #4).

We had some fun with my one-hundredth ranking in Senator seniority. I pitched for our congressional softball team made up of my staffers and staffers for Senator Baucus. When our team, called "Baucus-Tester Overdrive," made jerseys, they assigned me number 100.

But seniority, like everything else, quickly changes. On June 25, 2007, Wyoming's governor appointed Dr. John Barrasso to succeed Senator Craig Thomas, who passed away on June 4. Barrasso's appointment clicked me up to ninety-nine less than six months after I became a US senator. After my reelection in 2018, I ranked thirty-third in seniority—I was more senior than two-thirds of the Senate. It also meant two-thirds of the senators I originally served with in 2007 were gone.

I kept my number 100 jersey even after it no longer applied to my seniority rank. What really matters is how fast you can hurl the ball, not what number's on your shirt. Plus, I'm cheap.

4. PICKING AN OFFICE: "LIKE ELEMENTARY SCHOOL"

Speaking of seniority, the process of assigning offices to senators every two years is one of the strangest rituals among important people you will ever see. Every two years, every senator—one by one, in order of seniority—has the option of choosing a new available office suite in one of three grand Senate office buildings on Capitol Hill: Russell, the oldest and most distinguished-looking; Hart, the most modern and convenient; and Dirksen, which is between the two both physically and practically. Of course, the most senior members of the Senate have the nicest offices. When a senior member leaves or wants to move from Russell to, say, Hart, the next-most-senior member has a limited amount of time to decide whether to move into that vacated Russell space, to wait until another office opens up, or to stay put.

New senators are relegated to temporary offices in basements or in trailers for several months as their more permanent offices are custom-renovated. For the first few months of my time in the Senate, my nineteen staffers and I crammed into cubicles in windowless rooms in the basement of the Dirksen building, waiting our turn. It was so small we had to hold staff meetings in the cafeteria. Then we moved from the basement into the least desirable office suite in the Senate; as number one hundred, I got the office space the other ninety-nine senators didn't want: a very inconvenient collection of sometimes-connecting rooms on two different floors spread across two separate wings of the Russell building.

After every Election Day, the months-long process of what's called "suite selection" begins all over again. In the spring of 2009, after I had moved up the ranks a bit to number eighty-four in seniority, my turn finally came to choose a new office space. Joel Stein, the long-time humor columnist for *Time*, got wind of the process and asked if he could shadow me for a day as we made our move from Russell to Hart. So we put him to work cleaning out a minifridge, at least until he tried to throw away my Heineken minikeg. His March 26 *Time* column was another reminder that everything you say to a reporter is on the record, unless you say it isn't:

> In Montana, [Tester] explains, you don't throw away beer, even on office-moving day. In New Jersey, I tell him, you get pizza and beer when you help someone move. In Montana, I learn, people don't take obvious hints. . . . But nothing is crazier than the fact that every two years, the Senate must break from trillion-dollar bailouts and Iraq-war allocations so that everyone who wants to can switch offices.[2]

"It's like high school!" an apparently hungry Stein suggested as he helped carry an armful of stuff up to the seventh floor of the Hart building.

"I don't think it's like high school," I responded, in another comment that made the column. "I think it's more like elementary school."

Stein also pointed out that Senator Inouye was my new across-the-hall neighbor in the Hart building.

"I get to say aloha every morning," I told him. "Maybe he'll invite me to Hawaii."

5. TRY TO GET ON THE VICE PRESIDENT'S GOOD SIDE

During our orientation in mid-November 2006, Sharla and I and the rest of the newly elected senators and their spouses accepted invitations to the White House for a reception with President Bush and Vice President Cheney. Neither of us had ever been to the White House, and neither of us had met either man.

That evening my interaction with President Bush was uneventful but respectful. My new colleague Jim Webb had an entirely different experience at the White House. Webb, a former Republican secretary of the navy under President Reagan and the father of a marine fighting in Iraq, had also made President Bush's aimless war a signature campaign issue. That night Webb avoided standing in the receiving line, but the president tracked him down.

"How's your boy?" I heard the president ask. Webb tightened his face and looked the president in the eye.

"I'd like to get them out of Iraq, Mr. President."

"That's not what I asked you," the president responded. "*How's your boy?*"

"That's between me and my boy, Mr. President."[3]

Just as Sharla and I were leaving the White House, I realized I hadn't yet met Vice President Cheney—the president of the Senate—and I told her I'd be right back. The vice president of the United States, after all, also holds the title of president of the US Senate, a mostly ceremonial role that requires a vote only to break a tie. I quickly found Cheney and offered my handshake.

"Mr. Vice President, I'm Jon Tester." He unhappily shook my hand and glared at me.

"I know who you are," Cheney growled without a smile. He appeared to be pissed off. At first, I thought the vice president's reaction was just because he might be incapable of any warmth. It occurred to me later that perhaps he still hadn't gotten over the fact that my election was responsible for shifting control of the Senate to the Democrats, diminishing the power he had worked so hard to build. That was the first and last time I spoke with Cheney. I had to wonder if he had some sort of role in sticking me with the worst possible office in the Senate a few months later.

6. STOP AND READ THE SIGNS

When the Hart Building was constructed in the seventies, its designers carefully built it around one of the oldest buildings in the district, a redbrick house on the corner of Constitution Avenue and Second Street Northeast. That three-story building is now the Belmont-Paul Women's Equality National Monument, operated by the National Park Service. From my third-floor office in the corner of the Hart building, I could look out onto the US Supreme Court from the south windows and the Belmont house from the east windows.

Since 1929 the Belmont house served as the headquarters for the National Women's Party, the powerful organization that orchestrated the passage of the nineteenth amendment to the US Constitution. On Election Day 2016, dozens of women stuck their I VOTED stickers on the front gates of the building, a sign of respect after presumably voting for the candidate who millions of Americans hoped would be our first woman president. While admiring those stickers several weeks later, I stopped to read the small historical plaque I had never noticed before, tucked away in the bushes next to the Belmont house.

And that's when I learned that the building I look at every day was also the early-nineteenth century home of Albert Gallatin, a Geneva-born American who served as President Thomas Jefferson's treasury secretary. In that role, Gallatin funded the Lewis and Clark expedition, which traversed Montana and back following the Louisiana

Purchase. The explorers named one of Montana's premier rivers after their financier, and Montana's pioneers named the county surrounding Bozeman after the Gallatin River. Albert Gallatin also lent
his name to the small Missouri town where Senator Conrad Burns
grew up.

Lots of things in Washington, it seems, have some sort of Montana connection if you stop and read the little signs.

7. BRING YOUR OWN BEEF

One of the first things I noticed about DC was the high cost of red
meat in the supermarkets. And for the cost, the quality wasn't great,
especially when my high standard is beef I butcher myself. So early
on I brought my own steaks with me from Big Sandy to Washington,
frozen and stuffed inside a forty-pound roller-cooler that fits perfectly
into the overhead bin on the plane. They were still rock solid by the
time we arrived. Problem solved.

When the *New York Times* got wind of Sharla's and my preference
for Montana beef, they asked if a reporter could spend an evening
with us as we made dinner. Sharla and I shrugged at the idea, still
trying to understand the outside fascination with our preference for
superior food, made with simple ingredients familiar to most middle-
class Americans.

"The Testers prefer their grain-fed beef smothered in canned
cream-of-mushroom soup and a squirt of ketchup, cooked down in
a slow cooker," the *Times*' Jennifer Steinhauer wrote in early 2012.
"They like their purple barley, a staple of specialty food stores, boiled
up as a side dish and then set into a bath of Cool Whip and served
with a nice bottle of pinot noir."[4]

Of all the fancy meals I have had in Washington over the years,
including many inside fine restaurants known for serving beef, none
compare with the Big Sandy beef we prepare at home. In 2012, my
campaign team produced a TV ad about our preference for our own
beef. Though the script focused on cutting the deficit and college

affordability, the video showed me lugging my roller-cooler of meat through airport security.

8. GET USED TO KICKIN' THE CAN

In the summer of 2018, Majority Leader Mitch McConnell cancelled the traditional August recess, citing "a lot of important work to do."[5] No skin off my back, other than it mucked up my harvest schedule, and I've always figured out how to work around that. In fact I welcomed Senator McConnell's decision, because we did have a lot more work to get done that year. And folks across the country are fed up by the Senate's famous record of kicking the can down the road.

A year earlier, ten of my GOP colleagues fired off a letter as a press gimmick, publicly asking Senator McConnell to cancel the 2017 August recess.[6] "Our request is fully backed by our commitment to thoughtfully and diligently work," they wrote.[7]

Fast-forward to August 2018. I got my harvest in. I didn't miss a single vote. Senator McConnell decided not to get anything done. And seven Republicans skipped votes the entire first week of August (not including John McCain, whose failing health prevented him from voting all year). Two of those senators, Mike Lee of Utah and Thom Tillis of North Carolina, had signed the earlier letter.

The exodus of Republicans who chose not to show up in August 2018 was a pretty clear giveaway that McConnell's cancellation had nothing to do with actually getting work done. He cancelled the recess because that year, Democrats had twenty-six of the thirty-five seats up for reelection. Ten of us were considered vulnerable, meaning Donald Trump had won in our states in 2016. So, what better way to make it only tougher for all of us than to keep us from being at home among the people we work for? McConnell certainly didn't invent that play, and as majority leader, it's his every right. But man, if you're going to be part of a political gimmick, you'd better at least show up for the damn gimmick.

As for the Senate's ability to get work done quickly, reset your expectations. I introduced my first federal bill in the Senate on March 1, 2007—a bill to grant federal recognition to the Little Shell Band of Chippewa Indians. The Little Shell people, most of whom live in Montana, have sought federal recognition as a tribe for decades. I have reintroduced that recognition bill every session of Congress since 2007.

In 2018, Little Shell chairman Gerald Gray visited my office with an empty tin can. He put the can on my bookshelf to symbolize his frustration that his tribe's recognition bill had been kicked down the road for more than a century. My Senate colleague Steve Daines cosponsored the Little Shell Tribal Recognition Act, and in 2019 we got the language included in the larger National Defense Authorization Act.

There was a catch, of course. Senator McConnell agreed to include the Little Shell recognition language if we changed it from a "Tester-Daines" amendment to a "Daines-Tester" amendment. Of course I agreed. And President Trump signed the legislation into law on December 20, 2019.[8] I still keep Chairman Gray's tin can on my bookshelf as a reminder that diligence and patience pay off in the US Senate.

9. CELEBRITY DEATHS TRUMP REAL NEWS

On February 8, 2007, MSNBC invited me to the *Hardball* studio in Washington for what they said would be a live interview with the show's host, Chris Matthews. It was my first interview on national TV since my swearing-in, and Matthews wanted to talk about the remarkably brutal week in Iraq. General David Petraeus had just taken over command of the war. Violent car bombings dominated daily news. The day before, five US Marines and two US Navy hospital corpsmen died when their CH-46 helicopter crashed in Anbar Province; it was the fifth US helicopter to have gone down in three weeks.[9] That Thursday, US-backed forces arrested one of Iraq's top health leaders, who was accused of allowing death squads to use ambulances to carry out kidnappings and killings.[10]

I felt it important to talk about all these things, especially because so many Americans—even outside Montana—were looking to me to keep questioning America's involvement in Iraq. National TV interviews still made me nervous, so I spent a good amount of time practicing for *Hardball* with Matt McKenna, my communications director. And in the studio I prerecorded an interview with Matthews. Then, smack in the middle of our interview, MSNBC and all the other cable news networks switched over to announce breaking news: Someone had just found the supermodel Anna Nicole Smith unresponsive in a Florida hotel room. She died of a drug overdose, and the TV news media went bananas. After wrapping our interview about Iraq, Matthews rushed off to be part of what was clearly a more important story for MSNBC than a US senator's perspective on a bloody war. My interview never aired, which meant ninety precious minutes down the drain. McKenna flipped out at Matthews and his producer, screaming about the absurdity of a dead supermodel trumping war in Iraq. I shrugged it off, but it was a good lesson in the priorities of cable news coverage.

Three other Americans died that Thursday, February 8, 2007— heroes whose deaths got little attention as cable news channels obsessed over Anna Nicole Smith's overdose. All three young men were US Army reservists from the 321st Engineer Battalion based in Boise, Idaho. They were dispatched to the site of the CH-46 chopper that crashed the day before, to retrieve the bodies of other fallen Americans. In the city of Karmah, their vehicle exploded over a powerful bomb in the road.[11]

Lest they, among thousands of other Americans who paid the ultimate price in Iraq and Afghanistan, be forgotten, their names were:

- Specialist **Ross Aaron Clevenger**, from Melba, Idaho. Ross, twenty-one, was an aspiring entrepreneur, a writer, an avid snowboarder, and a movie lover. He had a "goofy grin which always brightened the room."[12]
- Sergeant **James Joseph Holtom**, from Rexburg, Idaho. At twenty-two, James was the oldest of seven siblings. Before

deployment, his soon-to-be fiancée took him to a Build-a-Bear Workshop, where he reluctantly made a camouflaged soldier bear for her. The stuffed animal featured a recording of James's voice saying, "I'll love you forever."[13]

- Private **Raymond Mitchell Werner**, of Boise, Idaho. Ray was an aspiring pastor when he died at the age of twenty-one, and he had a calling about serving in the military. His friend said Ray wanted to go to Iraq "so some other people could come back home." He got married two weeks before he left for training.[14]

10. EXPECT NEW FRIENDS OUT OF OLD ENEMIES

One of the most surprising moments of my first few months in office was when I returned to the Montana State Capitol to deliver my first ever address as a US senator to a joint session of the legislature on January 15, 2007. The Montana State Legislature has a long-held tradition of welcoming all members of its congressional delegation for speeches to both the House and Senate. I used the opportunity to talk about the need to wrap up the war in Iraq, to control government spending, and to reform the culture of Washington. Just a few days earlier, the Washington lobbying firm GAGE—run by Senator Burns's former chief of staff—announced it had hired the former senator as a senior adviser to "focus on increasing the firm's visibility and presence domestically and internationally."[15]

I told the assembly in Helena that our goal in Washington was to "stop the revolving door where former members of Congress walk out of the door of the nation's Capitol and into the office of a big, corporate law firm as millionaire lobbyists."[16]

But the most memorable moment of my first speech to the Montana Legislature was just before my remarks, after a meeting with the Democratic caucus in the basement of the Capitol. That's where I ran into a familiar face: "Coach," the man who decades earlier suggested

I was a "sheep" in high school, and who ultimately inspired me to attend college out of spite.

"*What are you doing here?*" I asked. He was the last person I expected to see.

"I came to hear your speech, Senator," he replied. He eagerly offered me his hand; for the first time I felt he had some respect for me. I don't believe Coach meant to teach me a powerful lesson over the course of several decades, but he did. He taught me to push myself, well beyond my own comfort zone, simply to prove wrong any assumption that I might never succeed. Sure, I did it out of pride and more than a little spite on my part. But seeing Coach come out of his way to greet me that day also showed me the power of proving myself *right*. I realized he had respect for me, and I had respect for him. I also realized the power—and danger—of stubborn determination in the face of doubt. I looked Coach in the eye, gave him a smile, grabbed his hand and squeezed it *hard*.

11. NEVER DARK, NEVER QUIET

Out on our farm twelve miles west of Big Sandy, the night sky is so dark the Milky Way is still milky. Our closest neighbor is nearly a mile away. Our farm is one of the quietest and, at night, darkest places on the planet. Ever since I was a boy, rarely a clear night goes by when I don't look up and admire the stars glittering across the sky. It's a view I realize I took for granted once I got to Washington.

Washington, DC, is never, ever dark or quiet. The night sky always glows orange. On virtually every street in the city, obnoxiously loud sirens wail throughout the day and night. During our first overnight in Washington, Sharla and I couldn't sleep. Amid the persistent sirens outside our bedroom, we heard birds chirping in the middle of the night. The birds were apparently confused by the city's light pollution, and they chirped away believing the sun—hours away from poking above the horizon—was just about to rise.

I know most Americans are used to life without stars, without solitude, and without the peace that comes with the quietness of a place like Chouteau County, Montana. It makes me realize how lucky I really am.

12. SET HIGHER STANDARDS

During my campaign in 2006, I ran against a member of the US Senate whose ethics and relationships with lobbyists came under sharp scrutiny. So during that campaign, I made a pledge to set higher standards for myself and for my staff should I be elected to the Senate. I did just that. My own internal ethics rules are more stringent than the Senate's.

While the Senate rules forbid members or staff from accepting gifts worth $50 or more, my own ethics rules require us to refuse all gifts, including meals and travel. The Senate rules forbid former members or former staffers from lobbying for one year after they leave office; my ethics rules forbid former staffers who become lobbyists from lobbying me *ever*. I will never rehire a staffer who works for me, then becomes a registered lobbyist. And I also vowed to publicize my daily public schedule, online, at the end of each workday in Congress—a practice I have kept up since my first day on the job. I was the first US Senator to do so.

These may be small things, but they're common sense. And Montanans expect them. Indeed, all Americans should have higher standards for their representatives in Congress.

13. GET OUT OF THE GREEN ZONE

In November of 2007, I joined Senator Jim Webb, a former Marine, for a trip to Iraq to see firsthand the progress of the war we both wanted to end. That year turned out to be the deadliest for US forces in Iraq; 899 Americans (and nearly 19,000 Iraqis) died in 2007.[17]

That visit to Iraq was the first time I had ever visited a war zone; in fact, it was the first time I had ever crossed the Atlantic Ocean.

"We're gonna get out of the Green Zone to see some real shit we need to see," Webb warned me. And boy, did we. He and I toured war zones in and around Baghdad in a darkened helicopter. With armed escorts and wearing heavy body armor, we visited an outdoor market that seemed haunted as the Iraqi locals glared at us with hatred in their eyes. Webb and I got to talk about the military's strategy over dinner with General Petraeus. We flew over bullet-battered buildings and piles of smoldering rubble in Ramadi. And I visited with some of the Montana troops stationed in Baghdad, one of whom told me that if American forces pulled out immediately, the entire country would collapse. Still, that tour of Iraq only hardened my opinion that America needed to find a way out of there quickly, to let Iraq's new government control its own destiny.

"As long as [the Iraqis] know we're here as a crutch, they're going to move at a snail's pace, and I think we need to pick up the pace," I told Montana reporters from Baghdad. "We need to apply pressure to the president as much as possible, to draw this thing down and bring it to an end as soon as possible."[18]

Even long after we left that awful place, I couldn't get the acrid smell of its air out of my brain. It smelled like burning, rotten flesh, gunpowder, and sewage, and it never really washed out of my clothes. My tour of Iraq outside the comfort and safety of the Green Zone was a turning point that colored my entire view of the war in Iraq. Though I'll never claim to know what actual servicemen and -women experience at war, I at least have a sense of how truly foreign and frightening it is.

14. REMEMBER THOSE WHO WORK WITH THEIR HANDS

One of the benefits of having temporary office space in the basement of the Dirksen building was my proximity to the skilled work that happens underneath the Senate complex. The US Senate has an old tradition of keeping many of its own services in-house. There's a bar-bershop, a clinic, a post office, a credit union, and numerous places to grab some grub. The Senate also makes most of its own furniture on site, and fabricates its own sheet metal inside the metal shop. Why? It's often more cost effective for the US Capitol complex to have its own specialized craftsmen and craftswomen who are specially trained to accommodate the unique needs and historical character of the old buildings. These carpenters, welders, machinists, upholsterers, and painters all work for the Architect of the Capitol, a sprawling division of Congress that quietly keeps both sides of Capitol Hill running smoothly.

In workshops tucked away in basement corridors, you'll find these folks hard at work with industrial equipment. After passing by the metal shop one day shortly after my arrival, I asked if I could take a tour. Of course, I was told. If a US senator had ever asked for a personal tour of the metal shop, it hadn't happened in anyone's recent memory.

On Capitol Hill, it's easy to forget that our nation is still powered by people who work with their hands, and it's far too common for members of Congress to forget or ignore that our own workplace is full of them. These workers spend their days in windowless rooms laboring behind the scenes without much recognition.

"Metal shop employees do lots of work for the Senate office buildings, including repairing roofs, designing and creating vents for air conditioning and heating systems, fabricating and installing stainless steel counters in Senate restaurants and overall maintenance duties," wrote a *Roll Call* reporter who came along on my tour.[19]

That afternoon, I felt more at home among those sheet metal workers, who were literally wearing work suits with blue collars, than anywhere else on Capitol Hill. We spoke the same language. After they got comfortable with the fact that I was genuinely interested in their work, they gave me shit about my Looney Tunes tie, then they showed me every corner of their shop. I even got to don a helmet and give the welding equipment a spin. I spot-welded a piece of metal and dripped some solder onto my boot, which one of the metalsmiths apologetically tried to clean off.

"Don't worry about that," I told him. "That's what boots are for, man."

15. SEEK THE GIANTS

The magnitude of my new role in the Senate didn't really hit me until I attended my first lunch with the Democratic caucus. I was still trying to put famous faces to famous names when Senator Jay Rockefeller of West Virginia walked over to me and introduced himself.

"You and I come from very different backgrounds, Senator Tester," he said, making me feel like a mouse from his height of six foot seven. "But we both ended up in the same place. Isn't that something else?"

That is *something else*. The more I think about Senator Rockefeller's observation, the more I realize how profound it was. Though one of the Senate's more modest members, Jay Rockefeller's family background was absolutely nothing like mine. Before becoming a senator, I made $30,000 a year—in a good year. I made a living as a dirt farmer. I once taught kids music in a school bathroom. I spent years without health insurance, because I couldn't afford it. Yet in terms of the great responsibilities entrusted to us as US senators, Jay Rockefeller and I were equals.

During my first year in the Senate, I often sought out Dan Inouye of Hawaii, Robert Byrd of West Virginia, and the four-foot-eleven Barbara Mikulski of Maryland, who impressed and scared the hell out of me. They too were giants, and I always learned from them. Senator Byrd, then eighty-nine, didn't always remember my name, but he affectionately greeted me by yelling "Mountain Man!" whenever he saw me. And on the other side of the aisle, I quickly befriended Johnny Isakson of Georgia, Olympia Snowe of Maine, Chuck Hagel of Nebraska, and Dick Lugar of Indiana. All of them showed me what the Senate used to be (and still is!) capable of: allowing strong relationships to trump partisanship. Years later, both Isakson and Hagel stood in my corner during one of the most difficult firestorms of my political career.

In those early days in the Senate I also watched with admiration as Barack Obama took command of his presidential race while also navigating the politics and demands of the Senate. After Obama became president, Interior Secretary Ken Salazar of Colorado, a former senator and another mentor of mine, challenged me to weekly basketball games at the gym inside the Department of the Interior (he's pretty damn good). I asked President Obama if he wanted to join us and he laughed it off.

"You'll hurt me, Jon."

"I'll be on your team, Mr. President."

"Doesn't matter, you'll hurt me anyway."

And then there was Senator Ted Kennedy, someone I had admired all my life. Mother admired him too, and even got to meet Senator Kennedy soon after I went to Washington. It was one of the proudest moments of her life. On several occasions I got to visit Senator Kennedy inside his "hideaway" office in the basement of the Capitol. That office was like a museum full of old photographs and mementos from decades of friendships with Republicans, Democrats, and countless foreign dignitaries. There he kept his brother John's cigar humidor and a sword given to him by Che Guevara.

I asked Senator Kennedy about an iconic photo taken in Miles City, Montana, in August 1960. The picture shows a grimacing twenty-eight-year-old Ted Kennedy riding a bucking bronco named Skyrocket, bareback, at the Eastern Montana Fair, with his right arm high in the air. While stumping for his older brother's presidential campaign, Ted Kennedy told me he had climbed up to the announcer's booth and asked the rodeo emcee to mention his brother's name.

"Nope," the announcer replied. "The only guys we announce are the ones riding the broncs." So Kennedy crawled back down, borrowed some appropriate rodeo attire and a black Stetson, went to the chutes and strapped himself to Skyrocket, and hung on for seven long seconds—not long enough to score points but enough time for a local news photographer named George Larson to snap the photograph, which ran in newspapers across the country.[20]

"The gate opened, and out I lurched, the world looking like a piece of film running through a broken sprocket," Kennedy wrote in his book *True Compass*. "I could hear the crowd—either cheering or laughing, I couldn't tell which."[21]

To this day, when I need uplifting, I click on to YouTube to listen to either of two of my favorite speeches. Both of them are from Senator Kennedy, delivered when he was only thirty-six years old. And both speeches resonate deeply with the political crises of today. The first is when Senator Kennedy addressed the Alaska Democratic Party on April 7, 1968, reflecting on the assassination of Martin Luther King Jr. several days earlier:

No matter how the most difficult questions of Vietnam are solved; no matter how we meet the future challenges in the Middle East; no matter how strong the controls we develop over the horror of atomic weapons; and no matter how we face the domestic problems of health for the poor, education for our young, and decent housing and better roads for the more distant parts of America—no matter how well we do these things, they will only be the epitaph of a great nation that could not bind its own wounds within itself, and as a result, lost itself.

If laws do not meet the need, and they don't; if speeches will not meet the need, and they won't; if marches and demonstrations won't meet the need, and they won't—where are we concerned? We can only turn to ourselves. We're in a moment of national crisis such as we are experiencing now; that is all that is left. Men in public life must be true to themselves—must be more candid with whomever they speak, regardless of the political consequences.[22]

The other speech I listen to frequently is the one Senator Kennedy delivered as a eulogy at his brother Bobby's funeral a few months later, on June 8, 1968:

My brother need not be idealized, or enlarged in death beyond what he was in life; to be remembered simply as a good
and decent man, who saw wrong and tried to right it, saw
suffering and tried to heal it, saw war and tried to stop it.[23]

Those are powerful words that move me to my core. It's guidance
I try to live by. I just thank the good Lord I got to spend a moment
of time on this planet serving alongside Senator Ted Kennedy—the
giant of the US Senate.

16. KEEP FAMILY FIRST

My cousin Roger Pearson passed away in November 2017. Roger's
family planned the funeral for Thursday, November 9. Attending the
service would mean I would miss four votes—generally a no-no, especially for someone whose reelection was a year away.

"Missing these votes is a big deal," advised Aaron Murphy, then
my chief of staff. "You sure?"

"Hell yes," I told him sternly. "At the end of all this, when I look
back on my life, am I going to wish I stayed here for four more votes?
Or am I going to wish I was home to celebrate the life of a guy I spent
Christmas Eves opening presents with?"

"Got it," Murph said. "We'll make it work." And that was that.
Missing those four votes was one of the easiest decisions I made since
joining the Senate.

The other rough patch that affected my Senate service came in
the summer of 2009. Mother came out to the farm for two weeks that
spring, during a painful battle with kidney failure. One afternoon she
sat alone in the cab of our parked Peterbilt, quietly looking out over
the progress that had been made over the past eighty-nine years.

"What's she doing out there?" Shon asked. I didn't think to tell
him what I know today and what she knew then: Mother's visit to the
farm that spring was her last. A few weeks later she told us she was
done undergoing dialysis. For the first time in my life and hers, she

decided to let go. And she did, gracefully as ever, on her own terms, on June 27. Mother came home to the Montana flatland, where the earth smells good after rain.

Helen Tester encouraged me to continue the balancing act of managing both the farm and the Senate schedules, because, she said, "the country needs you." She had been to Washington to see me sworn in as a US Senator, and she got to meet some of her heroes in politics. She's fully responsible for igniting the spark of politics that led me to where I am today.

Mother was brave and stoic. She plowed through her own emotions to keep our family growing together. She always thought ahead. She knew us better than we knew ourselves. And she never, ever put up with anyone's bullshit. We all got a good chuckle when we stumbled across her quote in her 1939 high school yearbook, which says:

Helen Pearson: She knows how to give a man her own way.[24]

CHAPTER 11

When We Need the Government . . . and When We Don't

Dad stopped going to school after he finished the eighth grade. What he lacked in formal education he made up for in the common sense required to survive an itinerant youth of manual labor with the Civilian Conservation Corps. That's a polite way of saying Dad didn't suffer bullshit. So when a state meat inspector arrived at our farm out of the blue in 1969, the meeting didn't go very well.

The inspector, from the Montana Department of Agriculture, drove down our mile-long driveway and parked his government pickup in front of our barn. Dad stepped out of the butcher shop where he had been hard at work.

"Howdy," Dad said. He greeted every stranger with warmth.

"You David Tester?" the inspector asked with an eastern European accent I'll never forget.

"Yessir. How can I help you?"

"On behalf of the State of Montana, I'm shutting you down."

"What the hell are you talking about?" This is where my father raised his voice.

"Because you're selling meat, Mr. Tester, and this business doesn't have a license for selling meat."

"We're not selling meat!" Dad snapped. "This is a custom butcher shop. People bring us the meat they already own and we just cut it up for them."

"Well, you're done doing that," the inspector replied. From here, the conversation turned into a shouting match until the inspector squealed out of our yard with Dad screaming after him.

Dad and Mother kept the butcher shop spotlessly clean and efficient. My folks never needed a license to operate it, because they provided a *service*, not a product. Nor could they afford the cost of burdensome regulations and standards that applied to larger meat processors. If they failed to meet the high quality of butchery services expected from their neighbors, word would travel quickly around our community and end their business forever. That meant my folks kept their own strict standards for the meat they cut.

The abrupt announcement from the State of Montana meat inspector rocked both my parents. All they had ever known was the business of making an honest living, and a government man just showed up in his government pickup to tell them they were doing it wrong. As Dad whipped up a storm of anger, Mother stood to the side and sobbed. She had realized the financial impact of our butcher shop shutting down with two boys in college. After the inspector left, my parents returned from their different parts of the emotional spectrum. They both realized common sense needed to prevail.

"Why don't we call Congressman Melcher?" Mother suggested. John "Doc" Melcher, a veterinarian, feedlot operator, and former mayor of Forsyth who had served in the Montana Senate, had just won the 1969 special election to serve Montana's second congressional district. Back then, Montana had two congressional districts, and Doc Melcher represented all of eastern Montana. He beat Montana House Majority Leader William Mather on June 24 to fill the seat vacated by Congressman James Battin, whom President Nixon appointed to the federal bench.[1]

Melcher, to my parents' surprise, immediately responded to our family's plight from Washington, and he agreed wholeheartedly that Dad and Mother did not need a state license for cutting—not selling—meat. Melcher, who still had plenty of connections within the state government, sent off a fiery letter to the Montana Department of Agriculture intervening in the situation. He reminded both my parents that Democrats, not Republicans, were far more concerned about the viability of America's family farms.

Doc Melcher's quick work as a new member of Congress kept our family business open. The Montana Department of Agriculture eventually came around and agreed we didn't need a license after all, and we never heard from that particular meat inspector again. I had just turned fifteen. My curiosity in politics had only grown since I'd peeked into the ballroom of the Hotel Finlen in Butte several months earlier to watch Senators Mansfield and Metcalf holding court with the Montana Democrats. Watching Doc Melcher save my family's business by simply sending a letter was the first time I had seen a politician go to bat for someone and actually make a difference. It's also when I realized when the government can very quickly go too far—by giving a single bureaucrat unchecked, unilateral authority to shut down a perfectly good, honest family business. It's much more difficult to operate a business in rural America, where pluck and common sense supersedes the hassle of government opinions and regulations. Of course, that doesn't mean we aren't concerned about sanitary butcher shops or unsafe conditions, but when governments impose more rules and requirements that work well for more condensed parts of our country, the impact is often much tougher on those of us in rural America. That's one of the reasons Donald Trump's promise of fewer regulations for small business resonated so clearly in Chouteau County and across rural America.

And like most Montanans who do honest work to make ends meet, I have a real problem when a single person thinks he can single-handedly unravel a family business with nothing more than a hunch or, in our case, an inaccurate assumption. And like most Montanans, I have an even bigger problem with a government that thinks it has business violating the privacy of ordinary, law-abiding citizens. That hit home for me in the aftermath of the attacks of September 11, 2001.

I woke up early that morning in Colstrip, Montana, for a daylong bus tour of remote coalbed methane wells near the Wyoming border with a group of other legislators. When word came down of the attacks in New York City and on the Pentagon, and of a survivorless airline crash in Pennsylvania, we all listened to updates over the radio. But none of us really felt the magnitude of the events of the day from the inside of a bus. None of us had seen the images.

After our tour ended late that afternoon, I embarked on the six-hour drive back to Big Sandy. By then I knew from the radio reports that the course of American history had changed. But it wasn't until almost twelve hours after the attacks that I felt the tragedy even more after seeing the collapse of the towers, desperate souls hurling themselves to their deaths, and black smoke rising above the New York skyline. I had stopped at a pizza joint in Billings for a quick bite to eat and everyone inside was glued to the news on TV.

For the first time that day—for the first time in my life—I was scared for the future of our nation and *terrified* of the uncertainty. I needed to get home to Sharla. I knew then that the United States of America was already on a swift march toward war, and that the attacks were going to change the way we go to war. I feared what it meant for my able-bodied, sixteen-year-old son. I worried how it would change our economy. Like millions of other Americans, I was bewildered by resentment toward America so profound that it resulted in the violent deaths of innocent civilians. I was pissed off, and I wanted revenge. I also knew, then, that it would change the way our government values, protects, and takes away our civil liberties.

One month later, on October 11, the US Senate passed the USA Act of 2001. Only Democrat Russ Feingold of Wisconsin voted nay, warning Congress must "be sure we are not rewarding these terrorists and weakening ourselves by giving up the cherished freedoms that they seek to destroy."[2] The US House of Representatives passed its version of the bill the following day with a vote of 337–79.[3] Congress then incorporated language from the Financial Anti-Terrorism Act and merged the bills into a sweeping, 132-page disaster of a policy it called the Uniting and Strengthening America by Providing Appropriate Tools Required to Intercept and Obstruct Terrorism Act. We know it by its less awkward acronym: The USA PATRIOT Act.

With Vice President Cheney to his right and his new FBI director, Robert Mueller, to his left, President Bush signed the Patriot Act into law on October 26, claiming it was "crafted with skill and care, determination and a spirit of bipartisanship for which the entire nation is grateful.[4]

"This bill was met with an overwhelming—*overwhelming*—agreement in Congress, because it upholds and respects the civil liberties guaranteed by our Constitution," Bush added. From Montana, many of us had an entirely different perspective. Congress was wrong. I have no problem whatsoever using lethal force to root out terrorism. But the moment law-abiding citizens lose their constitutionally guaranteed rights in the name of government strength is a moment we lose what it means to be an American. With the signing of the Patriot Act, we watched America kiss our sacred right to privacy goodbye.[5]

The most egregious provision in the Patriot Act allowed the federal government to expand nationwide wiretapping authority on phones, cell phones, and email accounts without first obtaining warrants. The law also allowed the government to hold non-US citizens for up to a week without charging them. The legislation earned the ire of the Montana chapter of the ACLU and even from a Montana field representative of the NRA, who warned "any expansion of government powers needs to be monitored, regardless of politics."[6] The NRA eventually said the legislation would not violate Second Amendment rights, but I couldn't disagree more. Without an independent check on the sweeping new powers of the federal government, there was no way to be certain.

Even Republican lawmakers agreed. During the 2005 session of the Montana State Legislature, we overwhelmingly passed a resolution condemning the Patriot Act. As Montana Senate president, on April 4, I signed the bipartisan Joint Resolution 19, which stated, in part, "it is the policy of the citizens of Montana to oppose any portion of the USA PATRIOT Act that violates the rights and liberties guaranteed under the Montana Constitution or the United States Constitution, including the Bill of Rights."[7] Our resolution added, "in the absence of reasonable suspicion of criminal activity under Montana law, the 59th Montana Legislature exhorts agents and instrumentalities of this state to not initiate or participate in or assist or cooperate with an inquiry, investigation, surveillance, or detention under the USA PATRIOT Act if the action violates constitutionally guaranteed civil rights or civil liberties."[8] Only ten of the fifty senators, and twelve of one hundred state representatives opposed Joint Resolution 19.

Government overreach sparked similar bipartisan resentment in Montana after Congress passed, and President Bush signed into law, REAL ID in the spring of 2005, mandating that states create what amounts to national ID cards—at their own expense—with "a common machine-readable technology, with defined minimum data elements."[9] In plainer words: States were now required to upgrade their drivers' licenses to include embedded information that could allow the federal government to track every person who had one. Lawmakers tucked the controversial REAL ID language into a critical emergency spending bill to fund the military. But before that happened, Congressman Dennis Rehberg voted yea on the stand-alone version of the unpopular REAL ID Act on February 10, 2005, stepping—not for the first or last time in his political career—into a steaming pile of goat shit.[10]

REAL ID did not sit well in Montana either, for Democrats, Libertarians, or Republicans. And ours became the first state in the nation to deny participation in the federal REAL ID program when all 150 members of the 2007 Montana Legislature approved a measure "opposing the implementation of the federal REAL ID Act and directing the Montana Department of Justice not to implement the provisions," which Governor Schweitzer eagerly signed into law.[11] In Congress that

February, I sponsored bipartisan federal legislation repealing REAL ID with Senators Dan Akaka of Hawaii, Patrick Leahy of Vermont, and Republican John Sununu of New Hampshire, though our bill never got the traction it needed to pass.[12]

"My state is opting out of the onerous regulation, blatant invasion of privacy, and the high cost of compliance that will come from implementing REAL ID," I said on the Senate floor that April, just after Schweitzer signed the bill. "Today, Montana adds its voice to those calling for the federal government to go back to the drawing board. Let's listen to what Montana has to say."[13]

Personal freedom, you could say, is a value that Montanans don't assign to a specific political party. With plenty of exceptions, it's fair to say that a strong Libertarian streak courses through the blood of even the most partisan Republicans and Democrats in our state. When it comes to our personal freedoms, the government should stay the hell out of the way.

Regrettably, I didn't always feel this way. In 1990, when Charlie Danreuther asked if I would consider running for his seat on the Chouteau County Commission, I considered myself "pro-life." Dad always considered himself pro-choice, and Mother never really talked about the issue of abortion. Nobody had ever really challenged me on the issue until a fiery, late-night conversation in the Montana State Capitol with my friend Senate Majority Leader Jon Ellingson of Missoula.

"I'm sorry," I told him. "You might like abortion, but I don't."

Ellingson stopped me right there, rejecting my assumption by raising his hand. He was calm but angry, and it wasn't clear to me why, at first.

"Don't you dare say I like abortion!" he said. "I'm sure I've never met anyone who has." Then Ellingson dug deep. "But it's not my decision to make, Jon, and it's not yours either. The government has no damn business making one of the most intimate decisions a woman can possibly make. The government has no business in deciding who you get to love or whether a woman can have a child. I'm not going to try to change your mind, but *don't say I like abortion*."

Ellingson, a lawyer who later worked for the ACLU, then went over the actual language of *Roe v. Wade*, which he knew almost by memory. And then he added, "Did you know Montana's Constitution is the only constitution in the country that protects human dignity?"

I stammered. I didn't know. Montana's Constitution indeed states: "The dignity of the human being is inviolable."[14]

"Human dignity *requires* an individual's right to make intimate decisions," Ellingson said. "And to me, that means the dignity to make a choice as intimate as whether to have a child is guaranteed by Montana's Constitution."[15]

That wasn't just a personal epiphany for me; it was the moment I became a proud advocate of protecting the freedom of choice and a woman's right to make her own decisions. That conversation changed my mind and struck me like lightning. I was, all along, pro-choice, and it took my careless accusation and someone else's smart mind for me to realize it. Being pro-choice is true to who I am and always was, what I have always believed, and where I believe the government has no business. In Montana, most of us agree on that.

By the spring of 2008 it was clear that America's economy had neared the edge of a cliff. That March the investment firm Bear Stearns went sideways, and the Federal Reserve committed $29 billion to back its assets to allow JPMorgan Chase to acquire it. Then in July I joined seventy-one of my colleagues in voting for the bipartisan Housing and Economic Recovery Act, designed to stem off the national housing crisis by throwing a line to the millions of Americans hurt by subprime mortgages.[16] The legislation also led to the federal government's takeover of Fannie Mae and Freddie Mac on September 7. Eight days later the Dow Jones Industrial Average plunged more than 500 points following news of the bankruptcy of investment bank Lehman Brothers. The next day the Federal Reserve took over AIG, risking $85 billion to bail out the insurance giant. I watched it unfold from my seat on the Senate Banking Committee, and the future looked treacherous.

For me, the government's role in the financial uncertainty became clear on September 23, during a four-and-a-half-hour Banking

Committee hearing with Treasury Secretary Hank Paulson and Fed chairman Ben Bernanke. They were asking Congress for the authority for the US Treasury Department to spend up to $700 billion in American taxpayer money to stabilize the worldwide financial markets by buying troubled assets. Outside the hearing room, everyone else called their request a bailout of Wall Street—a bailout for powerful banks and firms that had gotten greedy, took dangerous risks, then failed when the bubble burst. The Bush administration, most Republicans and, in fairness, most Democrats agreed these Wall Street banks were simply "too big to fail," a notion many of us small-business owners find insulting.

I finally got to ask questions at the very end of the hearing, and I asked Paulson and Bernanke about the impact of a $700 billion bailout on credit ratings and the impact of the consolidation on Wall Street on smaller financial institutions in rural America.

"When you have consolidation in any marketplace," I told Bernanke, "it tends to result in less benefits to the consumer—this is my perspective; you may disagree—less benefits to the consumer and need for more regulation. Do you see both things occurring, or needing to occur?"

Bernanke gave me a slick-sounding answer that still confuses me to this day: "Well, the financial supermarket approach has benefits and costs. It has some complementarities across different types of services. It has some, um, market issues like you're referring to. I think we need to look at the regulatory system very extensively."

I also asked about the role of American taxpayers bailing out Wall Street at a staggering cost, and whether America's G8 allies are committed to doing their part to twist the tourniquet on our bleeding the global economy. "Where are the other countries in this process?" I asked. "Because I think that unless their economies are cherry—and you said it's totally integrated, so if it's integrated they're in a mess too. Why aren't they ponying up?"

"All of them are dealing with their own economies," Secretary Paulson replied. "Economies are slowing down around the world. We have fragility in markets around the world. We have equity markets declining in various parts of the world. So again, every one of these countries is dealing with their own situation."

"You feel comfortable they've stepped up to the plate in a commensurate way?"

"I'd say that there are different approaches." Paulson gave me another nonanswer, but I was on borrowed time. And by then I knew the whole thing didn't smell right.

"I haven't been involved in government all that long—ten years," I told Bernanke and Paulson. "I've been involved in public service at the local level a lot longer than that. But I can tell you that every time— every time that I can think of—that we made a spur-of-the-moment decision that we didn't do our due diligence on, at the level of governments that I have been involved in, it has been a wreck." Both men looked at me from the witness table with flat, tired expressions on their faces. "I'm not sure we've got the whole sentence written, much less the i's dotted and the t's crossed. And I fully feel the urgency and I know you guys are frustrated, and I'm frustrated—everybody up here's frustrated. But the truth is we have to be given the time to do this right or it's not going to work."[17]

After the hearing I announced I wasn't sold on the proposed bailout of Wall Street.

"I want to know that this legislation fixes the root problems, so we're not doing this year after year," I said. "I want to know that no CEOs are getting big paychecks for running their companies into the ground. And I want to make sure that Main Street, not just Wall Street, is helped."[18] I had concerns about what I felt was an artificial time line to rush $700 billion into our economy, and I pointed out that our kids would get stuck with the bill. At home, Montanans were furious about the proposed bailout. And they let me know it.

I voted against the bailout of Wall Street, formally called the Emergency Economic Stabilization Act of 2008, one week later, joining only eight other Democrats in doing so. Only twenty-five Senators—fifteen Republicans, nine Democrats, and an independent, Bernie Sanders, rejected the measure on October 1.[19] Nonetheless,

Congress approved the law, which created the Troubled Asset Relief Program, or TARP.

On November 4, Americans elected Senator Barack Obama as their forty-fourth president. In Montana, though he never stepped foot in the state, John McCain beat Obama by just over eleven thousand votes (Obama came to campaign for Montana's three electoral votes several times). Max Baucus handily won his fifth term in the US Senate.[20] And in Minnesota, the race between Senator Norm Coleman and his challenger Al Franken remained too close to call. I followed that race closely, because my 2006 campaign manager and first chief of staff, Stephanie Schriock, took a temporary leave of absence to run Franken's campaign. Little did any of us know she wouldn't be able to return to my office until the following June.

Then in December 2008, Detroit came to Capitol Hill to ask for another bailout. The "Big Three" automakers—GM, Chrysler, and Ford—wanted $34 billion to stem off their own crisis due to months of skyrocketing oil prices. During a hearing on December 4, I had an opportunity to question Gene Dodaro, the refreshingly candid acting comptroller general of the Government Accountability Office.

"One of my big concerns is that if we do this bailout today, even after the plans, there is a potential we could be back here in a year, maybe less," I asked him. "Could you give me any assurances that if we allocate $34 billion today, that it will take care of the problem, assuming that the economic situation that we're in right now is where it's gonna be for the next year or maybe even a little longer?"

"We've not done the in-depth work that put me in a position to provide you that assurance, so I can't provide it," Dodaro answered.[21] Despite the lack of assurance, his reply was an honest moment. For the *Daily Show with Jon Stewart*, the clip of our exchange was featured as that evening's "Moment of Zen."[22] It takes a lot to impress me; I don't get starstruck and I don't find celebrities all that interesting. But as a fan and regular watcher of the *Daily Show*, seeing myself in that moment was a total surprise. As Christine, Shon, and Mel joked, that was the moment I had truly "made it" in politics.

As for the policy, my mind was made up. I voted against the auto bailout on December 11, and it failed. I became the only Senate Democrat who voted against both bailouts.[23]

"In order to ask Montanans to give their tax dollars to the automakers, I needed to see a solid business plan, a commitment to building more dependable, fuel-efficient vehicles, and a promise not to use taxpayer money to expand operations in other countries," I said in a statement after the vote. "But those were not in the Senate bill, and that is why I opposed it. No one—not the CEOs, labor unions, or outside experts—could assure me this plan would work."[24]

"I'd rather see the Treasury Department use the funds it already has from the Wall Street bailout before another bailout is passed," I added. On December 18 President Bush, with the support of President-Elect Obama, approved $17.4 billion to keep GM and Chrysler from collapsing, half of what the industry originally wanted, using taxpayer money already dedicated by TARP.[25]

Though I don't believe in bailouts, the American Recovery and Reinvestment Act was a whole different story. America's economy was still in a slide. The viability of rural America was at stake. After raising concerns about where exactly our Wall Street bailout money would go, word came down in March 2009 that AIG had awarded $165 million in bonuses to its top executives, even after accepting a $173 billion taxpayer bailout, citing employee contracts.[26]

"What would those contracts have been if the taxpayers wouldn't have bailed them out?" I steamed during a hearing a few days later. "That company would have been broke! Those people would be part of the 600,000 unemployed that occur in this country every month, and they would be out on the street." If this is the way Wall Street continues to do business, I added, we can't help with any amount of money. "They need to understand the only reason they have a job is because of the taxpayers."[27]

In Montana, small businesses barely scraped by. Contractors and construction workers were eager for work. College graduates found little work. Public schools and highways and water infrastructure systems needed to be repaired or replaced altogether. The recovery act offered an important fix, and tax breaks for ordinary Montanans to boot. Supporting the recovery act in February 2009 was a political hot potato, but also one of the easiest votes I cast during my time in the US Senate.[28] And with the benefit of hindsight, it worked.

As America slowly recovered and reinvested from the Great Recession, attention soon turned to President Obama's new health care proposal. As soon as the Minnesota Supreme Court officially gave Al Franken his 312-vote victory over Senator Coleman on June 30, 2009, Senate Democrats got the sixtieth vote they needed to overcome a filibuster of the Patient Protection and Affordable Care Act. It was an opportunity like the Montana Legislature had in 2005: control of both houses of Congress, the executive branch, and an agenda intended to improve the lives of ordinary people.

But unlike Montana in 2005, the Democrats lost steam quickly. In the six months between Senator Franken's swearing-in and the final vote on Christmas Eve, the Democrats publicly made sausage with Obamacare while the political Right stoked angry fires throughout the nation. The Right threw everything it had at the debate, including flat-out lies, like the infamous "death panels." With funding by Charles and David Koch, the newly formed Tea Party gobbled up much of the narrative and legitimized nationwide anger at the very notion of a government health care law. This anger seeped into every nook and cranny of our country. Montana was no exception.

Though there were several, fixable components of the Affordable Care Act I didn't love, one piece of the law was contrary to everything I believed in. The individual mandate requiring all adults to purchase insurance coverage flew in the face of what I believe a government can do for its citizens. Nonetheless, I believed the individual mandate was outweighed by the essential reforms it made—particularly in preventing insurance companies from limiting lifetime health care coverage or jacking up rates for folks with preexisting conditions. I realized why the mandate was necessary during a conversation I had with a long-haul trucker who came to my farm to pick up a load of wheat that autumn.

"I don't need your goddamn health care law," he snipped at me, while standing on my property.

"How long have you been driving this rig?" I asked him.

"Thirty years. Never needed to buy health insurance, and I ain't about to start."

"You've driven professionally for thirty years and you've never been in an accident?"

"Well, I had an accident once," the trucker said. "Broke my leg."

"How'd you pay for it if you didn't have health insurance?"

"I just went to the emergency room," he said. "Health care is free there."

That conversation was all I needed to finally realize why the individual mandate—a concept promoted by many Republicans in the early nineties—was written into Obamacare. No health care is free, but as long as an emergency room cannot deny health care to those who can't afford it, then everyone needs to have skin in the game in order to keep costs down. It's a simple concept, but I get why attacking it in the name of socialism or government overreach is red meat for the opponents of the Affordable Care Act.

Passing that law was, perhaps, the second-easiest vote of my political career. The right-wing think tanks quickly churned out a new talking point that my political opponents used ad nauseam. They claimed over and over again that I cast "the deciding vote" for Obamacare. Because we needed sixty votes to pass the law and we had sixty votes, they said the same thing about *every* Democrat in the Senate—manufacturing a false notion for voters that somehow I was solely to blame, as were my other politically vulnerable colleagues. I have no regrets. Government *should* be in the business of guaranteeing health care for its citizens, as long as we value health as a right for all and not a privilege for only those who can afford it. Thank God we are a nation that values the former.

Higher education, however, is a different story. I don't believe the government owes "free" college to everyone, for two reasons. I believe in the need for all students of higher education to have at least a little skin in the game. If they pay for at least part of their higher education, they will own it, and they will treat it accordingly—seriously and with a will to succeed. I also don't think any politician who promises the idea of free college really understands how the rest of America works. It is a hollow promise that sounds swell to the right people, but free college for everyone is simply unfeasible.

"My folks always said don't make a promise you can't keep," I told the progressive activists at the Center for American Progress' Ideas Conference in 2019. "Rural Americans appreciate hard work, and they appreciate talking truth. Unrealistic promises of things like totally free colleges or jobs for everybody at a living wage doesn't make sense in rural America, because it *doesn't make sense*. You've got to figure out how to get that done, and I don't see how you do it with just words."

In Big Sandy, as in so many communities across Montana, you lose the trust of your neighbors if you break a promise just once. Most of us also expect honesty, and we set reasonable expectations. If I'm going to buy a used pickup from someone in town, I expect the seller to tell me exactly what's wrong with it. If he doesn't shoot me straight, word will get out, and he probably won't be able to sell anything else ever again.

The US government is in a league of its own when it comes to broken promises for countless Americans who live in sovereign nations across rural America. It has a contractual duty to uphold its trust responsibilities to recognized Indian tribes. The federal agreements made with these governments weren't one-time deals; they were perpetual commitments to people who gave up their land, their cultures, and their languages in exchange for self-determination—a guarantee of health care, education, and economic viability. That's a promise that the US government has, for generations, denied to countless indigenous Americans.

Today the federal government must live up to those promises, because it made deals that don't sunset. Yet across many Native American communities in this country, access to basic health care is still dangerously subpar—to the point that US citizens *die* when they get sick. Jobs are scarce—to the point that US citizens have grown accustomed to destitution. Quality public education is a challenge—to the point that too many students simply give up. None of these things should ever happen in America, yet the federal government still lacks the resources and leadership it needs to fulfill these promises. It's why I lost my cool with Rear Admiral Michael Weahkee of the Indian Health Service in 2017. It's why I've always appreciated every minute of my time on the Senate Indian Affairs Committee. It's why I listen to the governments of Native American people. We have more work to do.

And of course, we need the federal government to serve as chief steward of the majority of America's vast public lands. Try as they might, and as bewildering as it is to me, powerful forces are still at work advocating the transfer of federally owned lands to the jurisdiction of individual states, which clearly don't have the financial resources needed to manage them. The idea, then, is to force states to sell off those lands for additional revenue and to relieve themselves of the financial burden of managing them, thus opening the door to private development, mineral exploration, and refusal of access. In this regard, the federal government protects our national parks, national forests, BLM lands, battlefields, wildlife refuges, and wilderness areas from wealthy individuals, corporations, and the constant zeal to extract and develop America's last best places.

Montana is home to about twenty-seven million acres of land owned by the federal government—much of it accessible to hikers, hunters, anglers, boaters, skiers, and wildlife watchers. In Montana, you don't have to pay private landowners to hunt or fish. You simply go outside and enjoy our public land with the proper paperwork and harvest what you're lucky enough to find or catch. You'll find out-of-work itinerants and billionaires fishing alongside each other on Montana's world-class rivers. Public lands are one of America's great equalizers; all of us own these places and have a right to access them; which means we also have a responsibility to them. We have a responsibility to use their resources judiciously; we have a responsibility to drink deeply but tread lightly; to leave them—as Dad taught us boys—better for our kids and grandkids. Over the years, the value of Montana's public lands has transcended partisan politics—as it should. We need the government to keep our public lands public.

And sometimes for the government, finesse and basic manners is what matters most to the people we serve. In 1990, another meat inspector arrived at the farm, just as one of my clients was leaving; their pickups passed each other on my long driveway. As soon as I saw the inspector's government plates, it felt like the story Dad had told hundreds of times about the inspector who arrived unannounced two decades earlier.

"You Jon Tester?" the man asked, getting out of his truck.

"Who's looking for Jon Tester?" I replied.

"I'm with the Montana Department of Agriculture," the man answered. "And I'm here to shut down the butcher shop on this property."

"Come on inside," I said. "I'm Jon Tester."

To my surprise, the inspector took me up on the invitation and sat down at my kitchen table. I intended to keep the meeting civil and to defuse the situation as best I could without losing my temper. I quietly promised myself not to react like Dad would have.

"Our business is a custom butcher shop," I coolly explained to the inspector, who sat back in his chair. "We don't sell meat. We custom-process the meat people already own and bring to us. If people don't want to bring their meat to me, they don't have to. They know what my place looks like. They've seen it. My folks went through this charade two decades ago and we got this all cleared up. What's changed?"

Then the inspector leaned forward and said:

"Let me tell you something. I have more authority than the Fish and Game or the Highway Patrol." The inspector paused and looked at me before adding, "You're showing me your butcher shop, Mr. Tester, because I have a gun. I have a permit to carry it. And I know how to use it."

I leaned forward in my chair and there we sat, eyes locked, at the kitchen table inside my house.

"*Let me tell you something,*" I replied. "If my father were here, he'd go get his .357 and he would see if you really knew how to use your goddamn gun. Now I'm not going to do that. But get the hell off my property."

"I'm going to need to look at your shop."

"The hell you will. You're no different from a common criminal on my property."

"I'll get a search warrant."

"You should have asked the Chouteau County attorney about that. You passed him on my driveway about five minutes ago. His beef's in my cooler." Then the inspector stood up. "There is one way I'll show you the place," I added.

"What's that, Mr. Tester?"

"Paul Williams is our county sheriff. You come back here with Sheriff Williams and I'll show you anything you want."

"That's the way it's going to be?"

"That's the only way it's going to be."

The inspector grumbled and finally left, teaching me a powerful lesson in government overreach. A few weeks later another State of Montana pickup truck pulled into our yard. *Here we go again*, I thought. The inspector parked in front of my butcher shop as I refueled my tractor, and he said my name at least five times as he walked up. I realized this inspector, unlike the last one, was trained in psychological disarmament by using my name. He was a much more respectful and reasonable guy who politely asked to see my shop without any threats or prejudgments. I happily showed the gentleman inside.

"You're good to go," the second inspector said. He told me we had a clean bill of health after I assured him that if any meat fell on the floor, which rarely happened, we threw it away.

"You don't need a license to operate this place," the new inspector concluded. "Thanks for the peek. Best of luck."

Our butcher shop as a family business didn't survive my entry into politics, anyway. We stopped cutting meat for neighbors in 1998, as I ran for the Montana Legislature. I simply ran out of time. We formally closed down the whole operation in 2006.

CHAPTER 12

Sleeping over a Volcano

Between June and October 2012, more than 89,000 ads influencing Montana's Senate race ran on local TV networks across our state, more than any other Senate race in the country.[1] The first ads attacking me actually started airing in 2011. During the first three weeks of October, when 25,000 ads bombarded the airwaves, virtually every commercial break featured back-to-back political ads.[2] Local auto dealerships and furniture stores complained there were no decent slots left for them to buy, and our race had driven up the overall cost of TV advertising statewide. TV stations profited handsomely. After Election Day, some of Montana's TV executives thanked me and my challenger, Congressman Dennis Rehberg, for helping bankroll the cost of their newly remodeled studios.

In all, a record $47 million was spent on Montana's 2012 Senate race, almost three and a half times more than the $14 million spent in 2006. That meant candidates and special interests spent a whopping $97 per vote in Montana in 2012.[3] And much of that money went to advertising—mostly on TV. As much as folks howl about their disdain for political TV ads, especially the negative ones, the ads aren't going away any time soon. That's because political TV ads, especially the negative ones, *work*.

Anonymously funded "dark money" organizations sponsored many of the TV ads that saturated our state in 2012 and again in 2018. The dark money ads were paid for by special interests—often wealthy individuals and corporations. Most of the ads in 2012 benefited Rehberg. But many of them were meant to benefit my campaign too. That's the problem with dark money; it's a race to the bottom. As much as I oppose the expenditure of unlimited, anonymous money in politics, I don't have any say in the matter. Because dark money is independently spent money, campaigns are, by law, not allowed to coordinate or to even know about the strategies of independent organizations that sponsor political ads on a candidate's behalf.

That's why it was a complete surprise to us when in October 2012 an unknown organization called the Montana Hunters and Anglers Leadership Fund launched a nearly $500,000 TV ad campaign propping up Montana's Libertarian US Senate candidate, Dan Cox. Even Cox knew his candidacy was a long shot, but like most Montana Libertarians, he was running on principle. The idea behind the Hunters and Anglers ads, apparently, was to siphon disenchanted conservative voters away from Rehberg, who struggled with low approval ratings. Fewer votes for Rehberg meant a better chance for me. Cox, who never paid a penny for a single TV ad, said he "couldn't have put together a better commercial against Rehberg."[4]

So what happened between 2006 and 2012? What turned on the firehose of political spending full blast? Why are we still in a rush to the bottom, where too many candidates win or lose by the powerful influence of special interests and their dark money? The need to reform campaign financing to shine light on dark money, rein in political spending, and limit corporate influence in politics is the most urgent issue facing America's political future. Montana's own political history, colored by the flamboyant Copper Kings, who made billions as the world became electrified at the turn of the last century, has already taught us powerful lessons about greed and power and corruption. All Americans can learn from them.

On the evening of June 28, 1907, the great Samuel L. Clemens attended a dinner party at the elite Union League Club in New York City. Clemens had reluctantly accepted an invitation to the banquet, held in honor of William Andrews Clark, one of the world's wealthiest men.

That small dinner party in New York City might have been lost to history had the seventy-one-year-old Clemens, writing under his better-known pen name, not described the evening in his *Autobiography of Mark Twain*. According to Twain, Clark had just lent to the Union League Club a small part of his priceless collection of European art—worth an impressive $100,000. But Twain pointed out that Clark made a staggering $30 million per year (more than $800 million per year in today's money).[5] When the club's president announced that the cost of exhibiting the art exceeded museum ticket sales, Clark dramatically reached into his pocket and gave the club $1,500, then delivered a painfully long, self-aggrandizing speech.

"With forty years' experience of human assfulness and vanity at banquets," a disgusted Twain wrote, "I have never seen anything of the sort that could remotely approach the assfulness and complacency of this coarse and vulgar and incomparably ignorant peasant's glorification of himself."[6]

Who was the coarse and vulgar man Twain despised so much? William Andrews Clark was at the time one of America's least popular US senators. Senator Clark, described by the historian Joseph Kinsey Howard as an "intelligent, efficient, ruthless" man who "had no humor and no vices," was one of Montana's three Copper Kings.[7] A brilliant businessman, Clark was a pioneer in the pursuit of copper mining, and he quickly amassed an enormous share of it along with his bitter rival, Marcus Daly, and the young Frederick "Fritz" Augustus Heinze. All three of these men called Montana home.

William Clark, a Democrat, first ran unsuccessfully for a seat in the US Senate in 1889, then again in 1893. He narrowly lost the second time and blamed his defeat on Daly's powerful influence over (and, apparently, bribery of) Montana legislators, who, back then, elected US Senators. So Clark threw his name into the hat again in late 1898. Then on January 10, 1899, state lawmakers held a hearing to investigate several concerning rumors about Clark's candidacy.

"People of Montana, you are sleeping over a volcano," Senator Fred Whiteside of Flathead County declared in a dramatic speech in the Montana State Capitol. "Are you going to elect a scoundrel unqualified to the United States Senate, or are you going to elect an honest man? The same corruption now existing in Montana caused the streets of Paris to run with blood. Have the people of Montana gone mad that they regard bribery as a virtue and condone the crime of a man because he is rich?"[8]

Then Whiteside held up three envelopes, which he said were given to him by Clark's operatives.

"Members of the joint assembly," he said, "I have in my hands $30,000 of bribery money; money used in the candidacy of W. A. Clark of Butte." The committee unsealed the envelopes and pulled out thirty crisp $1,000 bills, one by one, as spectators gasped.[9] For months to follow, questions swirled about exactly whose money it was and what, exactly, it was supposed to buy. This was, you might say, the most flagrant display of dark money in Montana's history.

Turns out, the cash was Clark's, and dozens of lawmakers accepted similar bribes in exchange for their support in sending the copper king to Washington. In fact, as history later revealed, Clark shelled out $431,000 to buy the votes of forty-seven lawmakers, who received an average of $9,100 apiece (more than $280,000 apiece in today's dollars!).[10]

Nonetheless, despite all sorts of unanswered questions, a majority of Montana legislators on January 28 elected William Clark to represent our state in the US Senate. Clark's own propagandist newspaper, the *Butte Miner*, reported that in snow-covered Helena that Saturday evening, "thousands of men, women and children were on the streets cheering, and the music of brass bands added to the noise."[11]

The US Senate had its own questions about the circumstances surrounding Clark's election and launched a months-long investigation. The entire country followed the scandal. On April 23, 1900, the Senate Committee on Privileges and Elections (a committee that no longer exists—maybe it should!) unanimously determined that Clark had bribed lawmakers and should be expelled from his seat.[12] On May 15, the committee's chairman called for a full Senate vote on a resolution to unseat Senator Clark.

Exactly a half hour before debate was scheduled to begin, Clark spoke on the Senate floor. A newspaper account says he spoke quietly as "tears welled to his eyes and his voice trembled with emotion." Clark accused the committee of "irrelevant, malicious and perjured testimony" as it reached the unanimous conclusion that he wasn't fit to serve in the Senate. Still, Clark announced he was stepping down. Then he shared his resignation letter, which read:

> Conscious of the rectitude of my own conduct and after a critical examination of all evidence taken by the committee . . . I am unwilling to occupy a seat in the senate of the United States. . . . Self-respect and due regard for the opinion of my associates, and a sense of duty to the people of the State of Montana, demand that I should return the credentials.[13]

And with that, Montana's US Senate seat became vacant—for a few hours.

Several days earlier, Clark had mailed his resignation letter to Montana, knowing that it would arrive while Montana's governor, Robert Smith, was away in California on official business. Smith was actually lured to California as part of Clark's elaborate plan, and his absence from Montana meant the lieutenant governor, Archibald Spriggs, Clark's friend, was temporarily serving in the capacity of acting governor. And on May 15, the *same day* Clark resigned from the Senate, Acting Governor Spriggs received Clark's letter and responded with a telegram back to Clark that read:

> *I have the honor to inform you that I have this day appointed you to fill the vacancy in Montana's representation in the senate of the United States.*[14]

Word of the scheme quickly spread across the country, and a pissed-off Governor Smith immediately boarded a train back to Montana to try to unscramble the mess.

"It is a sneaking and contemptible way to do business," Governor Smith fumed. "Clark, who is a millionaire, and his gang, are underhanded and a set of scoundrels, and would stop at nothing to gain their ends. I do not believe in sending a man to Congress who is not in harmony with the people and their interests."[15]

On May 18, immediately after returning to Montana and officially as its governor again, Smith sent his own telegram to Clark:

> *I have this day disregarded and revoked your appointment as United States senator made by Governor Spriggs on the 15th as being tainted with collusion and fraud, and have this day appointed Hon. Martin Maginnis, United States Senator, to fill the vacancy caused by your resignation.*[16]

Governor Smith sent a similar cable to the US Senate, igniting a constitutional crisis in Montana. For the remainder of the year both William Clark and Martin Maginnis, who previously served as a territorial representative to Congress, claimed to be Montana's US senators (along with Montana's *other* US Senator, Thomas Carter, who was duly elected without scandal in 1895). Credentials for both Clark and Maginnis were presented to the Senate, but the Committee on Privileges and Elections tabled those credentials, refusing to seat either man.[17]

In the middle of the scandal, on November 12, 1900, Marcus Daly passed away in New York City, just shy of his fifty-ninth birthday. With Daly out of the way and with a new state legislature in place, William Clark saw a fourth opportunity to finally win his prize. On January 16, 1901, with fifty-seven of ninety-three legislators' votes, Clark again won election to the US Senate.

This time Clark returned to Washington and took his oath on March 4, without objection. He served a single, uneventful six-year term in the Senate. Clark's tenure was mostly forgotten by history until Mark Twain suffered through Clark's speech at the Union League Club just a couple of months before the senator's retirement in 1907.

"He has so excused and so sweetened corruption that, in Montana, it no longer has an offensive smell," Twain wrote of Clark. "His history is known to everybody; he is as rotten a human being as can be found anywhere under the flag; he is a shame to the American nation, and no one has helped send him to the Senate who did not know that his proper place was the penitentiary, with a chain and ball on his legs."[18]

In 1899, not long before Marcus Daly's death, William Rockefeller (US senator Jay Rockefeller's great-great-uncle) and Henry Huttleston Rogers, both directors of the Standard Oil Company, formed the powerful Amalgamated Copper Company. Amalgamated bought most of Daly's interest in the Anaconda Copper Mining Company, which already owned most of the copper mines in Butte. Amalgamated Copper, one of the largest trusts ever created, was poised to grow even bigger.

Montana's third copper king, the young Fritz Heinze, wasn't about to be squeezed out by the massive trust. He called Amalgamated Copper "the greatest menace that any community could possibly have within its boundaries."[19] Heinze owned United Copper, a smaller, independent mining company, and he too knew how to grease the wheels of industry by buttering up judges who then ruled in his favor. Heinze leveraged those decisions to weaken Amalgamated Copper's growing power and influence.

So in 1909 the Amalgamated Copper Company turned to the Montana Legislature, dispatching shrewd lobbyists to Helena to successfully muscle through House Bill 160. The controversial legislation allowed corporations like Amalgamated to own stock in an unlimited number of other corporations, thus legalizing monopolies.

In December 1909 the *Montana News*, a now-defunct paper published by the Socialist Party of Montana, reported on a new $25 million enterprise, the Big Blackfoot Lumber Company, incorporated in the wake of House Bill 160.

"Every director in the company is an Amalgamated Copper company official," the *Montana News* reported on December 16. "The articles of incorporation give this company unlimited power. In fact it is a trust organized to gobble up the state and other corporations."

The long fingers of the Amalgamated Copper Company wrapped around the 1911 session of the Montana Legislature too. That session focused on electing a new US senator. The Republicans had lost in the 1910 legislative elections several months earlier, and through dozens of votes, their support went consistently to incumbent Thomas Carter. The Democrats, though, split their votes between Thomas Walsh, a lawyer from Helena, and W. G. Conrad, a banker from Great Falls. Conrad was Amalgamated Copper's choice, and the powerful delegation from Butte loyally stuck to him, resulting in a weeks-long stalemate. For seventy-nine ballots, no Senate candidate earned a majority.[20]

Then on March 2, 1911, someone threw a fourth name into the hat for the Democrats as a compromise: Henry Lee Myers, a relatively unknown, mild-mannered district judge from Hamilton, Montana. Moments later, on the eightieth ballot, Judge Myers earned all fifty-three votes from the Democrats—two more than he needed.[21] Suddenly a US senator-elect, Judge Myers wasn't even aware he had been nominated.

"If the news was a surprise to the state at large," the *Daily Missoulian* newspaper wrote after breaking the news to the judge with a rare long-distance phone call, "it was a surprise even greater to the recipient of [the] honor at the hands of the legislature."[22]

Though many considered Senator Myers friendly to Amalgamated Copper, he was also a progressive; he made early headlines for

supporting the popular election of US senators.[23] Indeed, he was one
of the last US Senators elected by a state legislature. Thomas Walsh,
the Helena lawyer, was Montana's last; lawmakers *unanimously* sent
him to the US Senate on January 14, 1913. Sixteen days later, on
January 30, the Montana Senate quietly approved House Joint Resolution 2, formally ratifying the Seventeenth Amendment. Montana
newspapers barely reported that our state had just done its part to
enshrine in the US Constitution the right of American citizens to vote
for their US senators.[24]

A remarkable group of fed-up Montanans (regrettably, all men)
convened in Deer Lodge, Montana, in June 1911 to form a ground-
breaking organization called the People's Power League.[25] Led by a
Republican newspaper editor, Miles Romney, the league picked up
steam throughout the year and into 1912, attracting hundreds of new
members from across the spectrum of political ideologies; among
them, three sitting judges, union leaders, the Socialist mayor of Butte,
future Democratic US senator Thomas Walsh, education leaders, and
other independent newspaper editors.

This new coalition had had it with the influence of the copper
empire, its billionaire kings, its "assful" senators, its surprise senators, its lobbyists, their stalemates, and their ability to buy influence
from lawmakers who were never truly held accountable to the people
they were supposed to serve. So the People's Power League collected
enough signatures to put on the November ballot a lengthy series of
election reforms it called the Corrupt Practices Act.

William Clark's newspaper, the *Butte Miner*, of course called the
Corrupt Practices Act "drastic" as it spelled out the law's sweeping
reforms.[26] Officially, the initiative was designed to "limit candidates'
election expenses; to define, prevent and punish corrupt and illegal
practices in nominations and elections; to secure and protect the pu-
rity of the ballot; to provide for furnishing information to the electors
and to provide the manner of conducting contests for nominations and

elections in certain cases."[27] That sounded pretty good to corruption-weary Montanans.

On November 5, 1912, voters overwhelmingly supported the measures by more than 75 percent of the vote.[28] Montanans that day sent a clear message about the future of politics in Big Sky Country: people and their ideas, not corporations and their money, would rule our democracy. A few days later the *Daily Missoulian* editorialized in favor of the Corrupt Practices Act, asserting the new law "will effectually end the system of saloon campaigning which has made possible the rule of the boss in Montana."[29]

Montana's Corrupt Practices Act stood on the books for nearly a century, until the US Supreme Court switched the track of American politics when it handed down its disastrous *Citizens United v. Federal Election Commission* decision in early 2010. The Supreme Court sided with the organization Citizens United, a conservative nonprofit that argued that secret spending by corporations, labor unions, and nonprofit organizations to influence American elections is free speech protected by the First Amendment. The court had already determined that money was speech in another disastrous decision, *Buckley v. Valeo.*

Citizens United was the decision that broke the dam and flooded the politics of our entire country with anonymous, unaccountable dark money campaign expenditures. It allowed so-called super PACs to spend unlimited gobs of money influencing our elections. My friend Bob Brown, a Republican and a former Montana secretary of state, had sharp, wise words in the days following the *Citizens United* decision, calling it a "mortal threat to Montana's 1912 people-made law, and similar laws in 22 other states":

> The [*Citizens United*] decision, dealing directly with laws banning corporate independent expenditures in political campaigns, affirmed that the legal personhood of corporations entitles them to the same First Amendment right to freedom of expression as is afforded to human beings . . . now corporations have the individual right to directly weigh into

any political campaign—federal, state or local—and spend as much as they want to. . . . The inequality of this is breathtaking. A multibillion-dollar, multinational "corporate citizen" can buy unlimited political air time while many living, breathing "common citizens" couldn't afford a high-powered megaphone.[30]

On October 10, 2010, a Montana district court judge twisted the knife, declaring Montana's 1912 law banning corporate influence over elections *unconstitutional*. The decision was in response to a lawsuit against then–attorney general Steve Bullock by the Western Tradition Partnership (WTP). Founded in Colorado in 2008 by a former Montana congressman, Ron Marlenee, and secretly funded, WTP described itself as "a no-compromise grass-roots organization dedicated to fighting the radical environmentalist agenda."[31] WTP launched vicious, anonymously funded attack mailers, often against Republicans in contested primaries whom WTP deemed impure.[32]

In late 2011 the Montana Supreme Court overturned the *Western Tradition Partnership v. Bullock* decision, saying the district court "erroneously construed and applied the *Citizens United* case." That meant the Montana Supreme Court effectively restored our ban on corporate spending by upholding the 1912 Corrupt Practices Act. Our corruption law specifically stated that corporations "may not make a contribution or an expenditure in connection with a candidate or a political committee that supports or opposes a candidate or a political party."[33]

Western Tradition Partnership had, by then, changed its name to American Tradition Partnership, and argued that "Montanans do not forfeit their freedoms of speech and association simply because they associate as a corporation." But as the Associated Press reported on December 31, a majority of the Montana Supreme Court sided with Attorney General Bullock:

The Montana court agreed with Bullock's argument that past political corruption, led by the famed Butte "Copper

Kings" that dominated state politics long ago, gives Montana a compelling interest in regulating corporate spending. . . . The Montana Supreme Court argued there are plenty of ways for corporations to engage in politics, without funneling anonymous money into the process.[34]

For the record, those state supreme court justices were Montana Chief Justice Mike McGrath and justices Brian Morris, Patricia Cotter, Mike Wheat, and Jim Rice.

The first test of *Citizens United* came just a few weeks after the Montana Supreme Court's decision. On February 9, 2012, lawyers for American Tradition Partnership asked the US Supreme Court to stay the Montana decision, claiming "immediate relief is needed to prevent irreparable harm to the Corporations' First Amendment free-speech right." They accused the Montana Supreme Court of "an obvious, blatant disregard of its duty" to follow *Citizens United*.[35]

Without even hearing the case, the US Supreme Court on June 25 responded by overturning the Montana Supreme Court's *American Tradition Partnership v. Bullock* ruling, saying "there can be no serious doubt" that the *Citizens United* decision applies to Montana's Corrupt Practices Act. That ruling hit Montana hard: the Supreme Court formally and finally threw out our century-old, people-passed law. Five justices—Kennedy, John Roberts, Samuel Alito, Antonin Scalia, and Clarence Thomas turned their backs on the will of Montanans who were fed up by the long history of our own corrupted government. Justices Stephen Breyer, Ruth Bader Ginsberg, Sonya Sotomayor, and Elena Kagan dissented.

"This Court's legal conclusion should not bar the Montana Supreme Court's finding, made on the record before it, that independent expenditures by corporations did in fact lead to corruption or the appearance of corruption in Montana," Breyer said.[36]

Back in Montana, that decision supplied more powerful weapons to the special interests battling over the airwaves and inside mailboxes of Montana voters. Many voters, saturated by messages from all sides, tuned out of important political discourse. I believe that is part of the overall strategy of those who believe corporations have the same rights as people: the more people shut themselves out of politics, the more powerful wealth becomes.

That summer an organization called Stand with Montanans launched another bipartisan effort to gather enough signatures to put a citizens' initiative on the 2012 ballot. Organizers successfully got the signatures needed to put Initiative 166 up for a vote that November. Its formal language said:

> I-166 establishes a state policy that corporations are not entitled to constitutional rights because they are not human beings, and charges Montana elected and appointed officials, state and federal, to implement that policy. With this policy, the people of Montana establish that there should be a level playing field in campaign spending, in part by prohibiting corporate campaign contributions and expenditures and by limiting political spending in elections. Further, Montana's congressional delegation is charged with proposing a joint resolution offering an amendment to the United States Constitution establishing that corporations are not human beings entitled to constitutional rights.[37]

I took that charge to heart. In June 2013 I introduced an amendment to the US Constitution stating, "The words people, person, or citizen as used in this Constitution do not include corporations, limited liability companies or other corporate entities."[38] That same day, I also cosponsored another constitutional amendment by Senator Tom Udall of New Mexico allowing the US government to "regulate and set reasonable limits on the raising and spending of money by candidates and others to influence elections."[39] Sadly, neither amendment has gotten any real traction in any Congress since. But I still bring up the importance of overturning *Citizens United* any chance I get.

"Some people think that *Citizens United* should be left alone because it helps Republicans, others will tell you that in time it will help

Democrats," I said during a Senate hearing before the 2012 election. "I will tell you today that this is disastrous for our democracy."

I also spoke about the history of Senator Clark and his success in literally buying his election in 1899. With this decision, special interests, dark money, and wealthy corporations again have free rein to do what they had done in the earliest days of our statehood. And they could do it without transparency.

"Transparency and accountability keep people like William Clark from being able to buy something that all Americans are entitled to no matter how much money they have: the power to vote," I added. "The Supreme Court's decision means we're back where we were in the past, when seats in Congress were up for sale."[40]

On Election Day 2012, Montanans overwhelmingly approved Initiative 166, which declared that corporations are not entitled to constitutional rights, with 75 percent of the vote share—the same margin by which voters had approved the Corrupt Practices Act a century earlier.[41]

As it was more than a century ago, campaign spending today is a rush to the bottom in Montana and across America. The billions of dollars spent today, however, are fueling an enormous imbalance in America's political landscape, pitting enormous, anonymous money against increasingly disenchanted voters in a stew of confusion, devious campaign tactics, and negative—but powerfully effective—messaging.

We should have learned from our past. Instead, we are forcing candidates to campaign against big money in their work to represent people. And while candidates spend countless hours raising money, away from the responsibilities they owe their constituents, special interests are at work even harder, bringing the unfortunate vicious cycle full circle. And in the end, the people lose.

Without a change to the Constitution, the political system in place today is only going to get worse. It creates a paralysis for lawmakers. In blue states, elected folks are afraid of being attacked by the Left. In red states, they're afraid of being attacked by the Right. Everyone is afraid of making decisions, because they worry that well-funded special interests will go after them. Big money creates an environment in which bills and amendments are brought to the Senate floor or kept off the floor because of the dollars supporting or opposing them. And in the judicial branch of government, political-minded judges are making the problem only worse. All of this has transformed the "world's greatest deliberative body" into a shell of what it once was. Senators Mike Mansfield, Lee Metcalf, or Burton K. Wheeler would have a hard time recognizing the US Senate today.

In addition to sponsoring a constitutional amendment to undo the *Citizens United* decision, I've pushed multiple bills to shine more light on dark money and to reform the way we spend money. Without champions on the other side of the aisle—champions like the late John McCain—such reforms will never be possible. I ask all my colleagues to put aside politics for just a minute to consider the fundamental reforms we owe our kids, or else we are doomed to be a nation run by rotten billionaires, not duly elected citizen-legislators.

America, we are indeed still sleeping over a volcano.

CHAPTER 13

The Maverick

A little over three decades before my grandfolks arrived in Chouteau County from the Red River valley, Edward and Amelia Rehberg arrived in the Montana Territory from Prussia and settled on a ranch outside Helena with their seven young kids. This was the first of the five generations of Montanans that Congressman Dennis Rehberg claimed in his political pedigree, and because Rehberg's family history was such a part of his campaign schtick, the journalist Ray Ring spent much of 2012 searching through old, handwritten archives. "The facts I discovered complete the picture in a startling way," Ring wrote in *High Country News*.[1]

Ring discovered that, in August 1885, Edward Rehberg took his ten-year-old daughter Clara into town to seek medical care after she was severely beaten at home with a belt and an iron "stove-lifter." Whoever was actually to blame for beating Clara is lost to history, but she died from painful, infected wounds a few weeks later. Both Edward and his second wife, Louisa, faced murder charges. A jury cleared Louisa, but after a series of trials, Edward was convicted of manslaughter and sentenced to five years of hard labor. But then the territory's supreme court released him in 1887, concluding, "The circumstances do not point to the defendant more than to any other of the persons capable of committing the crime (of whom there were several about the premises) as its perpetrator. The evidence does not certainly satisfy the mind to a moral certainty that the defendant was guilty."[2]

A couple of years before all this happened, amid whatever violence he may have faced at home, nine-year-old Albert J. Rehberg, the "second-generation Montanan" great-granddad of Dennis Rehberg, ran away and struck out on his own in Montana. And so began Rehberg's colorful story in the Big Sky State—a story he carefully cultivated over his long career in Montana politics.

Rehberg began that career in a politically muscular household. His father, Jack, a Montana legislator, unsuccessfully ran twice as a Republican for the US House of Representatives. Immediately after graduating from college in 1979, Dennis went to work for Montana congressman Ron Marlenee, then took over his family's sprawling ranchland in 1982. In 1984 he challenged and beat a veteran Republican incumbent named Harrison Fagg in the GOP primary for a Montana House seat. Rehberg and his team of volunteers knocked on every door in his Billings district and left behind flowers for "the lady of the house."[3] A few months later, after just turning twenty-nine, Rehberg handily won that seat with 77 percent of the vote.[4] As a state representative, Rehberg successfully and forcefully ran Conrad Burns's Senate campaign in 1988. And in June 1991, Governor Stan Stephens appointed the thirty-five-year-old rising star to be his lieutenant governor. That was also the year the Montana press started reporting Dennis Rehberg's status as a "fifth-generation Montanan."[5] He continued serving as lieutenant governor when Marc Racicot, a Republican, was elected governor in 1993.

Clearly, Rehberg groomed himself for a career in politics. He had his early licks with controversy too. In 1994, he faced stinging national criticism when he answered a question during a meeting in Anaconda, Montana, about the future of funding for the nearby state hospital. Whatever "going viral" was called back in 1994, that's what happened to Rehberg's unfortunate answer:

Some of the problems are probably even more serious than AIDS is, but it's the social ill that the public has determined on their behalf. The problem with AIDS is, you get it, you die—so why are we spending any money on the people that get it, when we can't even take care of the people who we can fix? Because we don't have enough money, yet society has made the determination we are going to spend money on AIDS.[6]

Rehberg quickly backpedaled and tried to clarify those remarks, telling a reporter the next day that it was "his way of pointing out the kind of choices he believes the American people will have to make under government-run health care."[7] This was the first of many brushes with careless and clumsy controversy that ultimately closed the book on Rehberg's storied political career.

Rehberg first took a stab at running for the US Senate in 1996, when, as lieutenant governor, he challenged Max Baucus. Back then, pundits said Baucus was one of the most vulnerable incumbents up for reelection. The race got so dirty that in its final days, Governor Racicot told his lieutenant governor's campaign that he was "disturbed and disappointed with the tone, timing and terms of the discussion that have appeared in some political campaign ads."[8] Rehberg had just sent a nasty campaign mailer to Montana households accusing Baucus of being a "deadbeat dad" over a child support dispute from years earlier.[9] But Baucus, a masterful campaign tactician, had more muscle and more hustle. He outraised Rehberg by $2.5 million. He had fifty-three full-time campaign staffers, compared with Rehberg's five. And Baucus had nine campaign offices, compared with Rehberg's one.[10] Bottom line: Baucus outworked Rehberg and ultimately defended his seat on Election Day, winning by just under twenty thousand votes.[11]

Following his defeat, Rehberg licked his wounds mostly behind the scenes until March 2000, when he announced his candidacy for the US House race. By then, Rehberg seemed to have warmed up his image a bit; he shed his given name, Dennis, and referred to himself by the more congenial nickname Denny, and he appeared in TV ads and on the campaign trail with his adorable baby daughter.[12] That November, Rehberg beat Democrat Nancy Keenan with just over 51 percent of the vote, launching a twelve-year career as Montana's sole member of Congress.[13]

Rehberg, however, wasn't my first challenger in the 2012 Senate race. Montanans hadn't even caught their breath after the 2010 election when a relatively unknown Bozeman businessman named Steve Daines suddenly announced his Senate candidacy on Saturday, November 13, just eleven days after one Election Day and 724 days before the next.[14] That announcement by an eager newcomer didn't sit well with Rehberg. So the congressman apparently struck some sort of deal to play musical chairs: In early February 2011, Daines announced he was switching his candidacy to run for Rehberg's vacant House seat. Problem was, Rehberg's House seat wasn't vacated yet, which confirmed the worst-kept secret in Montana: Rehberg was about to challenge me for the US Senate. And to no one's surprise, he made it official two days later at a GOP banquet on February 5.[15]

That night Rehberg hammered on his familiar themes. Speaking quickly with lots of nervous energy, he reminded his loyal supporters that he was a rancher. "So I know what it's like to fix fence, herd cattle, and be a good steward of the land—and make a small business profitable," he said.[16]

Rehberg also sharpened what became his chief attack over the next twenty months: to tie me to Barack Obama's unpopularity in Montana and to suggest my record was literally identical to the president's.[17] It reminded me of Senator Burns's efforts to suggest that my record was in lockstep with Senator Kennedy's. I've always thought Rehberg's attack strategy was an odd gamble. One of the benefits of my coming home to Montana every weekend and relentlessly working seven long days every single week, all while maintaining my unironic status as a farmer: It's tough to convince anyone who pays even a little attention that I've lost my way. Voters simply didn't believe it, nor should they—it wasn't ever true.

My strategy was to simply keep hard at work and to highlight my own record in Congress. After all, I'd managed to get a decent amount of work done over six years. And I'd managed to do it without becoming accustomed to Washington or giving up a single season on the farm. Early on, I emphasized my record of protecting our basic freedoms. That included my consistent opposition to the Patriot Act, a law Rehberg voted for. I talked often about my record of making decisions that resonated with Montanans—like protecting Social Security and Medicare, cutting debt and closing tax loopholes for the wealthy that Rehberg supported. Dennis Rehberg, I pointed out, also made some pretty self-serving decisions during his six terms in Congress. He accepted five automatic pay increases after promising he wouldn't as a Senate candidate in 1996, he took numerous taxpayer-funded trips overseas, and he leased vehicles in Montana at taxpayer expense, which he characterized as "mobile offices."[18] Worse, Rehberg voted to give tax breaks to the wealthy and to companies that outsourced American jobs. But two other issues sharply defined the 2012 Senate race in Montana between Dennis Rehberg and me, and both of them began years earlier.

On July 1, 2008, local firefighters successfully tackled a small wildfire burning on the Rehberg Ranch Estates, the former grass-and-sagebrush family ranchland that Rehberg had subdivided to create a neighborhood of high-end homes just north of Billings. The next day, City of Billings firefighters responded to another wildfire in the same lightning-prone area. They put it out, mopped it up, and stayed on scene overnight before leaving the next day. The day after that, on Friday, July 4, the mercury soared to 102 degrees as city firefighters battled the Independence Day rush. That's when another wildfire—presumably the same one—flared up again on the Rehberg Ranch Estates, fanning to 1,200 acres.[19] Billings firefighters again snuffed out the Rehberg Ranch fire before it destroyed any homes. And nobody was hurt—except, as you'll soon see, Rehberg himself.

The second defining event of the 2012 race happened on August 27, 2009. That evening Rehberg, two of his high-level staffers, a state senator named Greg Barkus and Barkus's wife joined the congressman for what he later described as a "working dinner" at a restaurant on the west shore of Flathead Lake. After dinner and drinks, Rehberg and his staffers climbed into the Barkuses' boat for a nighttime ride across the enormous lake to a marina outside Bigfork, Montana.

"I think I'm turned around," Barkus said as he sped his boat across the water, fiddling with his GPS equipment. His speedometer was broken, but he had the boat revved up to 4,000 rpm, which meant he was clipping along as fast as forty-five miles an hour.[20]

Moments later, at a lakeside campsite near Bigfork, campers huddled around a fire heard a loud crash: metal crumpling against solid rock and shattering glass over the roar of a powerful V8 engine. They raced down to the shoreline to see what happened.

"All they could see as they swung their headlamps and flashlights through the dark was a lot of seriously injured people, a lot of broken glass, a lot of blood," the *Missoulian* reported after extensive interviews with the witnesses. "And they could smell gas leaking from the boat, and hear its motor still running."[21]

You may have seen the striking photos from that evening: Barkus's twenty-one-foot boat fully ejected out of the water of Flathead Lake, resting 35 degrees up onto a jagged rock shoreline. I'll never forget when someone said the speedboat "James Bonded" right out of the water. This wreck, however, was no stunt. And this time multiple people were hurt, including Rehberg himself.

Senator Barkus had crashed full speed into the steep shoreline. When the campers ran to the scene, they found Rehberg's deputy chief of staff sitting on rocks nearby, screaming and bleeding from her head injuries. One of the campers found Rehberg's young state director facedown in the water and pulled him out. The twenty-seven-year-old staffer gasped for air and remained conscious for a while, but a helicopter eventually flew him to nearby Kalispell, where he stayed in a coma for ten days. Rehberg severely broke his ankle. He flopped himself out of the boat and dragged himself to the shore with only his cowboy boot keeping his foot connected to his leg. He too was sitting on the rocks when help came, and he had to be lifted up to an ambulance on a backboard. Senator Barkus shattered his pelvis and was still clinging to rocks in the water when he was rescued, and Mrs. Barkus was still on the floor of the boat.[22] Eventually she asked rescuers where her dog was, before realizing she'd never brought the dog.[23]

"I didn't lose consciousness, although I was rolling around like a rag doll," Rehberg, the maverick, recalled in a strange conference call with reporters two weeks after the wreck. "I'm a fast healer."[24] For weeks he hobbled around Capitol Hill with a walker and crutches.

Later, Montanans learned that Senator Barkus's blood-alcohol level clocked in at twice the legal limit—at least 0.16—following the crash.[25] He eventually pleaded no contest to felony criminal endangerment and paid a $29,000 fine. As for Rehberg, he said he downed a couple of pints of beer during the three-and-a-half hour dinner. He had a blood-alcohol level of 0.05, two hours *after* the wreck.[26]

Now fast-forward to the following summer. On July 2, 2010, just before the two-year statute of limitations expired, Congressman Rehberg filed a lawsuit against the City of Billings and the Billings Fire Department.[27] He claimed the firefighters "negligently or intentionally left the fire scene" on his property two years earlier, resulting in that 1,200-acre wildfire that damaged what was destined to become a housing development.[28] And now Rehberg wanted monetary damages from taxpayers. Whatever his reason, needless to say, suing his own constituents was a political disaster for Rehberg. It made Conrad Burns's blowup at hotshot firefighters four years earlier seem like a spark in a furnace.

"It's unfortunate that some folks are mischaracterizing this situation for political gain," Rehberg said after his unsuccessful House opponent that year called on him to apologize. For the rest of us, it was unfortunate that Dennis Rehberg mischaracterized the work of Billings firefighters for his own attempted monetary gain. He dropped his lawsuit in the fall of 2011, after the City of Billings called it "meritless litigation."[29] But for Rehberg, the political damage was already done. And it was about to get worse.

I brought on my 2012 campaign manager in early 2011. Preston Elliott, a Montana native, had worked for me in 2006 and had notched several high-profile campaigns in his stick by the time he returned home. A full year before Election Day, Preston had much of his team in place, and he headquartered the campaign in what we knew was the most politically strategic place for us to win: Rehberg's hometown of Billings. I also hired one of the smartest political minds in the country as my researcher. Christie Roberts spent countless hours carefully scrolling through old records, watching old debates, and reading through newspaper articles and complicated laws every minute of every day—learning everything she could about Dennis Rehberg: how he spoke, how he argued, how he legislated, and, most impressively, *how he thought.*

My campaign team insisted on referring to Rehberg by his full name, Dennis, on a hunch that the congressman switched his preference to "Denny" midway through his political career at the suggestion of some political consultant. "Denny," after all, sounded warmer. Neighborly. Jocular. More trustworthy. To test the theory, my staffers added a question to one of our early surveys asking a random sample of Montanans about the difference between "Dennis" and "Denny." Turns out Rehberg's likely advice was right. "Dennis," according to our own polling, was 3 percent less favorable than "Denny." So my campaign staffers set up a jar in the office stuffed with dollar bills; anyone who accidentally said "Denny" had to pay a dollar into the "Dennis Jar." Our using his full name seemed to have frustrated the Montana GOP, which for a short time called me Raymond, my given first name. The problem was, nobody knew who the GOP was referring to.

Our tactic of calling Denny Dennis reminds me of the Right's annoyingly subtle linguistic strategy of using the adjective "Democrat" instead of "Democratic." The "Democrat Party" sounds cold. Perhaps a tad authoritarian. Radical. Yet today that adjective is used by millions of Americans, even if innocently. So I considered my use of Rehberg's actual name my small, more polite way of giving 'em a taste of their own medicine.

Of course, Dennis and I had much more significant policy differences too. Early in 2011, John Boehner, the Republican Speaker of the US House of Representatives, ordained Rehberg chairman of the

House Appropriations Subcommittee on Labor, Health and Human Services, and Education. That meant Rehberg was one of the dozen House "cardinals" in charge of proposing federal spending levels. And Rehberg quickly told Montanans he would use his powerful new chairmanship to fulfill his promise to "defund Obamacare if we're not able to repeal it."[30]

Rehberg often had to walk the fine line of pulling conservative levers while also protecting himself from votes that he knew could hurt him in his Senate race. In the spring of 2011, he was one of only four Republicans who voted against Congressman Paul Ryan's "Path to Prosperity" budget resolution, which would have drastically cut Medicare and Medicaid—both of which remain popular in Montana. A year later in the thick of our Senate race, the Montana GOP leaned in to that decision and ran an ad pandering to Montana's independent voters. The TV ad painted Rehberg as a maverick who "refused to support a Republican budget plan that could harm the Medicare program so many of Montana's seniors rely on."[31] This bothered the hell out of principled conservatives, including the editorial board of the *Wall Street Journal*, which accused Rehberg of selling out. "The Montana Republican Party has been running 30-second TV spots touting Mr. Rehberg as an 'independent thinker,'" the *Journal* wrote in a smoldering editorial on June 27, "and neither word is true."

> The idea that Mr. Rehberg is some kind of maverick is as false as his Pelosi-like claims about seniors and Medicare. According to the National Journal's political rating system, he is more conservative than 81% of the House, while on the Congressional Quarterly's "party unity" scale he has joined his GOP colleagues more than 93% of the time every year except two. His claim to independence is a vote for Beltway business as usual on entitlements, which makes him another wildebeest in the herd that has created trillion-dollar deficits. . . . Better to let Mr. Tester keep the seat, if only for truth in advertising.[32]

At the same time, Rehberg tried his best to live up to his commitment to get rid of the Affordable Care Act. And then some. Chairman Rehberg's budget proposals would have blocked most funding for Obamacare, cut Pell Grants and low-income home heating assistance, and would have completely eliminated Title X funding, which provides family planning and lifesaving health services—like cancer screenings—for millions of Americans, mostly low-income women.[33]

"Without this program, some women would die, and unintended pregnancies would rise, resulting in some 400,000 more abortions a year and increases in Medicaid-related costs," the *New York Times* editorialized in 2012. The *Times* added that Rehberg's controversial spending proposal was "part of an alarming national crusade that goes beyond abortion rights and strikes broadly at women's health in general."[34]

Even worse for Rehberg—at least for his own political career—was his support for House Resolution 1505, a boneheaded piece of legislation that haunted him all the way through Election Day. Called the National Security and Federal Lands Protection Act, the controversial bill would have been worse than the Patriot Act in its scope. HR 1505 would have essentially given the US Department of Homeland Security "operational control" over all federal public lands within one hundred miles of America's borders, granting the federal government authority to build roads and fences, install surveillance equipment and sensors, fly aircraft, and even deploy "forward operating bases" in the name of whatever the DHS secretary considered national security. The bill would have also allowed the government to waive three dozen environmental laws.[35]

My old friend Vic Miller, a Blaine County commissioner who passed away in 2012, called HR 1505 "scary stuff" when he raised a flag about the bill in a 2011 newspaper column. Miller, who represented a county that butts up to the Canadian border, pointed out that the bill's one-hundred-mile security zone would encompass the entire top third of our state. "It's most of the Hi-Line, most of the Missouri River and the Flathead Valley, all of Glacier National Park and the Bob Marshall Wilderness, several national forests and five of the seven Indian nations in Montana," he wrote.

> If [Rehberg and other sponsors] get their way, the federal government would have incredible power to stop timber sales on Forest Service land. [The Department of Homeland Security] could prevent us from snowmobiling or fishing or hunting in our forests. The Department could prevent grazing on the C.M. Russell National Wildlife Refuge. Bureaucrats could kick all the cattle off of BLM land. It would be able to shut down Glacier National Park indefinitely. The Department of Homeland Security would also have the right to ignore all tribal protections for sacred sites. Why? The laws protecting these sites could be ignored.[36]

For a state like Montana, HR 1505 was a glaring example of what Montanans didn't want in their government. It could allow the government to commandeer public lands in a police state, and to literally fly black helicopters over them. Rehberg never successfully explained why he supported the legislation. And all at once he managed to piss off county commissioners, tribes, hunters, conservationists, and especially Libertarians, simply by throwing his support behind an overwhelmingly unpopular bill.

Even Steve Daines distanced himself from the legislation. Without mentioning Rehberg by name, Daines told a conservative radio talk show, "We've got people back in Washington that don't understand the importance here of states' rights."[37] My team and I tracked HR 1505 closely. Through Election Day we called it exactly what it was: a "federal land grab." As it turns out, the folks who supported me were closely tracking it too.

Early on, the outside efforts to help Rehberg kept stumbling. First there was that TV attack ad from the National Republican Senatorial Committee that featured a doctored photo of me shaking hands with President Obama with all five fingers. The blunder resulted in a national news story about the hilarity of the error and, in Montana at least, it destroyed the credibility of the NRSC. "From the made-up photo to the misleading message, the whole ad is an inaccurate picture of Jon," my campaign said.[38]

Several days before Montana's primary election in 2012, the Montana Newspaper Association asked if Rehberg and I might be available to participate in a debate on June 16, just eleven days after the primary. Though a traditional debate (the same one in which I debated Conrad Burns's empty seat six years earlier), the newspaper association hadn't done any early planning; it had appeared there would be no MNA debate in 2012. The head of the organization even admitted my participation might be a long shot given his late notice, and he said Rehberg hadn't committed either. Because I was scheduled to be out of state on the sixteenth, and because I had already committed to a debate hosted by the Montana Broadcasters Association a few days later, on June 24, my campaign told the Montana Newspaper Association no.

Apparently that word got back to the Rehberg campaign. And minutes after the Associated Press declared Rehberg the winner of the GOP primary (despite an alarmingly high 24 percent of Republican voters who supported an unknown challenger named Dennis Teske), Rehberg's people fired off a news release challenging me to the MNA debate.[39] It was a smart, shifty move on their part; they knew I had already said no, and they wanted to embarrass me—perhaps it would give Rehberg an opportunity to debate an empty seat, as I had done. And now I was getting requests from reporters asking if I was going to attend. After thinking about it for a few minutes, I called up Preston and Christie.

"Call their bluff. Cancel whatever we've got planned on the sixteenth and make this happen. Dennis won't expect it." After all, I had already been spending lots of time doing intensive debate prep sessions with my campaign team. Then I had another idea.

"Make sure Dan Cox gets an invite too so folks can hear his perspective. Call up the newspaper association and see if they'll have all three of us on stage. If they say yes, then call Cox and bring him in. Then we announce our first debate on June 16 with *both of them*."

And that's exactly what we did. The sudden likelihood of a real debate with all three candidates excited the Montana Newspaper Association, and sure enough, Cox, the Libertarian Party candidate, was eager to spend some much-needed time in the spotlight. As for our team, we knew the last thing Rehberg really wanted was an actual debate; he simply wanted to outwit me. And he certainly didn't want Dan Cox to be on stage asking tough questions about Rehberg's support for the Patriot Act, REAL ID, and his awful land-grab bill. So the day after the primary, we sent our own press release with the headline:

Tester announces first Senate debate with Rehberg, Cox[40]

By sending that press release, we locked Rehberg into attending a hastily planned, unexpected debate with *both* of his opponents. And it was just a few days away. For me, the suddenly scheduled debate meant only a few more hours of prep time, and I cleared my schedule for it. Debate prep involves locking yourself into a private room with a handful of trusted advisers who role-play a mock debate from start to finish—complete with a moderator who keeps strict time and people to play the parts of your opponents. Then they give you honest feedback. Christie Roberts played Dennis Rehberg. And though she looked nothing like the man, she nailed the part. Christie had studied Rehberg's speech so carefully that for every question, she had memorized his actual answers, with his specific speech patterns and phrases.

"At my town hall meetings I always ask the question: Are you better off than your parents or your grandparents?" Christie would say during each of our debate prep sessions, in full character as Dennis. "And almost every hand in the place goes up. And when I ask a second question: 'Do you think your children are going to be better off than you?' Nobody raises a hand."

The afternoon of the debate, in the wood-paneled banquet hall of Buck's T-4 Lodge in Big Sky, crowds of my supporters and Rehberg's supporters and even some of Cox's supporters flooded into the room, filling all seats and standing shoulder to shoulder against the walls, fighting for space with TV cameras. Christie and my communications team watched anxiously from folding tables along the side with their laptops opened up. Then, during Rehberg's opening statement, he said this about his town hall meetings:

"I started asking the question: Are you better off than your parents or your grandparents? And almost every hand in the place went up. And then I asked a second question: 'Do you think your children are going to be better off than you?' Hardly a hand in the place ever goes up."[41]

At that moment I looked over at Christie, who grinned at me. I grinned back as Rehberg finished his statement, speaking quickly and wearing a tight-fitting suit with all the buttons buttoned up. Whatever he was talking about, I knew I was going to win that debate.

When a panelist asked about Rehberg's support for the *Citizens United* decision, and how it conflicted with Rehberg's stated support for states' rights given that Montana's century-old Corrupt Practices Act was on the line, the congressman missed an opportunity to be an independent thinker. Maybe that's because the organization Citizens United had literally endorsed Rehberg.[42]

"I agree with the *Citizens United* decision because there should be nothing more free than political free speech," he responded as several people in the crowd booed. (This was, by the way, just nine days before the US Supreme Court struck down Montana's Corrupt Practices Act, citing *Citizens United* in its decision.) "When it comes to the federal government and money coming in and out of the state, *Citizens United* was the right decision on the part of the Supreme Court."[43]

On my high school debate team I learned to strike hard at false premises. And one of Rehberg's chief talking points, Christie had discovered, *was* a false premise: his very identity as a rancher. Despite his consistent and frequent claim of being a "fifth-generation rancher," we learned that Rehberg actually gave up cattle ranching when he was elected to Congress in 2000. In 2007, he claimed he was the only goat herder in Congress. But he even gave up his herd of cashmere goats in 2009. According to the Montana Department of Livestock,

Rehberg hadn't bought, sold, or registered any livestock in at least twelve years. His only business, it turns out, was converting his former family ranch into a housing development.[44]

"Agriculture is the number one industry in this state and I'm very, very proud to be a part of it," I said in my closing statement. Then I looked at Rehberg. "Building houses and 'mansion ranchin'' is not ranching."[45]

As soon as our debate in Big Sky wrapped up, I shifted my focus to the next planned debate on June 24. Notably, Rehberg had not yet committed to it, though we had it on our calendar for months. Then, a few days before, Rehberg backed out, citing "scheduling complications" over a couple of out-of-state fundraising events.[46] This forced the Montana Broadcasters Association to cancel the long-planned debate altogether, which resulted in relentless negative headlines for Rehberg.

The Montana Democratic Party made Rehberg's bad press even worse by putting together a video of someone dressed in a chicken outfit and making cameos all over Washington, DC, and Montana holding up a WHERE IS DENNIS REHBERG? sign, edited to the quick rhythm of a goofy song featuring clucking chickens. The video apparently impressed Chris Matthews, who played it on *Hardball*—the same show that had preempted my interview about Iraq to cover the death of Anna Nicole Smith.[47]

In August, Rehberg announced that Senator John McCain would be visiting Great Falls to stump with him. Though I had my share of disagreements with Senator McCain, I, like most Montanans, have always had great respect for the man. And his presence in Montana to campaign against me hurt. So I responded the best way I could: to highlight one of the biggest political differences between John McCain and Dennis Rehberg. McCain, that outspoken old maverick, broke with most in his party and publicly opposed the *Citizens United* ruling. So on August 17, the day of McCain's daylong visit to Montana, *Great Falls Tribune* readers woke up to a full-page, full-color newspaper ad. Our unmissable ad featured a good-lookin' picture of McCain, smiling, with the words:

SENATOR JOHN MCCAIN:
WELCOME TO MONTANA
AND THANK YOU *
FOR STANDING WITH
MONTANANS AGAINST
CITIZENS UNITED

The bottom half of the page featured a picture of Congressman Rehberg and read:

* PLEASE JOIN US IN ASKING CONGRESSMAN DENNIS REHBERG WHY HE SUPPORTS THIS DANGEROUS, OUT-OF-TOUCH SUPREME COURT DECISION.[48]

Our ad also featured Senator McCain's own words from a recent *Meet the Press* interview, when he called the *Citizens United* ruling "the worst decision of the United States Supreme Court in the twenty-first century." Of course, we also included Rehberg's quote from the debate calling *Citizens United* the "right decision."

That morning Senator McCain tweeted: "Pleased to be welcomed to #Montana with a full-page ad from Senator Tester!"[49] Even better, the local TV stations that covered the senator's visit also showed our newspaper ad to their viewers, and they reported on Rehberg's disagreement with McCain on *Citizens United*. That's when I realized it probably wouldn't be the last time I took out full-page newspaper ads to capture the public's attention during a high-profile visit to Montana.

I didn't rely on any high-profile visits to Montana in 2012—with one exception. That year, Pearl Jam held exactly one concert in North America. It was in Missoula on September 30. And once again, the band put on the show because my name was on the ballot. I had dialed up Jeff Ament early that year, and Pearl Jam agreed to host a performance that benefitted my campaign. And because it was Pearl Jam's only 2012 show in North America, it quickly attracted more than six thousand die-hard fans from across Montana and the country, again selling out the field house on the University of Montana campus.

"One thing about a small town is when someone needs help, they get it from all directions," I said while announcing the band's performance date. I needed help, because for star power, Dennis Rehberg had Karl Rove, Charles and David Koch, and John McCain on his side. I at least had Jeff, Eddie, Mike, Stone, Matt, and Boom on mine. "It's that kind of concerted effort that brings people together and gets things accomplished."[50]

Shortly before the show, Jeff and I met for a series of interviews together with local TV and radio stations. He wore a familiar T-shirt for our interviews—the exact same white shirt he had hand-made years earlier with TESTER 2006 in black marker across the front. He had crossed out "2006" and written "2012" underneath. For two boys from rural Big Sandy, we saw a lot in common, politically and practically.

"There's been an occasion when we're in Montana at the same time and we'll have a beer and maybe talk a little politics," Jeff told a morning radio show. "But mostly we'll talk about how the crops are doing in Big Sandy."[51]

In addition to tying me to President Obama, Rehberg relied on another political strategy in 2012: to draw attention to the number of contributions my campaign had received from registered lobbyists. It was hypocritical of me, Rehberg claimed, given that I had made such a stink about Senator Burns's questionable relationship with Jack Abramoff. My stink, Rehberg conveniently failed to mention, wasn't about the fact that Abramoff was a lobbyist; it was about the fact that Abramoff's gifts and favors and contributions *influenced* Burns, quid pro quo. In a rural state with just over a million people, and facing a race that ultimately totaled a whopping $46 million, both Rehberg and I had to rely on contributions from multiple sources, including lobbyists. I accurately disclosed all my campaign contributions and published all my public meetings to ensure accountability through transparency. Rehberg, we discovered, didn't even disclose the occupations of dozens of lobbyists who gave to his campaign as required by federal law.[52] That was his first careless and clumsy mistake in making his lobbyist attack on me stick.

Voters learned of his second mistake in late August, when my campaign was forwarded an audio recording from an anonymous source. The recording was of Rehberg's speech to the American League of Lobbyists during a lunchtime fundraiser in Washington in October 2011. He told the room about how he considered becoming a lobbyist after his 1996 Senate race.

"I almost did it," Rehberg recalled, with someone in the room recording every word. "But a lot of you all's type came to me and said, 'What are you, nuts?' You know, if we had the choice of either run for Congress or be a lobbyist, wouldn't you like to try the Congress first?' And I fell for it, and I ran for Congress. I probably—if I had been smart—I would've said, 'Nah, no, I think I'll stay out of the political arena and go into lobbying.'"

Then, the clincher, which never sounds good if you're running as a Washington maverick:

"I think lobbying is an honorable profession and I thank you for doing it," Rehberg told the lobbyists. "Many of you are part of the solution—are part of turning this economy around and ending the recession, except the government's in your way. They are, in fact, the enemy—they're your senior partner. And that is not what government was intended to do."[53]

Of course, pieces of that recording immediately appeared in TV ads, raising questions about what kind of political career in Washington Dennis Rehberg truly wanted.

In the fall my campaign team turned their attention back to Rehberg's frivolous lawsuit against the City of Billings and its firefighters. Christie had asked the city government how much taxpayers had to spend defending themselves from their congressman. The city attorney responded with an exact number: $20,761.60.[54] Of course, we made that number public, which ignited a whole new round of bad news for Rehberg. And it culminated in several weeks of TV commercials that ran across the state from my campaign and from independent organizations. Anyone who watched TV in Montana in October 2012 saw ad after ad after ad after ad about Rehberg's lawsuit. And for some reason, he insisted his lawsuit wasn't an issue that offended voters.

"I've traveled around Montana over the course of the last two years, in all fifty-six counties, and nobody has brought up the fire, except for *you*," Rehberg angrily claimed during our second debate, on October 8.[55] If that was Rehberg's truth, then his campaign team had done a terrific job of sheltering the congressman from the actual truth; from the opinions of countless angry Montanans, on both sides of the aisle, who were furious over the lawsuit. He made that claim minutes after I asked for a show of hands:

"How many people in this audience are from the city of Billings?" Most of the five hundred people crammed inside the college auditorium raised their hands. "Thank you very much. Congressman Rehberg has sued each and every one of you." Rehberg started fidgeting and rocking back and forth anxiously, which signaled that I had bested him again as I went on. "You don't respond and say 'Thank you' by filing a lawsuit with monetary damages, which is exactly what he did—that's not working together!"[56]

A few days after our Billings debate, Rehberg rolled his enormous campaign RV into Big Sandy for a brief stump speech to a crowd of about a dozen supporters, with an Associated Press reporter in tow. There, in my hometown, he boasted that he would win conservative Chouteau County—my home turf.

"Dennis Rehberg sued taxpayers and firefighters in his own hometown," my campaign spokesman warned, "so he should be careful if he thinks this race is a popularity contest among neighbors." The Associated Press also quoted a Rehberg supporter in Big Sandy who worried, on the record, that the wildfire lawsuit could cost the congressman the election.[57] Still, I couldn't argue with the likelihood that Rehberg could win both Chouteau County and his home turf of Yellowstone County, Montana's biggest.

As both sides fought the most expensive air-wave battle in Montana's history that fall, Preston Elliott and his team were busy making their own history. They assembled one of the most sophisticated field campaigns Montana had ever seen, putting to work thousands of volunteers who knocked on doors and made phone calls all day and every single night. My chief of staff, Tom Lopach, kept me on track raising money to keep up with the unlimited funding that poured in from who knows where to help Rehberg. And through it all, I stuck to my roots. I burned both ends of the candle to bring in the harvest that August, pushing the very limits of physical and mental endurance to run a top-tier Senate race, to be a full-time senator and a farmer—all at the same time.

Of course, all that work came at a cost. I broke down several times emotionally, usually in some motel room with Sharla. Every single minute of every single day had been strategically planned, with no room for flexibility. I was required to be "on" round the clock. There was no room for a single mistake or a slight misstatement. I ran on fumes for ninety days straight leading up to Election Day. But each time I sat in tears on some bed that wasn't my own, Sharla was there to catch me.

"You know what's at stake," she reminded me. Of course I did. The future of America's very democracy was on the line. So was the health care of millions of Americans. Our clean air and water. Opportunities for our grandkids. Those were outcomes that made the exhaustion all worth it. And that's how Sharla kept me going each morning after an emotional evening. By the final few weeks of that almost two-year campaign cycle I had hit a wall, but thanks to Sharla, I still kept my stride.

October brought a pair of unexpected curveballs. The first was that TV ad from the mysterious Montana Hunters and Anglers Leadership Fund. The ad was striking. It mimicked surveillance footage looking down on a boy camping with his dad in the woods. The footage displays "Department of Homeland Security Recording" on the screen. The boy notices the camera watching him from high in the trees and alerts his dad as a narrator says, "Congressman Dennis Rehberg would let the Department of Homeland Security monitor and control access on public lands—millions of acres." The dad spots the camera, grabs his rifle, and aims it at the lens as the narrator continues, "That may look good in Washington, but in Montana, not by a long shot." The dad pulls the trigger and the screen goes black, revealing the words:

VOTE COX
THE REAL CONSERVATIVE[58]

This was just one of several outside efforts to weaken Rehberg by bolstering our third opponent over Rehberg's obstinate support for HR 1505, the disastrous federal land-grab bill. And though the ad was entirely independent from our campaign, our own polling suggested the land-grab legislation was significantly hurting Rehberg. It too was another careless and clumsy mistake.

Also in October an organization called Citizens for Responsibility and Ethics in Washington, or CREW, made headway in its request to make public the presentence investigation report used in the 2011 trial of Senator Greg Barkus. The sealed, 155-page document included photographs, witness statements, toxicology information, and investigators' reports. CREW argued that there was "significant public interest" in disclosing the report, given the crash involved a current candidate for the US Senate.[59]

On Halloween night, less than a week before Election Day, Judge John McKeon released a redacted version of the report, saying:

> Neither this court nor Barkus can ignore the fact that Barkus and Rehberg were public officials at the time of this offense of criminal endangerment, this felony offense involved serious bodily injury and knowingly engaging in conduct that created substantial risk of serious bodily injury and that due to the contested U.S. Senate race, there remains considerable public interest regarding this offense.

Once unsealed, the court documents didn't deal a knockout punch to Rehberg, but they did shed more light on the events of the evening of August 27, 2009. Barkus, the report said, drank two scotches and an unknown amount of red wine that night, before crashing "full speed straight forward" into the rocks at forty-five miles per hour.[60] This raised questions for us about Rehberg's previous claim that he saw "no signs of impairment."[61]

"This report raises more questions about Congressman Rehberg's gross failure of accountability and his dishonesty with Montanans about what truly happened that night," Preston said.

On November 6, after a jam-packed day of getting out the vote, I held my Election Night watch party in Great Falls—this time at the Holiday Inn. And this time, I had no interest in holing up in my hotel room. Instead, I mixed it up with the hundreds of boisterous supporters who crammed into a ballroom-turned-campaign-headquarters full of blue and white balloons and TVs tuned to Election Night coverage. But in several cities across the state, long lines and delayed ballots prolonged results yet again. In Yellowstone County the new ballot-counting machines jammed up and delayed a final tally by days. It didn't take long to realize that we wouldn't know who won the US Senate race until Wednesday at the earliest.

Still, the returns looked good. The early numbers had me up. And the mood in the ballroom was festive. As expected, Montanans overwhelmingly voted for Mitt Romney over Barack Obama, whose race was managed by Jim Messina, Max Baucus's former chief of staff. Despite losing Montana's three electoral votes, Obama easily secured his second term. When one of the TV stations switched over to a live report from Rehberg's watch party in Billings, things in his camp looked dreary. His ballroom was empty, and deflated volunteers were already folding up tables and chairs. Rehberg was nowhere to be seen.

"Wake me up when you figure out who won," I told Preston. And Sharla and I went up to our room.

Working overnight, just as they did in 2006, my ace campaign team crunched the numbers in what they called the "boiler room" down in Billings. Early the next morning, they saw our undeniable victory; there was no way Rehberg could win, and the margin was already much more significant than my win over Senator Burns. Aaron Murphy, my communications director in 2012, spent the morning on the phone with the Associated Press, walking them through our own projections. The AP, however, refused to call our race. They needed more certainty on the numbers from Yellowstone County, which were still coming in.

"The numbers are *good*," Preston told me over the phone as Sharla and I ate breakfast in the hotel restaurant. He, like virtually everyone else on my campaign team, had stayed up all night. I could hear exhausted joy in his voice. "We're going to fuckin' *win* Yellowstone County!"

"No shit? By how much?"

"You win with one vote, boss."

"We're going to take this whole thing?"

"We're going to take this whole thing."

And not because we wanted to, we pulled a page from our own 2006 playbook. If the Associated Press wasn't going to call our race, we were confident enough to declare victory ourselves. We scheduled a news conference at nine a.m. at the Holiday Inn, during which I would announce that I had won reelection. Murph immediately told the AP about our plan. Either the AP could break the news of our win, or they would have to report that we were breaking the news. Moments later, Murph bolted into the restaurant, shaking and out of breath, and showed me the six-word AP news alert that had just blipped on his phone:

HELENA, Mont. (AP)—Montana Sen. Jon Tester wins re-election.

Our nine a.m. news conference suddenly turned into a victory speech, and dozens of local supporters took off work to cram into a little meeting room with a bunch of news cameras to be a part of it.

"Today ends an historic election in Montana," I said, with Christine, Shon, and Mel standing behind me. "Literally tens of thousands of TV commercials, radio ads, fliers in the mail—many of them from big corporations who spent millions of dollars trying to buy Montana's votes. This victory is our victory because it proves neither corporations nor billionaires can buy the state of Montana or buy elections."[62]

I also congratulated Rehberg, calling him "Denny." A few minutes later, President Obama called me from Air Force One to congratulate me, and I congratulated him back on his own reelection.

That morning down in Helena, things were still looking uncertain for Attorney General Steve Bullock. The AP had also refused to declare his victory, though Bullock's race was landing in his court. A couple of hours later, the AP declared Bullock Montana's new governor-elect. He had just beat Republican Rick Hill, a former Montana congressman, to fill the boots of Brian Schweitzer.

I won the 2012 Senate race by exactly 18,072 votes.[63] Rehberg didn't take his loss well. He was, I'm told, convinced he would win. In fact, he never even called to concede the race. Given the vitriol of the previous twenty months, I don't hold it against him.

I run into Denny in the airport every now and then; sometimes we even sit next to each other on the plane. We get along as most Montanans do when they check politics at the door. Sometimes we even exchange war stories with a laugh or two. We don't talk about the 2012 Senate race, when not only did I win Chouteau County, my turf, by 53 votes, but I also won Yellowstone County, his turf, by 488.[64]

CHAPTER 14

"Khaihawana Punk" and Other Game Changers

The most painful moment of 2012 didn't happen on the campaign trail. It happened on December 14. I remember exactly where I was: barreling west toward Bozeman from Billings on Interstate 90 in some rental car with a couple of my staffers.

"Ugh," my state director, Dayna Swanson, said quietly as she scrolled through the news on her phone. "Another shooting. *An elementary school.*" Our car stayed quiet for a moment.

"Kids?"

"Doesn't say. In Connecticut."

"How many?"

"Doesn't say." Dayna swallowed hard. And we didn't say much else for the rest of the drive. Every update throughout the day haunted us as we learned that a sick twenty-year-old man with three powerful guns and loads of ammo murdered twenty first-graders and six of their teachers at Sandy Hook Elementary. First-graders. My own grandson Brayden was in kindergarten, days away from turning six. That day

I kept thinking about him and all the first-graders I'd taught at F. E. Miley Elementary school. *First-graders still believe in Santa Claus.*

But the tragedy hit home several months later, when I met with several grieving parents of the Sandy Hook victims in my office in Washington. They told me about the pain of losing their children. Their families had been torn apart by a man who should never have had access to guns. They wanted limits on ammunition magazines. They asked me to support a ban on assault weapons. And they pleaded for my support for an upcoming amendment offered by Senator Joe Manchin, a Democrat from West Virginia, and Pat Toomey, a Republican from Pennsylvania. The Manchin-Toomey proposal would have ensured that "all individuals who should be prohibited from buying a gun are listed in the National Instant Criminal Background Check System," and that "criminals and the mentally ill are not able to purchase firearms."[1]

As the Sandy Hook parents left my office, Jennifer Hensel and her husband, Jeremy Richman, stayed behind to show me a photograph they carried with them.

"We want you to see this picture of our daughter," Jeremy said, his voice cracking. In the picture, six-year-old Avielle Rose Richman is smiling, sitting on top of a toy John Deere tractor and clutching a piece of watermelon with both hands. The sun lights up her wavy brown hair. Avielle, her parents said, had a spitfire personality and she was fascinated with naming things. She called herself "Bombs Galore" when she dressed up as a superhero, and she named her pet Siamese fighting fish "Khaihawana Punk."[2] I have no idea what that means, but any free-spirited six-year-old who names her fish Khaihawana Punk probably doesn't suffer fools.

After the Newtown parents left, I closed the door and sat down at my desk. My office seemed strangely large and quiet. And I broke down sobbing. It was the first and only time a meeting in my office resulted in that strong of an emotional response. I stayed in there alone for a good hour.

"You respect this like you respect your own life and everything you love," I remembered Dad telling me when I was about eight or nine, as he carefully placed a rifle in my arms. "Because it will take away you or everything you love with one mistake. Understood?" I nodded. "This gun takes away lives. That means you have a responsibility to respect the lives around you—even the gophers and sparrows you gotta shoot. Understood?" I nodded again.

I spent decades making a living with firearms—swiftly and carefully dispatching cows and hogs, each with a well-aimed single shot, before skinning them in my yard and butchering them in my shop. I shoot sparrows that shit all over my hay. Like millions of Americans, I keep guns in my own home. I still believe that the right of law-abiding citizens to keep and bear arms is one of the most powerful checks on the ever-present threat of a tyrannical government ever conceived, which is why our founders put it near the top of our Bill of Rights. Firearms are a deep part of Montana culture, and the third rail of our politics.

But so is some damn common sense.

In 2006 the National Rifle Association endorsed Conrad Burns, citing a tradition of siding with its endorsed incumbent, though I had a strong pro-gun record in the Montana Legislature and even though I considered my position on guns *stronger* than Burns's (he supported the Patriot Act!). In 2012 I tried again to earn the support of the NRA, which carries significant political weight in Montana. But that year the NRA conveniently forgot its tradition of endorsing incumbents. It stayed neutral, endorsing neither Rehberg nor me.

In the spring of 2013, several NRA lobbyists came into my office and asked me how I would vote for the Manchin-Toomey background check amendment. They told me they would score my vote on the measure, meaning a vote in favor would count against a possible endorsement. It was code for, "If you support this, we're comin' after ya." Though the compromise amendment was bipartisan, the NRA called it a "misguided 'compromise'" (with the word "compromise" in *its* quotes).

"Expanding background checks, at gun shows or elsewhere, will not reduce violent crime or keep our kids safe in their schools," the NRA's chief lobbyist wrote to me and all other senators prior to the vote.[3]

After hearing from the parents of the young victims of the massacre at Sandy Hook Elementary, I knew the NRA was wrong. On April 17, I gave the NRA a reason to come after me. I proudly voted for the Manchin-Toomey gun amendment. So did four of my Republican colleagues—Pat Toomey, Susan Collins of Maine, Mark Kirk of Illinois, and the old maverick John McCain of Arizona.[4] But it fell six votes short and failed.

That vote landed me on the NRA's shit list. I could care less. The NRA is no longer an organization committed to Second Amendment rights, or gun safety, or common sense. It's concerned about one thing: money. As with so many other things, the NRA has been corrupted by the broken cycle of money and politics, veering hard to the right with a focus on fundraising and extremism. Everything the NRA does now is designed to raise money by stirring the pot away from the middle, and by tapping into a deep root of distrust and fear. In fact, I believe the biggest threat to legal gun ownership is the NRA's stubborn zero-tolerance policy for common sense. It's forcing the pendulum to swing further to the right, which means at some point it will swing further the other way, swooping right past those of us in the middle who will be stuck wondering where our rights went.

To the National Rifle Association: I won't suffer fools either. Consider me your Khaihawana Punk.

Jeremy Richman never overcame what he and Jennifer called the "infinite pain" of their daughter's murder.[5] On March 25, 2019, he took his own life in the same building that housed the Avielle Foundation.[6] Jeremy and Jennifer started the nonprofit organization to prevent violence by "building compassion through brain research, community engagement, and education."[7] News of the suicide hit me hard; it was an ugly reminder of how cancerous mass gun violence and the aftermath of mass shootings are.

My colleague Max Baucus voted against the Manchin-Toomey amendment. Less than a week later, on April 23, he stunned Montana with surprising news.

"I will have served over forty years, and it's time to come home," Baucus told the *Great Falls Tribune* after announcing that he would not seek reelection in 2014.[8] Max Baucus, first elected to the US House of Representatives in 1974 as a thirty-two-year-old attorney, was elected to the Senate in 1978. Montanans had reelected him five times since. He also held the gavel as the powerful chairman of the Senate Finance Committee. The announcement from Baucus was a game changer in Montana. Which Democrat could successfully replace him?

For a few months, it looked like that candidate might be Brian Schweitzer, our former governor, who spent a few months assembling an entire US Senate campaign team before suddenly and mysteriously pulling the plug on a Saturday morning in July, with an explanation that only raised more questions.

"There are all kinds of people that I think ought to be in the United States Senate," Schweitzer said, adding that he was not one of those people. "I kicked the tires. I walked to the edge and looked over."[9]

Schweitzer's exit made room for a handful of other contenders, including Montana's newly elected lieutenant governor, to run for the vacant seat. Colonel John Walsh, after all, had a powerful profile for a Senate candidate. A native of Butte and the first in his family to graduate from college, Walsh had just wrapped up a solid career as adjutant general of the Montana National Guard. In 2004 and 2005 he commanded a battalion of seven hundred troops in Iraq which, the *Flathead Beacon* reported, meant that insurgents had a target on his back:

> On Oct. 15, 2005, the day Iraq ratified its new constitution, Walsh traveled to a local polling station between Kirkuk and Tikrit. As his five-vehicle convoy was traveling to the next polling place, an improvised explosive device, better known as an IED, detonated in front of Walsh's Humvee. The blast blew the bulletproof windshield into the vehicle and Walsh, who was sitting up front, hit his head on the dashboard.[10]

John Walsh also earned a master's degree from the US Army War College in Carlisle, Pennsylvania. Walsh formally announced his bid to replace Baucus on October 3, 2013, setting up a 2014 race against

Representative Steve Daines, Montana's newly elected congressman. Then, on December 20, another game changer.

"For more than two decades Max Baucus has worked to deepen the relationship between the United States and China," President Obama said while formally announcing that he wanted Baucus to become the next US ambassador to China. "The economic agreements he helped forge have created millions of American jobs and added billions of dollars to our economy, and he's perfectly suited to build on that progress in his new role."[11]

Baucus eagerly accepted the appointment. After becoming the longest-serving US senator in Montana's history, Baucus resigned on February 6, shortly after his colleagues unanimously confirmed him as ambassador.[12] That resignation left Governor Bullock with the rare responsibility of filling an eleven-month vacancy in the US Senate. Later that evening Bullock dialed up Walsh, his fifty-three-year-old lieutenant, and offered him the job. Bullock made his choice public the next day. And on Tuesday, February 11, Vice President Biden administered Walsh's oath of office as a United States senator, then added, "Look forward to working with you, pal."[13]

The *New York Times* delivered the next game changer on July 22, when one of its reporters, Jonathan Martin, confronted Senator Walsh in a hallway with a stack of papers. Martin had lots of well-documented research in his hands; it appeared Walsh had copied much of his 2007 final paper at the US Army War College, word for word from other sources, often without attribution. Turns out, anyone could look up Walsh's fourteen-page paper online. The *Times* broke its story the next day, complete with exhaustive, interactive internet graphics that highlighted Walsh's paper and each of its appropriated passages.[14] The War College immediately launched an investigation.[15] Two weeks later, facing unforgiving criticism, devastating headlines, a crippling slowdown in fundraising, late-night TV jokes, and a series of blistering editorials from Montana newspapers, Walsh ended his Senate campaign. He did so after personally driving from his home in Helena to his campaign headquarters in Billings so he could first tell his staff in person.

"I am ending my campaign so that I can focus on fulfilling the responsibility entrusted to me as your US senator," he then told supporters. He at least wanted to serve out the remainder of his appointed term.[16]

Several weeks later, Montana Democrats replaced Walsh with a state representative named Amanda Curtis as the Senate candidate they wanted on the November ballot. Though a charismatic candidate, Curtis never had the opportunity to catch up to Daines's name recognition or fundraising lead. "The National Democratic Party has effectively ceded the seat to Representative Steve Daines, the Republican nominee," the *New York Times* wrote.[17]

But even that didn't end the public punishment of John Walsh. The US Army War College in October revoked the senator's master's degree and even grinded his name off a plaque listing the school's graduates.[18] Walsh said he accepted the War College's decision, apologized for the plagiarism, and added he was "prepared to live with its consequences."[19]

Sure enough, on Election Day, Daines won by 18 percent—almost 65,000 more votes than Curtis.[20] Walsh called Daines to congratulate him and quietly kept hard at work fulfilling his responsibilities as a senator until early January 2015, when Daines took over. Today, US senator John Walsh is a real estate agent in Helena.[21]

Of course, the sin of plagiarism is a serious one, and you won't hear me defending it, nor will you hear me quickly blame the press about unsavory truths like so many in this country do. The press keeps our entire democracy in check. In the case of John Walsh, however, I have two observations.

First, it's worth noting that the *New York Times* apparently did not find the copied passages in Walsh's War College paper. In late October 2014, after Walsh's career had already unraveled, the head of the National Republican Senatorial Committee participated in a forum hosted by *Politico*. There, *Politico* reported, the NRSC admitted that one of its researchers had actually discovered Walsh's paper, then "gave it to the *New York Times*."[22] If that's true, why didn't the *Times* disclose it? Perhaps when flagship newspapers publish stories about plagiarism, they should disclose whether their research is *original* research.

Second, after Walsh had bowed out of his race amid a storm of media criticism, and as soon as it became clear that Representative Daines would win the 2014 race, most of Montana's political reporters essentially gave up asking Daines tough questions. In fact, Daines sailed right into the "world's most exclusive club" after only a single debate with Amanda Curtis. Now America's president is stress-testing our entire democracy, and millions of Americans don't even believe what the press reports. Today Steve Daines, a loyal and unquestioning supporter of the president, is frequently criticized by Montana's newspaper editorials (as am I, when I deserve it). I wish political reporters would have done a bit more diligence prior to the election of 2014. I'm not suggesting that Walsh was treated unfairly. I am suggesting that Steve Daines got lucky twice; once when GOP researchers gave the *New York Times* a silver bullet, and again when most political reporters simply gave up and wrote off his race.

I'll leave it to history to determine John Walsh's legacy as a US senator. But I hope history does not forget that for a few short months, Montana had as its senator an actual war hero—a man who survived a violent explosion in a Humvee and who commanded hundreds of American soldiers on the other side of the world, and who suffered severely and legitimately from PTSD. Walsh lost several soldiers under his command in war. Once, in the middle of a news conference, he told reporters he kept the names of soldiers he lost in Iraq in his briefcase. He paused, clutched the podium and cried until he collected himself.[23] Walsh told us he struggled to sleep at night and took prescription medications to blunt the pain. He was also the first Iraq veteran to serve in the US Senate, which is something history should celebrate, despite a fourteen-page college paper that wasn't original. And Walsh worked his ass off, for decades, "as a soldier, not an academic." Senator John Walsh is a good man who struck out in the dirty game of hardball politics. And he paid an enormous price for a sin that seems small—especially compared to the record of Donald Trump.

Another high-profile race in Montana changed the political

landscape in Montana in 2014. Montanans that year sent to Congress Ryan Zinke, a former Navy SEAL commander and state senator from Whitefish. As soon as Zinke handily won his election to the House, the political pundits started buzzing that he would be my formidable challenger for the Senate in 2018. As a member of Congress, Zinke steered away from his moderate record as a state senator and into the weeds of the Far Right. He also cultivated a tough-guy image, even going so far as to call himself "Commander Zinke" instead of Congressman (even the title of his 2016 book is *American Commander*).

In early 2014, before Democrats lost control of the Senate, Majority Leader Harry Reid asked me to chair the Indian Affairs Committee. I had served on the committee since my arrival seven years earlier, and I happily accepted the post, which came with its own separate staff and plenty of work to do. My role as chairman meant I worked more directly with Native American tribes, Native Hawaiians and other Pacific Islanders, and Alaska Natives, all of whom shared a common goal: self-determination. Other formidable challenges—including quality health care, nutrition, cultural preservation, community safety, education, and strong economies that provide job opportunities—all revolve around the linchpin of independent self-governance and effective government-to-government communication between tribal nations and the feds. It was also during my tenure on the Senate Indian Affairs Committee when I first heard a growing concern about an alarming trend: thousands of Native American women and girls across the United States and Canada simply vanish. No justice. No accountability. Hardly any investigation. Just . . . gone. Though the Missing and Murdered Indigenous Women and Girls movement had yet to become front-page news, Native communities were raising their voices. They were rightly fed up by decades of inaction.

After the Democrats lost the Senate that November, I became the chairman of an entirely different committee. My job as head of the Democratic Senatorial Campaign Committee required me to lead the way in protecting all incumbent Democrats. My other main task was to find, recruit, and support candidates across the country who could replace a handful of retiring Democrats or who could beat vulnerable incumbent Republicans. Ultimately, the Senate Democrats looked to me to win back the majority we lost in 2014. That meant we would need to win five seats in 2016 (winning four seats would tie the chamber, in which case the majority goes to the party of the vice president). Though the Republicans had twenty-four seats to defend and we only had ten, winning back the majority was one hell of a challenge.

My job at the DSCC required countless more hours of call time in a stuffy little office, dialing for dollars, finding and meeting with candidates, studying polling and voting trends, and working closely with Senate campaigns in all corners of the country. I had a good team in place: my chief of staff, Tom Lopach, became the DSCC's executive director. Christie Roberts started out as the research director and later became my political director, and my former campaign manager Preston Elliott became the DSCC's campaign director.

Together we scoured the country for good candidates, meeting with them in person whenever we could. After all, I had a unique perspective as someone who'd surprised the DSCC back in 2006. I wanted to find leaders who not only could win, but also had real-world experience, authenticity, and political savvy.

In 2011 I invited Lieutenant Colonel Tammy Duckworth—then assistant VA secretary—to speak to the Montana Democratic Party's annual Mansfield-Metcalf Dinner, and she graciously accepted. She gave that speech on her birthday. The next year Duckworth ran for and won a seat serving Illinois' Eighth Congressional District. As a badass congresswoman who lost both legs in an attack on her helicopter in Iraq, Duckworth easily gave incumbent senator Mark Kirk a run for his money in the Land of Lincoln.

I met with New Hampshire's governor, Maggie Hassan, who was eager to take on incumbent senator Kelly Ayotte. Governor Hassan and I both cut our teeth in politics as state senators, and I knew she would be another headache for the GOP. Down in California, Attorney General Kamala Harris was running a powerful campaign to replace Senator Barbara Boxer. And in Nevada, Catherine Cortez

Masto, another whip-smart attorney general, lined up to replace Harry Reid.

My good friend Claire McCaskill and I convinced Missouri's thirty-five-year-old secretary of state to also run for the Senate against incumbent Roy Blunt. Jason Kander, a veteran of Operation Enduring Freedom in Afghanistan, ran one of the toughest and smartest Senate races I have ever seen. In Pennsylvania, I worked closely with Katie McGinty, a former state secretary of environmental protection. In Arizona, Congresswoman Ann Kirkpatrick challenged John McCain. And in Florida, I recruited thirty-three-year-old Congressman Patrick Murphy, a former Republican, to run for Senator Marco Rubio's seat. I also coordinated with two familiar faces: former senators Russ Feingold of Wisconsin and Evan Bayh of Indiana threw their names back into the hat for their old seats in the Senate.

Being the chairman of the DSCC had its upsides too. Because it was a leadership role, I was asked to escort Pope Francis during his joint address to Congress on September 24, 2015—the first time in history a pope had done so. I am not a Roman Catholic, and I was one of several lawmakers who got to escort Francis, but the invitation moved me deeply. I consider the whole experience one of the most profound moments of my entire time in Washington.

After walking Pope Francis into the House of Representatives, I sat near the front and latched on to every word of his well-composed address. It occurred to me, sitting in the chamber among the nation's most powerful and influential people, that this ordinary, unassuming man in a plain white robe wielded more power and influence than any of us—arguably more than anyone else in the world—and he used it gently and frankly, to encourage all of Congress, and the entire country, to "defend and preserve the dignity" of our fellow citizens "in the tireless and demanding pursuit of the common good."

I still think about Pope Francis's speech. It's right up there with Ted Kennedy's speeches, and I listen to it often to remember his advice. Each time I listen, I discover new things about it, and I'm reminded where all of us continue to fall short.

"We must be especially attentive to every type of fundamentalism, whether religious or of any other kind," the pope told us. Today, I realize he was talking about the worsening polarization of the political ideals that divide America. Political fundamentalism, on the right and the left, is splitting us right down the middle. That doesn't mean there are blurred lines between right or wrong, nor does it mean we should always settle for feeble middle ground, nor should we avoid fighting like hell for what we know is right. To me, it simply means that extremism drowns out what the pope called the "spirit of openness and pragmatism."

Francis also spoke sharply about the treatment of immigrants more than thirteen months before the election of Donald Trump, and a full year and a half before President Trump ratcheted up his administration's harsh response to those who come to America with nothing. Long before the Trump administration separated young children from their families and kept them in cages like animals, the pope reminded Congress that America is "not fearful of foreigners, because most of us were once foreigners." Then he spoke to the treatment of America's first people with language I'll never forget:

> Those first contacts were often turbulent and violent, but it is difficult to judge the past by the criteria of the present. Nonetheless, when the stranger in our midst appeals to us, we must not repeat the sins and the errors of the past. We must resolve now to live as nobly and as justly as possible, as we educate new generations not to turn their back on our "neighbors" and everything around us.[24]

How quickly those in control of Congress forgot Pope Francis's words.

On the game-changing night of November 8, 2016, I watched the Election Night returns from my office at the DSCC with Senator Schumer and staffers, amid stacks of greasy boxes of cold pizza. The night dealt a humbling blow: We did not win the five seats we needed to gain a majority in the Senate. We did, however, flip two seats from red to blue. In Illinois, Congresswoman Duckworth whupped Senator

Kirk by 15 percent. And in New Hampshire Governor Hassan eked out a 1,017-vote win over Senator Ayotte.[25] Three Democrats—Jason Kander, Katie McGinty, and Russ Feingold—came close. We also held the seats of all three Democrats who retired from the Senate in 2014. Kamala Harris won Barbara Boxer's seat in California, Nevada's Catherine Cortez Masto captured Minority Leader Harry Reid's seat, and Maryland congressman Chris Van Hollen filled the seat Barbara Mikulski had held for three decades.

Like millions of other Americans, I felt more than disappointment in our political losses of 2016. For both Sharla and me, we felt dread and uncertainty about the future of our country. Our nation had just elected a man who had no business presiding over the United States of America. Donald Trump lost the popular vote but slid into Electoral College victory after Pennsylvania, Michigan, and Florida turned red. I couldn't ignore the fact that Montanans had overwhelmingly voted for Trump by a margin of nearly 21 points, while at the same time reelecting Steve Bullock as governor by four points.[26] Montana is remarkable that way. Tens of thousands of Montanans voted for a Republican to be their president and a Democrat to be their governor *on the same ballot.*

Montanans also reelected, overwhelmingly, Congressman Zinke. And the rumors about his plans to challenge me for the US Senate were no longer whispers. In fact, after I quickly and unceremoniously announced my plans to run for reelection in late November 2016, Zinke openly talked about the possibility of running against me.[27] Ryan Zinke and I got along with each other as members of Montana's three-person congressional delegation; for the most part, I found him to be a friendly straight shooter and a tactical politician. He had momentum on his side. Montanans liked him. And back then, though we disagreed often, he made very few mistakes.

I began preparing for a long campaign that I knew would be even tougher, uglier, and more expensive than my last. And I joshed Zinke several times about when he was going to announce his candidacy.

"I'm not going to run against you," he replied.

"I'll bet a steak dinner you do."

"I'll take that bet."

On November 21, Interior Secretary Sally Jewell came to Montana's Paradise Valley to make an announcement on behalf of the Obama administration. In a rustic banquet hall at Chico Hot Springs Resort, about twenty miles north of Yellowstone National Park, Jewell announced that the Interior Department would ban new mining claims on about thirty thousand acres of public land in the region for two years. The news came in response to a months-long campaign driven by local businesses and residents who opposed plans by Canadian mining companies to mine gold near Yellowstone's northern boundary. The hardrock mining operations would have severely affected tourism and threatened the famous Yellowstone River. America's first national park and the sensitive land and water around it, the Yellowstone Gateway Business Coalition argued, is "more precious than gold."

While a two-year moratorium was an important and welcomed step, permanently banning mining on public lands near Yellowstone would take an act of Congress. And when I got up to say a few words after Secretary Jewell, I announced plans to do just that. The jam-packed room roared with applause.

"Responsible mineral development plays an important role in Montana's economy," I said. "But there are simply some places where you should not dig and you should not drill, and the front porch of Yellowstone National Park is one of those places."[28]

About twenty minutes after I left Chico, Zinke called me up and told me he wanted to sponsor the House version of my bill. I thanked him and said I looked forward to working with him on the issue. Zinke didn't join us at Chico Hot Springs that day, but he knew right away how popular the issue was. And the legislation would need Zinke's full support in the House to become law. His phone call was a smart political move for a would-be challenger. And that's when I knew how difficult the next two years would be.

But then President-Elect Trump delivered the next game changer. On December 12, he summoned Ryan Zinke to New York City. The congressman arrived at Trump Tower with several gift copies of *American Commander* in hand. Trump had been leaning toward

Congresswoman Cathy McMorris Rodgers of Washington State to be his interior secretary until his greasy-haired kid stepped in. Apparently Don Jr. hit it off with Zinke and pulled some strings.

"Ryan Zinke, your former congressman—I put him at the Department of the Interior during the transition period!" he shouted during a fiery campaign speech in Montana in October 2018. Junior effectively reminded his audience that he'd personally secured Zinke's nomination to be his father's interior secretary, thus playing an unwitting role in steering Montana's 2018 US Senate race in my direction.[29]

In fact, after hearing that Zinke had become the front-runner for the Interior post, Majority Leader McConnell called up Vice President–Elect Pence and the incoming White House chief of staff, Reince Priebus, to protest the decision. But the *New York Times* reported that Trump "was not moved" by concerns that picking Zinke would take away the GOP's ace-in-the-hole candidate to unseat me. The president-elect, the *Times* reported, "was so taken with Mr. Zinke during their meeting on Monday at Trump Tower that he offered him the position."[30]

> The choice of Mr. Zinke, however, aggravated the party and vividly illustrated how Mr. Trump's improvisational, often impulsive style can collide with the best-laid plans of congressional Republicans. . . . With just one appointment, Mr. Trump snubbed the highest-ranking Republican woman in the House, Ms. McMorris Rodgers, imperiled the party's chances in a key Senate race and likely triggered a special election for Mr. Zinke's House seat.

The *Times* also quoted one of Zinke's consultants, Fred Davis. A Senate race between Zinke and me, Davis predicted, "would have been one of the biggest, toughest battles in the country and now I think Tester probably skates home free."[31]

Zinke knew full well he was the best shot at unseating me, and shortly before word of his nomination became public he sent me a text:

Jon, you owe me a steak dinner. Let's work together to get multiple use and reason back to our public lands. All the best and Merry Christmas. Z

But I knew I wasn't going to skate home free in 2018. Far from it. Trump's appointment of Zinke may have wiped the slate clean for the National Republican Senatorial Committee and the Montana GOP for 2018. But that December, almost two full years from Election Day, the first political ads started airing in Montana urging voters to contact me to support the president-elect's cabinet nominees. Several insiders warned me the NRA planned to come after me with everything it had.

A victory would require a perfect campaign. It would require me to reach as deep as I could to give my career of public service everything I had all over again. I would show Montanans that I was still the same, honest, hardworking farmer they'd sent to the US Senate in 2006. All that had really changed was a few more years under my belt, and a few more pounds over it. America's very democracy was on the line. Giving it all I had was going to be *worth it*.

CHAPTER 15

Holes in Soles

Whoa," the mild-mannered neurosurgeon remarked as he looked up and saw the massive, taxidermied bison head mounted over the desk in my Senate office. "I thought those were extinct!"

"Nope," I replied with a bewildered chuckle. "Just that one."

So began my preconfirmation meeting in early 2017 with Dr. Ben Carson, President Trump's nominee for secretary of housing and urban development. I went out of my way to meet with each of the president's cabinet nominees with a commitment to give them all a fair shake before deciding whether to confirm them. Dr. Carson may have been a brilliant doctor, but his lack of knowledge about western wildlife was just one of countless signs that President Trump and his new administration had a lot to learn about rural America. My goal during the president's first two years in office was to simply work with President Trump wherever I could and to hold him accountable whenever I had to. Election Day 2016, when he had won by 21 percent in Montana, also marked the official start of my reelection campaign. But I promised I would stay true to myself and to the people of Montana no matter which direction the political winds blew.

That meant I looked at every nominee through the lens of rural America. I wanted to know how well each of them understood issues affecting Native Americans, veterans, campaign spending, and the two pillars of a strong democracy: strong family-farm agriculture and good public education. Donald Trump's chaotic new presidency challenged all these things, but it also brought several opportunities to enact smarter policies for rural America, including reforming banking regulations to better serve smaller financial institutions, doing whatever I could to ensure the Department of Veterans Affairs fulfilled its promises to veterans, and addressing the epidemic of missing and murdered indigenous women and girls.

I had never met Dr. Carson before he stepped into my office for our preconfirmation interview. Despite the new president's unruly and unorthodox approach to governing, most of his nominees at least still honored the tradition of meeting in person with as many senators as possible prior to their confirmation votes. Dr. Carson arrived with a small entourage of assistants who anxiously took notes on our preconfirmation conversation. I kept our chat mostly focused on the importance of preserving the thirty-year fixed-rate mortgage for middle-class families and the need for more affordable housing on Native American reservations. And I found his interview satisfactory enough to earn my support.

General John Kelly, the former head of US Southern Command, told me he had never even met President Trump when he got a call from the transition team while watching college football at home one afternoon. They asked Kelly if he was interested in serving as President Trump's secretary of homeland security, months before the poor general ended up filling the tortuous role of White House chief of staff. General Kelly considered it a civic duty to say yes. I supported him too.

Steve Mnuchin, the billionaire investor who produced Hollywood blockbusters as a hobby, arrived with a larger entourage and spoke, it seemed, as if I wasn't even in the room. I didn't think he was qualified for a job that affects the lives of middle-class families, and I did not support his confirmation as treasury secretary. And then there was the education secretary nominee, Betsy DeVos, another billionaire whose interview didn't go so swell. When asked about public education, DeVos said it was failing, and that her solution would be to pull successful kids out of failing public schools and give them vouchers to attend private schools.

"If we do that, I am here to tell the people of the Senate today that we will destroy the foundation of this country and we will destroy—it may take a few years—we will destroy our democracy," I said on the Senate floor a few days later in early February, adding that it would be different if Betsy DeVos had spent a single second in a public education classroom. Then I folded up the prepared speech in front of me, because I wanted to speak from my gut about the importance of public education in rural America. I was pissed off.

I told my Senate colleagues how my Swedish-born grandmother Christine Pearson made sure her four kids understood the transformative value of public education, and how my mother, also a former teacher, passed that value down to me. I said I had to quit teaching elementary school in the late seventies because I could make more money on one Saturday butchering meat than an entire week of teaching music at my tiny hometown elementary school. Wouldn't it be smarter, I asked, to invest in schools like F. E. Miley Elementary instead of pushing for privatization of our public school system?

I am going to tell you what happens in a rural state like mine with privatization. My school system in my hometown of Big Sandy has about 175 kids. That is not an exception for Montana; there are a lot of schools that have 175 kids or fewer. By the way, that is not high school; that is K through twelve. Let's say that for whatever reason, somebody wants to set up a charter school a few miles down the road and suck a few kids out of Big Sandy, and maybe suck a few kids out of the Fort Benton school system, and a few more out of the Chester system. Pretty soon, they have their little charter school, and there is less money to teach the kids who are left in those public schools. What do you think is going to happen to those kids who are left there? That is going to take away from our public education system. Ultimately, it will cause those schools to close, because the money that funds our education is at a bare minimum right now.[1]

I added that I believed it was important that President Trump get the cabinet he needed to do a good job for the country, but I said I wasn't going to vote for a team that would destroy America's public education system.

I would not be doing a service to the people who came before me—the previous generations—and I certainly would not be doing a service to my kids and my grandkids and the generations to come after. This is a very important decision. If we want to do the tough work of debating our public education system and determining how we can make it better, get the best people in the classrooms, and get the best academic material in there for them to work off of, let's do that. But let's not destroy the public education system that has made this country great for generation after generation after generation.

Setting up an alternative charter school isn't a smart answer to a failing public school in rural America. The better answer requires concerned members of the community getting off their butts and going to public school board meetings and registering their concerns with elected board members.

A few days later we held a confirmation vote on Betsy DeVos. Two Republican women, Susan Collins of Maine and Lisa Murkowski of Alaska, joined all Democrats in voting against her, which meant Vice President Pence had to cast a tie-breaking vote.[2] And with Pence's fifty-first vote—the first time in history a vice president had to do so for a Senate confirmation—Betsy DeVos squeaked by as the nation's eleventh secretary of education.

It took only a matter of days before I heard the first complaint from Montana about Secretary DeVos. The US Department of Education had rejected critical funding for the University of Montana's Upward Bound program. The reason? A single page within the university's sixty-five-page application form was single spaced and not double spaced. The University of Montana had asked for $340,000 per year for five years to operate the program, which helps low-income and first-generation high school students get into college. Turns out, the University of Montana was among seventy-seven colleges across the country that didn't meet minor "formatting guidelines" for Upward Bound grant applications, and it quickly fixed the error and resubmitted its application.[3]

The Department of Education basically said, "tough shit." And in one of the stupidest excuses I have ever heard (I called it a "bull-manure response" on the record), DeVos's Department blamed the Obama administration for issuing the formatting guidelines in the first place. I wasn't going to have any of it. So I teamed up with Senator Collins to ask Secretary DeVos to quickly reconsider. Twenty-three other senators, including seven additional Republicans, signed on to our letter saying DeVos "should be supporting successful partnerships, not constructing bureaucratic roadblocks."[4]

I was also less diplomatic. I told the *Missoulian* newspaper the decision was "an example of bureaucracy at its very worst," adding, "When somebody directly hurts Montanans intentionally, that gets my blood boiling. . . . This is a direct assault on the next generation of leaders in this country."[5]

Overall, I supported most of President Trump's original cabinet—almost two-thirds of them.[6] I had a long and important talk with Sonny Perdue about the role of family agriculture in America. I felt very good about my support for Defense Secretary Jim Mattis. I even introduced Ryan Zinke before his confirmation hearing.

The biggest relief came when President Trump nominated Dr. David Shulkin for the daunting job of running the Department of Veterans Affairs. He was the only Trump nominee who earned the support of all one hundred senators, which I considered a nod to the nonpartisan nature of our progress on the Veterans' Affairs Committee. I had the honor of serving as the committee's ranking member with chairman Johnny Isakson of Georgia, and we got a lot of work done right away. While most of the nation's attention focused on Trump's wily first few weeks in office, I quietly worked with several Republicans to churn out bill after bill.

President Trump signed my first bill of 2017—his second as president—on January 31. The Senate unanimously passed the Government Accountability Office Access and Oversight Act, which I wrote with Senator Ben Sasse of Nebraska. Our bill allowed the GAO to audit key federal government programs and provide them access to unemployment insurance data and wage data.[7] In April, Trump signed my second bill—one I wrote with Chairman Isakson allowing certain veterans to get health care from private providers.[8] And from there, things really picked up. The president signed into law seven more of my bipartisan bills for veterans in 2017 alone, including the VA Accountability and Whistleblower Protection Act and the Gary Deloney and John Olsen Toxic Exposure Declassification Act.[9]

In the spring of 2017 I met with Jay Clayton, perhaps my favorite nominee among President Trump's slew of advisers, secretaries, and other appointed leaders. The president had tapped the high-powered lawyer to chair the Securities and Exchange Commission. And because of my status as a member of the banking committee, Clayton prioritized a face-to-face meeting with me. When he sat down, he rested an ankle over his other knee, exposing the sole of his shoe.

"Hey man," I told him, "you got holes in your feet!"

Clayton dropped his foot back to the floor, embarrassed. He had on a regular suit and tie (they all look "regular" to me), and the last thing he expected when he got dressed that morning was for someone like me to notice the bottoms of his well-worn shoes. I didn't mean to embarrass the guy.

"You can tell a lot from a guy who's got holes in his soles," I added, knowing full well that Jay Clayton made millions as a successful lawyer. The tension eased and we laughed it off. I lifted my cowboy boot and showed him the hole that had worn through my sole. "Farmers notice these things, Jay. I won't vote for or against you because of it, but I should warn you, the guy whose shoes looked like they just walked out of a Hollywood movie premiere—I didn't vote for him."

I lose no sleep over my wardrobe. I own lots of less-than-fashionable ties, all of which are secondhand, because I refuse to pay money for something as ridiculous as a piece of cloth I have to wrap around my neck. I also usually manage to dribble something down my shirt when I eat. I have a tie with a nice picture of a whale on it. For years I thought the whale had water spouting out of its head until someone inspected the tie closely and pointed out it was really just a smear of dried mashed potatoes from God knows when. But wearing good-looking clothes isn't what Montanans sent me to Washington to do. They expect me to burn the boot leather, both literally and figuratively.

I supported Jay Clayton's nomination, but not because he had holes in his shoes. I supported him because I truly believed he was a breath of fresh air in an administration that got swampier by the day. The holes in his soles only reminded me that Jay Clayton actually knew the value of a dollar.

Hours after President Trump signed my first bill into law on January 31, he held a news conference in the White House to announce his pick to fill the Supreme Court seat vacated after Antonin Scalia's death a year earlier. Neil Gorsuch struck me as a brilliant judge who reminded me a lot of John Morrison—the guy I beat in the Senate primary back in 2006. He wore sharp suits. He flashed a winning smile and had a polished way of speaking. I never doubted that he knew the law inside and out. In a word, Neil Gorsuch was brilliant. But was he fit to serve a lifetime appointment to the US Supreme Court?

I called up Murph, my chief of staff, and asked for as much information as possible because decisions as important as confirming a Supreme Court justice come along only a couple of times in a career. Judge Gorsuch came to my office for an in-person meeting less than a week after his nomination. He sat on the edge of a chair across from me, with both feet planted, and leaned forward—clear body language that he was listening and engaged in our conversation. He began each sentence with an abrupt "Senator," while looking me in the eye, which made him look and sound rehearsed with militaristic discipline. A few thin walls away, the young folks at my front desk were getting pounded with phone calls from Montanans asking me to oppose Judge Gorsuch's nomination, citing fears that he might eventually support undoing the *Roe v. Wade* decision. Some callers wanted me to support the judge with the unconvincing argument that he hailed from Colorado, which made him a fellow westerner and therefore automatically qualified to be on the Supreme Court.

My meeting with Judge Gorsuch was cordial. He had his talking points down pat. And just as he did in his closely scrutinized hearing a couple weeks later, he very slyly avoided any of my tough questions. He carefully dodged the issues of reproductive rights and the role of money in politics. After our meeting, I spent days poring over his judicial record and reading through decisions he had made in various lower-court rulings. I never doubted Gorsuch's intelligence. But confirming a Supreme Court justice for a lifetime term, especially after the Republicans scuttled President Obama's nomination of the equally qualified Merrick Garland, required full trust and diligence. With only fifty-two votes, Republicans would need the support of eight Democrats in order to break a filibuster and confirm Judge Gorsuch. Politically, Gorsuch's nomination put me in a tight spot: Should I vote for the pick of a president who'd just won overwhelmingly in Montana? Or should I vote against him, knowing it could end my political career?

So I called my most-senior staff into my office and sat them down around a table beneath the massive taxidermied bison head. A couple of my most trusted advisers joined by phone from Montana. Half of them were men; half were women. All of them had thoroughly read through Judge Gorsuch's records. They were well versed in what my polling suggested, what Montanans were calling my office about, and what the ads on TV in Montana were saying. During those few weeks pro-Gorsuch dark money organizations spent nearly $1 million on a

TV-ad blitz in Montana urging me to support the judge.[10] I shut the door of my office.

"I'm going to go around the room and I want to hear how you think I should vote," I said. "Let's start with my chief of staff," I added, looking at Murph. He took a deep breath.

"My recommendation would be to vote no," he finally said. "It's an important line to hold, given where he is on money in politics."

"No," said the woman next to him. "Remember how different his record on choice is compared with your record on choice."

"I recommend no."

"I think no. Your position on choice is too strong to throw into question with a vote for this guy."

"No."

"Well, I would advise a yes vote. It's important to show you're not just a typical Democrat. And this guy is as smart as they come."

"No."

"Thank you," I told them. I chewed on some of my fingernails. "Now we're going to go around the room again. This time, I want you to pretend I'm *not* running for reelection. And I'm going to ask the same question: How do you think I should vote?"

"Well, hell no."

"No."

"Absolutely not."

The recommendation from all of them was unanimous. Even the person who said yes moments earlier recommended no.

"*That* is the answer you should all have given me the first time around," I said. "This decision is much more important than a reelection." And on April 2, after reading everything I could about Neil Gorsuch and after studying his decisions, I formally announced my decision, saying, "It came with thoughtful deliberation, late nights, and the counsel of thousands of Montanans."

> Judge Gorsuch is a smart man but that doesn't make him
> right for a lifetime appointment to the Supreme Court. . . .
> With Judge Gorsuch on the bench, I am deeply concerned

that dark money will continue to drown out the voices and votes of citizens, the Court will stand between women and their doctors, and the government will reach into the private lives of law-abiding Americans. . . . When it comes to the letter of the law, he believes corporations are people. If that were true, then I invite Wells Fargo out to my farm to spend a few long days picking rock in the fields.[11]

By then the Democrats Heidi Heitkamp of North Dakota and Joe Donnelly of Indiana announced plans to support Gorsuch. Still, the Republicans had six more Democratic votes to find. Confirming a conservative to replace Antonin Scalia on the US Supreme Court—a priority for the GOP for decades—was within reach. And the Republicans finally got it by going nuclear. On April 6, the Senate Republicans voted to change our rules to allow the confirmation of Supreme Court justices with fifty votes instead of sixty.[12]

"This will be the first, and last, partisan filibuster of a Supreme Court justice," Majority Leader McConnell said after changing the long-held precedent for America's system of checks and balances on Supreme Court appointments.[13] The following day, on April 7, fifty-four senators voted to confirm Judge Gorsuch as a lifetime associate justice of the Supreme Court of the United States. I was not one of them.[14]

I was, however, responsible for overhauling the nation's banking regulations that year. I had long heard concerns from community banks and credit unions across Montana that the Dodd-Frank Wall Street Reform and Consumer Protection Act of 2010 had gone too far in over-regulating smaller financial institutions. I supported the Dodd-Frank law, a sweeping set of reforms that overhauled America's banking system in the wake of the financial crisis two years earlier. The law put the squeeze on Wall Street to prevent a crisis like that from ever happening again. But the law put the same powerful squeeze on smaller local and regional financial institutions. We didn't know then that in many cases, the Dodd-Frank law ended up squeezing the life right out of smaller banks and credit unions, forcing many of them to consolidate with bigger banks or go belly up altogether.

The chairman of the Banking Committee, Republican Mike Crapo of Idaho, heard the same concerns from community banks and credit unions in his state, and he was open to working with Democrats on a reform bill. The committee's top Democrat, Sherrod Brown of Ohio, wasn't interested in leading the effort. Some of our Democratic colleagues claimed that making any changes to Dodd-Frank would cede more power back to the big financial institutions that had almost collapsed our economy. I certainly didn't see it that way. And neither did Steve Turkiewicz, the head of the Montana Bankers Association.

"One size of regulation does not fit all," Turkiewicz said in 2017. "Our hometown Montana bankers, their employees and their customers have struggled and persevered for nearly a decade, as burdensome over-regulation threatened both economic opportunity and job creation in Montana. In most cases, Montana's hometown bankers have broken through and have been able to succeed on behalf of their customers. Yet the untold lost opportunity and stifled innovation that results from these burdensome regulations is, no doubt, significant."[15]

I told Senator Crapo that I wanted to start writing the regulatory reform bill, and I went to work rounding up support from both sides of the aisle. Among Democrats, Senators Heitkamp and Donnelly were both interested, along with Mark Warner of Virginia. After speaking at length with all of them, I spent many hours in my office with Kellin Clark, my economic policy adviser. After discussing all the provisions and components I wanted to see in the bill, I told Kellin on a Sunday in early November that I wanted to see a first draft on my desk in forty-eight hours.

"That's going to be tough," Kellin said. "We may not have the time."

"Bullshit," I told him. "I want it on my desk on Wednesday. If we don't get this thing written right now, it's not gonna happen."

"We'll get it done."

And sure enough, Kellin, working through two nights in a row with close input from his counterparts in other offices, and with the direction of their bosses, delivered on Wednesday the first draft of the seventy-three-page Economic Growth, Regulatory Relief, and Consumer Protection Act. A few minor revisions later, Chairman Crapo formally introduced the bill with me and eighteen other cosponsors on November 16.[16]

Before they even had a chance to read it, some of my Democratic colleagues quickly opposed our bipartisan proposal, suggesting that it went too far in rolling back Wall Street reforms of the Dodd-Frank law. Those of us who wrote the bill pushed back, noting that the consolidation of the banking industry—largely caused by Dodd-Frank—had significantly diminished the economic power of rural America, hurting rural communities across the heartland. Ultimately, small banks will be "swallowed up by the folks on Wall Street," I said on the Senate floor on March 6, 2018—a week before our final vote.

"Furthermore, when a community bank is bought out by a big bank, its business model changes and it is no longer tailored to fit that community." Worse, I added, a small community bank could board up altogether. "If you are a product of rural America like I am, you know full well the consequences when a bank leaves town. It is just a matter of time before that community shrivels up."[17]

Without a community bank to help a farmer finance a new combine for his small farm, that farm is more likely to go out of business or worse—to sell out to some corporate agricultural behemoth that wants nothing more than to buy up that small farm and turn it into another GMO fiefdom that churns out food from patented seeds. Community banks, I argued, were responsible for almost half of all small-business loans—and farmland and farm lending—in the country.

Some of my colleagues in my own party refused to see it that way. They had staked their reputations on standing up to the massive Wall Street banks at all costs, despite the unintended collateral damage suffered by small communities, and those reputations were more important to them than actual common sense. The whole debate immediately became a case study in the growing divide between rural and urban states. I admit I don't know the ins and outs of small communities in New England, but I know damn well that the original Dodd-Frank law had disproportionately hurt small towns across Montana by weakening the financial institutions that keep their small businesses open.

The politicization of our Economic Growth, Regulatory Relief, and Consumer Protection Act got ugly. One of my colleagues in my own party even raised money off of opposing it, which told me a lot about what was more important to her. In fact, the mischaracterization of our bill by some of my friends on the left prompted Dodd-Frank's namesake lawmakers, both of whom had retired from Congress, to publicly correct the record on my behalf.

"While we did not agree with everything in [Tester's] bill, its main purpose is to give relief to Main Street without taking the foot off the gas when it comes to regulating the big guys that caused the financial crisis," the former senator Chris Dodd and former congressman Barney Frank wrote to my supporters in 2018, adding the new bill "helps credit unions and community banks that are the lifeblood of rural communities. Frankly, these banks haven't been the problem and Jon knows that because he's from a rural community."[18]

The Senate passed the Economic Growth, Regulatory Relief, and Consumer Protection Act with sixty-seven votes, including fourteen Democrats, on March 14. It was the fourteenth bill of mine President Trump eventually signed into law.[19]

As we spent months in the Senate Banking Committee haggling and negotiating over the finer points of banking regulations, Native American communities continued to struggle with a much more dire concern: Between the beginning of 2018 and mid-August, twenty Native American women in Montana vanished; only one had been found.[20] Native American women faced a murder rate *ten times higher* than the national average.[21] The US Justice Department reported in 2016 that 84 percent of them experienced violence in their lifetimes (56 percent experienced sexual violence).[22] And in June 2017, the

Missing and Murdered Indigenous Women and Girls movement got a few powerful new voices.

At some point that month, Ashley Loring Heavy Runner, a twenty-year-old college student who had been preparing to move in with her sisters in Missoula, disappeared from the Blackfeet Indian Reservation in northwest Montana.[23] The only hazy clues: a tip that someone had last seen Ashley running from a vehicle along Highway 89 and reports that searchers had found her sweater, stained with oil and red marks that looked like blood, and a pair of boots in her size.[24]

I followed Ashley's disappearance closely after a young activist named Briana Lamb brought it to my attention during a roundtable meeting in Missoula. Briana pushed me hard for a response from Congress. She told me she was heartsick and fed up with inaction in Washington, especially because the hard work of women like Ashley's older sister, Kimberly Loring Heavy Runner, wasn't getting much traction. Kimberly organized more than 120 unsuccessful searches for Ashley, burning holes in her soles for months without answers. So I told Briana I would do whatever I could. A few days later I formally requested an Indian Affairs Committee hearing on the crisis—a decision that rested with the committee's chairman, Senator John Hoeven of North Dakota.[25] After Election Day in 2018, Senator Hoeven finally agreed to the hearing, and I invited Kimberly to Washington to testify.

Sitting before the Indian Affairs Committee on December 12, Kimberly Loring Heavy Runner nervously explained that the Bureau of Indian Affairs and tribal police officers had spent three days searching the area where Ashley was reportedly last seen but found nothing. After their initial investigation slowed down, Kimberly told us she got an offensive assessment about her sister's disappearance from the BIA.

"Two months after she went missing," Kimberly said, "the BIA was still stating that Ashley 'is of age and is able to leave whenever she wants to.' That is not a proper response when dealing with a woman that's been missing for two months and despite the fact that we found a sweater."[26]

Someone handed over that sweater to the BIA as evidence, Kimberly was told. And two weeks later, the BIA told Kimberly they no longer had it.

"They lost it!" she said. "They called us and told us they do not know where the sweater is." As for the boots? The BIA eventually claimed they were too small to have belonged to Ashley. But the worst part for Kimberly was what happened next: a simple, painful lack of communication. In fact, it seemed as if law enforcement agents gave up on the disappearance altogether. "We went weeks without speaking with them," she said. "They did not call and they did not give us any information."[27]

Stories like this are all too common for cases of missing Native Americans. I said during the hearing it was a failure of responsibility, and that cases like this would get much more traction outside Native American communities. To keep raising awareness of the epidemic of missing and murdered indigenous women and girls, I invited Briana Lamb to Washington as my guest to President Trump's State of the Union Address on February 5, 2019. Briana, I said, was a tireless organizer, researcher, and activist who had been raising awareness of the issue for six years through teaching and by organizing vigils and walks.

"This shouldn't be an Indigenous issue," Briana pointed out, "but an issue for everyone."[28] During his State of the Union Address in 2019, President Trump didn't mention the issue once.[29]

Maybe that's because the issue of immigration consumed most of the president's time and political capital during 2018. On January 9, the White House invited me and about two dozen other members of Congress to meet with the president for what his handlers billed as a bipartisan meeting on immigration. And thus began yet another very weird meeting with President Trump. Many of us wanted to see for ourselves the president's behavior, because earlier that week, with his mental health under national scrutiny, he'd tweeted that his two greatest assets were "mental stability and being, like, really smart."[30] Three minutes later he'd added that his rise to the presidency made him "a genius . . . and a very stable genius at that!"[31]

We all sat uncomfortably close to one another in the Cabinet Room, around the same table where the secretaries usually brief the president. I got wedged between Senators David Perdue of Georgia and John Cornyn of Texas, one of the palest white-haired men I've ever known. Numerous reporters and photographers filled the rest of the space, standing against the walls and clicking pictures constantly. It didn't make much difference to me, but nobody told us the meeting would be what felt like a press stunt. The White House billed the ordeal as a meeting with the president, but it was really just a strange, out-of-control news conference with a bunch of mixed messages that only made the confusing situation even worse.

Immediately the president launched right into immigration. For some reason, he had imposed a fast-approaching deadline of March 5 for Congress to "legalize DACA," the Obama-era Deferred Action for Childhood Arrivals policy allowing foreign-born children of immigrants to stay in America—the only country they have ever known.[32]

"I'm appealing to everyone in the room to put the country before party, and to sit down and negotiate and to compromise, and let's see if we can get something done," the president said.[33] *Off to a promising start*, I thought. And soon, Senator Dianne Feinstein, who sat directly across from me, saw an opening.

"What about a clean DACA bill now, with a commitment that we go into a comprehensive immigration reform procedure?" she asked the president. By "clean DACA bill," Senator Feinstein was referring to passing a DACA fix without any other strings attached—like funding for a wall along the southern border. What happened next was like watching a skilled hunter.

"I have no problem," he replied. "We're going to do DACA, and then we can start immediately on the phase two, which would be comprehensive." The hard-liners in the room squirmed in their chairs as they anxiously shot looks at each other. I could almost hear them say, *What the hell is he talking about?*

"Would you be agreeable to that?" Senator Feinstein asked, surprised by the president's amenable response. The hunter had just reached out and grabbed her prey by the neck.

"I would like to do that," President Trump said. "Go ahead. I think a lot of people would like to see that, but I think we have to do DACA first." Then the game warden swooped in.

"Mr. President, you need to be clear, though," House Majority Leader Kevin McCarthy interjected. "We have to have security."[34] By security, of course, he meant there would be no deal on DACA without funding for the wall. Apparently McCarthy and the other hard-liners got to President Trump shortly after our bipartisan meeting, because the president reversed course the next day when asked about an immigration deal in Congress.

"It's got to include the wall," the president said, back on script. "Any solution has to include the wall, because without the wall it all doesn't work."

The most remarkable part of our White House meeting, however, happened more than an hour after it began—*after* staffers ushered all the reporters and photographers out of the Cabinet Room. The doors closed, and the president continued insisting on building his wall, even despite questions about how to overcome the challenge of building the wall across sections of privately owned land that borders Mexico. President Trump responded by saying he would use expedited eminent domain—to seize privately owned land. Landowners would have no choice in the matter. I couldn't believe what I just heard, from a president and a party that preaches individual freedom, smaller government, and property rights.

Actually, I could believe it. As pro-Trump property rights advocates often forget, the president didn't think twice about using eminent domain powers to build his casino empire. In the mid-nineties, he wanted to buy up land next to his twenty-two-story Trump Plaza hotel in Atlantic City to build a parking area for guests' limousines. Several of the hotel's neighbors, including an elderly homeowner named Vera Coking, refused to sell. So Trump turned to a New Jersey government agency called the Casino Reinvestment Development Authority to try to condemn and claim the land under eminent domain. He thought Coking's three-story home was ugly.[35]

"Everybody coming in to Atlantic City sees that property, and it's not fair to Atlantic City and the people," Trump told the journalist John Stossel on an episode of *20/20* in June 1998. "They're staring at this terrible house instead of staring at beautiful fountains and beautiful other things that would be good."

"You're bullying these people out because they're—"

"Excuse me, that's wrong," Trump interrupted. "For you to use the word 'bully,' John, is very unfair. This is a government case. This is not Donald Trump."

"Yes, it's Donald Trump," Stossel fired back. "It's you and your cronies in government working together."

"We have been so nice to this woman," Trump said, referring to Vera Coking. "I offered her a lot of money," he continued, pointing to his chest, "out of this, a little thing called *heart*."[36]

On July 21, 1998, a New Jersey court ruled against the Casino Reinvestment Development Authority's condemnation order. Judge Richard Williams said his court "concluded that the primary interest served here is a private rather than a public one and as such, the actions cannot be justified under the law."[37] No wonder twenty years later, the president of the United States so callously suggested he had a right to seize private land for a wall along the southern border of America.

Six years before my second meeting with President Trump in the White House, Congressman Rehberg had paid an enormous price for supporting legislation giving operational control of federally owned land to the Department of Homeland Security. That wasn't nearly as bad as the use of eminent domain for private development, and it had shot a hole through Rehberg's political career, because Montanans accused him of supporting a "land grab." A president authorizing the federal government to forcibly take private land away from his own citizens to build a wall would be far, far worse—at least under any other president. I leaned over to Senator Cornyn.

"I sure in hell would hate to be a senator from Texas if he's using expedited eminent domain," I whispered with a grin.

John Cornyn turned even whiter than he already was.

CHAPTER 16

Whistleblowers Within

On April 28, 2018, the president of the United States called on me to resign from the US Senate. That Saturday morning, 192 days before Election Day, was the first time a sitting American president had ever called on a duly elected senator to step down from office.[1] Politically, in a state Donald Trump carried by nearly 21 points, it stung.

The president called for my resignation in a tweet he fired off at 3:07 a.m. Mountain Time.[2] Hours earlier, I arrived home at the farm after a very long week in Washington. Both Christie Roberts, my campaign manager, and Murph, my chief of staff, learned about the president's tweet within minutes and scrambled through the night, weighing various options for how best to respond before they even told me about it. I got up early that morning to begin a week of planting, and Murph called as I sat at our kitchen table with a cup of coffee.

"He went after you by name," he said nervously.

"Oh, really?"

"He's calling on you to *resign*."

"*Oh really?*" I chuckled. "It's all good."

I told Murph I wasn't going to sweat it, and neither should he or anyone else on my team. I knew that would be easier said than done, though. My entire campaign strategy had focused on my ability to work with the president and his administration—to rise above the chaos and to get important laws passed. If I had the luxury of running a reelection campaign in a perfect world, the president would have never paid much attention to me; he would simply keep signing the bills I quietly got passed. I never expected him to endorse me, but I also didn't expect him to go after me with the full heat and strength of the presidency.

On that Saturday morning in late April, President Trump was just getting started. Several hours after his first tweet he sent another: "A horrible thing that we in D.C. must live with, just like phony Russian Collusion. Tester should lose race in Montana. Very dishonest and sick!"[3] And a few hours after that, he skipped the 2018 White House Correspondents' Association dinner to hold a raucous campaign rally in Washington Township, Michigan. There the president railed on me for being "weak on the border" and for voting against his disastrous $2 trillion Tax Cuts and Jobs Act the previous December.

Then the president said this: "Well, I know things about Tester that I could say too. And if I said 'em, he'd never be elected again."[4] His crowd of thousands roared.

So how did I earn the top spot on President Trump's shit list in 2018? In a word: whistleblowers. Every day of his presidency, Donald Trump and his advisers and his media mouthpieces chipped away at the strength of our representative democracy; they lowered the standards of government and normalized chaos and uncertainty in an effort to keep as tight a grip as possible on their power. Thank God for the whistleblowers within, who understand that the office of the American president is more important than protecting the person of the American president. When a CIA whistleblower raised national security concerns about President Trump's July 25, 2019, phone call with Ukrainian president Volodymyr Zelensky, President Trump—like a threatened snake—curled up and hissed that the whistleblower was "close to a spy," and even suggested the whistleblower be executed for treason.[5] Indeed, whistleblowers are the truest patriots who may save our nation.

There's nothing unusual about federal government employees contacting a congressional committee to blow the whistle when they see trouble or want to report wrongdoing in an agency. Their ability to reach out to Congress is part of our system of checks and balances. Sometimes these employees are forced to go outside the chain of command out of fear of reprisal. That's what happened in late April 2018, when more than two dozen whistleblowers came directly to me and my office with complaints that humiliated and infuriated Donald Trump.

First, let's rewind to January 16, 2018. That's when many of us tuned in to watch one of the strangest news conferences I have ever seen. Press Secretary Sarah Huckabee Sanders first read to the White House press corps a letter from Brigadier General Dr. Richard Tubb, the White House physician emeritus, describing the president's current physician, Rear Admiral Ronny Jackson.

"Beginning on November 9, 2016, the members of the White House medical unit began shadowing the new president-elect, figuratively Velcroed to his side, 24/7," Tubb wrote. "On January 20, 2017, Dr. Jackson became that Velcro. Dr. Jackson's office is one of only a very few in the White House residence proper and is located directly across the hall from the president's private elevator."[6]

Then Sanders turned the podium over to Admiral Dr. Jackson. Aside from his carefully gelled graying hair, the doctor looked about two decades younger than his fifty years. He spoke confidently, with the speed and easy lilt of a Texas auctioneer, as he reassured reporters who were curious about the state of the president's physical and mental health, and the results from his recent four-hour physical exam.

Dr. Jackson smiled easily and laughed often as he took questions for almost an hour, seeming to relish every minute in the spotlight while praising the president's physical fitness. When a reporter asked how Jackson regarded President Trump as healthy despite an infamous diet of fast food burgers, fried chicken, and Diet Cokes, the doctor shrugged it off as simple genetics. "Some people have just great genes,"

Jackson said. "I told the president that if he had a healthier diet over the last twenty years, he might live to be two hundred years old."[7]

Like so many others who served at the pleasure of Donald Trump, Ronny Jackson seemed to be performing in front of the nation to an audience of one. Though Jackson had also served as a doctor for both presidents George W. Bush and Barack Obama, this was the first time he had ever taken the mic to directly brief the White House press corps. To many, the president's near-perfect bill of health seemed too convenient and even compromised. Maybe that's why most of the media missed Dr. Jackson's answer to a question about whether the president relied on any medication to help him sleep.

"The president does take some Ambien on occasion, like we all do, on overseas travel," Jackson admitted. "So when we travel from one time zone to another time zone on the other side of the planet, I recommend that everyone on the plane take a sleep aid at certain times so that we can try our best to get on the schedule of our destination."[8]

Other than a parody by *Saturday Night Live* the following weekend, the breakneck news cycles of the Chaos Presidency quickly moved on from Dr. Jackson's debut on the national stage. I didn't really expect to hear his name again. At the time, that news conference was just one more crazy story of one more crazy day unfolding sixteen blocks west of Capitol Hill.

Now fast-forward to March 28, when President Trump took to Twitter to dismiss his Veterans Affairs Secretary. Dr. David Shulkin was the only member of the president's cabinet who'd earned the confirmation vote of all one hundred senators. Secretary Shulkin had spent weeks dealing with his own unflattering headlines about inappropriate travel expenses and upheaval at the VA. When he knew his dismissal was imminent, Secretary Shulkin came to Capitol Hill to warn me that hardcore political operatives in the president's inner circle were threatening the VA; they wanted to fundamentally change how the VA delivers health care by bidding out the responsibility to private companies, putting profits ahead of doing what's best for veterans.

In 2017, President Trump had signed into law our legislation allowing certain rural veterans access to health care from private providers. This allows some veterans in rural America, where VA facilities are few and far between, quicker and more convenient access to health care. But as for privatizing the entire VA? Like most veterans and the service organizations that represent them, I agreed privatization would be disastrous. Removing the government's responsibility to provide health care for veterans and placing that responsibility in the hands of third-party, for-profit contractors would mean millions of veterans who live in inconvenient places would get worse care, or no care at all.

In the same Twitter announcement, President Trump said that he intended to nominate Rear Admiral Jackson to succeed Shulkin for the VA post. The news took Congress and all the veterans' service organizations by surprise. That's when I asked my team on the Veterans' Affairs Committee, "Who the hell is this guy?" My staff director, Tony McClain, said he'd research whatever he could find on Jackson's record and report back.

On April 16, Ronny Jackson came up to Capitol Hill for a meeting with the VA Committee chairman, Johnny Isakson.[9] And the following day, he came to my office for an in-person meeting. Since I was the ranking member of the Senate Veterans' Affairs Committee, the White House knew full well I could ultimately influence a positive vote recommendation among my colleagues.

Striding confidently into my office in his decorated Navy dress uniform, Dr. Jackson greeted me with a bleached smile and a firm handshake. He sat across from me attentively as we chatted about the challenges of the VA. Our meeting was friendly, but I still wasn't sold on the admiral, who had zero experience in running something as large and as complex as the Department of Veterans Affairs.

"I have concerns about whether his experience qualifies him to run the nation's largest health care system," I said afterward, adding that I looked forward to his preconfirmation hearing before the Senate Veterans' Affairs Committee.[10] Nonetheless, on that day, it appeared Dr. Jackson would succeed Secretary Shulkin without much resistance.

The following day, as we waited in gridlocked DC traffic, Murph got a phone call from a contact whose name I agreed to keep strictly confidential. We vetted the caller's identity before Murph put me on the phone with the person—a uniformed officer who had worked with Ronny Jackson.

"You cannot confirm this guy," the insider told me with a hushed voice. *"Ronny Jackson would be a disaster."*

I asked for details. The caller told me Dr. Jackson created a toxic work environment. He may have Velcroed his charm to the president, but he ran the medical unit with cruel vindictiveness. Those who worked under the admiral had even more stories to tell. He was hardly qualified to run the Department of Veterans Affairs. And other White House medical officers challenged Jackson's own practices as a physician.

"His nickname is 'Candyman' because of how loose he is with prescription drugs," the caller added. "And I'm certainly not the only one who knows it, Senator. There are a lot of other people who work with him who'd tell you the same thing. I'm telling you this because it's my *duty*."

I asked the caller to get in touch with my top researchers on the Veterans' Affairs Committee, who had the task of preparing for Dr. Jackson's upcoming hearing. The caller did exactly that. And from there, my staff had more than two dozen similar calls from current and former colleagues of Dr. Jackson, many of them fellow White House employees and many still high-ranking military officers. Many of them reached out to Chairman Isakson's office as well. The Veterans' Affairs Committee worked through the weekend on the phone, verifying identities and chasing down stories. On Monday, April 23, they came into my office with stacks of notes to brief me on what they had heard. Just when I thought the Trump administration could no longer surprise me, what they shared left me dumbstruck:

"We've broken the concerns down into three categories: the nominee's history of questionable prescribing practices, creating a hostile work environment, and alcohol abuse."

"Start with 'hostile work environment,'" I said.

"Well, here are some of the words all of our whistleblowers used to describe Dr. Jackson." One of my staff investigators looked at the other, who started reading through a list. "Explosive, toxic, abusive, volatile, despicable, dishonest, vindictive, belittling—"

"Got it. What else?"

"Our contacts said the nominee threw 'screaming tantrums' and 'screaming fits.' Another said the nominee is, quote, 'the worst officer I have ever served with.' Another described him as a 'kiss up, kick down' boss. More than one said working inside the White House Medical Unit should be a career highlight, but it was the worst assignment they've received. All of them are worried about reprisal. Let's just say the White House Medical Unit does not seem to be a place where it's easy to report problems up the chain of command."

"Why?"

"Because, Senator, Rear Admiral Jackson is at the top of that chain and he literally sits across the hall from the commander in chief. And the commander in chief *loves* him. They're Velcroed to each other, all right."

"What about the drugs?"

"Well, multiple contacts brought up the nickname 'Candyman.' Apparently folks at the White House can go to the nominee and he'll just give out prescription drugs. One told us he goes up and down the aisles of Air Force One casually handing out Ambien to passengers to help them sleep and Provigil to wake them up—without any screening, without any questions, without writing prescriptions. And multiple folks told us that he has an alcohol problem—even to the point of being intoxicated while on call."

"We even heard a report of a minor car wreck following a Secret Service going-away party."[11]

Of course, if any of these allegations were true, Dr. Jackson was most certainly not fit to serve as a cabinet secretary. To make matters worse, word started leaking that my office was sniffing around on various unflattering allegations, and various news reports started bubbling up that we were scrutinizing Jackson's nomination. John Kelly, the White House chief of staff, asked for an urgent phone call with me that afternoon. He wanted to know what exactly I was hearing and who I had heard it from. I gladly took up the call, but I had to protect my sources.

"It's really my job to find out if there's any there there," I told General Kelly. "And that's what my staff's doing at this moment in time. And if there's a *there* there, then we're gonna have a problem. If there isn't, then there won't be any problem." I suggested General Kelly have a come-to-Jesus with Dr. Jackson, to make sure the doctor had an opportunity to come clean before his hearing, which Chairman Isakson had initially scheduled for that Wednesday. Kelly said he'd already done so, then he questioned the veracity of what our sources were telling us. "There's no way to verify that," General Kelly said. "You'd have to take their word for it."

"If we get multiple people and they're telling the same story, that's pretty good verification," I replied.

"Well, to use a common word here in Washington, they could be colluding."

"They could be," I said, "but the question is *why*?"

What I didn't tell General Kelly was how much the White House had screwed up this particular nomination. "Normal" isn't a word anyone uses to describe the Trump administration, but normally, the White House will thoroughly vet a cabinet nominee before making its announcement official. Then the FBI conducts a background check before Congress begins its own vetting process. But because President Trump had announced Dr. Jackson's surprise nomination in a tweet, he'd punted the entire vetting process directly to Congress—specifically to Senator Isakson and me—in hopes the Senate would quickly confirm his nominee without tough questions.

The following day, Tuesday, April 24, 2018, changed the course of my political career. More important, it changed the course of the entire Department of Veterans Affairs. The day began with even more stories speculating about our investigation in the Veterans' Affairs Committee. But no reporter had any details about what exactly we had heard from Jackson's current and former colleagues. I met with Chairman Isakson in the morning. We had heard from our sources that Dr. Jackson had been the subject of internal investigations into allegations surrounding him. After consulting with me, Senator Isakson decided to postpone Dr. Jackson's Wednesday hearing.[12] Then we formally asked the White House for "all documentation pertaining to Rear Admiral Jackson's service in the White House Medical Unit and as physician to the president." We specifically requested to see all communications "regarding allegations or incidents" involving the doctor.[13] The White House, by the way, never provided that info.

During a news conference that afternoon, John Roberts, a reporter for Fox News, told the president that Jackson had "run into some serious political headwinds on Capitol Hill."

"I'm wondering what you know of those allegations," Roberts asked the president. "And do you intend to stand behind him?"

"If I were him—actually, in many ways, I would love to *be him*," President Trump said of Dr. Jackson in an odd, meandering answer. "But the fact is, I wouldn't [be VA Secretary]. I wouldn't do it. What does he need it for? To be abused by a bunch of politicians that aren't thinking nicely about our country? I really don't think, personally, he should do it."[14]

Meanwhile, in my office on Capitol Hill, I found it difficult to "think nicely," given the ballooning list of serious allegations. It felt like we were starting to lose control of our own tight-knit investigation. The question wasn't whether we'd bring the accusations to the public; the question was *how* and *when*.

On one hand, I was in the middle of a red-hot reelection campaign. With Ryan Zinke now serving in the cabinet, most pundits considered my race a likely win, even despite the fact that most Montanans supported Donald Trump. I had one of the most muscular campaign operations ever assembled in the history of our state. I raised plenty of funds to combat the forces of dark money. As far as politics goes, I hadn't made any fatal mistakes in almost a dozen years in the US Senate, and I treated the job with respect by working as hard as I could at it.

On the other hand, President Trump's White House had gotten away with scandal after scandal after scandal without suffering any real political consequences. He still enjoyed overwhelming popularity in Montana. The president challenged our very democracy every single day. Now he had just handpicked an unqualified naval officer to run the second-largest department in the federal government, with millions of lives on the line, without vetting him first. And more than two dozen whistleblowers—nearly all of them men and women in uniform—had just risked their careers, trusting me to provide the accountability expected of my position on the Veterans' Affairs Committee.

I sat at my desk for a long time. I thought about the first time I'd raised unpopular questions as an elected officeholder, when the Big Sandy school board strong-armed a sale of a house it owned to the superintendent without even an appraisal. I thought about the fall of the Montana Power Company and how its deregulation hurt the livelihoods of thousands of Montanans—*after* ratepayers were promised otherwise. I thought about all the dark money TV ads that had aired in Montana trying to influence my defeat, more than a century after the state of Montana already fought and won the fight over unaccountable money in politics. I thought about Betsy DeVos getting away with ruining our public education system, and how John Walsh's political career came crashing down over something as small, in comparison, as an unoriginal college paper. After considering all of these things, what I did next was the easiest most difficult decision of my life. I called my staff back into my office.

"This is serious shit," I told them.

"Yes it is."

"And you're confident in our sources?"

"Absolutely, Senator. These are high-level whistleblowers with high-level security clearances tasked with protecting the most powerful person on the planet. And they're risking everything to let us know."

Everyone in my office stayed quiet.

"Then we go *all in* now," I said. "We need to make this public. If we don't do it now and if we don't do it big, the White House is going to find a way to twist itself out of accountability. Trump and his people have too much control over stories like this, and they get away with lying about them, and I'm done with it. Ronny Jackson can discuss all of these allegations when he's in front of our committee. *Under oath.*"

And with that, I asked my staff to summarize many of the common allegations in a concise, two-page memo, which we shared with Chairman Isakson and his staff. Then I met with all the Democratic members of the committee to share with them what we'd learned. At that point the news media started hearing leaked details of our investigation, so we made our move. My communications director, Marneé Banks, took a deep breath and sent it to the growing number of interested reporters. *Click.* Within minutes, our phones started lighting up with news alerts from the Associated Press, the *New York Times*, and other media outlets detailing the allegations about Ronny Jackson. And the requests for news interviews started flooding in—more than one hundred of them within minutes. But the only interviews I accommodated that evening were a live interview on NPR's *All Things Considered*, then one with Anderson Cooper on CNN.

"The White House doctor's nickname, among some people in the White House, was 'the Candyman'?" Cooper asked with disbelief, live on *Anderson Cooper 360*. "That's not a nickname you want in a doctor."

"That's not a nickname you want in a doctor, and if you consider the prescription drugs we have a problem with in this country right now, it's not the example we need to have set," I replied.[15] "When we get reports of wrongdoing, it's our job as senators to make sure that we get to the bottom of it, and that's what we are doing right now. . . . I think it would be wise for the admiral to do some self-assessment and ask himself if this is out there, if this stuff is true, [then the confirmation is] certainly not going to happen for him."[16]

On the morning of Thursday, April 26, with his name leading the day's headlines, Rear Admiral Ronny Jackson withdrew his name from consideration as secretary of Veterans Affairs. He vehemently denied the allegations and said they had become a distraction. But now, at least, he wouldn't have to answer the allegations publicly and under oath. Minutes later, the president phoned into *Fox & Friends*.

He rambled for thirty minutes, but his softball interview began with Ronny Jackson's withdrawal.

"Last night the report was you had a huddle," the host, Brian Kilmeade, said of Jackson's decision to remove himself from consideration. "Is that what you decided last night?"

"Well, I even told him a day or two ago," Trump answered, apparently admitting that the decision for Jackson to step down may have been made before I even released my memo. "I saw where this was going."[17]

And then the president launched into me.

"I watch what Jon Tester of Montana—a state I won by like, over 20 points—you know, really," the president said, failing to complete his own sentence. "They love me and I love them. And I want to tell you that Jon Tester—I think this is going to cause him a lot of problems in his state . . . I think Jon Tester has to have a big price to pay in Montana."[18] Suddenly, the phones in all my offices across Montana and in Washington started ringing with angry Fox News viewers from across the country. Apparently their wrath was part of my big price to pay.

I didn't have much to add to the media storm that day. I did say it was my "constitutional responsibility to make sure the veterans of this nation get a strong, thoroughly vetted leader who will fight for them."[19] But a Republican friend of mine called me up with plenty more to add. Former defense secretary Chuck Hagel, the ex-senator from Nebraska, told me I did exactly what I was supposed to do as ranking member of the committee, then he came to my defense with a public statement:

> Fifty years ago today I was in Vietnam with my brother, and for fifty years I've been involved with veterans. . . . There is no one who cares more about veterans and looks out for their interests than my former colleague Jon Tester. As a veteran who has had the privilege of serving my country in many capacities, I've always admired Jon Tester's commitment to helping veterans—not using veterans for political purposes.[20]

The following day, Friday, April 27, President Trump used a news conference with German chancellor Angela Merkel to go after me again, saying he didn't think Montana "is going to put up with" my role in Admiral Jackson's withdrawal.[21] That afternoon, the US Secret Service disputed a CNN story, which cited four different sources, about an incident in 2015 that wasn't included in my memo. CNN reported that agents intervened when Dr. Jackson "was intoxicated and banged on the hotel room door of a female employee" during an overseas trip with then-president Obama.[22] But the agency carefully worded its response, without shutting the door on the alleged incident:

"A thorough review of internal documents related to all Presidential foreign travel that occurred in 2015, in addition to interviews of personnel who were present during foreign travel that occurred during the same timeframe, has resulted in no information that would indicate the allegation is accurate," the Secret Service said.[23]

The White House also claimed the Secret Service found no evidence that Jackson wrecked a car as the president's physician as described in my two-page memo. Jackson denied this too.[24]

"More than one of our sources told us about that car wreck," Murph told me before I left Washington for a week in Montana. His face was white and his voice deflated; clearly he hadn't slept much. "But if we screwed any of this up, I take responsibility for it."

Murph also told me thousands of angry Trump supporters (the vast majority of them non-Montanans) had called my office demanding my resignation. And many in our inner circle had questioned why I'd made the allegations public: Why did we turn a sleepy US Senate race without a serious challenger upside down by poking the biggest bear in politics? All of a sudden what was supposed to be an easy reelection victory had become much more difficult. Why didn't we just let this one go and play it safe?

"I can tell you're nervous," I told Murph. "Don't be. This is why I'm here. If this sinks my career then I'll be able to live with myself, and you will too, because lives are on the line. This is hardly the time to play it safe. I feel better about this than anything else I've done over the last twelve years." At least some of the color came back to Murph's face.

Senator Schumer wanted to know why the hell I would take such a risk given the vulnerability of my Senate seat. He was looking at the situation from the perspective of November's map.

"I don't understand why you had to be the one to make all this news," Schumer said in a call to the farm. Someone in a safer seat could have done it, he added.

"It's why I'm here, Chuck," I replied. "It's my *damn job.*"

And that brings us back to April 28, the Saturday morning Donald Trump called on me to resign. Chairman Isakson's office also chimed in that day, telling reporters that the Republican from Georgia "has a great relationship" with me, and adding that Senator Isakson "doesn't have a problem with how things were handled."

"I don't know for sure but highly doubt [Senator Isakson has] seen the president's tweets this morning," Isakson's spokeswoman added.[25] But President Trump's political rally in Michigan that night drowned out Senator Isakson's supportive words—when the president claimed to "know things" about me that would ruin my political career if he said them.

"Trump offered zero specifics—either in the speech or after it—to back up his charge against Tester," Chris Cillizza, a political commentator, pointed out on CNN. "There are no news reports suggesting there is some sort of major bombshell waiting to be dropped on Tester. His Republican opponents haven't—as far as I can tell—mentioned anything that hints at a skeleton in Tester's closet."[26] That's because, as Donald Trump and his people all damn well knew, there aren't any skeletons in my closet. I simply embarrassed the president and he responded the way he does best—by making shit up.

"I've got no secrets," I told a Montana Television Network reporter who came to interview me at the farm. I added I had no regrets about bringing the allegations against Dr. Jackson to light. "The president's going to do what the president does, and I'm going to continue to do what I do. And when it comes to working for veterans, I won't take a back seat to anybody."[27]

On April 30, CNN aired another exclusive report that changed the whole story again: Vice President Mike Pence's physician had apparently raised concerns about Rear Admiral Jackson in the fall of 2017:

> According to copies of internal documents obtained by CNN, Pence's doctor accused Jackson of overstepping his authority and inappropriately intervening in a medical situation involving the second lady as well as potentially violating federal privacy rights by briefing White House staff and disclosing details to other medical providers—but not appropriately consulting with the vice president's physician.
>
> The vice president's physician later wrote in a memo of feeling intimidated by an irate Jackson during a confrontation over the physician's concerns. The physician informed White House officials of being treated unprofessionally, describing a pattern of behavior from Jackson that made the physician "uncomfortable" and even consider resigning from the position.[28]

Senator Isakson referenced this story the next day, when speaking at a Rotary Club in Georgia about whether it was appropriate for the president to assert that the allegations against Jackson were "not true."

"Last night a story broke that made [what Trump said] a false statement," Isakson said. "The allegations that had been incorporated in some of the complaints that were held against Admiral Jackson were validated in that, so it looks like there's been a story that corroborates the fact that there were some of those allegations which were correct. . . . I did my job, and every senator has the responsibility, if they're presented with accusations, to try and seek the truth. And that exonerates everybody who seeks the truth."[29]

Johnny Isakson is a decent man, and his noble understanding of our role as lawmakers in a separate, coequal branch of government will never make sense to Donald Trump. The president's wrath and his personal attacks on me gave my political opponents a new opportunity. On May 1, just three days after the president's political rally in Michigan, a weirdo pro-Trump super PAC called America First Action started running TV ads across Montana using the president's comments.[30] The National Republican Senatorial Committee launched a similar TV ad the following day, featuring the angry president complaining, "What Jon Tester did to this man is a disgrace!"[31] Still, the ads didn't concern me too much. Despite the president's ability to rile up his supporters, plenty of veterans in Montana thanked me for sticking to my guns.

Unlike most stories of 2017 and the first half of 2018, my public vetting of Dr. Ronny Jackson seemed to have gotten stuck in the spin cycle of the news media. Networks dispatched reporters to Montana to gather sound-bite opinions from coffee shops and cowboy bars. Talking heads fought over whether I had just brought down my political career. Fox News played clips over and over again of Donald Trump railing against me at rallies. It was a good ten days before the news media stopped covering the president's anger with me, my suddenly tenuous campaign, and Dr. Jackson. And now, the entire country was paying attention to our little US Senate race in Montana. Supporters from across the nation started sending small donations to my campaign. But we were going to have to spend a lot more of that money to push back and to defend my record. Montana's primary election, when voters would determine which Republican would ultimately challenge me in November, was still a month away. Whoever won would have an automatic advantage, because Donald Trump knew who I was, and he thought he could push me around.

"What are you doing?" one of my longtime advisers asked. "This was supposed to be your easy win, Jon."

"When I was a kid, a gang of older bullies trapped us in the monkey bars and wouldn't allow us on the playground," I told him. "So I took my brother's advice. I found the biggest damn kid out there and socked him in the face as hard as I could. The big guys aren't used to getting a fist in the face. And the recess harassment went away."

"You punched the biggest bully in the face, all right. You humiliated him. But this is the president of the United States. And it's *this* president of the United States."

"Yeah." I sighed. "It's gonna be one hell of a year."

CHAPTER 17

How to Pronounce "Montana"

C hristie Roberts, my ace campaign manager who first started working for me in 2010, taped a Mike Tyson poster to the wall in her office on the weekend President Trump called on me to resign:

"EVERYONE HAS A PLAN UNTIL THEY GET PUNCHED IN THE MOUTH."

That message to her staff hung next to another poster of a cartoon goldfish warning, "If it seems fishy, it's probably phishy!"

For a couple of days, my scrutiny of President Trump's unvetted VA nominee was his punch in the mouth. And the president's sudden focus on me and the 2018 Senate race in Montana was mine. Then came the hook that knocked me back on my heels: new internal polling showed my numbers sliding down. I've never been a big believer in polling, especially after so many pollsters misfired in 2016, but it felt terrible. Soon, my own polling showed me outright losing. The wrath of Donald Trump was winning.

As a political narrative, the news media ate it up. The president's feud with me had all the ingredients for a sexy story: an explosive personality, a vulnerable underdog, and plenty more unanswered questions. President Trump and his team promised to do everything they could to deny me another term in the US Senate. They suggested I had no business serving a rural state that overwhelmingly elected President Trump. My role in taking down Dr. Ronny Jackson as a nominee was just a proof point. Soon the media narrative was so focused on my reelection that most folks glazed over news in June that the Pentagon's Inspector General had launched a formal investigation into the allegations against Dr. Jackson.[1] The doctor had quietly returned to the White House Medical Unit, though not to his former role as the president's physician.[2]

In Montana, all four Republican US Senate primary candidates vying for their party's nomination in 2018 leaned into the narrative, assuming that their best shot at unseating me was to align themselves squarely with the Chaos President. And on June 5, GOP voters in Montana finally chose their man: auditor and insurance commissioner Matt Rosendale. Rosendale won the primary election with a third of all votes cast, beating out former Billings judge Russell Fagg, state senator Albert Olszewski of Kalispell, and a well-to-do businessman named Troy Downing, who landed in hot water after claiming a primary residence tax exemption on his home in California.[3] This was, as many pundits noted, the B-team for the Montana GOP after Ryan Zinke left Montana to serve as interior secretary and popular attorney general Tim Fox passed on running for the Senate.

Rosendale, a successful real estate developer, moved to Montana from Centreville, Maryland, in 2002. Though he left the Chesapeake Bay behind, he never shed his chewy Eastern Maryland accent, which is unfamiliar in Montana, to say the least. He elongated certain vowels, curved his lips around certain words, and emphasized or even added certain syllables inconsistent with the way most Montanans speak—so much so that he nearly pronounced the president's name with two syllables: *TROO-ump*. Matt Rosendale even struggled to say "Montana." No matter how hard he tried, or didn't, Rosendale pronounced the name of our state with an *aw* in the first syllable and a long, nasally *tau* as the middle: *Mawn-TAU-nuh*. This may seem like small potatoes outside Big Sky Country, but when running for public office here, it's significant. I got nothing against folks from Maryland, but pronouncing "Montana" differently from Montanans is a clear way of saying, "I ain't one of you."

The Montana Democratic Party picked up on the quirk and had some fun with it in an online video stringing together a bunch of "Maryland Matt's" butchered pronunciations of *Mawn-TAU-nuh*. The party also included disparaging comments about his outsider status from his own Republican opponents.[4]

But what Matt Rosendale lacked in local history and dialect he made up for in ambition. He ran for and won a seat in the Montana House of Representatives in 2010, then a seat in the Montana Senate two years later. In 2014, he unsuccessfully challenged Zinke in the Republican primary to succeed Steve Daines for Montana's at-large seat in the US House of Representatives. For that campaign, Rosendale produced a TV ad that mimicked the TV spot supporting Libertarian Dan Cox in 2012. Rosendale's ad depicted him shooting down a government spy drone (which he pronounced *droon*). In 2016, as Donald Trump coasted to victory in Montana, Rosendale handily won a four-year term as our state's auditor and insurance commissioner. For that race, he never had to appear or say much in public. And on July 31, 2017, after just a few months into his term, Rosendale announced his candidacy for the US Senate.

"I am the best positioned person to take on Jon Tester because the people of *Mawn-TAU-nuh* don't feel that they have been served properly," Rosendale told Montana Public Radio that day. Then he claimed that Montanans were unsatisfied by how I represented them in Congress. "They feel like he comes home and tries to act like a farmer and yet he goes back to Washington and votes just like Chuck Schumer."[5]

Questioning my status as a farmer never made much sense to me as a campaign tactic, and it was the first mistake Rosendale and the Montana GOP made. Plenty of Montanans may disagree with my politics, but a majority of them know I am a farmer. I have never tried to *act* like one. And I'm well past the point of feeling like I need to prove it. Being a farmer is who I am.

Like being a farmer, being a *rancher* means more than just own-ing ranchland. Being a rancher means you raise livestock. Rosendale bought a ranch after moving to Montana from Maryland. And for years in press releases, TV commercials, stump speeches—even of-ficial paperwork—he regularly described himself as a rancher. He posed in front of cattle. He spoke about building fences and injecting growth hormones into livestock and working the land. But it turns out Rosendale had more in common with Congressman Dennis Reh-berg, who called himself a rancher because it was politically expedi-ent. The research organization American Bridge in 2018 requested and got public records on Rosendale's ranchland, then shared its find-ings with *Talking Points Memo*, which reported that Rosendale's claim appeared to be "all hat, no cattle":

> Rosendale hasn't registered ownership of any livestock since 2011—and before then it was limited to a few horses. It ap-pears that he's never owned any cattle. He similarly received a registered livestock brand when he bought his $2.2 million ranch in 2002, but let that lapse when it expired in 2011, and it doesn't appear that he ever used it.[6]

After that, the "rancher" references slowly and quietly disappeared from Rosendale's press releases, website, and social media descriptions.[7] Overplaying his rancher credentials was bad enough for Rosendale; then my own campaign researchers uncovered another document that questioned his commitment to being a Montana citizen.

In 2015—a full thirteen years after he moved to Montana—Matt Rosendale signed a form under penalty of perjury indicating he was a Maryland resident when selling a twenty-five-acre piece of property he still owned in Maryland. When a reporter asked him about it, the title company, The Atlantic Title Group, took the blame, stating it had completed the form and residency declaration *after* Rosendale had signed it.[8] For someone whose job title was literally "auditor," we found Rosendale's excuse unconvincing.

Still, as a Senate candidate, Rosendale commanded the GOP

field from the beginning. He lined up early support from the conservative Club for Growth, which pumped $1.7 million to make sure he emerged victorious from the primary election. Rosendale enjoyed the backing of the conservative financier Richard Uihlein. He got endorsements from Senators Ted Cruz and Mike Lee, and the pro-Trump Great America Alliance.[9] Then in the spring of 2018, with a solid lead, he put out a TV ad that looked awfully familiar. The ad showed Rosendale sitting in a kitchen, getting a flattop haircut. Pundits immediately compared the spot to my "Creating a Buzz" ad twelve years earlier. And moments after Rosendale won the GOP primary he declared, "The battle of the flattops has finally begun."

"Jon Tester is vulnerable and President Trump has made winning *Mawn-TAU-nuh* a priority," Rosendale continued that night, before returning to the GOP's recycled talking points. "He'll tell us one thing while he's here in *Mawn-TAU-nuh*, and then he goes back to Washington, DC, and he takes his counsel from Chuck Schumer and Nancy Pelosi."[10]

Making my race only about President Trump and national political leaders was Matt Rosendale's second mistake. Conrad Burns compared me to Ted Kennedy. Dennis Rehberg compared me to Barack Obama. Matt Rosendale compared me to Chuck Schumer and Nancy Pelosi. All those folks may not have been very popular in Montana, but comparing me to them was a weak strategy that rings hollow.

My strategy was to keep showing Montanans that despite the unpopularity and dysfunction of the swamp, I still knew how to get things done. After the Senate overwhelmingly passed our 2018 bipartisan banking reform bill, the Economic Growth, Regulatory Relief, and Consumer Protection Act, President Trump signed it into law at the White House on May 24. He surrounded himself with a number of lawmakers—mostly Republicans, though my friend Heidi Heitkamp of North Dakota got an invitation. I certainly did not get one; nor did I expect to. The hurt feelings over Dr. Jackson were still raw for the president. But in an obvious message to me, the president invited Montana's junior senator, Steve Daines, to stand at his side as he signed the bill I mostly wrote.

"Thank you, Steve," the president said. "Incredible job."[11] Senator Daines grinned, apparently forgetting that he had absolutely no role in crafting the bill. In fact, he never even cosponsored the legislation.[12] Some politicians are hardwired to sit back and accept credit for work they didn't do. That sort of thing doesn't come naturally to people who were raised on farms.

I kept introducing bills I thought were important to Montana: In 2017, I introduced the Yellowstone Gateway Protection Act in response to the work of the Yellowstone Gateway Business Coalition's efforts to permanently outlaw hardrock gold mining north of Yellowstone National Park—the legislation then-congressman Zinke wanted to sponsor in the House.

I introduced the Department of Education Accountability Act, which would have rescinded a half-million bucks from Education Secretary Betsy DeVos' personal office budget for every week she refused to reconsider the University of Montana's revised Upward Bound application.[13] I considered it only fair after her department rejected that application because a single page of it wasn't double spaced. A few days later, Secretary DeVos agreed to reconsider the application from Montana, and the university ultimately received its funding.[14] Then I introduced a bill to prevent the Education Department from rejecting such grant applications based on technical errors.[15]

In September 2017 the Center for Effective Lawmaking, a nonpartisan organization funded by the University of Virginia and Vanderbilt University, ranked me as the fourth-most-effective Senate Democrat.[16] The day after Montana's primary election in June 2018, President Trump signed into law my fifteenth bill, the VA MISSION Act, which replaced the VA Choice Program.[17] He signed my sixteenth bill the day after that, on June 7. That legislation formally named three VA medical facilities in Montana after the World War II heroes David Thatcher, Ben Steele, and Dr. Joe Medicine Crow.[18] But would any of these accomplishments matter in the age of fake news and distrust in Washington—especially when stacked against something as powerful as, say, the president himself coming to Montana to campaign against me?

"Trump's coming," Christie told me on the morning of June 29, 2018. She was confident, but she added with a sigh, "It's going to be ugly, boss."

"I bet it ain't the last time he comes here before Election Day," I replied.

"I won't take that bet. But we have a plan."

Of course Christie Roberts had a plan. After working as my 2012 campaign researcher and serving as political director of the Democratic Senatorial Campaign Committee, she knew exactly what it would take to run a campaign in a rural state that overwhelmingly supported Donald Trump. And when Christie agreed to manage my third US Senate campaign, I knew I'd gotten the best the country had to offer.

Donald Trump had first visited Montana two years earlier, on May 26, 2016. He flew his big black airliner into Billings and fired up a crowd of about 7,500 people. That day, Congressman Zinke spoke just before Trump, endorsing the billionaire candidate and invoking Senator Conrad Burns, who had passed away a month earlier.

"Before I took office Conrad called me and said, 'Son, I'm gonna tell you some really good advice,'" Zinke told the crowd in Burns's adopted hometown. "He said, 'Never, ever vote against ag in Montana.' You know what? We need a president who understands that agriculture makes this country great."[19]

On that, Ryan Zinke and I can agree. If only that president were Donald Trump.

Before that, the last time Montana welcomed a sitting US president was back in August 2009, when President Obama held a health care town hall meeting in a crowded airplane hangar near Bozeman. I forgot my tie that day and had to borrow Murph's, and then I had to sit on a little wooden stool on stage next to Senator Baucus, Governor Schweitzer, and the president *for hours*. Company aside, it was painfully uncomfortable.

Of course, I wasn't going to be anywhere near President Trump's latest rally in Montana, even though it was in my neck of the woods—Great Falls—on July 5, 2018. I planned to be in Billings that day, where I held a much quieter meeting at the local Chamber of Commerce about the impact of President Trump's trade war with China. After all, for a president who claimed to support agriculture, his trade war had already cost Montana farmers millions in lost revenue.

"If and when the tariffs are enacted tomorrow, we face significant duties of $65 million in wheat exports to China annually," Michelle Erickson-Jones, the president of the Montana Grain Growers Association, told me that day. "Right now, current daily impacts have been substantial: the price of bins, the price of steel, the price of equipment, the impacts to the used equipment market." And the pain didn't just hurt farmers. The executive director of the Missoula Public Library also weighed in about the rising costs of construction of a new library building: the tariffs on rebar alone had increased the cost by $100,000.[20]

But my event that day was no match for the hubbub underway in Great Falls, which was preparing for one of President Trump's famous rallies. That morning, readers of the *Great Falls Tribune* opened their newspapers to a familiar tactic. Christie and her team had purchased a full-page ad on the back of the newspaper, complete with a smiling mug of yours truly, with the words:

WELCOME TO MONTANA
& THANK YOU PRESIDENT TRUMP
FOR SUPPORTING JON'S LEGISLATION TO HELP VETERANS
AND FIRST RESPONDERS, HOLD THE
VA ACCOUNTABLE, AND GET RID
OF WASTE, FRAUD AND ABUSE
IN THE FEDERAL GOVERNMENT.

Underneath the large print, we listed all sixteen bills of mine President Trump had signed into law since he took office. Then:

WASHINGTON'S A MESS—BUT THAT'S
NOT STOPPING JON FROM GETTING
THINGS DONE FOR MONTANA.[21]

The ad was a page out of our own playbook. We also took out similar ads in smaller newspapers across Montana, and produced radio commercials with the same message. The national news media picked up on the cheeky tactic, which meant almost every story about the president's visit to Great Falls also included a mention of how many of my bills he had signed into law. That made the reaction from the National Republican Senatorial Committee all the more ironic: "No phony last-minute newspaper ads are going to be enough to cover up for his constant obstruction of President Trump's agenda," an NRSC spokesman replied.[22] The president's greasy-haired kid had weighed in a couple of days earlier, telling the *Great Falls Tribune* that I'm "nothing more than Chuck Schumer's liberal lapdog."[23]

The president's Great Falls rally drew a crowd of about 6,600 in the Four Seasons Arena. For a few moments, he handed the mic over to Auditor Rosendale. But for the most part, the president stuck to his familiar talking points about Ronny Jackson before taking his long, rambling speech all over the map. And then as quickly as he'd flown in on Air Force One, he flew out. The following Monday, he held a news conference at the White House to announce his nominee to replace Justice Anthony Kennedy on the US Supreme Court: Judge Brett Kavanaugh.

That summer I relied on star power a little too.

"We'll do another one for you, Jon," Jeff Ament told me earlier in the year. And the band folded a Missoula concert into their 2018 tour. This time Pearl Jam performed on August 13, under the stars in the sold-out stadium on the University of Montana campus. That day at the stadium, Jeff's dad, George, gave me a fresh haircut, just like he first did decades earlier at his barbershop in Big Sandy. Pearl Jam packed the house with tens of thousands of screaming fans. Their 2018 Rock2Vote concert didn't directly benefit me; it raised money for several progressive nonprofit organizations dedicated to getting young people to vote. And as such, lawyers advised the members of the band not to say my name onstage. Instead, during the second half of the show, all of them peeled off their outer shirts to reveal T-shirts that read TESTER in the shape of Montana.

"There is one crowd size that we would be proud of, and that we would brag about," the group's front man, Eddie Vedder, said between songs. "And that is if the state of Montana had the largest youth vote, the largest crowd, that came together in this upcoming election. That I would brag about all fuckin' day!"[24]

But the big news of that night wasn't the music; it was the artwork. Jeff conceptualized the official poster for the concert, then had it designed by an artist friend of his named Bobby Brown, known professionally as "Bobby Draws Skullz." As soon as word spread of how wild the posters were, fans stood in line for hours to buy them all up at $35 a pop. Christie showed me a copy, gritting her teeth.

The poster depicted a burning White House with the letters "P" and "J" on either side. In the foreground, a facedown skeleton with a mop of orange hair on his head reaches for a hammer-and-sickle briefcase as a bald eagle pecks at his foot. In the bottom-right corner is Matt Rosendale, holding a Maryland flag with a crab claw hand. On the lawn of the White House, an alien rests a broken foot while smoking a cigarette. Above the scene, white smoke spells the word "VOTE." And there's an unmistakable image of me, flying on my tractor above the fire and fury, waving with my two-fingered left hand.

"This is so . . . interesting," I told Christie. Though the poster was off message, I didn't want to admit to her that I actually loved it. None of us knew about the posters before we saw them on sale at the concert.

Republican political organizations immediately attacked the cartoon, claiming it was "gory" and "reprehensible." Matt Rosendale even called it an "act of violence," which was a stretch.[25] Though I agreed that the concert poster was going to cause an unnecessary headache for Christie, I thought all the GOP criticism was rich, given the president's frequent and much more blatant suggestions of violence without consequence. Jeff called me the next day to apologize for all the trouble surrounding the poster (the Secret Service even met with Jeff and Bobby Brown to discuss it), but I told him not to sweat it. Then Jeff stood up for himself as the GOP fumed:

The role of the artist is to make people think and feel, and the current administration has us thinking and feeling. I was the sole conceptualist of this poster, and I welcome all interpretations and discourse. Love, from the First Amendment, Jeff Ament.[26]

With love from the Second Amendment, the National Rifle Association came roaring into Montana in early September. They ran a TV ad claiming I was "two-faced" because I voted "against your right to self-defense," even though I support gun rights.[27] The NRA's dark-money lobbying arm, the Institute for Legislative Action, funded the spot. And a few days later, the *Daily Beast* broke a story indicating that Matt Rosendale may have illegally coordinated with the NRA-ILA before the ad appeared in Montana.[28]

Federal law strictly prohibits candidates like Rosendale from coordinating with independent electioneering organizations like the NRA-ILA on campaign spending plans designed to help that candidate or hurt that candidate's opponent. Yet the *Daily Beast* had somehow obtained an audio recording from July in which Rosendale suggested that he had inside information about air cover from the outside.

"I fully expect that the US Chamber is going to come in, and I fully expect that the NRA is going to come in," Rosendale said in the recording. "I think both of them will be coming in, probably, right here, at the end of August—sometime." Then he mentioned Chris Cox, the NRA-ILA's executive director. Again, federal law prohibits Rosendale from coordinating campaign spending plans with someone like Cox. So what he said next was telling: "But Chris Cox told me, he's like, 'We're going to be in this race.'"[29]

Though analysts said the audio made a clear case for an investigation by the Federal Election Commission, nothing ever happened.[30] Rosendale and the NRA-ILA claimed discussions were limited to the NRA-ILA endorsement and denied any allegations of improper coordination. Then, just as Rosendale predicted, the US Chamber of

Commerce came into Montana with a TV ad campaign attacking me, even though its eighty-year-old president, Tom Donohue, had met me in my office earlier that summer to praise my work on behalf of small businesses and community banks. Needless to say, that meeting was a waste of his time and mine.

As expected, President Trump returned to Montana on September 6 for another rally—at the same venue in Billings where he'd spoken in May 2016. The most remarkable part of his speech that night was his talk about his own possible impeachment—a full year before the US House of Representatives launched its impeachment inquiry into the president.

> I say, how do you impeach somebody that's doing a great job that hasn't done anything wrong? Our economy is good. How do you do it? How do you do it? How do you do it? "We will impeach him!" "But he's doing a great job!" "Doesn't matter!" . . . But if it does happen, it's your fault, because you didn't go out to vote, okay?[31]

I'm willing to bet most of the country doesn't remember the Make America Great Again rally in Billings that September because of what the president said about impeachment. I bet most folks know about that rally because of the hilarity happening behind the president's right shoulder. There, prominently standing in full view for the TV audience, was a seventeen-year-old high schooler wearing a blue and white plaid shirt, who scrunched his face, shook his head, refused to clap, and mouthed *what?* as the president said ridiculous things.

Fifty minutes into the president's speech, a young woman approached Plaid Shirt Guy and whispered something to him. Without resistance, he slipped out as she quietly took his place.[32] But Plaid Shirt Guy had already become a hashtag and a viral internet sensation. Turns out, he simply had wanted to experience hearing his president speak, then had gotten an email notifying him that he had been chosen as a VIP. His lucky placement directly behind the president, he told the *New York Times*, was "basically random."

"That was not me trying to protest," he said. "That was just my honest reactions to the things that he was saying."[33] By the way, Plaid Shirt Guy's older brother happened to be an intern in my Billings office.

Back in Washington, the big news that September was the upcoming confirmation of Supreme Court nominee Brett Kavanaugh, and news that Senator Dianne Feinstein of California had referred to the FBI a credible accusation from one of her constituents that Kavanaugh had, decades earlier, committed sexual assault.

For weeks, the White House had delayed scheduling my meeting with Kavanaugh, despite eight different requests from my office for a face-to-face sit-down with the judge.[34] The fact that the White House never accommodated my request to meet with a nominee who would serve a lifetime appointment on the Supreme Court wasn't just unprecedented, it was downright dangerous. I had questions about Judge Kavanaugh's record as an attorney in President George W. Bush's administration, when he played a role in shaping unpopular policies like the Patriot Act, warrantless wiretapping, and passenger profiling, though only a fraction of his records were made public.[35] As a federal judge, Kavanaugh had said the government's mass surveillance of Americans' phone records was constitutional.[36] During a 2016 forum with the conservative American Enterprise Institute, Paul Gigot, a *Wall Street Journal* columnist, had asked Kavanaugh, "Do you agree with the trend of the Supreme Court's jurisprudence that money spent during campaigns does represent speech and therefore deserves First Amendment protection, or at least strict scrutiny of any limits on that spending?"

"Absolutely," Judge Kavanaugh replied. "I think political speech is at the core of the First Amendment and to make your voice heard, you need to raise money to be able to communicate to others in any kind of effective way."[37]

Then, of course, there was the issue of choice. Confirming Brett Kavanaugh to the Supreme Court would finally complete the circle for many antichoice advocates, positioning the court to weaken or outright prohibit the freedom of choice with a conservative majority.

I had mostly made up my mind on Judge Kavanaugh by Thursday, September 27, when the nation watched Dr. Christine Blasey Ford's reluctant public testimony, followed by Kavanaugh's belligerent response, on live TV.

I shut the door to my office to watch the hearing underway on the floor below me, alone. Dr. Ford's account of the attack on her made me sick; it struck a chord deep within me. She was visibly scared, trembling, and sharing a painful story with millions of Americans simply because she had a patriotic responsibility to do so. During a pause in the testimony, I poked my head out of my office. There was Marneé Banks, my usually stalwart communications director, watching the hearing on four different TV screens in her cubicle. Tears streamed down her face, which I'd never seen before.

"Hey," I said. "*I believe her.*"

The next day, I announced my decision on Brett Kavanaugh, citing my concerns over his defense of the Patriot Act, his support of dark money, and "who he believes is in charge of making personal health decisions."

"And I have deep concerns about the allegations of sexual assault against Judge Kavanaugh," I added. "Unfortunately, Judge Kavanaugh couldn't find the time to discuss these concerns with me in person, so the only information I have is from what he said in his hearings. *I'll be voting against him.*"[38] And on October 6, I did.[39]

"No one should be surprised by this," a frustrated Matt Rosendale responded. "We always knew Jon Tester was never going to vote for Judge Brett Kavanaugh."[40]

Majority Leader McConnell held Judge Kavanaugh's hearing one month before Election Day to strategically inflict maximum political pain for vulnerable Democrats in red states. For me, voting against him was a more clear-cut decision than voting against Neil Gorsuch. Senator Joe Manchin of West Virginia was the only Democrat who supported Kavanaugh. Claire McCaskill of Missouri, Heidi Heitkamp of North Dakota, and Joe Donnelly of Indiana—all of whom represented states that President Trump won by at least 10 points—voted against him.

My decision to vote against Judge Kavanaugh formed the substance of the first question in my first debate with Matt Rosendale, on September 29. Rosendale and I originally agreed to debate each other on June 17, at the traditional Montana Broadcasters Association debate in Whitefish. Just like Dennis Rehberg did six years earlier, Rosendale backed out of that debate.

In early June, he told NBC Montana, "You'll see me in Whitefish." Then, a few days later, his campaign announced that Rosendale wouldn't participate after all, claiming that because the debate fell on Father's Day, "Matt is spending the day with his wife and sons, and he's not moving that around, nor should he."[41] My team didn't buy that excuse for a hot second. And neither did the media, which gave him relentless headlines about skipping his scheduled debate.

"Whatever the excuse is, it's disappointing," my campaign responded. "This debate is a Montana tradition, but of course Montana traditions mean nothing to Maryland Matt."

And so the Montana Broadcasters Association held a forum with just me, fielding questions in Whitefish. I had spent many hours preparing with my team for a debate that never happened, just as I had done in 2012 and in 2006. Pat Stranix, my campaign's research director, played the part of Matt Rosendale during our exhaustive debate prep sessions. Having memorized hours of speeches and previous debates, Pat went after me aggressively every time I lowered my guard. He even adopted Rosendale's unmistakable accent, which just pissed me off. Pat, we joked, made a better candidate out of Matt Rosendale than Matt Rosendale.

I continued having debate prep sessions through the summer, scheduling them around everything else packed into my day. That meant we held them early in the morning or late at night. After a long day of work or a short night of sleep, getting through two hours of intensive debate prep took everything I had, physically and emotionally. But it paid off.

When Rosendale and I finally met in Missoula for what should have been our second debate in late September, I was prepared. And I went after him on his unpopular support for transferring management of federal public lands to individual states—a position many of us public land supporters point out is the first step in ultimately selling them off. Rosendale conveniently said he changed his position when he became a candidate, even though he had a long record of opposing public land acquisitions by the state of Montana.

"I have since talked to people across the entire state and they have made it exceedingly clear that they do not want those lands transferred," Rosendale said. "I not only understand that, I agree with that."

"It is critically important that Montana has somebody in Washington, DC," I said, "who will not just speak whatever he thinks will get him the votes, but will fight for Montana values and fight for our public lands."[42]

Two weeks later we met for our second and final debate in Bozeman. That debate included the Libertarian candidate, Rick Breckenridge, who wore his signature buckskin vest and a stars-and-stripes necktie. We covered many of the same topics as the first debate, but with only twenty-three days until Election Day, Rosendale and I got feistier. We were both tired and irritated with each other. In my closing remarks, I made a case for Montanans to vote for someone who was born in Montana, who raised a family and ran businesses there; someone who understands that health care costs are too high in rural America; and someone who supported public education as the foundation of our democracy.

"Or, on the other hand," I added, "you can support somebody that was born in Maryland, made millions of dollars there developing property, bought a ranch in Montana, claims to be a rancher, but has no cows; somebody who has advocated for selling our public lands, advocated for kicking people with preexisting conditions off of insurance, advocated for making sure that transparency in our elections is minimal. He's not in it for Montana; he's in it for himself."[43]

Earlier that day, the Trump campaign announced a third visit to Big Sky Country by the president of the United States. He planned to hold another Make America Great Again rally in Missoula on October 18 for Rosendale. By late October, most Montanans had grown weary of—maybe even bored by—the president's political visits.

Between his rallies, Vice President Pence and the president's greasy-haired kid jetted into Montana to fire up their staunchest supporters, though they drew much smaller crowds. None of these speeches offered anything new, and they cost local taxpayers plenty of money. President Trump's visit to Billings alone cost city taxpayers an unbudgeted $59,000—mostly in law enforcement overtime.[44]

The following Thursday, the president arrived at the Missoula airport and spoke to eight thousand fans underneath a fiery orange Montana sunset.[45] For me and my team, the most striking moment of that evening got buried among other headlines. When riffing again about my "vicious" role in vetting Dr. Ronny Jackson, the president said this:

> And it's my fault. I said, "Admiral, how would you like to head up the VA? I want somebody great. You're an admiral, you're a leader." And he's fifty years old. He never had a problem in his whole life. Little bit like Justice Kavanaugh, you know, really a very fine, high quality, handsome guy. Never had a problem. And he said, "Sir, I had never thought of it, but I'll do whatever your wish is, sir." He didn't really want it. He didn't really want. And he might not have been qualified. But here's a doctor at a high level, and he's a man that everybody respected.[46]

"He might not have been qualified"? In what seemed like a half thought in a stream-of-consciousness string of scattered sentences, President Trump had just admitted aloud what so many whistleblowers in his own White House had warned us about. The president also made no mention of the fact that the Senate on July 23 overwhelmingly confirmed his new, much more qualified VA secretary, Robert Wilkie, with eighty-six votes.[47] I happily supported Bob Wilkie, who had served as acting VA secretary after President Trump dismissed Secretary Shulkin.

Halfway through his speech in Missoula, President Trump invited Rosendale up to the podium to say a few words.

"President Trump and all of his policies are on the line," Rosendale said before turning to an eight-year-old talking point. "So let's make history and retire Jon Tester and send President Trump the help he needs. Let's remember, it was Jon Tester who cast the deciding vote on Obamacare and got your premiums skyrocketing. I will never give up on repealing and replacing Obamacare!"[48]

And this was the third mistake Matt Rosendale and the GOP made in trying to win back the Senate seat once held by Conrad Burns: they staked too much of their strategy on a single political figure, assuming that Donald Trump could do no harm in a state that, for the most part, takes pride in prioritizing a politician's character over party.

No one who approached me at the airport, or in line at Costco, or while filling up next to me at the gas station, ever mentioned Ronny Jackson. Nobody in Montana I talked to wanted less health care, yet that was the only plan from Republicans in Congress. Montanans didn't want yet another federal representative to automatically rubber stamp the president and his breakneck agenda without at least asking questions. Maryland Matt, Mike Pence, Donald Trump, and Junior must have all assumed that at least more than 50 percent of Montana voters did. Yet again, they underestimated rural America.

After the president's third visit, Missoula County sent Rosendale a bill for nearly $13,000 to cover the cost of overtime for law enforcement officers.[49] Neither Matt Rosendale nor Donald Trump ever paid that bill.

Still, all those high-profile visits to Montana, paired with the onslaught of ads saturating the airwaves and tubes, took their toll. In early October, the *Cook Political Report* downgraded my race from "lean Democratic" to "toss-up."[50] They saw polling showing my race with Rosendale dead even. My internal polling suggested the same thing. Unlike 2012, either dog could win the scraps.

So, as I did in previous election years, I simply stayed focused on doing my work and visiting with as many Montanans as I could. My Senate staff kept hard at work doing what they could to tune out the noise and help Montanans navigate the VA and Social Security and federal student loans. On my campaign, Christie had spent the year building the largest field campaign in Montana's history, amassing thousands of volunteers who spent evenings and weekends going door to door or dialing up voters and turning out every vote they could.

Christie took no chances. She arranged for dozens of attorneys to be poll watchers on Election Day to ensure fair accounting for every single ballot cast in every corner of the state. She developed a sophisticated system for tracking which people voted and who still needed reminders. She even secured private funding to lease industrial snow-plows and operators to be on standby on all seven of Montana's reservations on Election Day, just in case it snowed. Given their physical remoteness, the reservations are never guaranteed timely plowing, and Christie certainly didn't want snowy roads to be the excuse for any voter who chose to stay home.

I knew we were doing something right when the *New York Times* published a column by the humorist Sarah Vowell, whose dad was a constituent of mine.

> Mr. Rosendale, a Maryland native, is such a meanspirited flake that my Republican father, a guy who wants his ashes shot out of a cannon he built from scratch in his backyard gun shop, plans to vote for Senator Tester, a Democrat. According to Dad, a Gallatin County voter, Mr. Tester, a second-term senator and third-generation farmer from Big Sandy, is "a Montanan who understands Montana." At least I think that's what he said. Once he told my mother and me he was voting for a Democrat I was distracted by determining if Mom needed medical attention. . . .
>
> In the State Senate, Mr. Rosendale's record on bills meant to lighten life's pressures included voting against funding the Southwest Montana Veterans Home; against giving scholarships to Purple Heart recipients; against assisting Gold Star spouses to secure home loans; against streamlining the process for firefighters to get medical treatment for work-related illnesses; and against requiring insurance companies to cover treatments for children with Down syndrome.[51]

Jeff "the Dude" Bridges, a friend of mine who for decades has called Montana home for at least several months a year, also weighed into the political landscape in October. The Dude held a public Q&A on the Montana State University campus in Bozeman in support of my campaign. He drew a crowd of hundreds—most of them students. Wearing a MONTANA ABIDES T-shirt, Bridges, who knew his star power would be broadcast far beyond that university ballroom, encouraged all young people to vote, telling them it's "very dangerous" to be complacent.[52] Bridges also praised my record of working with Republicans. "I just—man, I dig him," he said of me.[53] Jeff, I dig you too, man.

The weekend before Election Day, President Trump came to Montana for his fourth Make America Great Again rally, setting a record for the number of times a sitting president has visited our state. Notably, not one of those visits included any interest in what was actually happening in Montana; no visits to rural communities, no listening, no sight-seeing—just *talking*. And a whole lot of it. On November 3, President Trump, who was uncharacteristically flat and visibly exhausted, briefly spoke to a crowd of only five thousand near Bozeman. After that uneventful speech, he flew to Florida for another rally. None of us were convinced that his expensive jaunt into Montana changed a single vote.[54]

A snowstorm blasted into Montana on November 6, Election Day. I spent that day up at the farm, knowing my team and I had done everything we possibly could have done. I knew Christie and her army of volunteers had shifted into the highest gear possible to execute a game plan she had worked on for two full years. She called me the morning of Election Day to let me know that the snowplows she'd leased were clearing snow on the reservations, and that she felt good about where the race stood. Not certain; just good.

When I'm nervous, I fill my time with physical work. So Shon and I bundled up and spent most of the morning of Election Day in my shop, replacing the old motor in my 1986 Chevy three-quarter-ton pickup. I thought about how I'd bought the truck new at age twenty-nine, thinking I had made something of my life. And now, with my political career being put to the test, I was performing heart surgery on the old thing. I considered that precious morning makeup for the time I hadn't gotten to spend with Shon on Father's Day. The chore required us to stay singularly focused on coordinating tools and heavy equipment, keeping track of the guts of the machinery, and communicating with each other closely. Needless to say, both of us had clear heads that day.

In the afternoon Sharla, Shon, and I packed up and headed down to Great Falls, where we met Christine and James, Mel and Glen, Bob and Lois, Dave and Becky, grandkids and several of my cousins for that evening's watch party at the Great Falls Holiday Inn. The whole scene felt familiar—just like it did in 2012; we were, after all, in the same damn place. After the polls closed at eight p.m., hundreds of local supporters, volunteers, and exhausted campaign staffers showed up and crammed into a decorated ballroom to watch the returns. Christie set up shop with her seniormost staff in a "war room" away from the festivities, at a nondescript hotel across town. She covered all the windows with paper for privacy. Inside the war room they tracked—without a moment of rest—all the work of all the statewide volunteers and their coordinators, election returns, and communications efforts.

Back at our watch party, cheers filled the room as our TVs announced that Democrats had recaptured the US House of Representatives. It didn't take long for the Associated Press to declare Congressman Greg Gianforte, known for little more than physically assaulting a reporter in 2017, the winner of Montana's US House race. Senator Joe Manchin won his race in West Virginia, but Indiana's Joe Donnelly and Missouri's Claire McCaskill lost theirs. Then Heidi Heitkamp lost in North Dakota, and so did Republican Dean Heller of Nevada. Florida, where Senator Bill Nelson faced a tough challenge from Governor Rick Scott, was still too close to call. And so was our race.

At first, the early numbers showed me significantly ahead, giving us all an artificial sugar rush. Then ballots from the smaller counties started coming in, which narrowed the race to a dead heat. That's when we got word that we wouldn't know the final numbers until at least Wednesday. Voters in Gallatin County were still waiting in a long line to vote. For the third Election Night in a row, I went to the stage to thank all the supporters and volunteers who showed up. Donald Trump may have had the power of the American presidency in his corner, but I had thousands of volunteers across Montana in mine. I updated them on the status of the count, then, without knowing whether I had won, I told them to go home. Then Sharla and I went to our room for a glass of wine.

"Wake me up when you figure out who won," I told Christie.

A little before midnight, the Montana Secretary of State's official election website delivered its final update of the day. The new numbers showed Rosendale a few thousand votes ahead of me. Christie called to report that ballot counters still had tens of thousands of ballots to tally in Gallatin and Missoula Counties—two areas where we knew I would command a lead. But still, the official numbers showing Rosendale in the lead lingered on the official website all night long. At about three a.m. in Montana, my friends on the East Coast started waking up and saw headlines indicating Rosendale might just eke out a win in Montana.

Just after eight a.m. the following morning, Christie conferred with her data analysts and then stood up at the front of the war room, whose overcaffeinated staffers were already busy working on ballot chasing plans and even gearing up for a possible recount.

"Everyone!" She allowed herself a careful grin. "Close your laptops." Nobody in the room had slept in thirty-six hours. Few in the room knew what she was about to say.

"*We won this thing.*" I could almost hear the roar from that little room across town. The numbers were decisive, even before all the remaining ballots had yet to be counted. There was no way Rosendale could win. I had won, for the first time in my US Senate career, with *more than 50 percent of the vote.*

Moments later, Christie and Murph made their way back to the Holiday Inn and shared the news with Sharla and me. The Associated Press, they told me, was still reluctant to call the race.

"And you're sure of our numbers?"

"Yes we are."

I looked at both of them and smiled. They knew the deal. "So when do we go downstairs?"

"You're going to make a 'major announcement' at nine," Christie said. "The AP can decide whether it wants to break the news of our win, or they would have to report that we were breaking the news. We don't care. You won!"

Sure enough, at nine a.m., I went downstairs and into a jam-packed little conference room loaded with rolling TV cameras, reporters, misty-eyed supporters, and my family. The place erupted with cheers. Christine, Shon, and Mel spoke first. Then, literally seconds before I took the mic, Murph tapped my shoulder and showed me the news on his phone: the Associated Press had just formally declared me the winner.

That was the speech on live TV during which I had to fight back tears when speaking about the veteran who told me he wasn't going to let me forget about his fellow veterans. I added that Montanans spoke "loud and clear about the direction they want Montana to go."

And quite frankly, I hope the president comes back—many times. I do. But not for political rallies—in all seriousness—not for political rallies, but to see the challenges we have in our state. To take a look at that VA clinic in Missoula, Montana, to see how undersized it is. To take a look at the VA clinic here in Great Falls to see how undermanned it is. . . . But in the meantime, I can assure you all of this—and everybody that's watching—we need to get some things done in Washington, DC. We need to work together. We need to put aside the political pettiness and work together to get things done. And I will tell you why. Because as I have traversed this state—north, south, east, and west—the people I've talked to—the biggest issue they bring up is, "Why can't you guys work together?" Well, we can. And we will. And it will happen because the American people are demanding it.[55]

After all the hugs and handshakes, Matt Rosendale called me a few minutes after the hubbub died down.

"Senator," he said, "I'm not the type of guy who wouldn't call and say congratulations."

"Thank you, Auditor," I told him. "It means a lot to me."

Meanwhile, 1,800 miles east of Montana, a visibly annoyed President Trump hosted a combative postelection news conference in the East Room of the White House with a large gathering of journalists.

"It just came out that Jon Tester won," one of them told the president.

"Oh, congratulations to Jon Tester, congratulations," the president replied. "I'm sure you're very unhappy about that," he added, assuming the reporter wanted a more contentious response. And then the president moved on.[56]

Montana's 2018 Senate race broke new records, costing more than $73 million, all told.[57] For the first time in a statewide race, I had won with a majority of votes (50.3 percent), instead of a plurality. I earned about eighteen thousand more votes than Matt Rosendale.[58] Even if every person who voted for Rick Breckenridge had voted for Rosendale, I still would have won. It didn't take reinventing the wheel to win the most expensive race in Montana's history. But it sure as hell wasn't easy.

Looking back, I believe I won because of the same reason I won my seat on the Big Sandy school board, and in the Montana Legislature: I stayed truer and worked harder. Hard work and authenticity are what kept Fred and Christine Pearson on my farm a century ago. They're what keep Sharla and me on the farm to this day. They're Montana values, learned the hard way. And the communities of this state have come to expect them.

We expect accountability in our government and its leaders. We expect representatives who know the value of a dollar, and who could survive a day pickin' rock. We understand the sacrifices of public servants, from veterans to teachers, and we understand the pain of our most vulnerable citizens. We do it for the very survival of rural America, and our nation could learn a lesson—lots of lessons—from it. We know we've got no other choice but to keep slugging away when we're punched in the mouth.

Epilogue: Gone the Sun

Tonight, Sharla and I are sitting on our deck of our home near Big Sandy, looking east across the farmland. We just wrapped up the harvest. The air smells sweet. Not too hot. The birds are tweeting as the sun dips down behind us, lighting up the Bear Paw Mountains in the distance for a few minutes. I'm working on a cigar and we've opened up a bottle of wine. It's Kirkland wine from Costco. It's red and tastes like wine, and that's good enough for us.

This warm, blue evening reminds me of something Senator Chris Dodd once told me, several years after he had retired from the Senate. I don't even remember why I'd called him, but I worked myself up about whatever it was.

"Life is a gift, Jon," he told me, sensing the anxiety in my voice. "You've gotta enjoy it."

This night, enjoying the setting sun with Sharla, is a gift. As we sip our wine, I get to wondering. I wonder if my grandfolks ever enjoyed a late-summer evening like this, sitting in this exact same spot a century ago. What did they talk about? Of course they worried about the future. But was it the same kind of worry that Sharla and I worry about? Did they worry who would take over this sacred place when they were gone? Did they worry about the weather they couldn't forecast? What concerned them about their son and three daughters? Did they think of themselves as the people of rural America in a divided country? Or were they so focused on the simplicity of a hard day's work that they had little time to think about things like that?

In late 2018, after the razzmatazz of Election Day quieted down, the number crunchers pointed out that I'd won my third term in the US Senate having earned the support of 7 percent of self-identified Republicans across Montana. Despite millions of dollars spent to depict me as someone I'm not, a majority of Montana voters saw through the political pollution and the spin of dark money. At the end of the day, they voted for character and authenticity over political party. That, I believe, is one of the noblest characteristics of rural America: *character and authenticity matter.* If I ever lose sight of those things, I expect Montanans will let me know posthaste. As they should.

Since Election Day, numerous Montana Republicans have approached me in private to tell me that I earned their votes despite our political differences. Many said they may disagree with me, but they'd rather have representatives in Congress who ask questions rather than blindly follow orders. More than a few of my Republican colleagues in the Senate have, under their breath, whispered to me private frustrations with President Trump and his relentlessly controversial and bumbling administration. These colleagues have a tremendous responsibility to express their concerns with more than private whispers; the future of our republic is on the line. All of us swore an oath to support and defend the Constitution and the checks and balances it guarantees within our government. That oath became a whole lot weaker after the president's impeachment trial—after the Republicans refused to allow new witnesses who might've sunk the ship.

After President Trump's summit in Singapore with North Korean dictator Kim Jong-un in June 2018, I walked past a TV in my office tuned to a cable news channel. The banner on screen read, "Trump: North Korea No Longer a Nuclear Threat."

"That's the damnedest thing I've ever seen!" I said aloud, probably yelling at the TV. I've never been one to yell at a TV. A month later, on July 16, the president met alone with Vladimir Putin in Helsinki and defended the authoritarian president of Russia over America's

own intelligence agencies. That was the *new* damnedest thing I'd ever seen. Then it was the government shutdown over a senseless border wall. Then the phone call to Ukraine. Then the impeachment. Like so many Americans, I've had countless moments like that. Our country is being tested by this unprecedented cycle of developments that are dangerous at worst and amateur and embarrassing at best.

You don't have to be a political scientist to see that the members of Congress who protect President Trump, even at the expense of our nation's most foundational values, do it out of pride, or to keep clinging to their power, or to selfishly sidestep a steep political price.

All of us took another oath during the president's impeachment trial in early 2020, swearing to "do impartial justice according to the Constitution and laws." Yet several of my Republican colleagues announced how they would vote before the trial even started. I took some heat for telling *Politico* that I worried "the cake is already baked."[1] Then my colleagues proved me right.

They did their best to make the whole ordeal about process, not about information. Many of them fidgeted through or tuned out the trial itself—disrespecting or flat-out ignoring one of the most important responsibilities the Constitution requires of US senators. All but one of them cowered when it mattered most.

Soon after Trump's acquittal, his firing of Colonel Alexander Vindman and Ambassador Gordon Sondland, both of whom testified against the president, became the latest damnedest thing I'd ever seen. I kept thinking, *What would this be like if the president were a Democrat?* I'd run the SOB out of office, because I wouldn't want to be in the same party, and I ain't about to leave.

Throughout President Trump's impeachment trial, I also expected to take some heat from angry constituents in Montana. The fact is, I received very few phones calls and emails asking me to protect the president. When I came home to Montana after comfortably voting guilty on both articles of impeachment, I heard only thank-yous. That's because in Montana, *character* still matters in public service.

Donald Trump in 2016 claimed much of rural America *because* of character and what millions believed was authenticity. They trusted him to change a political system that felt artificial and distant to so many of us in rural America. Trump brought charisma to the politics of millions of ordinary people, making himself relatable, tough, and believable. That's why, when his own policies hurt American farmers and manufacturers, they marched in lockstep behind him, even despite their own self-interest. And there's no denying that racial tension was its undercurrent.

As Trump spoke directly to rural America, most Democrats ignored it. Trump elevated white voters who had struggled for years as their mostly white communities suffered, as jobs and opportunities disappeared, and as businesses boarded up. Trump turned to the old but effective strategy of lifting them up by pushing down *others*; by stirring up race-based fears and by giving angry and scared white voters permission to distrust other religions, other cultures, and other people.

Trump tapped into the deep, gnarly root of racism in rural America. While we can't uproot it overnight, we can't ignore it either. Rural America often refuses to examine the impacts of racism and the privilege that people like my homesteader grandparents benefitted from while the first Americans here were pushed away. Montana's Constitution mandates a program called Indian Education for All to ensure that all public school kids learn the accurate history of indigenous people. But we've got a hell of a lot more work to do to better understand one another, so that all communities can prosper without having to fear other communities, without having to push them down. That starts with the robust education that people like Christine Pearson and Helen Tester cared so deeply about.

Without our nation having built a foundation of respect and understanding through education, a populist like Donald Trump can easily convince rural America that the status quo in politics isn't working, and that *others* are to blame: nonwhite immigrants, the press, wackos who care more about bizarre politically correct–isms than the comfort of familiar traditions and cultures, and even Democrats. Trump told us the only way to make America great again would be to change direction away from the status quo—even if it meant we had to forgive or make excuses for his unforgivable behavior. Many of President Trump's supporters believed that his bluntness and gleeful ignorance of our political system was exactly what they needed to see the whole thing torn down and rebuilt. That would, they believed, preserve an America that looks like Big Sandy did when I was a kid—teeming with opportunity for white, mostly Christian, able-bodied families. Then as now, too many people were left out of that America. Then as now, we can't afford to ignore the very real problems hurting that America.

Our changing nation is a place where the symbolism of standing for the national anthem means something different to people who aren't privileged whites; where the word "Pocahontas" isn't a joke for people who've had Indian Education for All, where it makes sense to keep firearms out of the hands of people who shouldn't have them.

Democrats need to understand that we cannot give up on rural America. Making room for these changes won't be easy, but just as FDR did a century ago, we have no choice but to reach out and bring all of America along. After all, it saved the nation.

TO DEMOCRATS

So, to Democrats, I offer a few suggestions from a little farm in north-central Montana:

1. GO OUTSIDE YOUR COMFORT ZONES

"This is a fundamental problem with the Democratic Party," Bill Maher observed on his HBO show, *Real Time with Bill Maher*, on March 15, 2019. I was a guest on his show that evening. "They look weak running from a fight, when they should be in there throwing punches. Republicans never shy away from coming on this show. And they come with a smile on their face despite knowing that the only people in the crowd cheering them on are the three campaign aides they brought with them." Maher showed his left-leaning audience an image of thirty mostly smiling GOP guests he had hosted on *Real Time*. "The audience is against them and they don't care, because it's an opportunity to expose people to your side of the story," Maher continued. "So what if there are groans? Groans won't kill ya."[2]

In Montana, those of us in elected office happily speak to independents and Libertarians, Republicans and Democrats—and everyone in between. We put up with plenty of groans; that's a small price to pay. Nationally, the Democratic Party has lost too many people who are much more inclined to share most of our values than you might think. We have—for the large part—just stopped talking with people outside our comfort zone, whatever it is. We've forgotten how to speak to the folks who shower at the end of the day. Democrats have written off entire regions of our country, dismissing them as politically irrelevant or too small or too backward. I take issue with all those assertions. While Democrats have consolidated their priorities in the urban pockets of America, Republicans have been persistently communicating with and identifying with all of rural America.

Democrats, start speaking to everyone in America—something Donald Trump and his circle quickly figured out how to do, and do well.

2. LISTEN TO RURAL AMERICA

Not only do Democrats tend to stay in their comfort zones, they also tend to ignore the concerns and ideas and the very *promise* of rural America. Many in my party don't even listen. Showing up at the Iowa State Fair every four years doesn't count. Paying attention to only rural swing states doesn't count either. Part of why Donald Trump coasted to Electoral College victory in 2016 was because he at least showed up in rural America, and for millions, that was good enough. He *seemed* to listen to the part of America that Democrats not only ignored; they ridiculed. I'm not sure Secretary Clinton's campaign fully understood the irreversible damage done when she referred to half of Trump's supporters—presumably the interior of America—as "deplorables."

Not listening to those of us in rural America is toxic, but presuming the worst of us is fatal. As someone who's never lived in a town with more than a thousand people, I can tell you that rural America is as broad and diverse and colorful as any other part of America. In rural and frontier towns in every corner of this country, all people really want is for their elected leaders to *listen*. They want to see themselves in their representatives. They want to know people in power are fighting for and with them. They want authenticity. They've given up on whatever "normal" is in politics, because that normal has failed them. The status quo ain't working, and we ought to be listening—*truly listening*—to what rural America has to say about it.

Because what happens when we don't? A phony will come along and fake his way through it, and he will win hearts and threaten our democracy in the process. He will normalize all that we can never accept as normal. We cannot let that happen again.

"During planting season we think a lot about the phrase: 'You reap what you sow,'" I said at the Center for American Progress's Ideas Conference in 2019. "I live by the values of rural America. But make no mistake about it, those values sell in both rural America and urban America." That, I added, is why I believe that Montanans reelected me in 2018 after Trump won a presidential election in 2016.

> My parents always said you've got two ears and one mouth, act accordingly. And so I think that politicians are great at coming in and telling people what they should be believing. But the truth is in rural America I think you gotta start out by listening. And if you're able to meet the people where they are and listen, that's a good start. . . . I think rural voters believe that all politicians—*all politicians*—aren't fighting for their families or their way of life. And they're not listening to them. But the truth is rural America's values are things like accessible health care and good-paying jobs and affordable education. Those are our values. And quite frankly they are progressive values. And they are exactly the values we all need to fight for. And they are exactly the values that this administration has attacked time and time again.[3]

This is a ripe moment in America's story for Democrats to turn back to our heartland, to the flyover states and to the Rust Belt and to the Bible Belt and to the Deep South; to blue-collar factory towns and struggling coal towns and decaying industry towns. These Americans certainly know the difference between wasteful spending and smart investment. They struggle with paying for health care and they want good futures for their kids like we all do. They see the urgent need to address climate change, and the scourge of too much money in politics. To them, Washington always was and still is a dirty swamp, yet they still hold tight to the American optimism that promises to drain that swamp. That was *our* message.

3. DON'T OVERTHINK THE MESSAGE

Speaking of messaging, the way many of us Democrats tend to speak to most Americans is broken, clogged up by self-righteousness and identity politics. We overcomplicate things with wonky, abstract, or even impossible messages. But there's nothing complicated about what our party stands for: *opportunity for everyone.*

Though most Democrats have the best of intentions, we are getting whupped in the messaging war. We know it, yet we aren't very good at trying to win it. During the 2009 debate over the American Recovery and Reinvestment Act, most Democrats were happy to call it the "stimulus bill," a terrible phrase that suggests big government reigns over our economy. Even "recovery" and "reinvestment" aren't terms that jibe with ordinary folks—even if they were hurt by the Great Recession. I simply called the Recovery Act what it actually was: a "jobs bill." That term didn't get much traction among my colleagues, but it should have. When the Republicans passed their tax law in late 2017, what did they name it? "The Tax Cuts and Jobs Act." They sold their terrible policy to the public with much more success because they did it with simplicity, with relatable values, and with *power and speed.*

And while Republicans talk about good jobs, Democrats spend too much time talking about things like raising the minimum wage. Of course a higher minimum wage is a noble idea. But when you think about it, the message of demanding a higher minimum wage is like saying, "We want to make you less poor." Nobody *wants* to be less poor with a higher minimum wage! That's why the much more effective Republican message is "We want to make you wealthier." Where I'm sitting in Chouteau County, Montana, ordinary families aren't demanding a higher minimum wage; they simply want what so many others across rural America want: steady, fair-paying work they can be proud of, with fair benefits and opportunities.

4. RECLAIM FISCAL RESPONSIBILITY

Many of my Democratic colleagues in the Senate regularly suggest solving problems by throwing more money at them. Of course, certain things need more money, like the VA when veterans' lives are on the line. Certain times need more money too, like the thirteen-digit economic relief plans we passed during the COVID-19 pandemic in 2020, and our urgent passage of the Recovery Act ("the jobs bill") in order to stem off another economic depression in 2009.

But for the most part, Democrats are too quick to spend far too much money, and we do it without demanding the accountability that should always accompany the spending of taxpayer dollars. We tend to do it without demanding some skin in the game; without thinking about common-sense alternatives first. No wonder we've lost the confidence of many voters who struggle to balance their own personal finances every month.

My mother, Helen, washed dishes with a single cup of water; she hated the thought of Dad buying even a used Cadillac, and she never wasted a scrap. She saved up her money and sent her three sons to college. She knew the value of a dollar, and she taught me the same. She, like so many others who grew up in Montana in her generation, was a proud Democrat.

5. GIVE 'EM A REASON

On that *Real Time* episode in March 2019, Bill Maher asked me about the challenges I faced running a campaign as a Democrat in a state like Montana.

"I would imagine in Montana you feel like you're already five lengths behind your competition just because you have the 'D' next to your name," he said. "It is a bit of a badge of dishonor."

"Look, it's a red state," I admitted. "It will tend to vote Republican if you don't give them a reason to vote Democrat. We gave them a reason to vote Democrat. And they did."[4]

I've won each of my elections because I gave voters a reason. Good public education. Quality, affordable health care. Accountability. Freedom. Montana's way of life. Those are things that everyone can relate to, regardless of political party.

TO REPUBLICANS

I'd like to offer some suggestions to my Republican colleagues as well. I have counted many among my best friends and heroes throughout my life. But if we are to right the listing ship of our democracy, we have work to do. President Trump's election in 2016 was a symptom of a much larger disease: millions of Americans have understandably lost trust in our government—to the point where they removed their trust from whatever was normal and gave it freely to a reality TV star who made a name for himself with nothing more than luck and charisma. Now we have to get to work putting our democracy back. It simply requires returning to the basics.

1. ACCOUNTABILITY BEFORE PRIDE

The saddest part of watching Donald Trump isn't the fact that he has a fundamental problem with the truth, or that he has no idea how to run an administration, much less a country, or that he lacks curiosity, compassion, and any breadth of knowledge outside the confines of his diet of social media and Fox News. He's exactly what a majority of Electoral College voters preferred in 2016.

The sad part, for me, is the fact that the president has the entire Senate majority as his army. With little exception, my Republican friends in the Senate are refusing their constitutional responsibility of holding our commander in chief accountable—even when it comes to something as simple as demanding witnesses and new information at an impeachment trial. For years, President Trump has pulled at the threads of our nation, unraveling the fabric of America, and a slim majority of US senators have looked the other way.

I believe our two-party system of government serves a very important purpose that provides continual checks and balances on all of us. But if Republicans don't step up their accountability as our Constitution requires, we will either lose our democracy, or we will lose the Republican Party.

To my Republican colleagues: Many of you know our country deserves better; you have told me as much. You have the power to put this broken government upright again. Take a page from how a Democrat from Montana partnered with a Republican from Idaho to overhaul our banking laws: put pride aside and use the trust we have built together as colleagues to get back to work. You don't have to be scared of Donald Trump.

Sometimes pride means saving up for and buying a Cadillac. Sometimes pride means returning the Cadillac after realizing it could hurt your business. It's time to return the Cadillac.

2. SIMMER DOWN

Of course fingers can point at both parties when it comes to heated political rhetoric that eats away at our Democracy. I certainly can't claim to be a purist. But it's hard to argue that President Trump and his surrogates have rewritten the rules of engagement when it comes to overblown rhetoric, and in Montana, it backfired on the GOP in 2018.

At the same Montana campaign rally in late October during which Don Trump Junior called me a "piece of garbage," he also called me "swampy Jon Tester." Then, after announcing his success in shooting Montana prairie dogs for sport, he attacked me for not having a current hunting license.

"I'm the son of a billionaire, and I've got hunting licenses and fishing licenses in Montana!" Junior shouted, failing to see any irony as he tried to claim he fits in Montana "better" than me.[5] He pounded his fists and told his supporters that I was either a poacher or "the biggest fraud in the world" because I don't have a hunting license.

No, I don't have a hunting license. What Junior missed is that I don't claim to be much of a hunter. I've done a fair amount of hunting in the past, I enjoy the support of many hunters across Montana who care about protections for public land and wildlife, and I am quick to defend the rights of responsible hunters. I also have the support of Montanans who'd rather not see more wealthy outsiders coming into our state to bag trophies or to shoot prairie dogs for sport. I've never considered shooting prairie dogs a *sport*; farmers shoot them because they must. We hunt, after all, in large part to manage our wildlife.

But I'm not a hunter, because I prefer to eat my own beef over wild game. I'm not a hunter, because I'm a butcher, and years of harvesting animals has drained any desire to go out and shoot more of them. I'm not a hunter, because I'm a full-time US senator *and* a full-time farmer. And I ain't in the business of pretending to be someone I'm not—even if pretending to be a hunter would benefit me politically.

Junior's angry comments became another incendiary news story that appeared across Montana as voters prepared to cast their ballots, and I believe it actually worked against him. Junior's rhetoric had gone too far. No matter what words you use, Montanans know the difference between the son of a New York billionaire, a Maryland real estate developer, and a Montana farmer.

3. REFORM CAMPAIGN FINANCING

I'm often asked which issues are the most important facing Congress. For me, this is a difficult question with a simple answer. Sure, there are lots of major issues: the crisis of climate change, access to affordable health care, our national security, our food security, and the erosion of our constitutional rights. But we can address none of these effectively unless we first tackle the issue of money—far too much of it—flooding into our political system. It's the volcano we are sleeping over.

In late 2018, I told the *CQ on Congress* podcast that all this uncontrolled money is what's keeping Congress's wheels spinning in the mud. "Let's talk about how Congress works and why we have such low performance ratings—why we get very few things done that have any controversy around them," I said. "It's because of all this money coming into these campaigns, I believe. Why? It causes real paralysis. If I make this decision or that decision, either the Right or the Left [is] going to come after me with dark money, and I just don't think it's good for our democracy to be in a stage where we never ever take up big issues."[6]

Montana has a painful history colored by the corruption of money in politics, and the people of our state disinfected that corruption more than a century ago. Now the influence of money in politics—on both sides of the political spectrum—is roaring back, and it's keeping us at a stalemate in the US Senate. Senator John McCain, rest his soul, was a champion of campaign finance reform. This nation needs a new Republican champion to fill Senator McCain's boots. I hope that happens, because our most pressing challenges don't give a lick about which party scores the points.

4. DON'T IGNORE THE NATIONAL DEBT

Once we can find real common ground on reforming our campaign finance system, then all of us ought to return to the principle of fiscal conservatism—not just when a Democrat holds the keys to the White House.

When Barack Obama was president, my colleague Steve Daines had on display in his Senate office lobby an iPad featuring an upward-ticking national debt clock. Immediately after President Trump's inauguration, Senator Daines's national debt clock conveniently disappeared from his office. I thought it was a good idea, so I put an iPad in the lobby of my office showcasing the debt clock. The debt problem doesn't go away just because we have a new president in office.

On the day President Trump took office, our national debt clocked in at more than $19.9 trillion.[7] After the first twelve hundred

days of Donald Trump's presidency, our debt had grown $3 trillion to
$25 trillion—a staggering rate of more than $4 billion per day.[8] All
the outrage I heard about debt during the Obama years has quieted
down. It's concerning. I'm not looking to pick a fight over hypocrisy,
but for many of us in rural America, the urgency to get a handle on
our debt certainly hasn't gone away. If and when interest rates go up,
we are in for a slog, and our children will pay the price. If we don't
deal with our debt now, it's going to be too late.

The Tax Cuts and Jobs Act of 2017, which President Trump and
his GOP allies in the Senate rushed through without much public
scrutiny, certainly didn't help. That awful law ballooned our spending problem by giving tax breaks to the Americans who needed it the
least. While Democrats tend to throw money at problems, Republicans tend to keep giving the wealthy a pass. Neither of these make
any sense to those of us in rural America—the ordinary working-class
folks who run and innovate and feed and care for this country.

5. RECLAIM THE TRUTH

My God, facts matter. They always have and they always will.
The minute they don't is the minute our nation no longer belongs
to the people. I worry the GOP is losing its grip on the truth. My
mother read the newspaper every day and my grandmother read *The
Progressive* and *The Nation* religiously because they knew truth always prevails. Value independent journalism; it has kept our fragile
government in check for nearly 250 years. Demand accountability.
Allow the people we all serve to expect truth and transparency. They
deserve no less.

TO ALL

TRUST SCIENCE

As I close this chapter, the entire world is figuring out how to adapt
to the unfamiliar threat of COVID-19 and the economic devastation

that comes with closures, quarantines, unemployment, sickness, and uncertainty. On March 7, 2020, just days before en masse event cancellations and business closures, Dr. Neil deGrasse Tyson appeared on *The Late Show with Stephen Colbert* to discuss the looming threat of the coronavirus.

"I think we're in the middle of a massive experiment, worldwide," the popular astrophysicist said. "The experiment is: *Will people listen to scientists?*" The crowd laughed at first, then cheered. Tyson then noted that all of the worldwide coronavirus-related health precautions "are warnings offered by scientists for our own good.[9]

"It'd be interesting if we all paid attention to what scientists say," he added. "Maybe the coronavirus will just blow on by with a minimum of cases, and then we kicked its ass for obeying the recommendations of scientists on how to minimize your chances of getting it."

A few weeks later, on April 23, President Trump—not known for his commitment to listening to science or scientists—noted that disinfectants like bleach and isopropyl alcohol knock out the virus in "one minute" before he seriously wondered, aloud, whether there's "a way we can do something like that, by injection inside or almost a cleaning? Because you see it gets in the lungs and it does a tremendous number on the lungs." He also wondered whether hitting "the body, with a tremendous—whether it's ultraviolet or just very powerful— light . . . either through the skin or some other way" could treat a viral infection.[10]

Backlash was swift and severe. The companies that manufacture Lysol and Clorox warned Americans not to ingest their chemical products or to inject them into their bodies; doctors and scientists warned doing so could be fatal.[11] And the next day the president tried to claim he was "asking the question sarcastically . . . just to see what would happen."[12]

Of course, this is just one of countless examples of the president of the United States, and many of his allies, disregarding objective science. We are renting our planet from our grandchildren, which means we cannot afford the boneheaded luxury of ignoring science. I'm not a doctor. I'm not a researcher. But I am a farmer, and that means I'm beholden to science. I also know that Mother Nature always—*always*—bats last.

Like most reasonable people, I trust science to show us the way toward a future that our grandkids deserve. I trust it to show our world a future that looked a lot like the Montana of my grandparents' day— a place full of opportunity and hope.

Science disinfects ignorance, and as Neil deGrasse Tyson pointed out, we study it, discover it, make decisions from it, and save lives through it, *for our own good*.

We still have a lot of work to do to return to the principle of "opportunity for everyone," and we certainly can, if we all start rowing in that direction. I believe we can do that by speaking with real authenticity to rural America. When we do, we can loosen the grip of the rhetoric of Donald Trump that has for too long seeped into places that have been dismissed as "hillbilly" or "deplorable" or "gun loving."

America is far too extraordinary to be pigeonholed like that. Just look at a guy like me: A gun-owning, middle-of-the-road dad and grandpa who eats beef and grows organic food, who loves a good whiff of dirt, who questions elected leaders who think they're not accountable to this country, and who refuses to lose sight of the issues that will truly affect the future of our nation: inequality, intolerance, injustice, and the precipice of climate change.

In 2007, my daughter Christine and her husband, James, told me they had changed their minds about taking over the farm. In 2019, they moved their family to Indiana, where Christine got a job she couldn't refuse. My grandson Brayden, who's already older than the age I was when I decided I wanted to be a lifelong farmer, still tells me he wants to follow in his grandparents' footsteps on what would be his fourth-generation farm. If he wants it. Will that happen?

I wonder what will become of this little place twelve miles west of Big Sandy if life changes plans and dreams as it so often does. Sharla and I are only temporary stewards of this piece of dirt. On this glorious evening, I can think of no other place I'd rather be. We are only temporary stewards of this nation. And we owe its future the very best we've got.

"Hey," Sharla says to me as the bugs in the field begin to chirp. Her iPad lights up her beautiful face. "I'll be darned. Did you know 'Taps' has words?"

"No shit?" I had no idea.

Sharla kicks her feet up and scrolls through as she reads the words to "Taps" aloud:

Day is done
Gone the sun
From the lakes
From the hills
From the skies
All is well
Safely rest
God is nigh

Those twenty-four haunting notes I have heard and played thousands of times ring through my head. I take a puff from my cigar and look out across the fields again. I smile, even though I don't have any of the answers as to what will happen next.

But I know I am lucky. *All is well. Life is a gift.*

Acknowledgments

The fact that rural America continues to lose population, and the fact that once vibrant small towns are now just skeletons of their former selves, has always been a torment to me. Having lived my entire life on this farm west of Big Sandy has allowed me to witness the decline of rural America. It truly is a shame, because the rural areas of our nation have so much to offer—things like quality of life, appreciation and respect for Mother Nature, and the fact that in a rural community we truly are all in it together. It is a tough thing to see diminished.

To further add insult to this injury, rural America will feel the reckless trade policies and international acrimony President Trump has promoted for decades to come. If this book helps to reinvigorate rural America in any way, then it will be time well spent on my part and worth the read on your part. It is a small effort to restore strength and hope for the rural places good people call home.

I want to thank my wife, Sharla, for correcting history and adding to it during the journey of putting this book together. She is my soul mate, and this process has once again reminded me of that. My kids, Christine, Shon and, later in life, Mel: thanks to you and to your families for your support and input. My two older brothers, Dave and Bob, and their families, have had a tremendous impact on my decision making and my perceived success. I have had many friends through schools and adult life—too many to mention, so I'll only mention one: Steve Sibra, because you were there in first grade, and you have been there ever since.

Truth be known, this book would have never been written without Aaron Murphy. Aaron was able to organize my thoughts and put them on paper in a way that makes sense to these events and times in almost poetic terms. Thanks, Murph. You were a great chief of staff and an even better writer. Thanks also to Julie Stevenson, my agent, who soon became a good friend—the one who had enough faith to go the extra mile to make this all happen.

My parents always told me that we do what we do to make a better life for *you*—the next generation. We are renting this planet from our children and even more so from our grandchildren. Past generations worked for the greater good rather than for themselves. It is far past time to step up.

Notes

Chapter 1: Grit, Glue, and a Meat Grinder

1. "Tester Sends 8th Bill to Trump for Signature," press release, Senator Jon Tester, October 26, 2017, https://www.tester.senate.gov/?p=press_release&id=5604; "13 Bills," YouTube video, posted by "Jon Tester," March 12, 2018, https://www.youtube.com/watch?v=sbE7W-tcwkQ.
2. Joseph Kinsey Howard, *Montana: High, Wide and Handsome* (New Haven: Yale University Press, 1943), 167–77.
3. Howard, *Montana: High, Wide and Handsome*.
4. Robert W. Miller and Frank W. McKay, "Decline in US Childhood Cancer Mortality: 1950 through 1980," *Journal of the American Medical Association* 251, no 12 (March 23–30, 1984): 1567–70, https://doi.org/10.1001/jama.1984.03340360033025.
5. Population figures for Big Sandy are taken from the US Census Bureau, https://data.census.gov/cedsci/profile?g=1600000US3006250&q=Big%20Sandy%20town,%20Montana.
6. "Montanans for Tester Places Full Page Advertisement on Jon's 16 Bills Signed by President," press release, Montanans for Tester, July 5, 2018, https://www.jontester.com/news/press-releases/2018/montanans-for-tester-places-full-page-advertisement-on-jons-16-bills-signed-by-president/.
7. "President Trump Remarks at Rally in Great Falls, Montana," C-SPAN, July 5, 2018, https://www.c-span.org/video/?447876-1/president-trump-delivers-remarks-rally-great-falls-montana.
8. Jimmy Kimmel Twitter (@jimmykimmel), December 1, 2017, 5:13 p.m., https://twitter.com/jimmykimmel/status/936750077036478464.
9. John Bowden, "Red-State Dem: GOP Tax Bill 'One of Shittiest Bills' Ever," *The Hill*, December 20, 2017, https://thehill.com/homenews/senate/365895-red-state-dem-gop-tax-bill-one-of-the-shittiest-bills-ever.

10.   "Tax Cut and Spending Bill Could Cost $5.5 Trillion Through 2029," Committee for a Responsible Federal Budget, February 27, 2019, https://www.crfb.org/blogs/tax-cut-and-spending-bill-could-cost-55-trillion-through-2029.

Chapter 2: Pickin' Rock

1.   "Demo Political Rally Attracts 400 in Butte," *Montana Standard*, November 3, 1968.
2.   Associated Press, "Push Talks, Mike Urges," *Montana Standard*, November 3, 1968.
3.   John A. Farrell, "Nixon's Vietnam Treachery," *New York Times*, December 31, 2016, https://www.nytimes.com/2016/12/31/opinion/sunday/nixons-vietnam-treachery.html.
4.   "Mansfield, Michael Joseph (Mike) (1903–2001)," Biographical Directory of the US Congress, accessed March 25, 2020, http://bioguide.congress.gov/scripts/biodisplay.pl?index=m000113.
5.   An image of Mansfield's grave is available at https://images.findagrave.com/photos/2004/365/6001543_110450754982.jpg.
6.   "Maureen Mansfield Dies at 95," *Washington Post*, September 22, 2000, https://www.washingtonpost.com/archive/local/2000/09/22/maureen-mansfield-dies-at-95/b5ebe3f0-9d7b-4b40-bf1e-a6b573cf95dc/.
7.   Joe Biden, "Mansfield-Metcalf Address," Helena, Montana, March 10, 2018, via NBC Montana, https://www.facebook.com/watch/live/?v=1853707454640643.
8.   Joe Biden, *Promises to Keep: On Life and Politics* (New York: Random House, 2007).
9.   Biden, "Mansfield-Metcalf Address."
10.   *Congressional Record*, January 10, 2019, S122, https://www.congress.gov/116/crec/2019/01/10/CREC-2019-01-10.pdf
11.   "National Border Patrol Council Announces Endorsement for Tester," KTVQ, August 31, 2018, https://ktvq.com/news/montana-news/2018/08/31/national-border-patrol-council-announces-endorsement-for-senator-tester/.
12.   "Tester Demands Vote to Reopen the Government," YouTube video, posted by "Senator Jon Tester," January 10, 2019. https://www.youtube.com/watch?v=QYj-3FZ7HgI.
13.   Holly K. Michels, "Former VP Joe Biden Energizes Democrats at Sold-Out Event in Helena," *Billings Gazette*, March 10, 2018, https://billingsgazette.com/news/state-and-regional/govt-and-politics/article_16adc8d2-7bb3-5272-bf1a-9ef0a7acd005.html.

Chapter 3: 24 Notes

1.   Tom Lutey, "Montana Tribal Leaders: Trump's Offensive Remarks Worthy of Objection by Tester," *Billings Gazette*, February 19, 2017, https://billingsgazette.com/news/montana-tribal-leaders-trump-s-offensive-remarks-worthy-of-objection/article_e033128a-ee00-5aa0-8e97-1af6a33401e8.html.
2.   "About VHA," Department of Veterans Affairs, Veterans Health Administration, July 14, 2019, https://www.va.gov/health/aboutvha.asp.

3. Rob Chaney, "Tester Meets Trump, Seeks Relief from VA Hiring Freeze," *Missoulian*, February 9, 2017, https://missoulian.com/news/local/tester-meets -trump-seeks-relief-from-va-hiring-freeze/article_d9f2abe4-a2f8-5c9b-aa98 -b7d71b30d9bf.html.

4. "VA Releases National Suicide Data Report," press release, Department of Veterans Affairs, Office of Public and Intergovernmental Affairs, June 18, 2018, https://www.va.gov/opa/pressrel/pressrelease.cfm?id=4074.

5. Alan K. Simpson, *Right in the Old Gazoo: A Lifetime of Scrapping with the Press* (New York: William Morrow, 1997), 259.

6. Jon Tester, "2018 Election Victory Speech," November 7, 2018, Great Falls, MT, https://www.c-span.org/video/?454233-1/senator-jon-tester-delivers -victory-remarks.

7. "Montana Veteran Demographics," Veterans Health Administration, January 6, 2017, https://leg.mt.gov/content/Committees/Interim/2017-2018/State -Administration-and-Veterans-Affairs/Meetings/Sept-2017/Montana %20Veteran%20Demographics%20(as%20of%20Jan.%206%202017).pdf.

8. "Profile of Veterans: 2017," US Department of Veterans Affairs, March, 2017, p. 23, https://www.va.gov/vetdata/docs/SpecialReports/Profile_of_Veterans _2017.pdf

9. "Tester Taps Vets for Feedback," *Ravalli Republic*, January 29, 2007.

10. "Tester: An 'Historic Day' for Disabled Veterans," press release, Senator Jon Tester, January 31, 2008, https://www.tester.senate.gov/?p=press _release&id=1134.

11. "Tester Bill Brings Relief for Vets," *Helena Independent-Record*, April 24, 2010.

12. Tom Lutey, "Tester, VA Chief Hear from Veterans," *Billings Gazette*, February 20, 2008, https://billingsgazette.com/news/local/tester-va-chief-hear-from -veterans/article_7d9d9ebd-ca29-5ce1-83fa-8d53ab2dea9c.html.

13. Becky Shay, "Cramped VA Clinic Welcomes News of More Space," *Billings Gazette*, January 23, 2008, https://billingsgazette.com/news/local/cramped -va-clinic-welcomes-news-of-more-space/article_794c5582-57cb-5b58-a65b -222ea0154e82.html.

14. "Opinion: VA Building Up Billings Veteran Care," *Billings Gazette*, November 14, 2008.

15. Cindy Uken, "Ground Broken for Expansion of Billings VA Clinic," *Billings Gazette*, October 19, 2012, https://billingsgazette.com/news/local/ground -broken-for-expansion-of-billings-va-clinic/article_6d6d666d-9c1f-5406-87e5 -b2cfca2554cc.html.

16. "Tester Stands Up to Help Military Sexual Assault Survivors Get Benefits They Need," press release, Senator Jon Tester, March 26, 2015, https://www .tester.senate.gov/?p=press_release&id=3857.

17. "Joseph Medicine Crow," *The War*, PBS, 2007, https://www.pbs.org/video /war-joseph-medicine-crow/.

18. Becky Shay, "Crow Veteran Nominated for Medal of Freedom," *Billings Gazette*, March 18, 2008, https://billingsgazette.com/news/local/crow -veteran-nominated-for-medal-of-freedom/article_0202f212-048d-5192 -8131-cc80b023cebf.html.

19.   "Presidential Medal of Freedom Recipients," White House Archives, July 30, 2009, https://obamawhitehouse.archives.gov/blog/2009/07/30/presidential-medal-freedom-recipients.

20.   Derek Brouwer, "Medicine Crow Speaks at Groundbreaking for New Middle School," *Billings Gazette*, March 18, 2015, https://billingsgazette.com/news/local/education/medicine-crow-speaks-at-groundbreaking-for-new-middle-school/article_2b3d93e0-56d2-552b-a342-5bcb160ce590.html.

21.   Norman K. Risjord, *Giants in Their Time: Representative Americans from the Jazz Age to the Cold War* (Lanham, MD: Rowman & Littlefield, 2006), p.180.

22.   "Medal of Honor Citation for Daniel K. Inouye," US Army Center of Military History, June 21, 2000, https://history.army.mil/html/moh/ap-moh_citations.html#Inouye.

23.   "WATCH VIDEO: Sen. Inouye Punchbowl Memorial Pt. 6," YouTube video, posted by "KHON2 News," December 23, 2012, https://youtu.be/vWXjzucjCXo?t=171.

24.   "Tester: Politics Trumping Veterans in Washington," press release, Senator Jon Tester, July 24, 2014, https://www.tester.senate.gov/?p=press_release&id=3545.

25.   HR 3230, 113th Congress, Veterans Choice, Access and Accountability Act, https://www.congress.gov/bill/113th-congress/house-bill/3230.

26.   David J. Shulkin, "Privatizing the V.A. Will Hurt Veterans," *New York Times*, March 28, 2018, https://www.nytimes.com/2018/03/28/opinion/shulkin-veterans-affairs-privatization.html.

27.   "Legislative Presentation of Multiple VSOs," US Senate Veterans' Affairs Committee, March 14, 2018, https://www.veterans.senate.gov/hearings/legislative-presentation-of-multiple-vsos-03142018.

28.   US Senate Roll Call Vote No. 64, February 13, 2017, https://www.senate.gov/legislative/LIS/roll_call_lists/roll_call_vote_cfm.cfm?congress=115&session=1&vote=00064.

29.   Donald J. Trump, Twitter (@realDonaldTrump), March 28, 2018, 2:31 p.m., https://twitter.com/realDonaldTrump/status/979108653377703936; Donald J. Trump, Twitter (@realDonaldTrump), March 28, 2018, 2:31 p.m., https://twitter.com/realDonaldTrump/status/979108846408003584.

30.   Andrew Restuccia, "Did Shulkin Get Fired or Resign? This Is Why It Matters," *Politico*, March 31, 2018. https://www.politico.com/story/2018/03/31/did-shulkin-get-fired-or-resign-veterans-492877; "Former VA Secretary: Trump did not set me up for failure," YouTube video, posted by "CNN," April 1, 2018, https://www.youtube.com/watch?v=fYujioePqm4.

31.   US Department of Veterans Affairs, Office of Inspector General, February 14, 2018, https://www.va.gov/oig/publications/report-summary.asp?id=4034.

32.   Brandon Carter and Rebecca Kheel, "Shulkin Says He Has Reimbursed Government for Wife's Travel Expenses," *The Hill*, February 14, 2018, https://thehill.com/homenews/administration/373895-shulkin-reimburses-government-for-wifes-travel-expenses.

33.   Arthur Allen, "VA Audit: Aide Expensed Shulkin's Wife's European Travel Under False Pretense," *Politico*, February 14, 2018, https://www.politico.com/story/2018/02/14/david-shulkin-europe-travel-347064.

34.   Shulkin, "Privatizing the V.A."

Chapter 4: Falling Down, Marrying Up, Taking Over

1. Obituary, Jim C. Barsotti, 1940–2017, website of Holland and Bonine Funeral Home, accessed April 10, 2020, https://www.hollandbonine.com/obituary /james-jim-barsotti.
2. Associated Press, "Assembly to Receive 'New Blood' Infusion," *Missoulian*, May 17, 1974.; Associated Press, "James Elected President of Senate Pro Tem," *Great Falls Tribune*, January 7, 1963.
3. "Art in the House of Representatives," Montana Historical Society, accessed April 10, 2020, https://mhs.mt.gov/education/Capitol/Art/House-of -Representatives.
4. "Majority and Minority Party Numbers: 1889–Present," Montana State Legislature, accessed April 10, 2020, https://www.leg.mt.gov/civic-education /facts/party-control/.
5. "Tester Named for Music Scholarship," *Big Sandy Mountaineer*, May 16, 1974, http://mou.stparchive.com/page_image.php?paper=MOU&year=1974 &month=5&day=16&page=2&mode=F&base=MOU05161974P02&title =The%2520Mountaineer.

Chapter 5: A Slow-Burning Fuse

1. Opening Statement of Chairman Lisa Murkowski, Senate Interior Appropriations Subcommittee Hearing, July 12, 2017, https://www.appropriations.senate .gov/hearings/review-of-the-fy2018-budget-request-for-the-indian-health-service.
2. Opening Statement of Ranking Member Tom Udall, Senate Interior Appropriations Subcommittee Hearing, July 12, 2017, https://www.appropriations .senate.gov/hearings/review-of-the-fy2018-budget-request-for-the-indian -health-service.
3. Senate Interior Appropriations Subcommittee Hearing, July 12, 2017, https:// www.appropriations.senate.gov/hearings/review-of-the-fy2018-budget-request -for-the-indian-health-service.
4. "Spicer rips media's Trump coverage (Full remarks)," YouTube video, posted by "CNN," January 21, 2017, https://www.youtube.com/watch?v=Z3c8Fh8Fd GI&feature=youtu.be&t=151.
5. "Democratic Sen. Jon Tester on Health Care," *Weekend Edition Saturday*, NPR, July 15, 2017. https://www.npr.org/2017/07/15/537381196/democratic -sen-jon-tester-on-health-care.
6. "Farming Methods Justified, Controversial Greytak Says," *Great Falls Tribune*, June 9, 1983.
7. "About Montana's Conservation Districts," Montana Association of Conservation Districts, https://macdnet.org/about-us/district-info/.
8. US Congressional Record, December 21, 2009, S13652, https://www.congress .gov/crec/2009/12/21/CREC-2009-12-21-senate.pdf.
9. "Charles Edward Danreuther," *Great Falls Tribune*, November 18, 2012, https://www.legacy.com/obituaries/GreatFallsTribune/obituary.aspx?page =lifestory&pid=161111651.
10. "Democrats Were the Clear Winners in County, State," *Great Falls Tribune*, November 8, 1990.

11. "Valley Attorney, Blaine Sheriff Tossed Out," *Great Falls Tribune*, June 6, 1990.

Chapter 6: Preservers of the Past

1. "Dress Code for Students Relaxed," *Billings Gazette*, November 15, 1986.
2. "At Large: Will Big Sandy Schools Save Code of the Dressed?," *Billings Gazette*, March 9, 1986.
3. Associated Press, "ACLU to Challenge School Dress Code," *Montana Standard*, March 8, 1986.
4. "Big Sandy Settles Dress-Code Spat; Rules Loosened," *Great Falls Tribune*, November 15, 1986.
5. Associated Press, "Big Sandy Dress Code on Hold," *Great Falls Tribune*, March 15, 1986.
6. "Clothing Code Gets Revisions," *Billings Gazette*, March 21, 1986.
7. Mark Suagee, phone interview with Aaron Murphy, April 30, 2019.
8. "School's Dress-Code to Be Studied," *Great Falls Tribune*, March 21, 1986.
9. "Clawson At Large: Will Big Sandy Schools Save Code of the Dressed?," *Billings Gazette*, March 9, 1986.
10. "Clawson At Large: Preservers of the Past Receive Up-to-Date Advice," *Billings Gazette*, March 13, 1986.
11. "Roger Wayne Clawson," *Billings Gazette*, October 10, 2015, https:// billingsgazette.com/lifestyles/announcements/obituaries/roger-wayne -clawson/article_75252038-17bb-5039-b3de-2217cd980d32.html.
12. "Big Sandy Settles Dress-Code Spat; Rules Loosened," *Great Falls Tribune*, November 15, 1986.
13. Associated Press, "Big Sandy Students Defeat Dress Code with ACLU Help," *Missoulian*, November 15, 1986.
14. "Dress Code for Students Relaxed," *Billings Gazette*, November 15, 1986.
15. "Clawson At Large: Rebels need more than cause," *Billings Gazette*, November 18, 1986.
16. Website of Treasure Lodge #95, Big Sandy, MT, updated August 16, 2019, http://www.montanafreemasons.org/CMRussell/OffTreasure.htm.
17. "Class C: The Only Game in Town," YouTube video, posted by "MontanaPBS," March 5, 2008, https://www.youtube.com/watch?v=3FaULNDPFzU&feature =youtu.be&t=4341.
18. Melody Wall, "Tester Is the Appropriate Choice," *Great Falls Tribune*, October 6, 2012.
19. "Big Sandy Teens Die in Accident," *Great Falls Tribune*, April 20, 2000.
20. "Teens Who Died in Wreck Were from Havre, Big Sandy," *Great Falls Tribune*, April 21, 2000.
21. "The Simple Truth about the Gender Pay Gap," AAUW, Fall 2018, https://www.aauw.org/app/uploads/2020/02/AAUW-2018-SimpleTruth -nsa.pdf.
22. "The Simple Truth about the Gender Pay Gap: Fall 2019 Update," AAUW, Fall 2019, https://www.aauw.org/app/uploads/2020/02/Simple-Truth-Update -2019_v2-002.pdf.

23. "Household Food Security in the United States," US Department of Agriculture, September 2018, https://www.ers.usda.gov/webdocs/publications /90023/err-256.pdf?v=0.
24. "Cobell Nominated for Award," *Great Falls Tribune*, May 5, 2016.
25. "2016 Presidential Medal of Freedom Recipients: Elouise Cobell," White House Archives, November 22, 2016, https://obamawhitehouse.archives.gov /campaign/medal-of-freedom.
26. "Elouise Cobell awarded the Presidential Medal of Freedom," YouTube video, posted by "KRTV NEWS," November 22, 2016, https://www.youtube.com /watch?v=Ny1qOoDSXKI.
27. "Forest Jobs and Recreation Act," website of Senator Jon Tester, accessed April 10, 2020, https://www.tester.senate.gov/?p=issue&id=70.
28. Jennifer McKee, "Tester Unveils Forest Plan," *Missoulian*, July 18, 2009, https://missoulian.com/news/local/tester-unveils-forest-plan/article_e38d2be5 -14be-5bbd-9f51-271dea707080.html.

Chapter 7: A Peterbilt and a Prius

1. Associated Press, "Big Sandy farmer serves in Senate," *Montana Standard*, February 8, 1999.
2. Jim Robbins, "Tiny Invader, Deadly to Fish, Shuts Down a River in Montana," *New York Times*, August 23, 2016, https://www.nytimes.com /2016/08/24/us/tiny-parasite-invader-deadly-to-fish-shuts-down-yellowstone -river-in-montana.html.
3. Karl Puckett, "2017 Fire Season No. 1; Produced Largest Fire in State's History," *Great Falls Tribune*, February 8, 2018, https://www.greatfallstribune .com/story/news/2018/02/08/2017-fire-season-no-1-produced-largest-fire -states-history/319952002/.
4. "2017 Wildfire Season," Montana Department of Natural Resources and Conservation, 2017, http://dnrc.mt.gov/divisions/forestry/docs/fire-and -aviation/publications/SeasonReview_2017.pdf.
5. "2017 Census of Agriculture Highlights: Farms & Farmland," USDA National Agricultural Statistics Service, August 2019, https://www .nass.usda.gov/Publications/Highlights/2019/2017Census_Farms _Farmland.pdf.
6. "Tester to Introduce 'Common Sense' Amendments to Food Safety Bill," press release, Senator Jon Tester, April 14, 2010, https://www.tester.senate .gov/?p=press_release&id=1106.
7. US Congress, Public Law 111-353, FDA Food Safety Modernization Act, January 4, 2011, https://www.congress.gov/111/plaws/publ353/PLAW -111publ353.pdf
8. "Tester: Small Farms Won with Food Safety Exemption," *Food Safety News*, May 5, 2011, https://www.foodsafetynews.com/2011/05/tester-tours-fsma -victory-at-sustainable-food-conference/.
9. Lyndsey Layton, "Senate Advances Bill to Overhaul Food Safety," *Washington Post*, November 18, 2010. http://www.washingtonpost.com/wp-dyn/content /article/2010/11/17/AR2010111706101.html.

10. "Food Safety Key for All Farms," editorial, *Capital Press*, December 2, 2010, https://www.capitalpress.com/opinion/food-safety-key-for-all-farms /article_7eeeb470-6d8a-58ce-92e6-034a6108a85d.html.

11. "Letter to Senate Leaders," United Fresh Produce Association et al., November 18, 2019, https://www.agri-pulse.com/ext/resources/pdfs/u/n/i/t/y/United _Fresh_Food_Safety.pdf.

12. "United Fresh and Industry Allies Oppose Tester Amendment to Food Safety Legislation," *Inside United Fresh* (newsletter), November 23, 2010, http://iuf .unitedfresh.org/newsletters/2010/11/23.php.

13. Carolyn Lochhead, "Senate Set to Vote on Rigorous Food Safety Bill," *San Francisco Chronicle*, November 28, 2010, https://www.sfgate.com/politics /article/Senate-set-to-vote-on-rigorous-food-safety-bill-3244382.php.

14. Bill Marler, "Great quote by Eric Schlosser and Michael Pollan on S 510— Food Safety Act," *Marler Blog*, November 16, 2010, https://www.marlerblog .com/lawyer-oped/great-quote-from-eric-schlosser-and-michael-pollan-on-s -510-fda-food-safety-act/.

15. Michael Pollan and Eric Schlosser: "A Stale Food Fight," *New York Times*, November 28, 2010, https://www.nytimes.com/2010/11/29/opinion/29schlosser .html.

16. US Senate Roll Call Vote No. 257, November 30, 2010, https://www.senate .gov/legislative/LIS/roll_call_lists/roll_call_vote_cfm.cfm?congress=111&session =2&vote=00257.

17. US House Roll Call Vote No. 661, December 21, 2010, http://clerk.house.gov /evs/2010/roll661.xml.

18. "2017 Census of Agriculture—Table 52: Selected Producer Characteristics," USDA National Agricultural Statistics Service, 2017, https://www.nass.usda .gov/Publications/AgCensus/2017/Full_Report/Volume_1,_Chapter_1 _State_Level/Montana/st30_1_0052_0052.pdf; "2017 Census of Agriculture Highlights: Farm Producers," USDA National Agricultural Statistics Service, 2017, https://www.nass.usda.gov/Publications/Highlights/2019/2017Census _Farm_Producers.pdf.

19. "A Speech by HRH the Prince of Wales to the Future for Food Conference, Georgetown University, Washington, DC," website of the Prince of Wales, May 4, 2011, https://www.princeofwales.gov.uk/speech/speech-hrh-prince -wales-future-food-conference-georgetown-university-washington-dc.

20. "Senator Tester's Remarks at the Future of Food Conference," YouTube video, posted by "Senator Jon Tester," May 4, 2011, https://youtu.be/HmGC5 -wzlBE?t=344.

21. "Tester blasts Trump for China trade war, calls farmer bailout a 'Band-Aid," YouTube video, posted by "Face the Nation," May 26, 2019, https://www .youtube.com/watch?v=aXuWWMKF2f8.

22. US Congressional Record, September 17, 2019, S5504, https://www.congress .gov/116/crec/2019/09/17/CREC-2019-09-17.pdf.

Chapter 8: My One-Eared Dog

1. Montana Senate Journal, Addendum, 55th Legislature, 1997, https://leg.mt.gov /bills/1997/Journals/SADDEND.htm.

2. "Deregulation Costs Montana Hundreds of Millions of Dollars," *Great Falls Tribune*, December 7, 2014.

3. "Toole Selected Symbolic Date to File for PSC," *Missoulian*, March 24, 2006.

4. "Montana Legislature—1997: Geographic Information, Montana State Library, accessed April 10, 2020, https://mslservices.mt.gov/geographic _information/maps/legislature/LegislatureMap.aspx?yr=1997.

5. "A Guide to the Montana Legislature," Montana State Legislative Services Division, March 2017, https://leg.mt.gov/content/about-the-legislature/2017 guidetomontanalegislature.pdf.

6. "Fort Benton Man to Seek House Seat," *Great Falls Tribune*, December 28, 1997.

7. Charles S. Johnson, "Former Havre Legislator, Education Advocate Peck Dies," *Missoulian*, May 27, 2011, https://missoulian.com/news/ state-and-regional/former-havre-legislator-education-advocate-peck-dies/ article_4b5c8468-88d3-11e0-ab51-001cc4c002e0.html.

8. Lee Newspapers, "'Good Man' Leads Senate," *Missoulian*, November 21, 2004.

9. David C. W. Parker: *Battle for the Big Sky: Representation and the Politics of Place in the Race for the U.S. Senate* (Los Angeles: Sage Publications-CQ Press, 2015), p. 47.

10. "Candidate Accused of Deception, Pulls Campaign Radio Ads," *Great Falls Tribune*, October 31, 1998.

11. "Candidate Accused of Deception."

12. "Candidate Accused of Deception."

13. "Montana General Election Results," November 3, 1998, Montana Secretary of State, https://sosmt.gov/Portals/142/Elections/archives/1990s/1998/1998-General-County-Results.zip.

14. "Candidates: Door-to-Door Was Key," *Great Falls Tribune*, November 5, 1998.

15. "Candidates: Door-to-Door."

16. "CAP Ideas 2019: Sen. Jon Tester (D-MT)," YouTube video, posted by "see-progress," May 24, 2019, https://www.youtube.com/watch?v=FGpAYO9eQlY.

17. Associated Press, "End of Speed Law Puts Pressure on Lawmakers," *Independent Record* (Helena, MT), December 24, 1998.

18. Associated Press, "Big Sandy Farmer Serves in Senate," *Montana Standard*, February 8, 1999.

19. "Freshman Lawmakers Take Bold First Steps," *Great Falls Tribune*, February 28, 1999.

20. "Schweitzer Announces a Run for U.S. Senate," Lee Newspapers, March 25, 1999.

21. "Candidate Says He'll Take No Tobacco Money," Associated Press, April 10, 1999.

22. "Conrad Burns, 1935–2016," *Billings Gazette*, May 1, 2016, https://bil-lingsgazette.com/lifestyles/announcements/obituaries/conrad-burns/ article_99c13bc1-081a-5ccd-96c5-0d0eaa292295.html.

23. Parker, *Battle for the Big Sky*, 14.

24. Charles S. Johnson, "Republican Daines Announces U.S. Senate Bid," *Billings Gazette*, November 13, 2010, https://billingsgazette.com/news/state-and-regional/montana/republican-daines-announces-u-s-senate-bid/article_ ac93271a-8355-5e9c-9db3-6cf49b667984.html.

25.   "Meet Steve," Office of Senator Steve Daines, accessed April 6, 2020, https://
www.daines.senate.gov/meet-steve/biography.

26.   "Montanans' Anger over Drug Expenses Fodder in Campaign," *Great Falls
Tribune*, November 7, 1999.

27.   "Montanans Get Close Look at How Cheap Drugs Can Be," *Billings Gazette*,
November 20, 1999.

28.   "Schweitzer Raps Burns for Vote against Farm Aid," *Billings Gazette*, August 11,
1999.

29.   Lee Newspapers, "Schweitzer, Burns Debate," *Independent Record* (Helena,
MT), October 11, 2000.

30.   "Montana Trade Specialists Fear for Contracts," *Great Falls Tribune*, September 22, 1999.

31.   "Montana General Election Results: November 7, 2000," Montana Secretary
of State, https://sosmt.gov/Portals/142/Elections/archives/2000s/2000/2000
-GenState.pdf.

32.   "Montana General Election Results: November 5, 2002," Montana Secretary
of State, https://sosmt.gov/wp-content/uploads/attachments/2002-GenLeg.pdf.

33.   "David O. Tester," Kootenai Obituaries, April 12, 2004, http://www
.ruralnorthwest.com/artman/publish/printer_3440.shtml.

34.   Lee Newspapers, "Democrats Announce Economy Plan," *Montana Standard*,
January 27, 2004.

35.   "Schweitzer Victorious," *Great Falls Tribune*, November 2, 2004.

36.   Lee Newspapers, "Ruling Gives Democrat Seat in House," *Billings Gazette*,
December 29, 2004.

37.   "Montana General Election Results," Montana Secretary of State, November 2,
2004, https://sosmt.gov/wp-content/uploads/attachments/2004-GenState
.pdf; Constitution of the State of Montana, article XIII, section 7, "Definition
of Marriage, 2017," https://leg.mt.gov/bills/mca/title_0000/article_0130
/part_0010/section_0070/0000-0130-0010-0070.html.

38.   "'Good Man' Leads Senate."

39.   Lee Newspapers, "Supreme Court Says Funding Is Inadequate," *Independent
Record* (Helena, MT), November 10, 2004.

40.   "Renewable Energy Mandate Praised, Condemned," Lee Newspapers, April 12,
2005.

41.   "2005 History & Final Status of Bills and Resolutions," Montana State Legislature, pp. 165–66, https://leg.mt.gov/content/publications/sales/2005
_history_final_status_vol.pdf.

42.   "Renewables—Rewards and Risks: A Report to the 64th Legislature," Mon-
tana State Legislature, September, 2014, p. 2, https://leg.mt.gov/content
/Committees/Interim/2013-2014/Energy-and-Telecommunications/Legislation
/RPSFinal.pdf.

43.   Associated Press, "Drug Makers Take Aim at Governor's Prescription Plan,"
Great Falls Tribune, February 10, 2005.

44.   "Montanans Killed in Iraq, Afghanistan Since 9/11 Attacks," *Missoulian*,
September 10, 2011, https://missoulian.com/news/local/montanans-killed
-in-iraq-afghanistan-since-attacks/article_79cb804a-dc27-11e0-818c-001cc
4c002e0.html.

45. Susan Schmidt, "Tribal Grant Is Being Questioned," *Washington Post*, March 1, 2005, https://www.washingtonpost.com/wp-dyn/articles/A61436 -2005Feb28.html.

46. Schmidt, "Tribal Grant Is Being Questioned."

Chapter 9: More Zeroes

1. Lee Newspapers, "Burns Clings to His Roots," *Billings Gazette*, October 9, 1994.

2. "Conrad Burns Dies," *Great Falls Tribune*, April 29, 2016.

3. "Burns Beats Gorton for Commission," *Billings Gazette*, November 5, 1986.

4. "Burns Promises 'Different Attitude,'" *Billings Gazette*, February 26, 1988.

5. Associated Press, "The Wilderness Bill Veto Draws Strong Reactions," *Independent Record* (Helena, MT), November 3, 1988.

6. "Montana General Election Results: November 8, 1988," Montana Secretary of State, https://ia800901.us.archive.org/2/items/reportofofficial1988mon-trich/reportofofficial1988montrich.pdf.

7. "An IR View: A Fickle Lot," *Independent Record* (Helena, MT), November 11, 1988.

8. Associated Press, "Burns: Senate to Be 'No Real Difference,'" *Great Falls Tribune*, November 10, 1988.

9. "America's Worst Senators—Conrad Burns: Shock Jock," *Time*, April 14, 2006, http://content.time.com/time/nation/article/0,8599,1183991,00.html.

10. Jennifer McKee, "Burns Changed Position after Donation," *Billings Gazette*, December 2, 2005, https://billingsgazette.com/news/state-and-regional/montana/burns-changed-position-after-donation/article_f1aa1666-b046-57d0-99da-0eb6d1e8b540.html.

11. "Burns' Burden," *Missoula Independent*, March 23, 2006.

12. Lee Newspapers, "State Auditor Announces Run for U.S. Senate Seat," *Missoulian*, April 26, 2005.

13. Lee Newspapers, "Tester Announces Bid to Take Burns' Senate Seat," *Ravalli Republic*, May 25, 2005.

14. "Senate Hopeful Tester Brings Campaign to Missoula," *Missoulian*, May 26, 2005.

15. "Pearl Jam Show Backs Tester," *Missoulian*, August 30, 2005.

16. Associated Press, "Pearl Jam Raises $85,000 for Tester," *Montana Standard*, October 5, 2005.

17. Associated Press, "Burns' Foes Raise $1.2M Total," *Billings Gazette*, October 15, 2005.

18. "Senate Race in National Spotlight," *Great Falls Tribune*, October 15, 2005.

19. "Okay, I'm Definately [sic] On Board," *A Chicken Is Not Pillage* (blog), October 10, 2005. https://wulfgar.typepad.com/a_chicken_is_not_pillage/tester_06/.

20. Lee Newspapers, "Democrats: Special Session Is Move in Right Direction," *Missoulian*, December 6, 2005.

21. Lee Newspapers, "Special Session's Funding Increase Not Biggest," *Billings Gazette*, December 19, 2005.

22. James Risen and Eric Lichtblau, "Bush Lets U.S. Spy on Callers Without Courts," *New York Times*, December 15, 2005, https://www.nytimes .com/2005/12/16/politics/bush-lets-us-spy-on-callers-without-courts.html.

23. Lee Newspapers, "Democrat Tester Says Burns Should Resign," *Billings Gazette*, March 9, 2006; "Burns Calls for Democrats to Address Issues," *Great Falls Tribune*, April 5, 2006.

24. Associated Press, "Keenan Confirms He'll Challenge Burns in Primary," *Independent Record* (Helena, MT), March 22, 2006.

25. "Why the Morrison Affair Matters," *Missoula Independent*, April 20, 2006.

26. Lee Newspapers, "Democratic Senate candidates spar over ethics, electability," *Billings Gazette*, May 5, 2006.

27. Mike Dennison: *Inside Montana Politics: A Reporter's View from the Trenches* (Charleston, SC: History Press, 2019), 153.

28. David Margolick, "Washington's Invisible Man," *Vanity Fair*, April 2006, https://www.vanityfair.com/style/2006/04/abramoff200604.

29. "Jon Tester—Creating a Buzz," YouTube video, posted by "Matt Singer," May 9, 2006, https://www.youtube.com/watch?v=joQi27QG7Cs.

30. "Montana Primary Election Results: June 6, 2006," Montana Secretary of State, https://sosmt.gov/wp-content/uploads/attachments/2006_State_Primary.pdf.

31. Lee Newspapers: "U.S. Senate race gets rough early," June 8, 2006. https://newspapers.com/image/392468979/.

32. "Shirley You Can't Be Serious," *The Daily Show with Jon Stewart*, November 4, 2002, http://www.cc.com/video-clips/6g49ll/the-daily-show-with-jon-stewart-shirley-you-can-t-be-serious.

33. "Burns' absence makes the barbs grow sharper," *Great Falls Tribune*, June 11, 2006, https://newspapers.com/image/243491889/.

34. "Sen. Burns' Comments Detailed in Reports," Lee Newspapers, August 1, 2006.

35. Lee Newspapers, "Burns Criticism Cut from Report," *Independent Record* (Helena, MT), July 28, 2006; Lee Newspapers, "Sen. Burns' Comments Detailed in Reports," *Missoulian*, August 1, 2006.

36. Lee Newspapers, "Senator Chastises Hotshots," *Missoulian*, July 27, 2006.

37. "Sen. Burns' Comments."

38. Lee Newspapers, "Burns Defends Right to Question Fire Tactics," *Missoulian*, August 15, 2006.

39. "Conrad Burns' Naptime," YouTube video, posted by "arrowhead77," August 17, 2006, https://www.youtube.com/watch?v=a_B0i2LukP4.

40. "Immigration is a joke for Conrad Burns," YouTube video, posted by "arrowhead77," August 22, 2006, https://www.youtube.com/watch?v=lWxEhDau5D0.

41. "Sen. Spouts off Again," *Rapid City Journal*, August 24, 2006.

42. Associated Press, "Burns Staffer Explains Recent 'Terrorist' Quote," *Missoulian*, September 2, 2006.

43. "Jon Tester Sen. Burns Bozeman Debate Part 1," YouTube video, posted by "arrowhead77," October 9, 2006, https://youtu.be/CP7D2rPbu5k?t=536.

44. "Burns-Tester Debate in Butte, Part 2," YouTube video, posted by "Don Pogreba," September 24, 2006, https://www.youtube.com/watch?v=67G0rWDtDVI.

45. "Burns-Tester Debate in Butte, Part 7," YouTube video, posted by "Don Pogreba," September 24, 2006, https://www.youtube.com/watch?v=8QzZG4IGePE.

46. "Tom Ridge Criticizes Tester for Remarks on the Patriot Act," *Great Falls Tribune*, September 28, 2006.

47. "Jon Tester Sen. Burns Billings Debate Part 4," YouTube video, posted by "arrowhead77," October 21, 2006, https://youtu.be/rRr5PMV1W2c?t=301.

48. Associated Press, "Burns Isn't Sharing President's War Plan," *Missoulian*, October 19, 2006.

49. Jennifer McKee, "Unlicensed Tester Butchered Neighbors' Animals, Wasn't Cited," *Billings Gazette*, October 30, 2006, https://billingsgazette.com/news /state-and-regional/montana/unlicensed-tester-butchered-neighbor-s-animals -wasn-t-cited/article_eab9c4db-1dd2-5087-b418-e192374bab9f.html.

50. Associated Press, "Democrats Rally for Tester," *Billings Gazette*, November 4, 2006.

51. Terence Samuel, *The Upper House: A Journey behind the Closed Doors of the US Senate* (New York: Palgrave Macmillan, 2010), 26.

52. Samuel, 36.

53. "Olbermann Election 2006 Recap," YouTube video, posted by "snufflesjetc-ity," November 8, 2006, https://youtu.be/JWVE9cCyAIc?t=170.

54. Associated Press, "Burns Vows to Stay Active in State Affairs," *Billings Gazette*, December 1, 2006.

55. "Conrad Burns," obituary, *Billings Gazette*, May 1, 2016, https://billingsgazette .com/lifestyles/announcements/obituaries/conrad-burns/article_99c13bc1 -081a-5ccd-96c5-0d0eaa292295.html.

Chapter 10: A Farmer's Guide to the US Senate

1. Charles S. Johnson, "Going Broke is a 'Wonderful Learning Experience'," *Billings Gazette*, October 9, 1994.

2. Joel Stein, "Moving On Up: The Senate Shifts Offices," *Time*, March 26, 2009, http://www.time.com/time/magazine/article/0,9171,1887870,00.html.

3. Michael D. Shear, "In Following His Own Script, Webb May Test Senate's Limits," *Washington Post*, November 29, 2006. https://www.washingtonpost .com/archive/politics/2006/11/29/in-following-his-own-script-webb-may -test-senates-limits/4b3e74d7-97d7-4970-8b76-17c401d78cc4/?utm_term =.8703353b21ec.

4. Jennifer Steinhauer, "Loyal to his 4-Legged Constituents," *New York Times*, January 10, 2012. https://www.nytimes.com/2012/01/11/dining/senator-jon -tester-brings-dinner-from-montana.html.

5. Jordain Carney, "McConnell Cancels Senate's August Recess," *The Hill*, June 5, 2018, https://thehill.com/homenews/senate/390784-mcconnell-cancels -senates-august-recess.

6. Joe Perticone, "Republicans Pushed to Cancel the Senate's August Recess— Then Skipped Town," *Business Insider*, August 17, 2018, https://www.business insider.com/republicans-pushed-to-cancel-august-congressional-recess-then -left-2018-8.

7. "Tillis Joins Group of Senators Calling for Senate to Cancel August Recess to Make Progress on Major Issues," press release, Senator Thom Tillis, June 30, 2017, https://www.tillis.senate.gov/2017/6/tillis-joins-group-of-senators -calling-for-senate-to-cancel-august-recess-to-make-progress-on-major-issues.

8. National Defense Authorization Act for Fiscal Year 2020, S. 1790, 116th Congress, https://www.congress.gov/bill/116th-congress/senate-bill/1790.

9. "Flying Iraq's Deadly Skies," *Baltimore Sun*, February 8, 2007.

10. US Department of Defense, Defense Casualty Analysis System, https://dcas .dmdc.osd.mil/dcas/pages/report_oif_namesalp.xhtml.

11. "Idahoans Do a Year of Roadside Bomb Patrol," *Idaho Statesman*, January 20, 2008.

12. "Ross Aaron Clevenger," obituary, *Idaho Statesman*, February 16, 2007, https://www.legacy.com/obituaries/idahostatesman/obituary.aspx?n=ross -aaron-clevenger&pid=86462646.

13. Vickie D. Ashwill, "Loved Ones Mourn Loss of Soldiers," *Idaho Statesman*, February 12, 2007, https://www.idahostatesman.com/news/local/military /article40684536.html.

14. Ashwill; Associated Press, "Families Remember Fallen Soldiers," *South Idaho Press*, February 12, 2007.

15. Associated Press, "Burns Takes Job with Lobbying Firm in Washington," *Billings Gazette*, January 11, 2007; GAGE Press Release: "Senator Conrad Burns joins growing International Consulting Company," January, 2007, https://gage.cc/senator-conrad-burns-joins-growing-international-consulting -company/.

16. Lee Newspapers, "Tester Opposes Bush's Iraq Plan," *Billings Gazette*, January 16, 2007.

17. Allegra Stratton, "2007 Is America's Deadliest Year in Iraq," *The Guardian*, December 31, 2007, https://www.theguardian.com/world/2007/dec/31/usa .iraq.

18. Lee Newspapers, "Tester Visits Iraq, Backs Withdrawal," *Billings Gazette*, November 30, 2007.

19. Elizabeth Brotherton, "For Sen. Tester, Not Your Average Day in the Senate," *Roll Call*, March 2, 2007, https://www.rollcall.com/news/-17282-1.html.

20. Joseph Boushee, "Local Captures Kennedy Ride," *Miles City Star*, September 2, 2009.

21. Edward M. Kennedy, *True Compass: A Memoir* (New York: Twelve, 2009).

22. "Ted Kennedy on the Assassination of Martin Luther King Jr.," YouTube video, posted by "TPM TV," August 26, 2009, https://youtu.be/aQ4 _kTc7uIc?t=949.

23. "Ted Kennedy's Eulogy For Robert F. Kennedy Ft. Hans Zimmer," YouTube video, posted by "Zach Stott," May 14, 2018, https://youtu.be /aV0MKikJraE?t=255.

24. *The Centennial: 1938-1939*, Big Sandy High School yearbook, p. 16, available at https://mtmemory.org/digital/collection/p16013coll16/id/7113/rec/12.

Chapter 11: When We Need the Government . . . and When We Don't

1. Associated Press, "Early Returns Give Margin 2,500 More than Mather," *Harve Daily News*, June 25, 1969.

2. US Senate Roll Call Vote No. 302, October 11, 2001, https://www.senate. gov/legislative/LIS/roll_call_lists/roll_call_vote_cfm.cfm?congress=107&ses

sion=1&vote=003,02; "Montanans Wary of Security Laws," *Billings Gazette*, October 28, 2001.

3. U.S. House of Representatives Roll Call Vote No. 386, October 12, 2001, http://clerk.house.gov/evs/2001/roll386.xml.

4. "Signing of the PATRIOT Act Anti-Terrorism Legislation October 26, 2001," YouTube video, posted by "US National Archives," April 24, 2012, https://www.youtube.com/watch?v=dXAvGE0eMKE.

5. The USA PATRIOT Act, U.S. Congress, Public Law 107-56, October 26, 2001, https://www.congress.gov/107/plaws/publ56/PLAW-107publ56.pdf.

6. "Montanans Wary of Security Laws," *Billings Gazette*, October 28, 2001.

7. "2005 History & Final Status of Bills and Resolutions," Montana State Legislature, p. 208, https://leg.mt.gov/content/publications/sales/2005_history _final_status_vol.pdf.

8. "2005 Montana Legislature: Senate Joint Resolution 19," Montana State Senate, April 4, 2005, https://leg.mt.gov/bills/2005/BillHtml/SJ0019.htm.

9. Emergency Supplemental Appropriations Act, US Congress, Public Law 109-13, May 11, 2005, p. 11, https://www.congress.gov/109/plaws/publ13/PLAW -109publ13.pdf.

10. US House of Representatives, Roll Call Vote No. 31, REAL ID Act, February 10, 2005, http://clerk.house.gov/evs/2005/roll031.xml.

11. House Bill 287, Montana State Legislature, 2007, https://leg.mt.gov/bills /2007/billhtml/HB0287.htm.

12. US Congress, 110th Congress, S. 717, https://www.congress.gov/bill/110th -congress/senate-bill/717/cosponsors.

13. US Congressional Record, April 17, 2007, S4589–S4590, https://www .congress.gov/crec/2007/04/17/CREC-2007-04-17-senate.pdf.

14. Montana Code Annotated, State of Montana Constitution, article II, part II, section 4, https://leg.mt.gov/bills/mca/title_0000/article_0020/part_0010 /section_0040/0000-0020-0010-0040.html.

15. Jon Ellingson, phone interview with Aaron Murphy, June 17, 2019.

16. US Senate, Roll Call Vote No. 186, Housing and Economic Recovery Act, July 26, 2008, https://www.senate.gov/legislative/LIS/roll_call_lists/roll_call _vote_cfm.cfm?congress=110&session=2&vote=00186.

17. "Turmoil in US Credit Markets," US Senate Banking Committee Hearing, September 23, 2008, https://www.banking.senate.gov /hearings/turmoil-in-us-credit-markets-recent-actions-regarding -government-sponsored-entities-investment-banks-and-other-financial -institutions.

18. "Tester: Government's Bailout Plan Doesn't Smell Right," press release, Senator Jon Tester, September 23, 2008, https://www.tester.senate.gov/?p=press _release&id=2140.

19. US Senate, Roll Call Vote No. 213, October 1, 2008, https://www.senate.gov /legislative/LIS/roll_call_lists/roll_call_vote_cfm.cfm?congress=110 &session=2&vote=00213.

20. "Montana General Election Results: November 4, 2008," Montana Secretary of State, https://sosmt.gov/wp-content/uploads/attachments/2008_State _General.pdf.

21. "State of the Domestic Auto Industry 2," US Senate Banking Committee hearing, December 4, 2008, https://www.banking.senate.gov/hearings/the -state-of-the-domestic-automobile-industry-part-ii.

22. "Moment of Zen: No Assurances," *The Daily Show with Jon Stewart*, Comedy Central, December 4, 2008, http://www.cc.com/video-clips/b1ve9g/the -daily-show-with-jon-stewart-moment-of-zen---no-assurances.

23. US Senate, Roll Call Vote No. 215, December 11, 2008, https://www.senate .gov/legislative/LIS/roll_call_lists/roll_call_vote_cfm.cfm?congress=110 &session=2&vote=00215.

24. "Tester Statement on Auto Bailout 'No' Vote," press release, Senator Jon Tes- ter, December 12, 2008, https://www.tester.senate.gov/?p=press_release &id=1223.

25. David M. Herszenhorn and David E. Sanger, "Bush Approves $17.4 Billion Auto Bailout," *New York Times*, December 19, 2008, https://www.nytimes .com/2008/12/19/business/worldbusiness/19iht-20autoB.18826530.html.

26. Edmund L. Andrews and Peter Baker, "A.I.G. Planning Huge Bonuses After $170 Billion Bailout," *New York Times*, March 14, 2009, https://www .nytimes.com/2009/03/15/business/15AIG.html.

27. "Tester Blasts AIG for Using Bailout Money for Bonuses," YouTube video, posted by "Senator Jon Tester, "March 17, 2009, https://www.youtube.com /watch?v=oNK52-gv1j4.

28. US Senate, Roll Call Vote No. 64, February 13, 2009, https://www.senate. gov/legislative/LIS/roll_call_lists/roll_call_vote_cfm.cfm?congress=111 &session=1&vote=00064.

Chapter 12: Sleeping over a Volcano

1. Mike Dennison, "Outside Money Spent on Rehberg/Tester Race May Surpass $30 Million," *Independent Record* (Helena, MT), November 4, 2007, https:// helenair.com/news/local/outside-money-spent-on-rehberg-tester-race-may -surpass-million/article_8d9632ce-2603-11e2-af50-001a4bcf887a.html.

2. "2012 Shatters 2004 and 2008 Records for Total Ads Aired," Wesleyan Media Project, October 24, 2012, https://mediaproject.wesleyan.edu/releases/2012 -shatters-2004-and-2008-records-for-total-ads-aired/.

3. Associated Press, "Spending in Montana Senate Race Reached Record $47 Million," *Missoulian*, December 10, 2012, https://missoulian.com/news/local /spending-in-montana-senate-race-reached-record-million/article_707af262 -42e4-11e2-8a31-001a4bcf887a.html.

4. Lee Newspapers, "Group Sympathetic to Tester Drops $500k on TV Ad—For Libertarian," *Billings Gazette*, October 26, 2012, https://billingsgazette.com /news/state-and-regional/montana/group-sympathetic-to-tester-drops-k-on -tv-ad-for/article_44197da9-b6d2-5e8a-ae05-7442aef0a45d.html.

5. US Inflation Calculator, data retrieved via in2013dollars.com, accessed April 10, 2020, http://www.in2013dollars.com/us/inflation/1907?amount=30.

6. Samuel Clemens (Mark Twain), *The Autobiography of Mark Twain*, vol. 2 (Berkeley: University of California Press, 2013), 389.

7. Howard, *Montana*, 58.

8. "A Damnable Conspiracy," *Butte Miner*, January 11, 1899.

9.   "$500,000 for Seat in Senate," *Boston Globe*, August 3, 1899.

10. Howard, *Montana*, 67.

11. "People of Helena and Legislators Honor the Senator-Elect," *Butte Miner*, January 29, 1899.

12. "The Election Case of William A. Clark of Montana (1900)," US Senate, accessed April 10, 2020, https://www.senate.gov/artandhistory/history/common/contested_elections/089William_Clark.htm.

13. "Senator Clark Resigns His Seat," *Morning News* (Lancaster, PA), May 16, 1900.

14. "Clark Reappointed," *Morning News* (Lancaster, PA), May 16, 1900; "Clark Outwits the Senate and the Governor of Montana," *San Francisco Examiner*, May 16, 1900.

15. "Clark Outwits."

16. "Gov. Smith Writes a Card to the People," *Helena Independent*, May 22, 1900.

17. "Election Case of William A. Clark."

18. Clemens, *Autobiography*, 387–88.

19. Howard, *Montana*, 77.

20. Jeff Wiltse, "The Origins of Montana's Corrupt Practices Act: A More Complete History," *Montana Law Review* 73, no. 2 (Summer 2012): 317, https://scholarship.law.umt.edu/cgi/viewcontent.cgi?article=2377&context=mlr.

21. "Ravalli County Judge Legislature's Choice," *Daily Missoulian*, March 3, 1911.

22. "Editorial: Senator Myers," *Daily Missoulian*, March 3, 1911; "Gasp of Surprise Myers' Answer," *Daily Missoulian*, March 3, 1911.

23. "Senator Myers to Washington," *Fergus County Democrat*, April 11, 1911.

24. "University Bill Dies in Senate," *Anaconda Standard*, January 31, 1913; "Plea of Whiteside Fails to Influence Result," *Daily Missoulian*, January 31, 1913.

25. "People's Power League Organized," *Anaconda Standard*, June 12, 1911.

26. "Montana Now Has Drastic Corrupt Practice Law," *Butte Miner*, November 17, 1912.

27. "Separate Official Ballot," *Butte Miner*, November 5, 1912.

28. "Montana General Election Results, November 5, 1912," Montana Secretary of State, https://sosmt.gov/Portals/142/Elections/archives/1910s/1912_General_Statewide.pdf.

29. "Never Again," editorial, *Daily Missoulian*, November 9, 1912.

30. Bob Brown, "When Corporations Become People, Montanans Have Much to Fear," *Great Falls Tribune*, February 25, 2010.

31. Lee Newspapers, "Who Is ATP?" *Billings Gazette*, June 25, 2012, https://billingsgazette.com/news/state-and-regional/montana/u-s-supreme-court-strikes-montana-ban-on-corporate-donations/article_ddb5f485-1c06-5a33-8f06-846134e11a75.html.

32. Kim Barker, "Documents Found in Meth House Bare Inner Workings of Dark Money Group," *ProPublica*, October 29, 2012, https://www.propublica.org/article/documents-found-in-meth-house-bare-inner-workings-of-dark-money-group.

33. "Opinion: *Western Tradition Partnership v. Bullock*," Montana Supreme Court, December 30, 2011, p. 8. http://electionlawblog.org/wp-content/uploads/MT-expenditures-decision.pdf.

34. Associated Press, "Corporate Spending Limit Restored," *Great Falls Tribune*, December 31, 2011.
35. "Application to Stay Montana Supreme Court Decision Pending Certiorari," Barg & Bopp, February 9, 2012, https://www.jamesmadisoncenter.org/cases/files/2012/01/Application-for-Stay-final.pdf.
36. "On Petition for Writ of Certiorari to the Supreme Court of Montana," US Supreme Court, No. 11-1179, June 25, 2012, https://www.supremecourt.gov/opinions/11pdf/11-1179h9j3.pdf.
37. I-166 Ballot Language (2012), Stand with Montanans, accessed April 10, 2020, http://www.standwithmontanans.org/ballot_language.
38. "S.J. Res. 18," US Congress, 113th Congress, 1st session, June 18, 2013, https://www.congress.gov/113/bills/sjres18/BILLS-113sjres18is.pdf.
39. "S.J. Res. 19," US Congress, 113th Congress, 1st session, June 18, 2013, https://www.congress.gov/113/bills/sjres19/BILLS-113sjres19rs.pdf.
40. "Tester: Citizens United a threat to democracy," YouTube video, posted by "Senator Jon Tester," September 12, 2012, https://www.youtube.com/watch?v=HyqBf6d_g6Q; "Tester: Citizens United a Threat to Democracy," press release, Senator Jon Tester, September 12, 2012, https://www.tester.senate.gov/?p=press_release&id=2615.
41. Montana General Election Results, Montana Secretary of State, November 6, 2012, https://sosmt.gov/wp-content/uploads/attachments/2012_General_Canvass.pdf.

Chapter 13: The Maverick

1. Ray Ring, "Who Is Denny Rehberg, Really?," *High Country News*, September 3, 2012, https://www.hcn.org/issues/44.15/who-is-denny-rehberg-really.
2. *Cases Argued and Determined*, Supreme Court of Montana Territory, vol. 6 (1887), via *High Country News*, https://www.hcn.org/external_files/rehberg/rehberg_1887_court_ruling.pdf.
3. Parker, *Battle for the Big Sky*, 62–65.
4. "Yellowstone County Results," *Billings Gazette*, November 8, 1984.
5. *Ravalli Republic*: "Rehberg Is New Lt. Gov.," *Ravalli Republic*, June 27, 1991.
6. "What Rehberg Said," *Montana Standard*, January 8, 1994.
7. "Rehberg Says AIDS Remarks Were Rhetorical," *Montana Standard*, January 8, 1994.
8. Associated Press, "Racicot Blasts Rehberg, Baucus for Nasty Ads," *Great Falls Tribune*, November 2, 1996.
9. "Baucus, Rehberg Trade Accusations over Campaign Ads," *Great Falls Tribune*, November 2, 1996.
10. Lee Newspapers, "Baucus Defeats Rehberg, Serves Another 6 Years," *Independent Record* (Helena, MT), November 6, 1996.
11. Montana General Election Results: November 5, 1996, Montana Secretary of State, https://sosmt.gov/Portals/142/Elections/archives/1990s/1996/1996gen.pdf.
12. Lee Newspapers, "Rehberg Formally in House Race," *Billings Gazette*, March 22, 2000.

13. Montana General Election Results: November 7, 2000, Montana Secretary of State, https://sosmt.gov/Portals/142/Elections/archives/2000s/2000/2000-GenState.pdf.

14. Charles S. Johnson, "Republican Daines Announces U.S. Senate Bid," *Billings Gazette*, November 14, 2010, https://billingsgazette.com/news/state-and-regional/montana/republican-daines-announces-u-s-senate-bid/article_ac93271a-8355-5e9c-9db3-6cf49b667984.html.

15. Charles S. Johnson, "Republican Steve Daines Switches to House Race," *Missoulian*, February 4, 2012, https://missoulian.com/news/state-and-regional/election-republican-steve-daines-switches-to-house-race/article_13e53864-2fae-11e0-9ca7-001cc4c03286.html.

16. "Denny Rehberg Official Announcement Video for United States Senate Part 1," YouTube video, posted by "Montanans4Rehberg," February 6, 2011, https://youtu.be/jP7TMVcCjhU?t=353.

17. Charles S. Johnson, "Rehberg Officially Enters 2012 Senate Race," *Missoulian*, February 6, 2011, https://missoulian.com/news/local/rehberg-officially-enters-race-for-u-s-senate/article_89deb39c-3143-11e0-8e8b-001cc4c002e0.html.

18. Lee Newspapers, "Ad Watch: Group Criticizes Rehberg's Votes on Pay Increases," Billings Gazette, March 25, 2012, https://billingsgazette.com/news/state-and-regional/montana/ad-watch-group-criticizes-rehberg-s-votes-on-pay-increases/article_4bbc2ca7-b0af-521c-8933-bd45c4dd7f3e.html.

19. Lee Newspapers, "Report Reveals Details of Wildfire," *Missoulian*, July 19, 2010.

20. Pre-Sentence Investigation Report, Gregory Duane Barkus, Montana Department of Corrections, January 10, 2011, p. 3, via *Missoulian*, https://bloximages.chicago2.vip.townnews.com/missoulian.com/content/tncms/assets/v3/editorial/1/3b/13bc5b4a-23ba-11e2-96db-0019bb2963f4/5091c0cc8a5a0.pdf.pdf.

21. Vince Devlin, "Quick Action by Campers Saved Lives in Rehberg Boat Crash," *Missoulian*, September 13, 2009, https://missoulian.com/news/local/quick-action-by-campers-saved-lives-in-rehberg-boat-crash/article_bbd4bb38-a028-11de-8dd1-001cc4c03286.html.

22. Devlin.

23. Pre-Sentence Investigation Report.

24. Associated Press, "Rehberg Returns to Work with Walker, Crutches," *Montana Standard*, September 10, 2009.

25. Lee Newspapers, "Barkus Sentenced in Boat Crash, Avoids Jail Time," *Billings Gazette*, January 11, 2011, https://billingsgazette.com/news/state-and-regional/montana/barkus-sentenced-in-boat-crash-avoids-jail-time/article_7cfc7282-24c2-11e0-bddc-001cc4c03286.html.

26. "Rehberg Returns to Work."

27. Associated Press, "Rehberg Defends Lawsuit," *Great Falls Tribune*, July 7, 2010.

28. *Rehberg Ranch v. City of Billings*, July 2, 2010, via *Billings Gazette*, https://bloximages.chicago2.vip.townnews.com/billingsgazette.com/content/tncms/assets/v3/editorial/7/a0/7a0a070c-895d-11df-9199-001cc4c002e0/4c33c85a949fb.pdf.pdf.

29. Associated Press, "Rehberg Drops Lawsuit against City of Billings over Wildfire," *Missoulian*, November 11, 2011, https://missoulian.com/news /state-and-regional/rehberg-drops-lawsuit-against-city-of-billings-over-wildfire /article_2e06365c-0beb-11e1-a9d2-001cc4c03286.html.

30. Charles S. Johnson, "Rehberg Gets Key Chairmanship, Targets 'Obamacare,'" *Independent Record* (Helena, MT), January 7, 2011, https://helenair.com /news/rehberg-gets-key-chairmanship-targets-obamacare/article_1e76949c -1a84-11e0-b335-001cc4c03286.html.

31. Michael Warren, "Montana Republicans: Ryan Plan 'Could Harm' Medicare," *Washington Examiner*, June 22, 2012, https://www.washingtonexaminer .com/weekly-standard/montana-republicans-ryan-plan-could-harm-medicare.

32. "What Good Is a GOP Senate?," editorial, *Wall Street Journal*, June 27, 2012, https://www.wsj.com/articles/SB10001424052702304765304577483133930 695476.

33. Lee Newspapers, "Highlights of Rehberg's budget proposal," *Missoulian*, October 9, 2011. Lee Newspapers, "Highlights of Rehberg-Led Spending Proposal," *Missoulian*, July 18, 2012.

34. "Republicans vs. Women," editorial, *New York Times*, July 29, 2012, https:// www.nytimes.com/2012/07/30/opinion/republicans-vs-women.html.

35. "H.R. 1505: National Security and Federal Lands Protection Act," US Congress, April 11, 2011, https://www.congress.gov/bill/112th-congress/house -bill/1505/.

36. Vic Miller, "Rehberg's Security Bill Is Scary Stuff," *Billings Gazette*, September 28, 2011.

37. "Daines Joins Chorus of Critics Blasting Rehberg's Federal Land-Grab Bill," press release , Montanans for Tester, March 13, 2012, https://www.jontester .com/news/2012/daines-joins-chorus-of-critics-blasting-rehbergs-federal-land -grab-bill/.

38. Associated Press, "GOP Ad Portrays Tester with Five Fingers," *Great Falls Tribune*, September 30, 2011.

39. Montana Primary Election Results, June 5, 2012, Montana Secretary of State, https://sosmt.gov/wp-content/uploads/attachments/2012_PRIMARY _STATEWIDE_CANVASS.PDF.

40. "Tester Announces First Senate Debate with Rehberg, Cox," press release, Montanans for Tester, June 6, 2012, https://www.jontester.com/news/2012 /tester-announces-first-senate-debate-with-rehberg-cox/.

41. "U.S. Senate Debate," YouTube video, posted by "ivotelibterariancom," June 16, 2012, https://youtu.be/jN7ZOfPKDoo?t=332.

42. "Citizens United Political Victory Fund Backs Congressman Denny Rehberg for U.S. Senate," press release, Citizens United Political Victory Fund, September 21, 2011, http://www.cupvf.org/press-releases.aspx?article =3002.

43. "U.S. Senate Debate."

44. "Dennis Rehberg: Not a Rancher After All," press release, Montanans for Tester, June 16, 2012, https://www.jontester.com/news/press-releases/2012 /dennis-rehberg-not-a-rancher-after-all/.

45. "U.S. Senate Debate."

46. Associated Press, "Rehberg 'No-Show' Leads to Debate Cancelation," *Great Falls Tribune*, June 22, 2012.

47. "'Rehberg Chicken' Featured on Hardball," YouTube video, posted by "Montana Democratic Party," June 26, 2012, https://www.youtube.com /watch?v=7yErjW5agJc.

48. Montanans for Tester newspaper ad, Great Falls Tribune, August 17, 2012, p. A5.

49. John McCain, Twitter (@SenJohnMcCain), August 17, 2012, 10:17 a.m., https://twitter.com/SenJohnMcCain/status/236512086635712512.

50. Tristan Scott, "Small-Town Ties between Ament, Tester Bring Pearl Jam Back to Missoula," *Missoulian*, June 14, 2012, https://missoulian.com/entertainment /music/small-town-ties-between-ament-tester-bring-pearl-jam-back/article _dd2e8b16-b69f-11e1-9148-0019bb2963f4.html.

51. "Jeff Ament & Senator Jon Tester Interview," YouTube video, posted by "The Big J Show," June 14, 2012, https://youtu.be/FLTsL_zamDs?t=190.

52. Associated Press, "AP Investigation: Rehberg Underreports Lobbyist Donations," *Missoulian*, February 5, 2012, https://missoulian.com/news/state -and-regional/ap-investigation-rehberg-underreports-lobbyist-donations/ article_355289a6-500b-11e1-a630-0019bb2963f4.html#ixzz1p73AGg9z.

53. Rehberg at American League of Lobbyists fundraiser, audio recording, October 2011, via *Huffington Post*, http://big.assets.huffingtonpost.com/Rehberg EventAudioPART1.mp3.

54. "City Spends $21k in Rehberg Lawsuit," *Billings Gazette*, March 7, 2012.

55. "Jon Tester and Denny Rehberg spar in second U.S. Senate debate," YouTube video, posted by "Dustin Hurst," October 10, 2012, https://youtu.be /JMKX6E-pcwg?t=3422.

56. "Jon Tester and Denny Rehberg spar."

57. Associated Press, "Rehberg Campaigns in Tester's Hometown," *Montana Standard*, October 12, 2012.

58. "Montana Hunters and Anglers Leadership Fund—Surveillance," YouTube video, posted by "MTHuntersandAnglers," October 26, 2012, https://www .youtube.com/watch?v=xFzxnWJfTGw.

59. "Barkus Report May Be Released," *Great Falls Tribune*, October 11, 2012.

60. Pre-Sentence Investigation Report.

61. Lee Newspapers, "Court Releases Investigative Report on Barkus, Rehberg Boat Crash," *Missoulian*, October 31, 2012, https://missoulian.com/news /local/court-releases-investigative-report-on-barkus-rehberg-boat-crash/article _d9e94018-23b4-11e2-b7fd-0019bb2963f4.html.

62. "Jon Tester Senate Victory Speech," YouTube video, posted by "Jon Tester," November 7, 2012, https://www.youtube.com/watch?v=DQj_1CAVvdA.

63. Montana General Election Results, November 6, 2012, Montana Secretary of State, https://sosmt.gov/wp-content/uploads/attachments/2012_General _Canvass.pdf.

64. Montana General Election Results (Chouteau County), November 6, 2012, Montana Secretary of State, http://mtelectionresults.gov/ResultsSW.aspx?type =CTYALL&cty=08&eid=4&map=CTY; Montana General Election Results (Yellowstone County), November 6, 2012, Montana Secretary of

State, http://mtelectionresults.gov/ResultsSW.aspx?type=CTYALL&cty
=56&eid=4&map=CTY.

Chapter 14: "Khaihawana Punk" and Other Game Changers

1. Senate Amendment 715 to the Safe Communities, Safe Schools Act of 2013, April 11, 2013, p. 16, https://www.congress.gov/113/crec/2013/04/11/CREC -2013-04-11-pt1-PgS2598-3.pdf.

2. "Avielle Rose Richman," Avielle Foundation, accessed April 10, 2020, https:// aviellefoundation.org/about-the-foundation/avielle-rose-richman/.

3. Paul Bedard, "NRA Threatens Senators Who Back Toomey-Manchin Deal," *Washington Examiner*, April 11, 2013, https://www.washingtonexaminer.com /nra-threatens-senators-who-back-toomey-manchin-deal.

4. US Senate Roll Call Vote No. 97, April 17, 2013, https://www.senate.gov /legislative/LIS/roll_call_lists/roll_call_vote_cfm.cfm?congress=113&session =1&vote=00097.

5. Tovia Smith, "A Newtown Family's Campaign to Change How We Think about Violence," NPR, December 12, 2017, https://www.npr.org /2017/12/12/569060702/a-newtown-familys-campaign-to-change-how -we-think-about-violence.

6. Michael Gold and Tyler Pager, "Sandy Hook Victim's Father Dies in Apparent Suicide in Newtown," *New York Times*, March 25, 2019, https://www .nytimes.com/2019/03/25/nyregion/sandy-hook-father.html.

7. "Welcome to the Avielle Foundation," The Avielle Foundation, accessed April 10, 2020, https://aviellefoundation.org/about-the-foundation /avielle-rose-richman/.

8. "Baucus to Retire at End of Term," *Great Falls Tribune*, April 23, 2013.

9. Associated Press, "Schweitzer says he won't run for Senate," *Ravalli Republic*, July 14, 2013.

10. Justin Franz, "The Rise and Fall of John Walsh," *Flathead Beacon*, October 29, 2014, https://flatheadbeacon.com/2014/10/29/rise-fall-john-walsh/.

11. "President Obama Announces His Intent to Nominate Senator Max Baucus as Ambassador to the People's Republic of China," White House Archives, December 20, 2013, https://obamawhitehouse.archives.gov/the-press -office/2013/12/20/president-obama-announces-his-intent-nominate -senator-max-baucus-ambassa.

12. US Senate Roll Call Vote No. 25, February 6, 2014, https://www.senate.gov /legislative/LIS/roll_call_lists/roll_call_vote_cfm.cfm?congress=113&session =2&vote=00025.

13. Associated Press, "Walsh Sworn in As Senator," *Montana Standard*, February 12, 2014.

14. Jonathan Martin, "Interactive: How Senator John Walsh Plagiarized a Final Paper," *New York Times*, July 23, 2014, https://www.nytimes.com/interactive /2014/07/23/us/politics/john-walsh-final-paper-plagiarism.html.

15. Jonathan Martin, "Senator's Thesis Turns Out to Be Remix of Others' Works, Uncited," *New York Times*, July 23, 2014, https://www.nytimes. com/2014/07/24/us/politics/montana-senator-john-walsh-plagiarized-thesis .html.

16. Lee Newspapers, "Senator Will Finish Term, Which Ends in January," *Missoulian*, August 8, 2014.

17. Jonathan Martin, "Plagiarism Costs Degree for Senator John Walsh," *New York Times*, October 10, 2014, https://www.nytimes.com/2014/10/11/us/politics/plagiarism-costs-degree-for-senator-john-walsh.html.

18. Associated Press, "Plagiarism Report Not Very Likely to Affect Senate Race," *Montana Standard*, October 12, 2014.

19. Martin, "Plagiarism Costs Degree."

20. Montana General Election Results, November 4, 2014, Montana Secretary of State, https://sosmt.gov/wp-content/uploads/attachments/2014-General-Official-Statewide-Canvass.pdf.

21. "John Walsh, Realtor," website of Big Sky Brokers, Helena Montana, accessed April 10, 2020, https://www.bigskybrokers.com/john-walsh-realtor/.

22. James Hohmann, "NRSC Cops to Walsh Plagiarism Leak," *Politico*, October 30, 2014, https://www.politico.com/story/2014/10/strategists-peel-back-curtain-on-oppo-112358.

23. Associated Press, "Walsh Releases Military Records," *Great Falls Tribune*, January 27, 2014.

24. "Transcript: Pope Francis's speech to Congress," *Washington Post*, September 24, 2015, https://www.washingtonpost.com/local/social-issues/transcript-pope-franciss-speech-to-congress/2015/09/24/6d7d7ac8-62bf-11e5-8e9e-dce8a2a2a679_story.html.

25. New Hampshire General Election Results, November 8, 2016, New Hampshire Secretary of State, http://sos.nh.gov/2016USSGen.aspx?id=8589963690.

26. Montana General Election Results, November 8, 2016, Montana Secretary of State, https://sosmt.gov/wp-content/uploads/attachments/2016GeneralStatewideCanvass.pdf.

27. Associated Press, "Zinke: Senate Run vs. Tester Possible," *Independent Record* (Helena, MT), November 29, 2016.

28. Michael Wright, "Obama Administration Blocks New Mining Claims on 30,000 Acres in Paradise Valley," *Bozeman Daily Chronicle*, November 21, 2016, https://www.bozemandailychronicle.com/news/environment/obama-administration-blocks-new-mining-claims-on-acres-in-paradise/article_d1895a45-fa90-5fd6-98ce-c7e852efe7d5.html.

29. "Donald Trump Jr. in Montana," YouTube video, posted by "Redoubt News," October 30, 2018, https://www.youtube.com/watch?v=2hkxvLH7tjg.

30. Jonathan Martin and Alexander Burns, "McConnell Eyed Ryan Zinke for a Senate Seat. Donald Trump Had Other Ideas," *New York Times*, December 16, 2016, https://www.nytimes.com/2016/12/16/us/politics/ryan-zinke-mitch-mcconnell-trump-cabinet.html.

31. Martin and Burns, "McConnell Eyed Ryan Zinke."

Chapter 15: Holes in Soles

1. US Congressional Record, February 3, 2017, S672, https://www.govinfo.gov/content/pkg/CREC-2017-02-03/pdf/CREC-2017-02-03.pdf.

2. US Senate Roll Call Vote No. 54, February 7, 2017, https://www.senate.gov

/legislative/LIS/roll_call_lists/roll_call_vote_cfm.cfm?congress=115&session =1&vote=00054.

3.   Keila Szpaller, "UM Not Alone in Losing Upward Bound Funds for Double-Spacing Error," May 1, 2017, https://missoulian.com/news/local/um-not-alone-in-losing-upward-bound-funds-for-double/article_6cedeb94-4c2f-503d -beb4-6ea871c82808.html.

4.   "Tester Fights for First-Generation College Students at University of Montana," press release, Senator Jon Tester, April 28, 2017, https://www.tester .senate.gov/?p=press_release&id=5237.

5.   Szpaller, "UM Not Alone."

6.   Wilson Andrews, "How Each Senator Voted on Trump's Cabinet and Administration Nominees," *New York Times*, May 11, 2017, https://www.nytimes.com /interactive/2017/01/31/us/politics/trump-cabinet-confirmation-votes.html.

7.   "Congress Unanimously Clears Tester's Transparency and Accountability Bill," press release, Senator Jon Tester, January 17, 2017, https://www.tester. senate.gov/?p=press_release&id=4949; US Congress, Public Law 115-3, GAO Access and Oversight Act, January 31, 2017, https://www.congress.gov/115 /plaws/publ3/PLAW-115publ3.pdf.

8.   "President Trump Signs Tester's Bipartisan Bill to Improve Veterans Choice Program," press release, Senator Jon Tester, April 19, 2017, https://www.tester. senate.gov/?p=press_release&id=5213; US Congress, Public Law 115-26, VA Choice Improvement, April 19, 2017, https://www.congress.gov/115/plaws /publ26/PLAW-115publ26.pdf.

9.   Jon Tester, "Tester Passes 20 Bipartisan Bills into Law this Congress," Medium, June 11, 2018, https://medium.com/@sen_jon_tester/trump-has -signed-16-of-testers-bills-into-law-this-congress-f4289c16912b.

10.   Tom Lutey, "Tester Will Oppose Neil Gorsuch," *Billings Gazette*, April 2, 2017, https://billingsgazette.com/news/state-and-regional/govt-and-politics/tester-will -oppose-neil-gorsuch/article_2d8a04f7-7596-5527-a4f7-bcd32dc582c5.html.

11.   Jon Tester, "Why I Cannot Support Judge Gorsuch," Medium, April 2, 2017, https://medium.com/@sen_jon_tester/why-i-cannot-support-judge-gorsuch -70c7b460cd7e.

12.   US Senate Roll Call Vote No. 109, April 6, 2014, https://www.senate.gov/ legislative/LIS/roll_call_lists/roll_call_vote_cfm.cfm?congress=115&session =1&vote=00109.

13.   Susan Davis, "Senate Pulls 'Nuclear' Trigger to Ease Gorsuch Nomination," NPR, April 6, 2017, https://www.npr.org/2017/04/06/522847700/senate -pulls-nuclear-trigger-to-ease-gorsuch-confirmation.

14.   US Senate Roll Call Vote No. 111, April 7, 2014, https://www.senate.gov /legislative/LIS/roll_call_lists/roll_call_vote_cfm.cfm?congress=115&session =1&vote=00111.

15.   "A 'CLEAR' Path toward Meaningful, Fair Reform of Hometown Banking Regulation," *Banking on Montanans* (blog), Montana Bankers Association, June 9, 2017.

16.   Public Law 115-174: "Economic Growth, Regulatory Relief . . . ," US Congress, May 24, 2018, https://www.congress.gov/bill/115th-congress/senate -bill/2155/cosponsors.

17. US Congressional Record, March 6, 2018, S1356, https://www.govinfo.gov /content/pkg/CREC-2018-03-06/pdf/CREC-2018-03-06.pdf.

18. "News from Christopher Dodd and Barney Frank," Montanans for Tester email, March 20, 2018.

19. Tester, "Tester Passes 20."

20. "Tester Calls for Senate Hearing on Missing and Murdered Indigenous Women," press release, Senator Jon Tester, August 29, 2018, https://www .tester.senate.gov/?p=press_release&id=6382.

21. Tristan Scott, "Polson Woman Honors Missing and Murdered Indigenous Women," *Flathead Beacon*, March 27, 2018, https://flatheadbeacon .com/2018/03/27/polson-woman-honors-missing-murdered-indigenous -women/.

22. "Violence against American Indian and Alaska Native Women and Men," National Institute of Justice, September 2016, https://www.ncjrs.gov /pdffiles1/nij/249822.pdf.

23. Evan Simon, "A Family's Desperate Search for a Missing Young Woman Highlights Questions about Justice on Tribal Lands," ABC News, November 1, 2017, https://abcnews.go.com/US/familys-desperate-search-missing-young -woman-highlights-questions/story?id=50737963.

24. Testimony of Kimberly Loring Heavy Runner, US Senate Indian Affairs Committee, December 12, 2018 (at 2:07:23), https://www.indian.senate.gov /hearing/missing-and-murdered-confronting-silent-crisis-indian-country.

25. "Tester Calls for Senate Hearing on Missing and Murdered Native American Women," https://www.tester.senate.gov/?p=press_release&id=6382.

26. Testimony of Kimberly Loring Heavy Runner.

27. Testimony of Kimberly Loring Heavy Runner.

28. "Missoula's Briana Lamb, Advocate for Missing and Murdered Indigenous Women, to be Tester's Guest at State of the Union," press release, Senator Jon Tester, February 1, 2019, https://www.tester.senate.gov/?p=press_release &id=6606.

29. "Transcript: Remarks by President Trump in State of the Union Address," The White House, February 5, 2019, https://www.whitehouse.gov/briefings -statements/remarks-president-trump-state-union-address-2/.

30. Donald J. Trump, Twitter (@realDonaldTrump), January 6, 2018 5:27 a.m., https://twitter.com/realDonaldTrump/status/949618475877765120.

31. Donald J. Trump, Twitter (@realDonaldTrump), January 6, 2018 5:30 a.m., https://twitter.com/realDonaldTrump/status/949619270631256064.

32. Donald J. Trump, Twitter (@realDonaldTrump), September 5, 2017 6:38 p.m., https://twitter.com/realDonaldTrump/status/905228667336499200.

33. "Transcript: Remarks by President Trump in Meeting with Bipartisan Members of Congress on Immigration," The White House, January 9, 2018, https://www.whitehouse.gov/briefings-statements/remarks-president-trump -meeting-bipartisan-members-congress-immigration/.

34. "Transcript: Remarks by President Trump."

35. David M. Herszenhorn, "Widowed Homeowner Foils Trump in Atlantic City," *New York Times*, July 21, 1998, https://www.nytimes.com/1998/07/21 /nyregion/widowed-homeowner-foils-trump-in-atlantic-city.html.

36. "TRUMPED: The Donald, the Widow and Eminent Domain," YouTube video, posted by "InstituteForJustice," May 16, 2011, https://www.youtube.com/watch?v=SmM4ZBoppNQ.

37. Herszenhorn, "Widowed Homeowner."

Chapter 16: Whistleblowers Within

1. John T. Bennett, "White House Mum about Trump's Unprecedented Call for Senator's Resignation," *Roll Call*, May 2, 2018, https://www.rollcall.com/news/politics/trumps-call-senators-resignation-called-unprecedented.

2. Donald J. Trump, Twitter (@realDonaldTrump), April 28, 2018, 5:07 a.m., https://twitter.com/realDonaldTrump/status/990200773232529413.

3. Donald J. Trump, Twitter, April 28, 2018, 12:11 p.m., https://twitter.com/realdonaldtrump/status/990307626784362496.

4. "Trump goes after Tester - Michigan rally, April 28, 2018," President Trump Remarks at Michigan Rally, C-SPAN user-created clip, April 28, 2018, https://www.c-span.org/video/?c4818137/trump-tester-michigan-rally-april-28-2018.

5. Maggie Haberman and Katie Rogers, "Trump Attacks Whistle-Blower's Sources and Alludes to Punishment for Spies," *New York Times*, September 26, 2019, https://www.nytimes.com/2019/09/26/us/politics/trump-whistle-blower-spy.html.

6. "Donald Trump physical examination results full press conference," YouTube video, posted by "Global News," January 16, 2018, https://youtu.be/OBZieO9fycE?t=111.

7. "Donald Trump physical examination results."

8. Ibid.

9. "Isakson Meets with VA Secretary Nominee Rear Admiral Ronny Jackson, M.D.," press release, Senator Johnny Isakson, April 16, 2018, https://www.isakson.senate.gov/public/index.cfm/2018/4/isakson-meets-with-va-secretary-nominee-rear-admiral-ronny-jackson-m-d.

10. "Tester: I Need to Know If Admiral Jackson Has What It Takes to Run the VA," press release, Senator Jon Tester, April 17, 2018, https://www.tester.senate.gov/?p=press_release&id=6097.

11. "Summary of Accusations Against Ronny Jackson," Senator Jon Tester, April 24, 2018, via *Washington Post*, https://apps.washingtonpost.com/g/documents/politics/ronny-jackson-summary-of-allegations/2922/.

12. "Tester/Isakson Statement on VA Secretary Nomination," press release, US Senate Veterans' Affairs Committee, April 24, 2018, https://www.veterans.senate.gov/newsroom/majority-news/isakson-tester_statement-on-va-secretary-nomination.

13. "Isakson/Tester Letter to White House re: Ronny Jackson," US Senate Veterans' Affairs Committee, April 24, 2018, https://www.veterans.senate.gov/imo/media/doc/20180424102245104.pdf.

14. "Trump on Ronny Jackson as VA nominee: 'It's totally his decision,'" YouTube video, posted by "CBS News," April 24, 2018, https://youtu.be/um4QhKxG3RI?t=300.

15. "Anderson Cooper: Trump fails to 'get the best people,'" YouTube video, posted by "CNN," April 24, 2018, https://youtu.be/_beA5vPkjdA?t=401.

16. "Anderson Cooper: Trump fails.'"

17. "Exclusive Interview: President Trump on Fox and Friends," YouTube video, posted by "FOX News," April 26, 2018, https://youtu.be/_lu_Hgw60Ns?t=183.

18. "Exclusive Interview: President Trump."

19. "Tester Statement on Jackson Nomination Withdrawal," press release, Senator Jon Tester, April 26, 2018, https://www.tester.senate.gov/?p=press_release&id=6119.

20. "Former Secretary of Defense Chuck Hagel Issues Statement on VA Secretary Nominee Withdrawal," press release, Senator Jon Tester, April 26, 2018, https://www.tester.senate.gov/?p=press_release&id=6121.

21. "Trump on Dr. R. Jackson," C-SPAN user-created clip, September 21, 2019, https://www.c-span.org/video/?c4818078/trump-dr-r-jackson.

22. Juana Summers and Manu Raju, "VA Nominee Drunkenly Banged on Female Employees Door During Overseas Trip, Sources Say," CNN, April 27, 2018, https://www.cnn.com/2018/04/24/politics/ronny-jackson-door-allegations/index.html.

23. "Response to Reports Secret Service Personnel Forced to Intervene During President Protective Mission Visit," press release, US Secret Service, April 26, 2018, https://www.secretservice.gov/data/press/releases/2018/18-APR/CMR_19-18_final.pdf.

24. Amy Gardner and Seung Min Kim, "White House: No Evidence That Ronny Jackson 'Wrecked' a Vehicle as President's Physician," *Washington Post*, April 28, 2018, https://www.washingtonpost.com/politics/white-house-no-evidence-that-ronny-jackson-wrecked-a-vehicle-as-presidents-physician/2018/04/27/083cc9e8-4a39-11e8-9072-f6d4bc32f223_story.html.

25. Jeff Zeleny, Twitter (@jeffzeleny), April 28, 2018, 6:25 a.m., https://twitter.com/jeffzeleny/status/990220398586458112.

26. Chris Cillizza, "Donald Trump Hints He Has Dirt on This Senator," CNN, April 30, 2018, https://www.cnn.com/2018/04/30/politics/jon-tester-donald-trump-ronny-jackson/index.html.

27. "Sen. Tester Gives First TV Interview Since Trump Called on Him Resign," YouTube video, posted by "KPAX-TV," May 4, 2018, https://www.youtube.com/watch?v=ZlPZ69Fn4-4.

28. Manu Raju, "Exclusive: Pence's Doctor Alerted WH Aides about Ronny Jackson Concerns Last Fall," CNN, May 1, 2018, https://www.cnn.com/2018/04/30/politics/karen-pence-doctor-privacy-ronny-jackson/index.html.

29. Anderson Cooper and Gary Tuchman, "AC360" (Transcript), May 1, 2018, transcripts.cnn.com/TRANSCRIPTS/1805/01/acd.02.html.

30. "Disgraceful," YouTube video, posted by "America First Action Super PAC," May 1, 2018, https://www.youtube.com/watch?time_continue=16&v=eVKHxlsYnXE.

31. "Jon Tester's Got to Go | Montana Senate," YouTube video, posted by "NRSC," July 2, 2018, https://www.youtube.com/watch?v=mk9jNtIQs78&feature=youtu.be.

Chapter 17: How to Pronounce "Montana"

1. Barbara Starr, "Pentagon Opens Investigation into Ronny Jackson Allegations," CNN, June 4, 2018, https://www.cnn.com/2018/06/04/politics/pentagon -investigation-ronny-jackson/index.html.

2. Ashley Parker, "Ronny Jackson Won't Return to Job as Trump's Physician," *Washington Post*, April 29, 2018, https://www.washingtonpost .com/politics/ronny-jackson-wont-return-to-job-as-trumps-physician /2018/04/29/101d2bfe-4c0e-11e8-84a0-458a1aa9ac0a_story.html.

3. Freddy Monares, "Montana U.S. Senate Candidate Claims Primary Home Tax Break in California," *Bozeman Daily Chronicle*, November 17, 2017, https://www.bozemandailychronicle.com/news/politics/montana-u-s-senate -candidate-claims-primary-home-tax-break/article_a0be62e3-2ba1-5396

4. -a3fc-ff70da1f1dd6.html.

5. MT Democratic Party, Twitter (@MT Dems), March 23, 2018, 11:06 a.m., https://twitter.com/MTDems/status/977245239474774016.

6. Edward O'Brien, "Matt Rosendale Announces Run for Montana Senate Seat," Montana Public Radio, July 31, 2017, https://www.mtpr.org/post/matt-rosendale -announces-run-montana-senate-seat.

7. Cameron Joseph, "Montana Senate Candidate's Claims to Be a Rancher Are Partly Bull," *Talking Points Memo*, May 29, 2018, https://talkingpointsmemo .com/dc/montana-gop-senate-candidate-matt-rosendale-claims-to-be-a-rancher -are-partly-bull.

8. Cameron Joseph, "Montana GOP Senate Candidate Quietly Scrubs 'Rancher' from His Campaign Bios," *Talking Points Memo*, September 6, 2018, https:// talkingpointsmemo.com/dc/montana-gop-senate-candidate-quietly-scrubs -rancher-from-his-campaign-bios.

9. Holly Michels, "Title Company Error Leads to Incorrect Form for Rosendale," *Independent Record* (Helena, MT), April 25, 2018, https://helenair.com /news/state-and-regional/govt-and-politics/title-company-error-erroneously -described-rosendale-as-maryland-resident-long/article_dc7ece75-32aa-598e -99a9-32cd1ea6dcd7.html.

10. Simone Pathé, "Matt Rosendale Wins Montana GOP Senate Primary," *Roll Call*, June 6, 2018, https://www.rollcall.com/news/politics/rosendale-wins -montana-gop-senate-primary.

11. "Matt Rosendale addresses supporters after winning Montana Republican U.S. Senate primary," YouTube video, posted by "KTVH Helena," June 6, 2018, https://youtu.be/XLjrnt5JKic?t=125.

12. "Transcript: Remarks by President Trump at Signing of S.2155, Economic Growth, Regulatory Relief, and Consumer Protection Act," The White House, May 24, 2018, https://www.whitehouse.gov/briefings-statements /remarks-president-trump-signing-s-2155-economic-growth-regulatory-relief -consumer-protection-act/.

13. Public Law 115-174, Economic Growth, Regulatory Relief and Consumer Protection Act, US Congress, May 24, 2018, https://www.congress.gov /bill/115th-congress/senate-bill/2155/cosponsors.

14. "Tester to DeVos: Your Decision Has Serious Consequences," press release,

Senator Jon Tester, May 16, 2017, https://www.tester.senate.gov/?p=press
_release&id=5261.

15. "After Tester's Demands, DeVos Reverses Course on University of Montana
Upward Bound Application," press release, Senator Jon Tester, May 24, 2017,
https://www.tester.senate.gov/?p=press_release&id=5277.

16. "Tester Defends Montana Students Against DeVos' Harmful Decisions,"
press release, Senator Jon Tester, October 1, 2018, https://www.tester.senate
.gov/?p=press_release&id=6469.

17. "Tester Named One of the Most Effective Senators in Washington," press
release, Senator Jon Tester, September 28, 2017, https://www.tester.senate
.gov/?p=press_release&id=5566.

18. Tester, "Tester Passes 20."

19. "President Trump Signs Montana Delegation's Bill to Rename Three VA Facilities in Honor of Montana Veterans," press release, Senator Jon Tester, June 7,
2018, https://www.tester.senate.gov/?p=press_release&id=6213.

20. "FULL EVENT: Donald Trump Billings Montana Rally (5 26 16)," YouTube
video, posted by "Chris Stevens," September 3, 2016, https://youtu.be
/q4zpBiUivOQ?t=238.

21. Tom Lutey, "Montanans Share Concerns over US-China Trade War with
Tester," *Billings Gazette*, July 6, 2018, https://billingsgazette.com/news/state
-and-regional/govt-and-politics/montanans-share-concerns-over-u-s--china
-trade-war/article_b7d68bbd-6b23-5b94-bf97-8ec2d16e0792.html.

22. Montanans for Tester newspaper ad, *Great Falls Tribune*, July 5, 2018, p. S4.

23. John Verhovek, "Democratic Sen. Jon Tester Thanks Trump in Full-Page Ad
ahead of Rally," ABC News, July 5, 2018, https://abcnews.go.com/Politics
/democratic-sen-jon-tester-trump-full-page-ad/story?id=56382201.

24. Don Trump Jr., "Jon Tester Is No Partner of President Trump," *Great
Falls Tribune*, July 3, 2018, https://www.greatfallstribune.com/story/opinion
/2018/07/03/donald-trump-jr-jon-tester-no-partner-president-trump-rally
-great-falls-montana/756781002/.

25. Cory Walsh, "Pearl Jam Concert Had Hometown Feel, from Ament to
Montana Flags to Missoula Lyrics," *Missoulian*, August 14, 2018, https://
missoulian.com/news/local/pearl-jam-concert-had-hometown-feel-from
-ament-to-montana/article_fe5be2e4-19fd-52c1-8749-b408c0aee7c5.html.

26. Matt Volz, "Republicans Blast Pearl Jam Poster of Burning White House,"
Associated Press, August 15, 2018, https://www.apnews.com/bcd3b47b1a
2b4106bb7557aeb03168a5.

27. Volz, "Republicans Blast."

28. "Defend Freedom. Defeat Two-Faced Tester!" YouTube video, posted by "NRA,"
September 6, 2018, https://www.youtube.com/watch?v=AuqwhCm_MZs.

29. Lachlan Markay "Exclusive: Audio Reveals Potentially Illegal Coordination
between NRA and Montana Senate Hopeful Matt Rosendale," *Daily Beast*,
September 13, 2018, https://www.thedailybeast.com/exclusive-audio-reveals-
potentially-illegal-coordination-between-nra-and-montana-senate-hopeful-
matt-rosendale.

30. Lachlan, "Matt Rosendale on NRA support," Soundcloud, September 13,
2018, https://soundcloud.com/user-379527848/matt-rosendale-on-nra-support.

31. John Adams, "Daily Beast Audio Reveals Potential Illegal Coordination between NRA and Matt Rosendale," Montana Public Radio, September 13, 2018, https://www.mtpr.org/post/daily-beast-audio-reveals-potential-illegal -coordination-between-nra-and-matt-rosendale.

32. "Speech: Donald Trump Holds a Political Rally in Billings, Montana - September 6, 2018," YouTube video, posted by "Factbase Videos," September 6, 2018, https://youtu.be/Fbg4Cs7wgZc?t=2162.

33. "Speech: Donald Trump."

34. Sarah Mervosh, "How 'Plaid Shirt Guy' Got Prime Seating at a Trump Rally," *New York Times*, September 9, 2018, https://www.nytimes.com/2018/09/09 /us/politics/trump-rally-vip-tickets.html.

35. "AP FACT CHECK: Emails show Tester did try to meet with Kavanaugh," Associated Press, October 4, 2018, https://www.apnews.com/a80ea097dca 0471b81108d52843590fd.

36. EPIC, "National Archives Confirms Existence of Numerous Kavanaugh Records on Surveillance Programs," October 3, 2018, https://www.youtube .com/watch?v=GCtR0OyHiK8.

37. Hina Shamsi, "On National Security, Kavanaugh Has a History of Extreme Deference to the President," ACLU blog, August 29, 2018, https://www.aclu .org/blog/national-security/national-security-kavanaugh-has-history-extreme -deference-president.

38. "Judge Brett Kavanaugh - The Court: Power, policy, and self-government | LIVE STREAM," YouTube video, posted by "American Enterprise Institute," March 31, 2016, https://youtu.be/GCtR0OyHiK8?t=2647.

39. "Tester: 'I Have Concerns about Kavanaugh's Record,'" press release, Senator Jon Tester, September 28, 2018, https://www.tester.senate.gov/?p=press _release&id=6466.

40. US Senate Roll Call Vote No. 223, October 6, 2018, https://www.senate.gov /legislative/LIS/roll_call_lists/roll_call_vote_cfm.cfm?congress=115&session =2&vote=00223.

41. Associated Press, "Montana Sen. Tester a 'No' Vote on Kavanaugh Confirmation," *US News & World Report*, September 28, 2018, https://www.usnews .com/news/best-states/montana/articles/2018-09-28/montana-senators-split -on-accusations-against-kavanaugh.

42. "Montana U.S. Senate Candidates Trade Barbs over Debate Plans," NBC Montana, June 11, 2018, https://nbcmontana.com/news/local/rosendale -wont-debate-tester-sunday-cites-fathers-day.

43. "Tester Rosendale on Public Lands," C-Span user-created clip, October 5, 2019, https://www.c-span.org/video/?c4821156/tester-rosendale-public-lands.

44. "Montana's U.S. Senate candidates debate," YouTube video, posted by "KRTV News," October 14, 2018, https://youtu.be/C182vB2ucKw?t=3281.

45. Mike Ferguson, "President Trump's Billings Visit Cost Taxpayers $59K in Law Enforcement Overtime," *Billings Gazette*, September 14, 2018, https:// billingsgazette.com/news/state-and-regional/govt-and-politics/president -trump-s-billings-visit-cost-taxpayers-k-in-law/article_9e4bd177-a16d-5edb-b 18c-21eef7ad9507.html.

46. Nicholas Deshais, "Trump Reminds Missoula Crowd of His 2016 Win, Lauds

GOP Senate Candidate, Praises Assault of Journalist," *Spokesman-Review* (Spokane, WA), October 18, 2018, https://www.spokesman.com/stories/2018/oct/18/rallying-supporters-in-missoula-trump-gathers-mome/.

47. "Speech: Donald Trump Holds a Political Rally in Missoula, Montana - October 18, 2018," YouTube video, posted by "Factbase Videos," October 18, 2018, https://www.youtube.com/watch?v=uAePpc9-OrM&feature=youtu.be&t=3520.

48. US Senate Roll Call Vote No. 163, July 23, 2018, https://www.senate.gov/legislative/LIS/roll_call_lists/roll_call_vote_cfm.cfm?congress=115&session=2&vote=00163.

49. "Speech: Donald Trump Holds a Political Rally in Missoula, Montana - October 18."

50. Tommy Martino, "Missoula County Seeks $13K for Costs during Trump Rally," *Missoulian*, October 25, 2018, https://missoulian.com/news/local/missoula-county-seeks-k-for-costs-during-trump-rally/article_1ea96b64-8a6a-542f-ad7b-8a18af136e6b.html.

51. Lisa Hagen, "Cook Political Report Shifts Three Senate Races toward Republicans," *The Hill*, October 4, 2018, https://thehill.com/homenews/campaign/409969-cook-political-report-shifts-three-senate-races-towards-republicans.

52. Sarah Vowell, "Did Hell Freeze Over? My Republican Dad Is Voting for a Democrat," *New York Times*, October 12, 2018, https://www.nytimes.com/2018/10/12/opinion/sunday/jon-tester-democrat-montana-senate-west.html.

53. Corin Cates-Carney, "Jeff Bridges Campaigns for Jon Tester in Bozeman," Montana Public Radio, October 17, 2018, https://www.mtpr.org/post/jeff-bridges-campaigns-jon-tester-bozeman.

54. "Actor Jeff Bridges endorses Jon Tester at Montana State University," YouTube video, posted by "KTVH Helena," October 17, 2018, https://youtu.be/_bK6r6Ug_d4?t=40.

55. Larisa Casillas "5,000 Attend Donald Trump Rally in Belgrade," NBC Montana, November 3, 2018, https://nbcmontana.com/news/local/5000-attend-donald-trump-rally-in-belgrade.

56. "Senator Jon Tester Victory Speech," C-SPAN, November 7, 2018, https://www.c-span.org/video/?454233-1/senator-jon-tester-delivers-victory-remarks.

57. "Watch Now: President Trump's full press conference after Midterm Elections results," YouTube video, posted by "CBS News," November 7, 2018, https://www.youtube.com/watch?v=-67ZrVAX58A&t=4562.

58. "More Than $70 Million Spent in Montana US Senate Race," Associated Press, December 10, 2018, https://www.apnews.com/68d7dab124f44fbf91afe12695fc3d24.

59. Montana General Election Results, November 6, 2018, Montana Secretary of State, https://sosmt.gov/wp-content/uploads/2018GeneralReportStateCanvass.pdf.

Epilogue: Gone the Sun

1. Burgess Everett and Heather Caygle, "Senate Democrats Break with Pelosi over Impeachment Trial," *Politico*, January 8, 2020, https://www.politico.com/news/2020/01/08/senate-democrats-break-pelosi-over-impeachment-096224.

2. "REAL TIME WITH BILL MAHER S17 • E8," YouTube video, posted by "Real Time with Bill Maher," March 28, 2019, https://www.youtube.com/watch?v=ztuTVWQ42Js&.

3. "CAP Ideas 2019: Sen. Jon Tester (D-MT)," YouTube video, posted by "see-progress," May 24, 2019, https://www.youtube.com/watch?v=FGpAYO9eQlY.

4. "REAL TIME."

5. "Donald Trump Jr. in Montana," YouTube video, posted by "Redoubt News," October 30, 2018, https://www.youtube.com/watch?v=2hkxvLH7tjg; Thomas Plank, "Donald Trump Jr. Headlines 'Montana Victory Tour' in East Helena," *Independent Record* (Helena, MT), October 26, 2018, https://helenair.com/news/local/donald-trump-jr-headlines-montana-victory-tour-in-east-helena/article_e0ada12f-228a-5e7e-9157-3fa3f0cb2071.html.

6. "Sen. Tester Targets Dark Money," *CQ on Congress* (podcast), via *Roll Call*, December 21, 2018, https://www.rollcall.com/news/podcasts/sen-tester-targets-dark-money.

7. "Debt to the Penny," TreasuryDirect.gov, May 5, 2020, https://treasurydirect.gov/NP/debt/search?startMonth=05&startDay=05&startYear=2020&endMonth=&endDay=&endYear=.

8. "Debt to the Penny," TreasuryDirect.gov, October 16, 2019, https://treasurydirect.gov/NP/debt/search?startMonth=10&startDay=16&startYear=2019&endMonth=&endDay=&endYear=.

9. "Neil deGrasse Tyson On Coronavirus: Will People Listen To Science?" YouTube video, posted by "The Late Show with Stephen Colbert," March 7, 2020, https://www.youtube.com/watch?v=jB4FUHHMI24.

10. "4/23/20: Members of the Coronavirus Task Force Hold a Press Briefing," YouTube video, posted by "The White House," April 23, 2020, https://youtu.be/PsQnfpfIa_o?t=1588.

11. Katie Rogers, Christine Hauser, Alan Yuhas, and Maggie Haberman, "Trump's Suggestion That Disinfectants Could Be Used to Treat Coronavirus Prompts Aggressive Pushback," *New York Times*, April 24, 2020, https://www.nytimes.com/2020/04/24/us/politics/trump-inject-disinfectant-bleach-coronavirus.html.

12. "President Trump Participates in a Signing Ceremony," YouTube video, posted by "The White House," April 24, 2020, https://youtu.be/m4_wdAY8opM?t=1421.

Index